INVENTING EXOTICISM

MATERIAL TEXTS

A complete list of books in the series is available from the publisher.

INVENTING EXOTICISM

Geography, Globalism, and Europe's Early Modern World

BENJAMIN SCHMIDT

PENN

University of Pennsylvania Press

Philadelphia

Published by
University of Pennsylvania Press
Philadelphia, Pennsylvania 19104-4112
www.upenn.edu/pennpress

Printed in the United States of America on acid-free paper
10 9 8 7 6 5 4 3 2

Library of Congress Cataloging-in-Publication Data
Schmidt, Benjamin.
    Inventing exoticism : geography, globalism, and Europe's early modern world /
Benjamin Schmidt. — 1st ed.
        p. cm. — (Material texts)
    ISBN 978-0-8122-4646-9 (hardcover : alk. paper)
    1. Europe—Civilization—Foreign influences. 2. Geography—
Europe—History—17th century. 3. Geography—Europe—
History—18th century. 4. Exoticism in art—Europe. 5. Exoticism in
literature. 6. Europe—Civilization—History—17th century. 7. Europe—
Civilization—History—18th century. 8. Netherlands—Civilization—
History—17th century. 9. Netherlands—Civilization—History—18th
century. I. Title. II. Series: Material texts.
    CB203.S337 2015
    940.2′52—dc23   2014030162

Finally, to them both, with boundless gratitude—
Louise and Isabel

[CONTENTS]

Plates follow page 220

[ILLUSTRATIONS]

PLATES

FIGURES

I will present . . . something new: no monster dragged out of the African wilderness, but a *delightful* and no less useful history, or description, of the fresh young flora that can be observed in this most distant corner of the world and have been hitherto unknown to *us Europeans*.

—GEORGIUS RUMPHIUS, *Herbarium Amboinense* (1690)

But then the *Dutch* must be understood to be as they really are, *the Carryers of the World*, the middle Persons in Trade, the Factors and Brokers of *Europe* . . . they *buy* to *sell* again, *take* in to *send* out; and the greatest Part of their vast Commerce consists in being supply'd from all Parts of the World, that they may supply all the World again.

—DANIEL DEFOE, *A Plan of the English Commerce* (1728)

Not much Arctic exoticism.

—VICTOR SEGALEN, *Essai sur l'exotisme* (1904)

INTRODUCTION

On the Invention of Exoticism and

the Invention of Europe

Europe's Exotic World

They arrive in pairs, single file, and snake around a large, central orb that rests on a pedestal, each couple bearing riches from afar: ivory tusks, tortoise shells, and a claw-footed casket from a tandem of muscular Africans; large rolls of tobacco and a finely decorated coffer borne by a feather-decked duo of Indians from America; a hefty ceramic urn (filled with frankincense or myrrh, one imagines) from the two Asian delegates who bring up the rear (figure 1). They deliver their wares to a lavishly attired, splendidly coiffed, daintily gesturing woman, who sits—stage left—surrounded by objects that mark her distinctive status: books, maps, compasses, and other specimens of both learning and imperial technology. She represents Europa, the allegorical embodiment of what used to pass under the banner of Christendom, and she now receives the marvelous gifts and gracious homages of the exotic world. This last is signified more literally and graphically—geographically—by the print's central device, a plainly discernible terrestrial globe, which announces the oeuvre's grandiose ambitions by way of its title: *La galerie agreable du monde*.[1]

By the year of this global gallery's opening in 1729, the conceit of a magisterial Europa receiving the treasures of the exotic world had grandly landed on the cover of what surely counts among the most stupendous published works of the early modern period. In fact, the *Galerie agreable* may rank among the most fabulous books ever printed, early modern or not, and its appearance marked the culmination of several decades of highly impressive publications and productions—of books, prints, and maps; of material objects, natural specimens, and foreign curiosities—in the terrain of exotic geography. The gallery's impresario, Leiden printer extraordinaire Pieter van

FIGURE 1. After Romeyn de Hooghe, frontispiece (etching) to Pieter van der Aa, *La galerie agreable du monde* (Leiden, ca. 1729). Collection Antiquariaat Forum BV, 't Goy-Houten, The Netherlands.

der Aa, stood out among his peers, even in the book-rich milieu of the early modern Netherlands, for his extravagant publications. He produced some of the most elegant atlases of the period, along with numerous other picture-filled descriptions of Europe's known world. The aptly named *Galerie agreable* boasted some four thousand "very precise" and "very beautiful" illustrations, printed on more than 2,500 double-folio leaves—a printing feat rarely matched.[2] (The sixty-six "tomes" into which the book was organized were apportioned into thirty or so separate volumes, yet this arrangement could vary according to the buyer's preference.) The cover illustration designed to launch this monumental enterprise derived from the atelier of Romeyn de Hooghe, a renowned graphic artist and himself a prolific producer of sought-after prints: over five thousand, including dozens of spectacular compositions depicting the exotic world, many of which appeared in the publications of Pieter van der Aa.[3]

The frontispiece to the global *Galerie agreable* certainly offered a spectacle—a swirling drama of the "agreeable" world as it was meant to be seen and grasped by early modern Europeans. For despite the typically busy, slightly dizzying, Baroque composition, the message for the European spectator circa 1730 would have been clear. The allegorical figures of the continents—four by tradition, which had been revived in the Renaissance and ironed out over the ensuing age of European discovery and expansion—stage a performance of material transaction and global order.[4] And while there may be a clear directional flow to these exchanges and affiliations, with the parade of figures circulating from the exotic world toward Europa, this is not presented as simpleminded subservience. The exotic ensemble approaches the seated continent in a fashion that is not self-evidently servile, submissive, obeisant, or "disagreeable" so much as generously attentive and perhaps even ceremonial. There is an almost balletic elegance to the manner in which these emissaries from distant realms approach Europa and present her with their exotic bounty; it is vaguely ritualistic. And it is vaguely religious, as well: subtly so, in the background architecture, which features a mosque and pagoda, thereby hinting at the diverse faiths of the globe; and allusively so, in the way the worldly drama of the gift-bearing continents evokes the sacred story of the visiting magi—three delegations who likewise arrive with goods from distant realms (albeit from the East in that pre-Columbian world).[5] Yet the narrative of global encounter has by now shifted: a plainly secular and geographically inquisitive Europa—note how her accoutrements encourage both learning and global exchange—accumulates the profuse exotica of an agreeable world.

Over a period spanning the final third of the seventeenth century and first third of the eighteenth, a new conception of the world and of Europe's relationship to it developed in sources of exotic geography. These new materials—a vast body of textual, visual, and material objects—presented the world as distinctly "agreeable" and thus accommodating in various ways. They addressed, moreover, a singular *European* spectator, or consumer, of this world—neither identifiably Protestant nor Catholic; not particularly Spanish, British, French, or Dutch—who both engaged with and cheerfully accumulated the delights of this appealingly exotic world. This scenario is visualized just as vividly on another contemporary frontispiece, in this case by the French Huguenot and Amsterdam-based engraver Daniel Marot, for a volume that candidly offered its readers the "pleasures" of the exotic world (as the book's title labeled them; figure 2). With one arm resting on the telltale bull of ancient mythology, Europa receives, literally on a platter, the riches of the non-European world—the "pleasurable exotica" advertised on the tray's silk drapery—which arrive in the form of pearls and porcelain, ivory and lacquer, parrots and other *naturalia* from around the world.[6] In the background, one can just make

FIGURE 2. Jacob Gole after Daniel Marot, "Amoenitates exoticae" (engraved frontispiece), in Engelbert Kaempfer, *Amoenitatum exoticarum politico-physico-medicarum fasciculi V* (Lemgo, 1712). Beinecke Rare Book and Manuscript Library, Yale University.

out a pagoda and mosque—hints, once again, of global religions (and the curious shapes of their temples)—yet there is no corollary allusion to European Christianity. Rather, as in the *Galerie agreable* print, Europa is framed by her affiliation with various forms of learning (two montages of the arts grace the museum-like rotunda above, while a second female allegorical figure represents the science of geography);

with the science of navigation (which appears in the guise of Poseidon, flanking Europa on the right; the other bearded figure, Father Time, holds a ship's compass); and with the evident "pleasures" of the titular *exoticae*. Europa is defined not by any bluntly imperial role in the world, in other words, but by her association with geography and with the pleasures of exotica.[7] The two, moreover, are inherently connected: in both frontispiece images, Europe gains its identity *through* the exotic world; in both, global exotica and their pleasures coalesce around a freshly constituted idea of "Europe." These twin portrayals emphasize the agreeable quality of the non-European world, presented as a site not of conflict and competition but of desire and delight. They underscore, in short, Europe's pleasure in the exotic.

This book describes how this happened: how a new conception of the exotic world and a new conceit of Europe came to be, and how these two imaginative constructs also came to shape and rely on one another during this pivotal moment of mounting European expansion in the world.[8] In the decades surrounding 1700—from roughly the mid-1660s through the early 1730s—a novel form of exoticism developed in European ateliers, particularly those of the Netherlands, through a series of broad-ranging, multimedia, and commercially successful products that engaged with the non-European world in both word and image. The swirling aesthetic of Pieter van der Aa's frontispiece is emblematic for these products. The new exoticism emphasized variety, abundance, and agreeably digressive concoctions that mixed and matched the wonders of the world—mosques with pagodas, pearls with porcelain—rather than distinguishing among them. It aimed to "delight." This innovative formulation of Europe's overseas world functioned both as an attractive product—the prodigiously illustrated books of van der Aa being the culmination of a much larger trend—and, taken collectively, as an argument for how the world should appear to the early modern reader and viewer of these sources. It shaped Europe's world circa 1700, and it set the stage for Europe's imperial moment in the coming years. The new mode of exoticism entailed, furthermore, a freshly invented and expressly *European* audience, which could imagine itself not merely as consumers of exotic things but also as partakers of the pleasures of an agreeably exotic world. That these consumers spanned national borders and confessional divides is particularly remarkable: the articulation of a new form of exoticism helped to instigate, as well, a new form of *Homo europaeus*.[9]

Who, What, When, Where, and Why (Not Quite in That Order)

Exotic geography, in a strikingly broad range of forms, became enormously popular in Europe beginning a decade or so following the Peace of Westphalia of 1648—a series of treaties that brought a sustained period of relative concord to much of Europe following more than a century of unrelenting, intercontinental war—and enduring several decades into the eighteenth century.[10] A surge of sources that described, depicted, or otherwise engaged with the non-European world flooded the market from around the 1660s, crossing several genres, multiple media, and an impressive variety of material forms. Books furnishing all manner of extra-European history and ethnography; printed anthologies describing myriad global religions, political regimes, and cultural habits; illustrated volumes offering personal travel narratives and geographic descriptions; grandly designed prints depicting foreign buildings, famous monuments, cityscapes, and various forms of *vedute*; engraved, etched, and sketched representations of exotic flora, fauna, and other *naturalia*; decorated maps of the cities, kingdoms, and continents, and maritime charts of the ports, seas, and oceans of the world; panel paintings of exotic peoples, landscapes, and still lifes; an abundance of tin-glazed earthenware and imported porcelain, adorned with patterns and imagery evocative of the overseas world; woven tapestries, dyed and painted textiles, lacquered and inlaid furniture, adroitly embellished with exotic motifs; tropical woods, rare gems, and an assortment of natural specimens and rare artifacts redolent of the exotic world from which they claimed to derive: all became more commonly accessible and more pervasively available by the final decades of the seventeenth century. These materials cast their attention eastward as well as westward—in the previous century, novelty and wonder may have been more instinctively and typically linked with the new worlds of America—and they incorporated, or perhaps sought to mimic, visual motifs from across a wide spectrum of global traditions. Exotic geography also enjoyed broad appeal. Books appeared in multiple languages and in numerous editions, pitched to elite and popular audiences alike, while cartographic sources circulated as readily obtainable, single-sheet prints as well as deluxe, multivolume atlases. Exotic décor could be had by way of inexpensive delftware—perhaps the single most common medium of exoticism in this period—or pricier porcelain; in the form of cheaply painted fans no less than magnificent tapestry (see plate 1 and plate 20).

All of this indicates an exceptionally wide range of consumption—exotic geography circulated across much of Europe and to a vast range of consumers—yet it was markedly the opposite in terms of production: a disproportionate amount of exotica, in the form of books, maps, paintings, and ceramics, issued from workshops located predominantly in the Netherlands, which served as Europe's leading producer of exotic geography. Meanwhile, a substantial quantity of exotic goods—including porcelain, lacquerware, tropical shells, rare woods, and other foreign specimens—reached European consumers via Dutch shipping. The Netherlands became in this period an entrepôt of exoticism.[11]

Why the Netherlands, and why then? In part, one can point to the superb supporting resources of the Dutch Republic, for example, when it came to printing—the pulsing heart of the industry, Amsterdam, reached a productive high point precisely in the period 1680–1725, when an influx of Huguenot printers, engravers, and publishers bolstered that city's already vibrant book trade—and when it came, more particularly, to the sort of graphic and cartographic output that characterized the picture-rich geography works made in Dutch ateliers.[12] Dutch workshops also excelled in handling products related to natural history—this was a golden age not only for collecting exotic shells and other natural specimens but also for the publication of those herbaria, florilegia, and shell books that described these collections—and the Netherlands served as a hub for a vibrant trade in foreign flora, fauna, and conchological rarities.[13] Ceramics, from at least the mid-seventeenth century, streamed from factories in Delft along with other Dutch cities—Haarlem, Amsterdam, and Rotterdam also manufactured tin-glazed earthenware—and popular Dutch-made blue-and-white pottery soon came to dominate the European market (the true Ming and Qing porcelain that delftware mimicked being a strictly high-end product).[14] Painting, of course, had long prospered on the open art market of the Dutch Republic, but it is worth noting that the specialized genres of *pronk* (sumptuous) still life, with their ostentatious display of rich imported goods, and of exotic landscape, which featured a wide range of extra-European scenes, burgeoned only in the second half of the seventeenth century (Frans Post, the popular painter of Brazil, being but one of several artists who concentrated on images of the Indies, both East and West).[15]

More generally, these products in their various forms flourished not merely in the markets of the Netherlands but also throughout much of Europe. And this prompts a finely recalibrated version of the question: Why did *Dutch*-made presentations of the exotic world enjoy such phenomenal *Europe*-wide success? The answer lies in the qualified Dutchness of the products, the European perspective of their pitch, and the new form of geography that resulted. Among the most important shifts in the brand of exotic geography devised over this period in Dutch ateliers is its relative *un*-Dutchness: the considerable effort extended by producers in the Netherlands to efface any parochial Dutch presence in their works and to adopt a broadly European view of things. For despite the manufacture of so many of these materials in the Dutch Republic, they did not necessarily derive from Dutch authors, Dutch draftsmen, or even Dutch travelers. Plainly, van der Aa's thousands of images had been culled from scores of sources of extensively scattered provenance; the final product, all the same, carried the stamp and look of his brand of "exotic" geography (van der Aa acknowledges himself merely as the printer). Yet even in the case of more narrative-driven products, which bore authorial credit or pointed to a specific journey—Johan Nieuhof's bestselling description of China, for example, or Olfert Dapper's immensely successful geography of Africa—the sources on which the narratives had been constructed often came from elsewhere.[16] Dutch-made geography not infrequently rested on the foundations of Habsburg reports, Jesuit letters, and other far-fetched materials that had been cannily collected and smartly repackaged by publishers in the Netherlands. Publishers deftly disguised this background matter, however, to create a generically pitched account, focused more on China or Africa than on any specific (and invariably colonial) events that may have taken place there. And when the geography in question pointed ineluctably toward Dutch-impinged portions of the globe—when Dutch actors irrefutably occupied the foreground of their global theater—this fact was blotted out as much as possible. From Arnoldus Montanus's "pleasingly" designed, if meanderingly sketched, geography of Japan (circa 1670), which generously narrates the preceding Portuguese, Spanish, and English ventures in that distant land and the "tragic" saga of Catholic persecution and martyrdom under the early Tokugawa regime—and which promptly became the foremost early modern book on Japan, produced in several French, German, and English editions—one barely gets the impression that, by this moment in colonial history, the Dutch had won exclusive European access to Japanese trade, having ousted their (chiefly Catholic) rivals earlier in the century. Montanus's geography goes out of its way to suppress the story of Dutch success and to avoid any parochial—which is to say, Dutch—narrative of European interventions overseas. This results in a far more "agreeable" and far more "European" fashioning of the exotic East.[17]

This moment of exotic geography, which takes off explosively right around the time of Montanus's publication—like Nieuhof's and Dapper's, produced originally in Amsterdam in the mid- to late 1660s—marks a fundamental departure in Europe's descriptive and narrative engagement with the world. Previous forms of European geography had been pointedly and polemically parochial; the genre of geography most typically provided a perspective of the world that accorded with the national, colonial, or imperial agenda of its makers. Richard Hakluyt's *Principal navigations, voiages, traffiques and discoueries* (1598) famously celebrated the fledgling British empire, Antonio de Herrera y Tordesillas's *Historia general* (1601–1615) offered a history-cum-geography of the world from an unambiguously and triumphalist Habsburg perch, and André Thevet's *Les singularitez de la France antarctique* (1557) conveyed a singularly French take on South ("antarctic") America.[18] This was standard for the field. Just a few years before the innovative turn of exotic geography in the later seventeenth century, Peter Heylyn would address the expressly "English reader" of his *Cosmographie* (1652) by offering a full-throated endorsement of its purposefully patriotic agenda:

In the pursuance of the Work, as I have taken on my self the parts of an *Historian* and *Geographer*; so have I not forgotten that I a[m] an *English-man*, and which is somewhat more, a *Church-man*. As an *English-man* I have been mindfull upon all occasions to commit to memory the noble actions of my Countrey; exployted both by Sea and Land, in most parts of the world, and

INTRODUCTION

represented on the same *Theaters*, upon which they were acted. . . . I have apprehended every modest occasion, of recording the heroick Acts of my native Soil, and filing on the Registers of perpetuall Fame the Gallantrie and brave Atchievements of the People of England.[19]

Heylyn's geography was naturally never translated for a non-English audience, and the same can be said for Richard Hakluyt's and Samuel Purchas's works—an English cleric like Heylyn, Purchas authored the massive *Hakluytus posthumus, or Purchas his pilgrimes* (1625)[20]—and for most other major English contributions to geography produced in the century or so preceding Nieuhof, Dapper, and Montanus, whose own books all became routinely successful in their English-language editions. Nor would there have been any point in promoting a rousing English take on the world to any beyond the borders of Britain—or, for that matter, a Spanish, French, or German *Weltanschauung* to unsympathetic audiences beyond those linguistic boundaries. This is how the genre of geography generally functioned: by offering an interested angle on the world from an explicitly provincial perspective; by producing what the sociologist of science Bruno Latour refers to as "local" knowledge, thereby underscoring precisely the parochial approach of such projects. The new form of geography that developed in the second half of the seventeenth century, by contrast, even while crafted within the confines of Dutch ateliers, generated an ostensibly wider vision of the world, or what constituted "universal" knowledge in Latourian terms—"universal," it bears emphasizing, from a European perspective.[21] The new exotic geography delivered a new way to see, read, consume, and comprehend the non-European world. It marked a significant shift from earlier modes of description, characterized by intense contestation—national, confessional, colonial, imperial—to modes that allowed a generically "European" consumer to enjoy a generically "exotic" world. Hence the invention of exoticism and the invention of Europe—and the broad repercussions these developments would have.[22]

The Dutch role in staging this exotic world correlates closely to the Dutch role in the world itself. A changing status for the Netherlands overseas, where circumstances had been evolving, likewise, over the later decades of the seventeenth century, afforded a changing perspective on the world—or, at any rate, more leeway for publishers, engravers, and others in the Netherlands to reconceptualize their images of the globe and to devise a new mode of representing the non-European world. Dutch colonial fortunes had been in a state of flux from the mid-seventeenth century, when a series of crises knocked the Republic and its overseas companies—the Dutch West India Company (WIC) and Dutch East India Company (VOC)—back on their heels, particularly in the West. Beginning around 1650—shortly after the Peace of Westphalia finally granted the Republic political independence—the WIC and its not insubstantial territorial possessions began to disintegrate. Prior to that, for a brief interval from the 1620s through the 1650s, the WIC had established an impressive Atlantic empire: colonies in North America (New Netherland) and along the Brazilian bulge of South America, together with trading posts in West Africa and the Caribbean. Yet by 1654 the Company was forced to forfeit its Brazilian colonies to the Iberians; by 1664 it had entered into an ultimately losing sequence of wars with the British over New Netherland (soon to be rechristened New York); and by 1674 the WIC itself was compelled to declare bankruptcy. "Nu zijn wij dit alles quijt"—Now all of this has been lost to us—observed the leading Dutch economic theorist of the day, Pieter de la Court, grimly and succinctly.[23] Meanwhile, over the final third of the seventeenth century and into the early eighteenth, the Dutch began to lose relative market share in Asia to the rising (and protectionist) empires of England and France.[24] It was not so much that Dutch merchants wholly yielded their stake in the traffic of exotic goods—hardly the case. Yet Dutch overseas companies and the States General of the Netherlands had all but abandoned by this time a territorial approach to overseas expansion, as they shifted to a more plainly trade-based model. This had arguably been a key part of the Dutch commercial strategy from the start (compare Portuguese expansion), yet this trend began to accelerate in the final years of the seventeenth century and into the eighteenth. In the meantime, just as Dutch colonialists jettisoned whatever earlier notions of territorial empire they may have nurtured, Dutch makers of geography fostered a new and revised sense of the overseas world. They began to cultivate not a narrowly Dutch perspective, but a broadly European one, focusing less on this or that imperial testing ground than on an "exotic" world that seemed to supersede national and imperial projects. In a sense, the Dutch exchanged an empire of territory for an empire of geography: they began to trade also in the *image* of the world.[25]

Their pivot was both quick and compelling. When the Dutch physician Willem Piso published the *Historia naturalis Brasiliae* in 1648, a survey of the flora and fauna of Brazil studied under the auspices and patronage of Johan Maurits of Nassau-Siegen—the cousin of the stadtholder Frederick Henry, Prince of Orange, and the illustrious governor of Dutch Brazil during its glory years in the early 1640s—Piso prefaced the work with effusive praise of his commander and his noble service in Dutch Brazil. The volume was one of several published in the wake of the Dutch adventure in South America that fulsomely hailed the valiant deeds of Nassau and the tropical triumphs of the Netherlands at the height of its colonial American power—prime examples, in other words, of Dutch imperial geography. Yet when a new edition of the natural history appeared just a few years later, following the fall of Dutch Brazil and recalibration of the Dutch West Indies strategy, the patriotic preface was briskly revised—the paean to Nassau's brilliance disappears— and Piso's study of the tropical West was now augmented by a survey of nature in the tropical East, thus diluting the hotly provincial focus of the original book. The

Indiae utriusque re naturali et medica (1658) spreads its attention far beyond the Netherlands' imperial scope, encompassing a broader spectrum of the exotic world. A once conspicuously Dutch-centered work now affords a more coolly European perspective on exotic *naturalia*. Parochial prerogatives give way to continental— that is, European—curiosities.[26]

The presentation of the exotic world in these works aspired in this manner to a brand of "European" geography. This shift sometimes required only such basic bibliographic tricks—excising a patriotic preface, for example—yet in other instances it called for more rhetorically dexterous maneuvers. Talal Asad once observed that "Europe did not simply expand overseas; it made itself through that expansion."[27] This protean process took place, too, in sources of geography, where Europeans overseas *rhetorically* coalesced. Consider one remarkable global encounter that took place on a beach of Ternate, a small island in the Maluku Sea strategically located at the imperial crossroads of Spain (to the north, in the Philippines) and the Dutch Republic (to the south, in Java). Seventeenth-century Ternate brought together two of the most ardent antagonists of early modern Europe, who had waged perhaps the fiercest conflict of that era, a war that pitted the Catholic monarch of Spain against the Calvinist provinces of the Netherlands. The exhausting Eighty Years' War (as it came to be known) also extended overseas, notably—and rhetorically— to the Americas. Dutch polemicists spent the first half of the seventeenth century all but fetishizing the image of Spanish "tyranny" in America, a trope they tirelessly enlisted to blacken the Habsburg imperial program and to challenge it at every opportunity, including in numerous early seventeenth-century works of geography. Now, however, by the 1660s, these one-time enemies shared a tropical island—as declares the narrative of a lavishly illustrated geography volume, *Oost-Indische voyagie* (East Indian voyage)—and this encouraged one Wouter Schouten to pay a social visit to the administrator of Fort Calamatta in Spanish-held Ternate.[28] There the two men engaged in a genial conversation on—of all things!—the *amity* of Europeans and the need for Europeans abroad to cooperate in the conversion of indigenous peoples. The "good" Spaniard—such phrasing would have been unimaginable in Dutch literature of the previous decades—is given his due and more than cordial respect. Schouten does recollect hostilities past, yet he ultimately agrees with his Catholic colleague that the former nemeses should join in their mutual pursuit of a "Christian world." At this point, however, the text turns abruptly from European history to exotic geography—yet with a purpose. After a brief review of the state of the Spice Islands, the narrative addresses the tropical landscapes and wonders of Ternate: the volcano and thick jungle covering the island's verdant slopes; the splendid royal palace with its opulent interiors; and the menagerie of the local prince, which housed parrots and parakeets of fabulous colors, among the best of the Indies. The text now moves candidly to the point. These exotic species and "the beautifully

FIGURE 3. Johannes Kip, "'t Eyl. Tarnate" (etching), in Wouter Schouten, *Oost-Indische voyagie* (Amsterdam, 1676). Special Collections, University of Amsterdam (OG 77-17).

colored and no less spectacularly feathered Birds of Paradise [the quasi mythical bird of endless flight]" attract merchants from Bengal, Persia, Surat, and beyond, and if properly dried and preserved, could be traded "throughout the East Indies and in Europe, too," where they would fetch a high price. On this the two former adversaries agree, and so the promise of commercial profits trumps the animus of religious and imperial difference.[29]

In Schouten's text as in numerous other similarly pitched narratives set in the exotic world—and similarly manufactured in ateliers of the Netherlands—such passages of soft internationalism serve to dull the sharp edges of confessional, national, and even imperial difference. Commerce in exotica will succeed, it was insinuated, inasmuch as European competitors cooperate (and perhaps even outmaneuver their Asian counterparts, as Schouten's reference to Indian and Persian traders implies). They did not, of course, yet the texts themselves and their rhetorical flourishes did succeed by promoting a vision of imperial comity (or by ignoring imperial rivalry altogether), and they quickly became successful products of globalism in their own right: popular representations of a world indubitably rich in exotic wonders and ostensibly absent of imperial discord.

The Grammar of Sameness and the Hyper-Imperial World

Sources in the manner of Schouten's and the new mode of geography they embodied strove to underscore global differences, yet in ways that suggest a significant departure in terms of how early modern Europeans described and imagined the world. The older mode of geography—the modus operandi of post-1492 Europe, fashioned in the wake of the initial forays to the West and the expansions in the East that occupied Spain and Portugal, and to a lesser extent England and France, in the century and a half following Christopher Columbus and Vasco da Gama—sought strategically to *reduce* differences across the immense oceans, to shrink the cultural and conceptual gaps between expansion-minded Europeans and those distant places and peoples they aspired to colonize and rule. Geography sought to bridge the pressing challenge of "incommensurability," and its texts adhered to what Anthony Pagden has called the "principle of attachment": rhetorical strategies developed by Europeans in these early years expressly to forge connections between the colonizer and the colonized and thus to smooth the path to imperial progress.[30] Earlier sources at once generated and resolved the "marvel" instigated by encounters in the New World, as Stephen Greenblatt has described it, a register that first challenged and later reassured imperial-minded Europeans of their ability to flourish abroad. Sixteenth-century rhetoric of geography—the prior discourse of exoticism—enabled Europeans to minimize the gulf between themselves and the "wonder" of the New World, and thereby make extra-European spaces more amenable to those who would possess them.[31]

This approach encouraged those who described the world to render overseas places and peoples *more*, not less, familiar to the Europeans who voyaged to them, to the metropolitan powers that sponsored them, and to the readers and viewers who followed them. When Columbus first arrived in the Caribbean, he compared the unfamiliar landscapes he witnessed to "Valencia in March," while the mainland near the Orinoco would later appear to him like "Valencia in April"—the season had mildly adjusted, yet the Old World standard not at all. The rich fields of the New World shimmered, he averred, like "the farmlands of Córdoba," and the mountains were "very similar to Castile."[32] Likewise, Hernán Cortés perceived in the colorful vendors' stalls of Tenochtitlan scenes from "the silk markets of Granada," and the Mexican city reminded him more generally of "Seville or Córdoba."[33] In all of these instances, exotic encounters evoked touchstones from the fatherland. They also invoked, surely not by accident, sites of Castile's recent exploits in expanding that fatherland in their just concluded peninsular wars of conquest (the so-called *Reconquista* against the Moors). In the much the same spirit, engravings "of the Cheif mene [*sic*] of Virginia"—the Algonquian-speaking hunters and warriors encountered by British colonists in North America—were juxtaposed in early English printed accounts to pictures "of the Pictes which in the Olde tyme dyd [in]habite one part of the great Bretainne," and this cross-cultural affiliation, with its convenient suggestion of transatlantic kinship, became a standard trope of description in subsequent accounts.[34]

It suggests, as well, another characteristic of this earlier mode of geography: its sense of time and history. For not only do the New World topographies in these sources bear strategic resemblances to Old World locales, but geography also fixes these relationships in terms of temporal progress. The New World regions described in initial reports by Columbus and Cortés soon became codified on Old World maps as *New* Spain and *New* Granada, just as other Europeans would soon christen the spaces of their respective imperial aspirations as New England, New France, New Netherland, New Sweden—new outposts, in short, of the Old World's global imagination. Earlier habits of geographic description and nomenclature in this way produced thinly disguised imperial narratives, which were offered as implicitly "progressive" narratives (as the critic Ania Loomba has described them).[35] Renaissance geography thus served, as the sixteenth-century humanist and cartographer Abraham Ortelius elegantly put it, as the eye of history.[36]

The newer, post-1650 form of geography took a notably different tack. Rather than trying to bridge distances and erase global distinctions, it sought to extend and expand those qualities that differentiated Europeans from the exotic world, emphasizing precisely the diversions and attractions of an enticingly unfamiliar globe. Descriptions of exotic settings placed an accent on the distinctive and unusual stuff that separated Europeans from those who had lately entered their geographic (and colonial) orbit; on the peculiar habitats and curious habits of outlying places and peoples; on the wondrous nature and sometimes ineffable qualities that constituted the exotic world. What Arnoldus Montanus called Mexico—in preference to the vigorously Habsburgian *New Spain*—was juxtaposed in that author's rambling tomes of geography not with sites in Old Castile but with things, for example, in exotic Japan: both landscapes had spectacular, volcanic mountains; both endured phenomenal, temple-flattening earthquakes; both hosted immense, dragon-like lizards; and so on. In place of drawing tighter bonds between Europeans and the far-flung topographies they encountered, Montanus allied the mutual remarkableness of exotic spaces—in this case, the land of the rising sun and the land of the venerated sun (in the guise of the god Huitzilopochtli, as he delighted to explain). He made explicit the linkages imagined among non-European landscapes and cultures, and he set these implicitly in opposition to things "European."[37] In this and copious similar cases, exotic geography cultivated a characteristic analogistic logic: a strong degree of correlation flourished among non-European spaces, which bore a stamp of exotic sameness that could imply ties between tropical Mexico and Edo Japan. And the converse also held sway: a strong degree of *European* sameness prevailed among those who shared an interest in the broadly exotic world—the growing audience for exotic geography—which could produce a convivial summit among former enemies on the island of Ternate.

This shift in geography had broad implications. It denoted a change in both how Europeans looked at the world and how they looked at themselves. It marked an important transition, as well, for the epistemological underpinnings of early modern geography. If time and history had played a critical role in framing prior descriptions and perceptions of non-European places—overseas lands branded as "newer" satellites of European empires; exotic peoples presented as "olde tyme" variants of European colonists; geography identified as the eye of (European) history—then space and distance (from Europe) served as key organizing principles for this later moment of geography. Geography now moved laterally across non-European landscapes, rather than vertically through European-cum-global history. Images and accounts and material arts mixed and matched foreign peoples and polities, curious cultures and specimens, all lumped together as collectively, generically, congenially exotic. If geography had served in the sixteenth century as the eye of history, it was by the latter half of the seventeenth century the eye—or perhaps the outstretched arms or long loping legs—of ethnography, cultural anthropology, comparative religion, natural history, and the innumerable other subjects that fit within its capacious boundaries. The effect was to reconstitute both the subject and object of geography. Whereas earlier modes of geography took a more neatly chronological approach, which could devolve into a progressive narrative of this or that European power's expansion overseas, the newer mode adopted a more haphazard and chaotic style, reveling in the messy variety and splendid richness of the exotic world. And while earlier forms of geography might frame their subject in polemically narrow and explicitly imperial terms, pitching to a clearly demarcated and plainly partisan audience—be these Spanish, Portuguese, British, French, or Dutch consumers—the newer form avoided such a parochial focus. It was, nonetheless, just as partisan, albeit from a commonly *European* viewpoint. It offered what might be construed as a *pan*-colonial, or *hyper*-imperial, perspective; it fashioned an agreeably exotic world for a universally European consumer.

This raises one further quality of exotic geography: its formulation of global "difference." Difference, as a heuristic device, has long played an instrumental role in the influential field of colonial (and postcolonial) studies. The articulation of difference between Europe and those parts of the world it engaged with over the long-going, so-called age of empire—the "grammar of difference," "the reproduction of difference," "the construction of cultural difference," as Frederick Cooper and Ann Stoler identify it in their canonical study of Western imperialism—has served as a touchstone for countless inquiries into the ways Europe engaged with and represented those parts of the world it endeavored to control and colonize. It lay at the heart of Edward Said's seminal writings on culture and empire, and it undergirded, before that, Victor Segalen's precocious *Essay on Exoticism*, an early twentieth-century exploration of the "aesthetic of diversity [*esthétique du divers*]" that, as Segalen proposed, shaped and guided the West's engagement with the tropical Other. For Cooper and Stoler, it is self-evident that the "reproduction of difference" supported "the universalizing claims of European ideology"; that "the colonial experience shaped what it meant to be . . . 'European'" and hence "different"; and that "the production of colonial knowledge"—geography in its myriad forms—took place in Europe "across imperial centers." Difference—"European distinctiveness"—centrally defined the modern project of empire.[38]

These assessments, however, while certainly apt for the modern, post-1750 cases that interest Cooper and Stoler (and, of course, Said), apply less sensibly for earlier sources of empire and geography. First, they take for granted the prior existence of a fully formed and distinctive "European" who could in the first place be differentiated from the exotic world and "shaped" by colonial experience. The a priori formulation of Europeanness (and thus alterity) is peremptorily assumed. They miss, furthermore, the role of geography in constituting this *Homo europaeus* and the productive process of *making* both a subject and an object for geography.[39] Their analysis begs the question of *how* a consensual "European ideology" came into existence, and it skips over the necessary inverse of imperial "difference": exotic sameness. The form of exotic geography produced over the final decades of the seventeenth century and first few of the eighteenth—during a period that postdated the more sharply parochial focus of Renaissance geography, as it circulated in the early decades of colonial rivalry, yet a period that predated the assumed "European" ideology of modern colonialism: the post-Columbian, pre-Saidian moment of geography—strived to generate both difference and sameness. Difference between Europe and the world was indubitably conveyed, but so too and perhaps just as crucially was a sense of global sameness: of a mutually recognized European perspective on the world, which subtly suppressed— or carefully camouflaged—imperial rivalries; and of an effectively homogenized, blithely blended exotic world, which rendered the attractions of the globe, east and west, comparably and pleasingly exotic. To create this deftly mixed cocktail required crafty middlemen, and herein lies one final accomplishment of exotic geography and its makers. For the ateliers of the Dutch adopted and designed the end form of exotic geography from an enormous assortment of sources. They produced both the "gallery" of the world and the visitors who came to view it. They issued an enormous range of materials from which so many of the later representations of the world would be built: the foundations of "colonial knowledge" on which European imperial power would be constructed. Modern criticism, starting with Said, misses this moment of production: there is not a single mention of the Dutch in *Orientalism*.[40]

This modernist oversight may reflect the success of early modern, largely Dutch producers of exotic geography, who skillfully concealed their role in shaping the world. They presented a global spectacle—a gallery of exotica—yet did so in ways at once subtle and cunning. While the hard-headed English trader Daniel Defoe, who approached the incipient globalism of his age with the mindset of a merchant, well understood the Dutch part in the project of world trade—"*the Carryers of the World*, the middle Persons in Trade, the Factors and Brokers of *Europe*," he intoned with barely suppressed envy—he neglected to notice their role in *making* Europe's world. They "supply'd from all Parts of the World, that they may supply all the World again."[41] Yet their workshops also supplied the images, forms, and ideas of the world that would have been most readily recognizable to Defoe and his contemporaries from the numerous editions and translations, pictures and objects, that issued from the cultural warehouses of the Netherlands. Meanwhile, the politically oriented Baron de Montesquieu, likewise attuned to global matters, barely perceived a Dutch presence when he cast his eye to the geopolitical affairs of his day. "The most powerful states in Europe," remarks Usbek to Ibben, in analyzing the structures of Europe's imperial ambition, "are those of the German Emperor and the kings of France, Spain, and England." That he declined even to invoke the Dutch speaks to their success in disguising their enterprise of constructing "European" knowledge and power. That the exuberant exotic world fashioned by Montesquieu in the *Lettres persanes* issued originally from the print shops of Amsterdam speaks not only to the politics of Enlightenment publishing, but also to the prevailing role of Dutch ateliers in printing, presenting, manufacturing, and marketing all variety of exotic worlds.[42]

Exotic Geography and Its Imperatives

Exotic geography proliferated in the decades surrounding 1700, spanning several genres and media, and providing a mounting number of readers and consumers across Europe with a fresh vision of their expanding world. The various sources of exotic geography, which were generated preeminently in the ateliers of the Dutch Republic, shared certain characteristics and modes of presentation. These, in turn, reflected certain sensibilities and strategic imperatives. First, from an ideological standpoint, exotic geography affected a seemingly neutral, or at least apolitical, approach to the affairs of the non-European world—with the critical caveat that this neutrality had a distinctly European cast to it. Sources offered a global perspective that endeavored, insofar as possible, to expunge European colonial rivalries and to efface European cultural differences. They endorsed a view of the world meant to appear studiously non-national, nondoctrinal, and supraconfessional; their outlook and frame of reference were pointedly pan-European. Indeed, exotic geography did much to promote an idea of "Europe" in the world. Its sources had the dual effect of rendering the globe in binary terms—imperial Europe and the broadly exotic world—while forging, in the process, both a European consumer and an exotic subject for consumption. Rather than the provincial approach common to so many earlier modes of geography, sources of circa 1700 evinced a generically European conception of the world and promoted a "universal" form of geography.

This raises a second quality of exotic geography: its discursive style, analogistic design, blended format, and overall strategy of presenting the extra-European world as a vast, intermingled hodgepodge of exotic peoples, places, and things. This had the effect of diluting any single perspective, authorial voice, or national narrative. Textual accounts, cartographic depictions, visual representations, decorative objects: all tended to conflate the parts of the world, to concoct a diverse yet delightful, digressive yet agreeable, global product. Exotic geography in this way reflected a basic commercial imperative: it appealed broadly, and it sold widely. It was an attractive product. And it was a salable product. Exotic geography marketed itself enthusiastically by emphasizing the curious and salacious—there is an inordinate amount of attention to the exotic body and to the corporeal qualities and sexual habits of the non-European world—and by doing so with a Rabelaisian flair for the pungent and racy detail. In its published form—books above all, yet also printed collections of maps, engravings, and etchings—exotic geography came larded with pictures, paratexts, inventories, and other devices, meant to encourage the reader to nimbly "skim" and promiscuously "taste" the world's exotic offerings (as more than one editor advised his readers).[43] This reflected both packaging and branding. Exotic geography presented the world as an agreeable product—an image of the world as commodity, an affordable form of consumable globalism assembled for an eager European audience. And sources marketed and branded this format—so adroitly and consistently made in Holland—in visually sumptuous and winningly designed volumes. Exotic geography ushered in coffee-table books at the dawn of the age of coffee.

All of which suggests, as well, an aesthetic imperative. Exotic geography, even as it crossed genres and media, shared a distinct look and style. Sources of geography jumbled together the sundry parts of the globe and gleefully reproduced these in swirling compositions and meandering narratives, bringing into a single frame or text varied and far-flung exotica. Exotic geography boasted of its capaciousness and abundance; variety, as one editor pitched it in the preface to a collection of exotic miscellany, was the spice of geographic life.[44] And exotic geography lingered on the varied, the unusual, the strange—all trademarks of the exotic style. Arnoldus Montanus reveled in the "strange" mores of the exotic world, which he recorded in his volumes on Japan and America: the "strange" properties of exotic nature, the "strange stories" of exotic religions, the "strange entertainment[s]" of exotic rulers, and, more generally, the "strange novelties" and "[strange] varieties" of the world.[45] For Adam Olearius it was the "the strange Circulations of humane Nature" and—equally imperative—the "divertisment" and "pleasure" that sold his narrative (in Olearius's case, on Muscovy). For Charles de Rochefort, the "delightful variety of things" ensured the value and appeal of his descriptions of the Caribbean: here it is variety *as* delight.[46] Sources in the mode of Rochefort's made this mélange of amusements more tangible by recourse to images, and the exotic style is identifiable, as well, by its emphatic visuality. Printed volumes advertised both the abundant quantity and the superb quality of their pictures, and tomes of Dutch-made geography from this period are in fact exceptionally well illustrated. Many of these exotic images moved, moreover, from medium to medium: from a book's illustrated frontispiece, to a map's baroque cartouche, to the design of a panel painting, to the décor of Delft-made ceramics, and to numerous other material arts—lacquerware, glassware, tapestry, wall panels, carved woods, embellished shells, and so on. In this way, exotic geography generated some of the most powerful and iconic images of the non-European world—exotic clichés and stereotypes (as these would come to be known in the jargon of the printer's atelier), which would endure well into the eighteenth century and beyond.

This book traces several of these exotic images, along with exotic descriptions in textual form, and investigates the manifold processes of their production and consumption in early modern Europe. It considers the making and deployment of exotic motifs, and the causes and effects of their widespread diffusion in the period around 1700. It does so across multiple genres and media encompassing texts, images, and material objects, and it lingers on more than a few particular instances of geographic representation: of exotic peoples and polities, exotic habits and mores, exotic plants and animals, and the exotic body itself. It further explores the changing register of exotic motifs and meanings over time, and the gradual evolution of the concept of a diverting, enticing, "agreeable" world, which was so extensively and enthusiastically embraced by eighteenth-century Europeans. It seeks, in short, to understand what counted for "exotic" and why: to explicate a rich chapter in the history of Europe's engagement with and formulation of the wider world, and of Europe's understanding of its place in the world at this pivotal moment of global history from circa 1670 to 1730.

The ensuing chapters progress more or less chronologically, with the earliest materials dating from the mid- to late seventeenth century, and the final chapter and epilogue investigating issues and sources that extend well into the mid-eighteenth century. The chapters also vary in the evidence they invoke—texts, pictures, objects—although with considerable overlap among them. Chapter 1 ("Printing the World") concentrates on geography texts and geography books and some of the important distinctions between them. It considers two essential questions for the history of printed geography: How was geography produced in its published, textual form, and why, more particularly, did the exceptionally rich and exceedingly popular volumes of exotic geography of this period derive so commonly from Dutch ateliers? The complex processes of production examined in this chapter suggest a need for greater nuance in our assessment of those sources that have traditionally bolstered arguments addressing "European" colonial expansion and the knowledge/power dynamics of this critical imperial moment. Scholars have been perhaps overly quick to make statements about colonial "texts" and their ideological interests, while paying only meager attention to the books that housed them. The manufacture of these books—and, ultimately, of printed textual geography—entailed numerous twists and turns of production and equally many authorial shifts, and this undermines assumptions made about the relationship between geographic literature and colonial action. This chapter explores these twists and turns by providing a textual and bibliogonic study of exotic geography: of the form and brand of book so briskly manufactured in these years, typically in Dutch workshops, which presented European consumers their most influential and durable descriptions of the world.

The intensively visual quality of exotic geography—its insistent presentation of the world in pictorial terms—forms the subject of the second chapter ("Seeing the World"). While the first chapter concerns texts and reading, the second chapter focuses on pictures and looking. It demonstrates how exotic geography established a look—a brand identity—that was highly pictorial and strikingly visual. It was, in this sense, the veritable ancestor of *National Geographic* (the first book printed with four-color illustrations was, in fact, an early modern Dutch-made volume of geography).[47] Works produced by the Dutch circa 1670 to 1730 bore ever more graphic content—engraved, etched, charted, graphed—and they promised to illustrate the exotic world as never before: the Dutch put the *graphic* back into *geographic*, as it were. This suggests *not* an Alpersian art of describing—not an exercise of verisimilitude, a desire to record, replicate, and reproduce faithfully the world for all to see (despite the persistent promise of book after book to deliver "the truth": chapter 1 demonstrates that these were hardly "true" or personal accounts and not at all "Dutch" in terms of their original authorship).[48] Rather, it was an art of packaging: a strategy adopted by the producers of these materials, who keenly understood the benefit of delivering a visual version of the world, designed to entice and engage the broadest possible reading—or better, viewing—public. Rather than delivering bona fide eyewitness accounts, exotic geography produced the *semblance* of sight. The semblance of sight and the semblance of truth would play an instrumental role in the reporting of exotic *naturalia*, and this chapter also explores a central question in the history of early modern science: How do pictures relate to truth claims? It interrogates how witnessing and picturing—both on site and in the atelier—functioned in sources of geography and instigated, accordingly, Enlightenment debates on seeing and believing.

The third chapter moves from words and pictures to sensory experiences and human bodies ("Exotic Bodies"). It analyzes how the distinctive approach of geography in the exotic mode and the manner in which exotic materials were designed and presented led to several critical formulations of the non-European: literally, of the non-European body. In sources of geography from the late seventeenth and early eighteenth centuries—this goes for texts and pictures as well as material arts—the exotic body is characterized by its sensual allure, capacity for pain, and racial ambiguity. The exotic body, in this way, was primed for imperial control. Sex and violence feature centrally in sources of exotic geography, as do several seemingly paradoxical presentations of the non-European body: a simultaneous revulsion and fascination with exotic sexual "perversions"; the intersecting motifs of exotic bodily pain and exotic bodily pleasure; and the pervasive inclination to stage the exotic body as lurid spectacle. These motifs and fascinations offer insight into one of the key concerns of colonial studies—namely, how conceptions of non-European corporality and "race" are articulated in early modern sources. In probing the rhetorical treatment and figurative abuse of the exotic body, this chapter also presents an argument on the evolution of somatic pain and physical torture as motifs in European sources. It sketches out a subtle yet meaningful shift in the register of early modern torture: from religious representations—largely the case in pre-1648 sources, where the *European* body serves as the key site of pain and suffering in depictions of the confessional conflicts of the period—to the representation of the *non-European* body, which becomes an increasingly common place to stage the spectacular violence and "tyrannical" abuse that was meant to prevail in the exotic world.

After pain comes pleasure, and the fourth chapter ("Exotic Pleasures") returns to the conceit of an agreeable world: the identification of the exotic world with the sentiments of desire and pleasure. This chapter turns more squarely to the material arts, which over these years assiduously borrowed exotic motifs and incorporated exotic techniques (lacquer and porcelain are the most obvious examples) and exotic materials (woods, shells, gems, ivory, silk) into their products.[49] It also returns to the subject (broached in chapter 1) of exotic stereotypes: motifs and iconographies that moved readily and effectively among genres and media, transferring typically from two-dimensional, graphic arts (book illustrations, engraved prints, map cartouches) to three-dimensional, decorative arts (ceramics, textiles, furniture). Indeed, exotic imagery produced in this period had a distinctive form and style that readily lent itself to the material arts. More generally, exotic geography was perceived as "decorative," and just like the so-called decorative arts, it was understood to impart diverting pleasures. These tendencies indicate how exotic geography ultimately came to function against its putative purpose. By the early eighteenth century, scholarly critics of Dutch-made geography—this goes particularly for printed books—complained that the field had become, ironically, an indistinct discipline, an imprecise science, and a

FIGURE 4. Jan van der Heyden, *Room with Curiosities* (1712); oil on canvas; 75 × 63.5 cm. Museum of Fine Arts, Budapest.

deceptive mode of representation that effectively disordered and jumbled the globe rather than accounted for its differences. Exotic geography served not so much to delineate the parts of the non-European world as to render them generally "agreeable" to a European consumer.[50]

The book concludes by peering ahead to the middle decades of the eighteenth century, when there was a broad backlash against the form of exotic geography that had flourished in previous years—yet which also saw the persistence of many of the exotic forms that had been forged over the previous century. On the one hand, there was a call for "order and method" and a more "enlightened" approach to the geographic description of the world. Demands for reform came from "learned men," commonly writing from the perspective of metropolitan London and Paris; they denounced the digressions and embellishments of earlier sources of geography. On the other hand, an aesthetic of exoticism carried on in other quarters and other bodies of sources—for example, in the enormously popular design book *The ladies amusement*—where it retained its "decorative" approach to global matters. One set of materials—those focused on "order" and "method"—are taken up by Foucauldian and postcolonial critics, while the other, with its distinctly gendered formulations, is largely ignored by modern scholars. The epilogue ("From Promiscuous Assemblage to Order and Method") demonstrates how the form of exoticism invented in the prior period all but instigated later responses from "enlightened" critics. Exotic geography created a cheerfully disordered world that would ultimately require ordering. Contextualizing these later eighteenth-century sources and debates reveals the subtle political, cultural, commercial, and aesthetic reverberations of the earlier moment of "exoticism." It highlights a history that not only has been overlooked (or misunderstood) by modern critics of European expansion and empire, but is one with broad implications across numerous fields of study and scholarly debate.

A final note: This book offers an inquiry into the origins of European exoticism as they developed in the second half of the seventeenth century, identifying and analyzing a style of presentation and an attitude toward the world that would become immensely influential over the course of the eighteenth century. It does not, however, provide a systematic study of the immense corpus of print geography produced in this period, the copious output of extra-European maps and globes, the profusion of material objects embellished with exotic motifs, and so on. Paintings incorporating exotic subjects—to take but one obvious example—proliferated in this period across several genres. Still lifes with exotic objects, landscapes set in exotic locales, shell and flower paintings centered on exotic *naturalia*, depictions of collectors' cabinets and other assemblages of exotic things—all were pioneered in these very years, chiefly in ateliers of the Netherlands (figure 4 and see plate 16).[51] In so many ways, the Dutch—"*Carryers of the World* . . . and Brokers of *Europe*," as Defoe deftly dubbed them—formulated and fashioned, invented and advanced, the prevailing sense of Europe's exotic world at the turn of the eighteenth century. They supplied the images of the world so that the rest of Europe could launch out and supply itself (to tweak Defoe's characterization). And the rest of Europe duly did assimilate and incorporate this "poetics of space" (as Said would term it), which guided who and what Europe would ultimately become. This book offers a history of this poetics of space, a study of its formulation and the various forms of its expression, and a suggestion of how this earlier moment of engagement with the world may have shaped ideas of global space that have lingered well beyond Defoe and his visions of European expansion.

Talking of the Russians and the Chinese, he advised me to read Bell's travels. I asked him whether I should read Du Halde's account of China. "Why yes, (said he) as one reads such a book; that is to say, consult it."

—JAMES BOSWELL, *The Life of Samuel Johnson* (1768)

CHAPTER ONE

PRINTING THE WORLD

Processed Books and Exotic Stereotypes

The Van Meurs Brand of the World

On 19 May 1664, Europe's exotic world expanded dramatically. This was not the date that saw a particularly far-reaching exploratory voyage launched from a European port (although surely several would have been dispatched at that time). Nor was this the moment when an exceptionally rich vessel returned from the Indies, to be unloaded at the warehouses of Amsterdam, London, Seville, or La Rochelle (again, not an unlikely scenario). Rather, this was the day on which the States of Holland granted the Amsterdam publisher Jacob van Meurs (circa 1618–1680) an exclusive, fifteen-year privilege to publish a large-format book on China based on the journals and on-site sketches of Johan Nieuhof (1618–1672), who had embarked on a quasi-official embassy to the imperial court in Beijing nearly a decade earlier. The story of that publication and the impact of its several, extensively circulated printed editions—and of the broader influence of these books on a wide range of sources of geography, cartography, visual arts, and more—marks the debut, in an important sense, of a new form of European engagement with the non-European world. Van Meurs launched more than a just a ship, and he furnished more than mere commercial profits: he pioneered a new form of descriptive transaction with the exotic world. He hit upon a "printerly" formula for presenting the world—large, lavish, visually ornate books; filled with enticing figures, decorative maps, and other smartly designed paratexts; spanning in their coverage a staggering expanse of the globe; and printed in multiple editions, languages, and formats—thereby establishing a product and a mode of production that would prove phenomenally successful and vastly influential for years to come.[1]

FIGURE 5. Jacob van Meurs, frontispiece (engraving) to Johan Nieuhof, *L'Ambassade de la Compagnie Orientale* (Leiden, 1665). Special Collections, University of Amsterdam (OF 86-10).

Van Meurs's road to China was paved with good, savvy, entrepreneurial intentions. Looking back at this transitional moment without the benefit of hindsight, it is hard to detect the avalanche of geographic production that was rumbling just over the horizon. In the coming fifteen years (the period covered by the States' privileges), van Meurs would publish or oversee the publication of over a dozen volumes of his trademark, large-format geographies, and these would appear in dozens of editions—this on top of the several (at least eight) variations he produced of Nieuhof's best-selling China book.[2] At this pivotal moment of bureaucratic business in 1664, however, Jacob van Meurs was hardly a prominent printer, nor was Johan Nieuhof a particularly well-known traveler. The latter had visited Amsterdam for only a few weeks in the summer of 1658, on his return voyage from the Far East, before heading off on another journey to the Indies. (Nieuhof, who also served in Brazil, would ultimately die overseas, in Madagascar, when his search for fresh water ended with his presumed murder at the hand of the native islanders, a colonial drama that in many ways anticipated the death of Captain Cook a century later.)[3] Before setting off for Asia, however, Nieuhof left his journal with his brother Hendrik, an Amsterdam portrait painter and brick dealer.[4] Johan claims that interested parties had "daily" beseeched him to make his materials available, and while this may be a standard trope of the genre (his comments echo almost precisely those of Jan Huygen van Linschoten in the preface to his famous *Itinerario*), it does indicate the basic commercial value of his journal.[5] Hendrik, in any case, held on to it for a few more years before striking a deal in 1663 or 1664 with van Meurs—likely for cash, yet there is no record of this transaction—who had been actively seeking to expand his business in travel literature.

As it turns out, the journal itself was not as critical to the enterprise as the method of its presentation—or better, transformation—and here one discerns the mediations of van Meurs and just how innovative they were. For the journal of Johan Nieuhof, as produced by Jacob van Meurs, was a bona fide "journal" in name only: it provided, literally, a name, and it assigned a coherent authorship to a disparate set of narratives. And even as it assertively advertised the Dutch embassy to China and made much of the on-spot reporting of Johan Nieuhof, its titular author and credible narrator, the book comprised in fact several texts, many of them derived from earlier Jesuit sources (an irony of sorts, since the eventual failure of the Dutch embassy and its commercial-diplomatic initiative in China was likely engineered by the Jesuits, who were deeply antagonistic to their Protestant rivals). These non-Nieuhof sources were disguised and embedded in the narrative, a technique that van Meurs would employ over and over again in his books. Authorship was bestowed upon a single figure, thereby establishing a trustworthy authority for the volume's contents—an authorial beachhead, as it were, a viable figure to take on the author-function for the volume—while several otherwise authored texts were adopted and augmented, massaged and manipulated, such that the end product offered something more akin to a hodgepodge "description" (as this genre of geography was sometimes called) than a personal travelogue.[6] More important than the text, moreover, were the paratexts, and above all the copious and well-engraved illustrations, which sometimes bore only tangential connections to the prose they purported to delineate. For these van Meurs relied on a group of skilled draftsmen who worked under his direction (van Meurs himself had trained as an engraver), just as he employed a stable of *afschrijvers*—the Dutch word translates as copyist, yet it implies more accurately someone who writes anonymous copy for a publisher, or perhaps even a ghostwriter—to convert his miscellaneous manuscripts into books.

This energetic, interactive, highly interventionist process of bookmaking was hardly new. Printers had played an active role in the authorship of books since the invention of movable type (compare, in this regard, the work of modern book packagers). What was new in the 1660s was the perfection of this modus operandi in the field of geography and the evident success with it enjoyed by van Meurs. For van Meurs sold the public not only on this and several other printed descriptions of the world, which fully dominated the market for the next few decades; he also sold them on a style of publication and a form of exotic geography. Van Meurs's books were easily identified and eagerly anticipated. They had a recognizable appearance that highlighted the consumer's role in *looking* at geography, which was delivered in notably visual packages: swirling frontispiece prints, showing the peoples and products of the globe; full-page engraved illustrations, invariably advertised on the title page; fold-out maps; trademark city views; ethnographic portraits; and so on. Van Meurs's products also emphasized textual matters, particularly the "truth" of the account, the on-site presence of the designated author, and, by extension, the "credit" of the narrative. These techniques, pioneered in Nieuhof's trendsetting China volume and then tinkered with and perfected in subsequent publications on Japan, India, Persia, Africa, America, and many more exotic locales, launched the van Meurs brand of geography. They established a type of geographic product that consumers readily recognized and cheerfully embraced. Melchisédech Thévenot, van Meurs's colleague and (lesser) rival in Paris—Thévenot published a series of travel accounts that sought to emulate Dutch-publishing techniques—singled out the quality of Dutch geography of this time and expressed his admiration for the Nieuhof book in particular, the publication of which Thévenot himself anxiously awaited (and promptly pirated, albeit in a less successful format). He and others looked forward to the new "narrative of one of their [Dutch] merchants, whose reports in the past have so often turned out to be truthful; they describe things just as they are," he pronounced approvingly. Dutch volumes of geography were the standard-setting, sought after sources for the exotic world.[7]

FIGURE 6. Jacob van Meurs (atelier), "Asia" (engraved frontispiece), in Olfert Dapper, *Asia: of Naukeurige beschryving van het rijk des Grooten Mogols* (Amsterdam, 1672). Special Collections, University of Amsterdam (OM 63-115).

Malabaarse Lantlopers die Slangen Laten Danßen

FIGURE 7. Willem vander Gouwen, "Malabaarse Lantlopers die Slangen Laten Danssen" (engraving), in Johan Nieuhof, *Gedenkwaerdige zee en lantreize door de voornaemste landschappen van West en Oostindien* (Amsterdam, 1682). Special Collections, University of Amsterdam (KF 61-4601).

This chapter explores how and why this was so. Van Meurs and the numerous other, mostly Holland-based bookmakers who followed in his footsteps endeavored to create a new mode of describing the world and, in the process, forged a new genre of geography. They established a format, or style, of printed description, which exercised exceptionally far-reaching appeal. This appeal was based, to a large degree, on the distinctive look of their books, their typographic construction, and their high "credit"—a term that applied both to the names on the title pages, printer no less than author, as well as to the materials presented within. Moreover, by designing such broadly printed, distributed, translated, emulated, and pirated books, and by crafting such pervasively imitated forms of geography, Dutch publishers established new ways of replicating and engaging with non-European places, peoples, and artifacts. They developed a new process of reproducing the world. Their innovations greatly influenced how exotic knowledge was conveyed, framed, and presented in this period (roughly the final third of the seventeenth and first third of the eighteenth centuries). More than inducing a mere generic shift, their efforts instigated a wholesale transformation of how Europeans consumed their expanding globe.[8] The publishing practices of van Meurs followed a certain commercial logic—as does all publishing—and many of these "Dutch" sources were anything but Dutch: Spanish, Portuguese, and Italian materials on the Indies were expertly transformed for French, English, and German markets. Yet the end product emanated, by and large, from Holland, the hub of exoticism. Holland and above all Amsterdam printers, illustrators, cartographers, and bookmakers in this way invented a fresh form of exoticism. They produced a profoundly influential form of the world, which would endure for years to come.

Processed Books and Processes of Production

The production of European books describing the non-European world took off spectacularly in the decades approaching 1700. Certainly the field of geography had grown appreciably in the period following Europe's overseas expansion of the late fifteenth century. Yet this later moment of exotic geography witnessed a whole new order of bookmaking, in terms of both quantity and quality. From the final third of the seventeenth century and through the first third of the eighteenth, the large-scale manufacture of wide-ranging, superbly printed volumes of geography flourished, particularly in Holland, which issued some of the most attractive and desirable accounts available of the globe—of global nature, global religion, global culture, global history, and so on. While there are several microclimates to be discerned in this terrain of exotic geography, certain general patterns—hot spells of production, lofty figures of bookmaking, salubrious subjects for publication—may

FIGURE 8. Jacob van Meurs (atelier), "America" (engraved frontispiece), in Arnoldus Montanus, *De nieuwe en onbekende weereld* (Amsterdam, 1671). Koninklijke Bibliotheek, The Hague.

be readily identified. Jacob van Meurs played a pivotal role in launching this moment of descriptive print, and his output from the mid-1660s through the early 1680s is truly staggering (he died in late 1679 or early 1680, leaving several projects to be published posthumously by his widow and his sometime partners). Van Meurs and his fecund atelier produced stupendously illustrated folio volumes on America, Africa (one apiece on northern and sub-Saharan), India, China (two separately authored publications), and Japan—all in the seven dynamic years following Nieuhof's groundbreaking China book. Additional volumes (also printed in folio) on the Levant, the Mediterranean islands, the Near East, and Persia followed; and three more books of travel literature (as opposed to descriptive geography) covered the West and East Indies, South and Southeast Asia, and Central Asia—albeit some of these published by van Meurs's widow or with occasional partners, with whom van Meurs sometimes collaborated in the competitive world of Amsterdam publishing.

If van Meurs unleashed this flood of geography in the 1660s, the other figure who stands out, occupying the other end of this bibliographic landscape, is Pieter van der Aa. Van der Aa (1659–1733) occupies an enviable place in the history of early modern print; he was the leading bookmaker of Leiden from the 1690s through the early 1730s and perhaps the most ambitious European publisher of his day. He mastered a slightly different form of geography than van Meurs, issuing massive, serial compilations, often comprising previously published texts, which were generously embellished with engraved maps, city views (or *vedute*), exotic *naturalia*, ethnographic scenes, and the like. Indeed, by the end of his career, the visual component of van der Aa's remarkable body of work had nudged out the textual, a process that culminated in the almost wholly pictorial, sixty-six-tome *Galerie agreable du monde* (circa 1729), a staggering graphic production that boasted in the range of four thousand illustrations. Van der Aa issued several other multivolume (and multilingual) compilations of geography, which became highly sought after on the international market: a mammoth "Collection of the Most Memorable Sea and Land Travels," which appeared in 130 installments or as a twenty-eight-volume set; a series of smaller-sized travel "guides" (as opposed to travelogues), which sold under the catchy brand name "Les Délices"; several "grand" atlases, including the sumptuous *Nouveau theatre du monde, ou La geographie royale*, printed on extra-large folio paper (figure 9); and a smaller-format *Atlas soulagé*, pitched to the lower end of the market. Van der Aa also collaborated on the publication of a gorgeous *florilegium* that depicted global plants ("terrestrial flora"), some 250 of which merited full-page engraved illustrations; and on a *thesaurus*, or treasury, of marine fauna that featured the invertebrate animals and mollusks of the East Indian seas.[9]

FIGURE 9. François van Bleiswyk, "Le Nouveau Theatre du Monde" (engraved frontispiece), in Pieter van der Aa, *Le nouveau theatre du monde, ou La geographie royale* (Leiden, 1713). Beinecke Rare Book and Manuscript Library, Yale University.

In between these two towering figures of exotic typography, whose careers so eloquently bookend this geographic moment, stood several other exceptional printers, engravers, and booksellers active in the field. Some of these in fact teamed up with van Meurs and van der Aa—not an uncommon practice when undertaking such high-cost print projects. Others simply come under the rubric of "important printers of the late seventeenth and early eighteenth century" who recognized the obvious commercial opportunities in the business of geography. Johannes Janssonius van Waesberge—a scion of two illustrious bookmaking families and the printer of Athanasius Kircher's *China illustrata*—and Johannes van Someren of Amsterdam both competed and cooperated with van Meurs in the 1670s and 1680s.[10] Van Someren joined forces with van Meurs in the publication of two high-profile travel accounts, one by Wouter Schouten and the other by Jan Jansz Struys, each of which appeared in multiple languages and editions.[11] Van Someren also produced important travel accounts on his own, and he partnered in the publication of Hendrik Adriaan van Reede tot Drakenstein's monumental *Hortus Indicus Malabaricus*, a twelve-volume study of South Asian *naturalia* (figure 11). Janssonius van Waesberge and van Someren pooled their resources to print Philip Baldaeus's best-selling description of Malabar and Coromandel, which, like most of their other printed endeavors of the period, mimicked van Meurs's trademark visual approach to geography and in some ways even challenged the master's dominance of the market.[12] François Halma, who specialized in learned publications and spent twenty-five years as "printer for the academy" in the university town of Utrecht, contributed several extraordinary geography publications, including editions of Nicolaes Witsen's two-volume description of "Tartary" (figure 12) and Georg Rumphius's stunning natural history of Ambon.[13] And Jan Claesz ten Hoorn, who concentrated on "popular" travel narratives (a Dutch tradition from the early seventeenth century) and overseas "handbooks" (exhaustive lists of, for example, medical plants, natural products, or commercial goods available in the Indies), also found a niche in the rough and tumble world of Amsterdam bookselling in the 1680s and 1690s.[14] Add to this list the Netherlands' well-known printers of cartographic materials—the ateliers of Blaeu, Janssonius, Visscher, de Wit, Danckerts, van Keulen, and so on—and its outstanding cohort of graphic artists—the likes of Romeyn de Hooghe, Jan Luyken, and Bernard Picart all flourished in these years and in the context of these publications—and one gets a keen sense of the phenomenal contribution made by the Dutch in these years to the field of geographic print.

The scope of geographic publishing, as all of this might suggest, was also impressively broad. This goes for the range of generic subfields, the span of geographic coverage, and even the breadth of market reach. To begin with the last of these, even as van Meurs and his imitators perfected the art of the thick, illustrated, folio "descriptions," which mostly appealed to well-to-do consumers—these were ample

FIGURE 10. Idol in Arakan (etching), in Wouter Schouten, *Oost-Indische voyagie* (Amsterdam, 1676). Special Collections, University of Amsterdam (OG 77-17).

volumes designed to highlight their full-page and often double-page engravings; their fold-out maps, tables, and explanatory charts; their various textual synopses delivered in tables of contents, chapter overviews, marginalia, and indices—other printers pitched their products to more modest buyers. In the case of geography, it should be emphasized, hard distinctions between "elite" and "popular" are not especially useful. Even while some products sold for a princely sum and thus exclusively to the princely classes and most elite merchants—van der Aa's *Galerie agreable* fetched a cool 416 guilders (about the average annual salary for a master

FIGURE 11. "Horti Indici Malabarici" (engraved frontispiece), in Hendrik Adriaan van Reede tot Drakestein, *Hortus Indicus Malabaricus* (Amsterdam, 1678–1679). Peter H. Raven Library, Missouri Botanical Garden. Image courtesy of the Biodiversity Heritage Library.

Noord ooster gedeelte
van
ASIA en EUROPA
Door
Nicolaes Witsen

IN AMSTERDAM,
By FRANÇOIS HALMA, Boekverkoper.
MDCCV.

FIGURE 12. Frontispiece (engraving) to Nicolaes Witsen, *Noord en Oost Tartarye, ofte bondig ontwerp van eenige dier landen en volken, welke voormaels bekent zijn geweest*, 2nd ed. (Amsterdam, 1705; 1st ed. 1692). Special Collections, University of Amsterdam (KF 61-1504-05).

craftsman), which approximated the price of Joan Blaeu's *Atlas major* when ordered in a deluxe edition[15]—down-market publications could also draw buyers from the ranks of privileged collectors, who were hardly less interested in the less expensively produced journals of exploration than in the high-end geographies. More to the point, inexpensive products, just like costly ones, featured plentiful illustrations (albeit sometimes in woodcut) and strategic paratexts, which were meant, likewise, to entice the consumer and usher the reader through the book. Some works appeared concurrently in high- and low-end editions, the same text effectively packaged in competing formats (folio versus quarto, for example). And a book's discrete components—this goes especially for engraved maps and *vedute*—could be marketed and sold separately by the publisher, who often did good business selling individually printed sheets as well as full-fledged books (and who might have doubled as an engraver: van Meurs is a fine example, and several printers in the cartography trade also trained as engravers).

As for their geographic and generic range, Dutch materials covered virtually all of the known world—from a European standpoint, to be sure—which they approached from assorted perspectives and in myriad forms. This meant the production of several categories of books that contended with the exotic world, genres that became closely aligned with the dynamism of Dutch print. Holland-made travel journals proliferated in this period, as did global "descriptions," a title word that was invoked with growing frequency in this period, its usage meant to denote a form of geography that was not expressly personal (as was the travel journal).[16] Cartographic printing, which culminated in the celebrated "grand" atlases manufactured in Amsterdam from the 1660s, flourished as well in the form of maritime atlases; colossal world maps; regional, and hence more affordable, sheet maps; terrestrial globes (crafted from printed gores); and the mixed form of geography perfected and promoted by van der Aa, which interspersed maps with city views, exotic landscapes, and vignettes of foreign "mores," sprinkled throughout with brief and perfunctory text. Van der Aa also dabbled in another specialty of Dutch geographic printing: anthologies of "curious" texts and images, which were typically recycled from sundry publications or perhaps reconstituted by a so-called *veelschrijver* (the word translates loosely as "'prolific writer," yet its meaning comes closer to "hack," or someone who combines the attributes of a hired scribbler with the energy of a Trollope). These collections presented vast, sprawling compendia of seemingly haphazardly arranged wonders, which approximated in their construction a printed form of the *Wunderkammer*. They bore titles that commonly played on this spatial analogy: "The Great Cabinet of Curiosities," "The Wonder-Filled World," or, more prosaically (and more commercially candid), "The Warehouse of Wonders."[17] This geographic moment also generated a gush of publications in the field of exotic natural history. The high-water mark of this production around the

FIGURE 13. Maria Sibylla Merian, Banana plant (hand-colored engraving), in *Metamorphosis insectorum Surinamensium* (Amsterdam, 1705). Special Collections, University of Amsterdam (OL 63 1090).

turn of the century—the publication, from around 1695 to 1705, of stupendous volumes on South American insects, South Indian plants, and Indian Ocean crustaceans—has been identified as the *decennium mirabilis* of early modern natural history, and Amsterdam draftsmen, engravers, and printers were central to this astonishing publishing achievement.[18] Finally, there were several thematically oriented books produced in these years addressing exotic "mores": the religions of the world, the social customs of the world, the dress ("habits") of the world, the polities of the world, and so on.[19]

The variety and extent of publication in the field of geography was further amplified by the manner in which printers expanded their reach, churning out multiple editions and translations of books and prints, while adopting strategies that also sought to maximize circulation and audience. Print runs in the Dutch Republic were relatively high in the first place, and books in the field of geography were no exception. While not all printers have left evidence of their output, and while some made a point of advertising the *limited* distribution of certain deluxe, status-imparting products—Louis Renard's princely volume on tropical fish was available (so Renard claimed) in a mere one hundred copies, five of which went to the royal dedicatee, King George I of England; and van der Aa restricted the audience of his regal *Galerie agreable* likewise to one hundred wealthy buyers[20]—extant data suggest substantial print numbers. Broadly speaking, publishers in the business of geography produced somewhere between 750 and 2,000 copies per title, the higher number corresponding to lower-cost products and the lesser figure to the most deluxe editions.[21]

Quite remarkably, several of the intensively illustrated folio volumes, which fetched well-above-average prices (reflecting the high costs of paper no less than the engravers' labor), justified print runs of well over a thousand. Cornelis de Bruijn, who authored, illustrated, and directed the publication of his *Voyage to the Levant*, advertised a subscription list that showed a print run of at least 1,350. This represents a *minimum* estimate, since copies would also have been printed to be sold on the open market (namely, to nonsubscribers).[22] A public auction in 1735 following the death of Pieter van der Aa revealed not only a healthy stock of titles that had been printed earlier in the century—the printer's widow possessed hundreds of copies of travel books published some thirty years earlier, indicating the ongoing sale of these books. It also showed print runs of books only recently, or not yet, offered for sale. Van der Aa had on hand around 1,200 copies of a not-yet-advertised work on tropical Florida, and his shop had close to 1,000 copies of several recently published titles. Taken together, the van der Aa data indicate print runs between 1,000 and perhaps 1,500.[23] Records of a van Meurs family dowry dispute in 1678, generated by the marriage just a few years earlier of Jacob's only daughter, divulge the presence in van Meurs's print shop of some 500 copies of books on India, China, and Africa (along with hundreds of other books), which had been published around 1670. This number presumably represents only a fraction of the original production, which would have been about twice as many copies, if not more.[24]

Once they launched a book into print, publishers generated ever more editions and translations over the coming years. The privileges granted to booksellers typically specified a course of publication—such as those issued by the States of Holland to Jacob van Meurs in 1664—and, accordingly, a plan for market expansion. This was more or less expected: printers in the business of geography aggressively established, and then defended, their market share. So, of course, did printers of other genres, and it can hardly be claimed that revised editions and foreign-language translations were new developments in printing; nor were these practices special to the field of geography (religious books could go through scores of editions) or to the book trade in the Netherlands.[25] What was innovative, however, and especially impressive in this period and for this field was the all but invariable republication of the large-format, intensively illustrated, tough-to-produce volumes that were the hallmark of Dutch-made geography, and the control that a single printer or consortium of printers retained over their product. What is striking is how commonly this occurred and how uncommonly difficult it was to produce these books in the first place.[26]

The publication by van Meurs of a string of exotic geographies, authored by the stay-at-home tandem of Olfert Dapper (1636–1689) and Arnoldus Montanus (1625–1683), is fairly typical. All of the Dapper and Montanus titles—on America, Africa, "Syria" (the Middle East), the Levant (including southeastern Europe), Persia, India, China, Japan, and so on, ten volumes in all, depending on how you tally them[27]—appeared in fat folios (often closing in on 1,000 pages); all included a superlative body of graphic work (plus, invariably, an expertly engraved frontispiece); and all carried an extensive battery of paratexts. All, in short, were expensive to make—not least on account of the paper they were printed on, which, in this period of exorbitant paper costs (the 1660s through 1680s), drove up prices.[28] All but one, however, came out in multiple editions, one appeared in *nine* editions (and several more in the range of half a dozen editions), and almost all of these various editions came out under the auspices of van Meurs's enterprising atelier in Amsterdam (rather than with a competing printer). All but one, too, were translated—regularly into French, German, and English, and once into Greek—and the process of translation, remarkably enough, almost always remained under the control of van Meurs himself rather than foreign printers, as was otherwise typically the case for early modern imprints. (Van Meurs generally commissioned the work to Holland-based scholars and translators; for English editions, he sent plates or ready-printed illustrations to the London office of John Ogilby, the Royal Geographer, who organized the translations.)[29] There were invariably, in later years, revised editions done by other printers (sometimes former collaborators), and some of the texts were ultimately pirated. Yet the scope of control exercised by van Meurs over his product is exceptional—as was the extent of his products' reach, the vastness of which surely must have justified his considerable material investment. Van Meurs's entire opus was even "digested" in an extraordinary publication, *Dapperus exoticus curiosus* (the title conflating, in this instance, the two authors Dapper and

Montanus), which offered a sort of readers' digest of the "much-read" corpus, as the title page asserts, of van Meurs–made geography.[30] The presumably over-whelmed consumer could herewith obtain abbreviated, note-like synopses of the entire Dapper-cum-Montanus output, not merely summarized but also referenced with page citations to the original books: a handy owner's manual to van Meurs's empire of geography.

As impressive as the van Meurs output may have been, it was not an isolated phenomenon. Several other large-scale projects of printed geography radiated from the Netherlands in these years: bulky books, produced in plentiful editions, and cir-culated widely by bookmakers such as Janssonius van Waesberge and van Someren; Gillis Joosten Saeghman and François Halma (the former working at the lower end, the latter at the higher end of the market); van der Aa (based in Leiden) and the other Holland atlas makers (mostly in Amsterdam); Jean-Frédéric Bernard and Ber-nard Picart (who teamed up to produce massive books on global religion); and the many other printers and engravers active in the decades around 1700.[31] Indeed, the energetic production in the field of geography, and the fierce ambition and compe-tition among Dutch booksellers, induced some of the many printerly innovations that van Meurs and his colleagues developed in these years. The practice of solicit-ing book subscriptions, for example, had existed earlier in the century, in England no less than Holland (Dutch printers in this case borrowing from their London colleagues). Yet this somewhat experimental strategy of book-dealing, which of-fered printers a hedge against the immense resources needed to invest in large-scale publications, was greatly refined in the context of Dutch geography.[32] Cornelis de Bruijn used subscription for both of his sumptuously illustrated travel books, as did François Valentyn for his monumental five-volume description of the East In-dies. De Bruijn's prospectuses for potential subscribers of his *Klein Asia* (Asia Minor) and *Muscovy*—both of these volumes offered far more extensive coverage than their titles imply (*Muscovy* became famous for its engravings of Persepolis), and both rank among the most richly illustrated books of their day[33]—provide sharp detail of the costs and payment options for specific editions. They also allude, inter alia, to the markets de Bruijn aspired to reach. The books could be ordered large or extra large—in regular folio or on "great paper," as it was known—and payment could be made in installments. Size definitely mattered, with the larger-paper edi-tion raising costs by 25 to 30 percent. Illustrations were critical too, with the more opulently engraved pages of *Muscovy*, which boasted about one and half times the pictures of *Klein Asia* (circa 300 versus 200), costing nearly twice as much.[34] The list of subscribers reveals a distinctly international market, even for the Dutch-language editions (the books also appeared in French and English). And it also reveals a built-in secondary market for the books: the seventy-nine orders for seven or more volumes of *Klein Asia* strongly suggest that certain subscribers purchased

ZUIDLANDER.

FIGURE 14. Cornelis de Bruijn, "Zuidlander" (engraving), in *Cornelis de Bruins Reizen over Moskovie, door Persie en Indie* (Amsterdam, 1711). Special Collections, University of Amsterdam (KF 61-1546).

copies with the intention of reselling them for profit (and the vast majority of these bulk orders did *not* come from fellow booksellers).[35]

De Bruijn also innovated, in this case almost wholly originally and quite spectacularly, by printing two copies of his Asia Minor book in color, one in Dutch and another in French (see plate 2). This was not only a highly inventive and arguably unprecedented development in the annals of printing, but also an enormous outlay of resources that produced stunning results; it shows the critical standing of Dutch-made geography in the history of the book. A technique for four-color printing had been tinkered with a few years earlier by Johannes Teyler, a draftsman from Nijmegen. This entailed using a single imprint to reproduce mechanically a colored page (rather than making multiple impressions for each color, as had earlier been done), and Teyler had used this method to produce several miscellaneous loose prints. There is a chance that Teyler and de Bruijn met in the Levant during the latter's travels, and there is no doubt that de Bruijn was able to learn and apply Teyler's technique to the process of printing an entire book—with outstanding results. The two color editions of the Asia Minor book became a sensation in the world of bibliophiles, art enthusiasts, and—not least—lovers of geography. They were an attraction in their own right, enticing visitors to de Bruijn's atelier in Amsterdam. The German traveler Zacharias Conrad van Uffenbach passed through in March 1711 and admired these "wondrous" volumes, which he celebrated in his journal. Others had printed perhaps rudimentary works in color or single-sheet color prints, van Uffenbach observed, and others had produced hand-illustrated geographies. Yet none had published a color volume as impressive as de Bruijn's. "There was nothing to compare," he enthused, with the astonishingly engraved and vividly colored images in de Bruijn's geography. De Bruijn's book depicted in "true" detail and more remarkably than any other Uffenbach had seen the peoples and places of the exotic world.[36]

To label a book "incomparable" in the context of the Dutch printing industry of circa 1700 was high praise indeed. For the publication of de Bruijn's exotic geography took place during one of the most extraordinary moments in the history of early modern publishing, when Holland in general and Amsterdam more particularly enjoyed an unrivaled, unassailable position of supremacy in the book trade.[37] Over the course of the seventeenth century, the Dutch Republic transformed itself into the hub of the European book trade, and by the final decades of the century, circumstances allowed Holland to become still more dominant in the production of those large-scale print projects that had become the hallmark of exotic geography. Several factors supported the rise and reign of Dutch printing. Economic conditions, for the most part, greatly bolstered the industry, although some qualifications are necessary for certain later intervals in the century, when the Republic's economic health weakened. At the opening of the century, to be sure, printing in Holland received an invaluable boost in the form of capital—printing is an exemplary capital-intensive industry—which migrated from the South Netherlands to the north along with those Flemish war refugees who fled the Spanish army. Paper, often a printer's greatest expense, entered the Republic from France and in such abundance that there remained enough left over to support a thriving export trade out of Amsterdam.

Later in the century, when French supplies ran dry, the "Hollander" method of pulping and paper production, an innovative process that took advantage of wind-driven mills, developed in the gusty Zaan region and produced some of Europe's finest white paper. Type cast by Amsterdam typefounders supported not only Holland's thriving ateliers, but also London's, well into the eighteenth century; and several other technicians and artists vital to the business of print were amply available in Holland (and, in many cases, available for export, too): typesetters, draftsmen, engravers, colorists, cartographers, and many more, who made the Dutch print industry a well-oiled machine throughout the century.[38]

Many of these factors speak to the supply of printed materials, yet there were other dynamics that spurred demand, as well. Cultural and political conditions alike favored the Republic's business in books, although in many cases these were circumstances that sustained, more pervasively, the Netherlands' strong early modern economy. Unusually high literacy rates in the exceptionally urban setting of the United Provinces—this goes particularly for the province of Holland—meant that there was a ready domestic market for reading material. Half of adult Dutch men in this period could read, and a third of adult women; the brisk Dutch economy of the seventeenth century meant, furthermore, that this reading public had the disposable income actually to acquire books. The influence of printers' guilds—or rather the lack thereof—also provided booksellers with comparatively greater flexibility. The Amsterdam guild was organized only in 1662—until then printers could join the St. Lucas guild, which primarily served painters—and this meant that regulation of the industry was lax. This also goes for political and religious meddling, which was relatively limited; and this points to larger societal factors of the sort that distinguish the Republic's development in the Golden Age more generally. These factors include a loose and decentralized political structure, which provided for greater local autonomy and less intrusive mechanisms for censorship; relative religious tolerance, which permitted skilled artisans of virtually all stripes (including foreign-born) to participate in the printing industry and, at the same time, assured a multilingual and heterodox reading public that could support a range of printed products; an excellent internal distribution system centered on Amsterdam, which transported publications to other Dutch cities as well as to the Dutch countryside; and the all-important role of Amsterdam as a global entrepôt (and an accessible European commercial center), which meant that merchants and travelers, products and ideas, from across the continent and around the globe could enter the Dutch Republic and contribute, in various ways, to the business of books.

The international character of the Republic's commerce and the centrality of Amsterdam as a hub of trade became particularly important in the second half of the century, when the domestic economy went through several rough patches. It seems particularly striking that the emergence of printed exotica took place *not* during one of the commercial peaks of the Netherlands but during the crisis-filled decades of the 1660s and 1670s, which coincided with two Anglo-Dutch wars, a French invasion, and the *Rampjaar* (disaster year) of 1672. As the domestic market for books faltered, however, the international market expanded, something that becomes more pronounced in the final third of the seventeenth century. By the 1660s and especially from the mid-1680s, when the revocation of the Edict of Nantes sent a flood of Huguenot refugees flowing out of France and into the Netherlands, Dutch printers increasingly published French titles, a trend that partly displaced the earlier pattern of Dutch-issued Latin titles and a trend that carried on well into the eighteenth century. For several decades, too, booksellers in Holland furnished the market in England with printed materials, both Dutch-made or otherwise imported from the Continent.[39] As the economic climate became less hospitable, moreover, printers felt the need to innovate in order to create more profitable products. It is in this context that printers experimented with novel forms and strategies of publication: profusely illustrated accounts of foreign lands, serialized and large-scale publications sold per subscription, rapid translations of texts into other European languages, handsomely turned-out volumes on exotic natural history, global religions, and so on. They experimented, that is to say, with those forms of geography that streamed off Dutch presses beginning in the mid 1660s. In the final third of the seventeenth century and the early decades of the eighteenth, the Republic became not only "le Magasin de l'univers," as it was famously known, but also the leading purveyor of *images* of the universe. The Dutch, in short, printed the world.

Making Exotic Geography: Impresarios of Print

The much sought-after volumes of geography printed in the Netherlands over these years were concocted out of several ingredients, all expertly prepared. Or rather—to use a more workmanlike metaphor—they were manufactured by enterprising bookmen (and occasionally bookwomen) who smartly assembled the various components of these volumes into a demonstrably appealing whole.[40] Early modern books were generally produced, not written—manufactured, not authored—and this process of production took place in well-organized ateliers, under the guidance of artisan-entrepreneurs: the printer-cum-bookseller (in the Netherlands the two positions were commonly combined in a single person or, in later years, in a corporation). Roger Chartier has written of the "textual tyranny" of traditional literary approaches to early modern books and of the "imperialism of close reading."[41] In both cases, he has in mind the way critics tend to privilege the text over the book and, in the process, pay at best passing attention to the forms (or even genres) in which a text is delivered. Chartier's typographically sensitive, quasi-formal approach certainly applies to travel literature, a relatively new genre in the early modern period, and it applies even more so to the particularly "constructed" form of geography that developed in the second half of the seventeenth century (with roots in the sixteenth century, to be sure). In analyzing the social and cultural functions of literature, Chartier singles out the importance of editorial practices and publishing strategies. (The two are not the same, even when undertaken by the same person, and while the first gets more attention than Chartier sometimes admits, the second gets almost none.) Both are essential to understanding that which gets glibly referred to as "literature." "Forms effect meaning," Chartier posits, citing the New Zealand historian of the book Donald McKenzie, who makes this essential point by way of introducing the groundbreaking literary subfield that McKenzie terms (and has done so much to instigate) "the sociology of texts."[42] Underscoring the role of the bookmaker makes all the more sense for the form of printed geography produced circa 1700, which tended to entail—to a greater degree than other forms of books, almost by definition—an impressive array of paratexts, visual apparatuses, printerly appendages, and the like. These were less composed than *processed* books.

One final insight from the innovative work of book historians. Chartier borrows from Michel de Certeau the concept of "poaching," recast by Chartier as "appropriating."[43] In both cases, their strategy for analyzing literary artifacts encourages them to grant the reader a greater role in the process of consuming books; in both cases, as well, early modern literature is shown to be less stable than might otherwise be allowed by its critics, who are inclined to fetishize "the text" at the expense of the book and thus to devalue the "readerly" process of constructing meaning outside of authorial control. Chartier's and Certeau's hermeneutics cast salutary light on the *consumption* of books; they move away from the critics' narrow focus on texts and their application to putative authors, and toward a broader concern with books and their hands-on readers. Yet they may inadvertently leave in the shadows another process of "poaching," which takes place in the *production* of books: the role played by bookmakers in gathering, appropriating, manipulating, and, of course, setting into type those materials that are ultimately presented in final printed form as books. This exercise of bookmaking generally falls under the rubric of "editing," and the "editor" of a book sometimes earns acknowledgment for his or her literary labors—yet more often does not, or earns it only halfheartedly. More often, too, the dynamic process of reformulating texts (and images) to create books goes unexamined. The later variants of an "original," appropriated text often go undistinguished, and editors and publishers—bookmakers—go largely unrecognized for what might accurately be thought of as an authorial role. We tend to ignore editors at the expense of titular authors and to downgrade "editorial practices" in preference to the alchemy and romance of writing.[44]

"Editors," "publishers," "printers," and "booksellers" are all somewhat inaccurate and inadequate terms to describe the architects and engineers of printed geography, who might best be called simply bookmakers or perhaps impresarios of print. These were the entrepreneurs of exotic geography—versatile and creative, astute and ambitious. In the book world of the early modern Netherlands, a single figure generally filled the duties of both printer and bookseller; volumes printed in one's atelier might be made available for purchase in one's adjacent shop. The printer/bookseller might also fill the role of engraver. Jacob van Meurs was trained and originally registered as a *plaatsnijder*, or engraver (1649), a professional status he continued to hold at least until he obtained the privileges for Nieuhof's book, at which time (1664) he entered the guild as a merchant of books and art. In truth, his far-ranging skills—and professional identities—are not so easily categorized. On the title page of the first Dutch edition of Nieuhof's China book (1665), van Meurs fashions himself a "Boekverkooper [*sic*] en Plaatsnijder" (bookseller and engraver), while for the French edition (also 1665), he fills the role merely of "Marchand Libraire" (bookseller), and by the German edition (1666), he reverts to a "Buch- und Kunst-händlern" (book and art dealer). His widow retained her guild membership only as a "bookseller."[45] Johannes Janssonius van Waesberge, who married into the well-established (and well-off) Janssonius family of atlas makers, earned his stripes as a bookseller and printer. He barely bothered with the manual craft of engraving, yet he did buy and sell plates made by others. He also pioneered the business of collaborative publishing: a corporate approach to large-scale, jointly financed print projects that were directed by consortia of bookmen and investors and came to be called "compagnies."[46] Then there is the case of Pieter van der Aa, who trained as a printer, was licensed as a bookseller, and may rank as the most impressive bookmaker of his age. His innovative approach to publishing indicates an important role as book designer, as well, and as a book promoter. His *Galerie agreable* offered a fresh take on book formatting—apart from the book's gargantuan bulk, it also innovated in its prodigiously pictorial form, with many of the images smartly engraved within trompe l'oeil "frames" (figure 15 and see figure 149)—and his serialized publications reveal a knack for marketing and advertising (and an appetite for financial risk). Virtually all of his publications give evidence, too, of editorial selection, intervention, interpolation, and augmentation, which applies to the graphic (especially cartographic) materials no less than the textual. In his myriad guises, van der Aa brilliantly inhabited the role of impresario of print.

The editor-figure occupied several roles and performed many tasks, yet he or she also assumed an organizational function that might be likened to a director of operations ("les directeurs de l'ouvrage," as one preface phrased it), the overseer of a highly complex commercial enterprise.[47] There was, to begin with, the composition of the text—what we tend to think of as authorship, yet which involved, in truth, far more. Manuscripts attracted fierce competition in the ruthless world of Dutch publishing,

FIGURE 15. "Animalia diverse generis" (engraving with etching), in Pieter van der Aa, *La galerie agreable du monde* (Leiden, ca. 1729). Collection Antiquariaat Forum BV, 't Goy-Houten, The Netherlands.

and travel journals in particular sparked the seventeenth-century equivalent of bidding wars for the next potential best seller. Several authors' prefaces allude to this heated environment, offering tantalizing glimpses into the early modern art of the book deal: the incessant visits from "dealers," the pressure to make texts and drawings available to publishers, the anxiety over deadlines, and so on. Nieuhof writes in this vein—"Daily I had numerous visits from various *liefhebbers* [literally "amateurs," yet in this context "interested parties"] who wished to see the manuscripts and sketches I had brought back from China"—echoing similar comments made by the great Dutch traveler-writer Jan Huygen van Linschoten.[48] There were "fights" over freshly imported travel narratives, and this induced printers to secure official privileges—as van Meurs promptly did from the States of Holland upon acquiring Nieuhof's "precious treasures" from China.[49] In some cases, journals were obtained in an underhanded fashion—rival printers accused one another of outright stealing—and in many instances they were simply copied or pirated: hence, again, the value of autho-

CHAPTER ONE

rized privileges. In nearly all cases, materials were altered on their way to publication, whether this entailed substantial revisions to an original text, the grafting of one text with several others (a blending that could create a wholly different narrative), or emendations that effectively reframed a text for varying local audiences (this goes for originally Dutch texts made to appeal to non-Dutch readers and the reverse). In the case of Nieuhof, more than one surviving manuscript attests to the strenuous massaging undertaken by the editors (van Meurs and others) of the "author's" notebooks and sketchpads.[50] Virtually all of the "shipwreck accounts"—this genre was especially popular in the second half of the seventeenth century—involved co-writing, to put it charitably. Willem Bontekoe's phenomenal best seller, which described his stormy adventures in the Indian Ocean and went through some seventy-five editions, was likely the work of an *afschrijver* hired by the printer. This was also the case with the disaster tale ascribed to Hendrick Hamel, which included scattered descriptions of Korea and Japan, and this likely explains the making of Jan Jansz Struys's picaresque, rambling travelogue surveying large swathes of Asia.[51] To take a somewhat different case, the Dutch version of Charles de Rochefort's influential "natural and moral history" of the Caribbean (*Histoire naturelle et morale des iles Antilles de l'Amerique*), which fits into a slightly more learned genre, was substantially rewritten by the Rotterdam poet and painter Heiman Dullaert, who is listed merely as the book's translator. And practically all of the vast oeuvre of stay-at-home Olfert Dapper is derivative and revised, the product of an imaginative (and perhaps also collaborative) cut-and-paste job by one of the best horses in van Meurs's stable of scribblers (namely, Dapper).

Borrowing texts, reworking texts, interweaving texts, and even plagiarizing (as we might put it) texts: these techniques are not at all exceptional in the context of seventeenth-century printing, Dutch or otherwise, and garden-variety editorial intervention is not the issue here. More to the point is how common these practices were to the field of exotic geography and how inherently counterintuitive both the process and the results could be. Textual intercessions by an editor-printer not only were frequent—rare was the travel journal that did *not* undergo some manner of manipulation on its road to publication—but were effectively routinized, with those in the business of printing geography regularly engaging some form of *afschrijver* or *veelschrijver* to manage their texts, and a cadre of engravers and draftsmen to handle their graphic material. That this was done to the expressly idiosyncratic genre of travel literature is all the more notable. An account of a voyage to the Indies, advertised as a personal journal or diary of a particular expedition, often arrived to the reader refracted through the eyes of a landlubbing publisher who had substantially reworked the prose. The peregrinations of Johan Nieuhof's manuscript—composed originally in situ on behalf of the Dutch East India Company (VOC), yet later handed over in some form to Johan's brother—are well documented, as are the sly insertions of the Jesuit-authored texts that made it into the final, van Meurs–

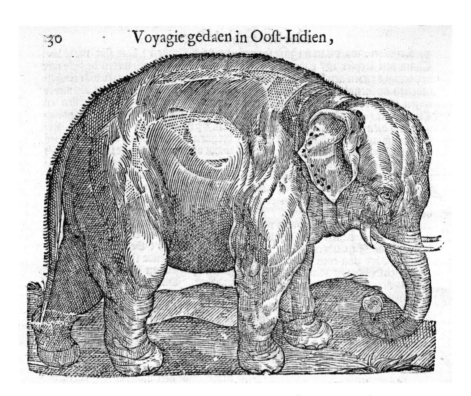

FIGURE 16. Elephant (woodblock print), in Hendrick Hamel, 't Oprechte journael, van de ongeluckige reyse van 't jacht de Sperwer (Amsterdam, ca. 1670). Koninklijke Bibliotheek, The Hague.

published book.[52] Further cases of textual tinkering abound. Hendrick Hamel's account of a shipwreck off the Korean island of Jeju, just south of the peninsula, appeared in print in Amsterdam (1668) well before Hamel himself, who returned to Europe only two years later. The several versions of the book that came out over the coming years combined a captivity narrative centered on Hamel's experience (based, in turn, on his VOC-mandated journal) with miscellaneous prose snippets, composed for altogether other purposes, which described the isolated Choson ("hermit") kingdom of Korea; materials on Japan were added, as well. The most popular edition of the work appeared in three separate printings at the address of Gillis Saeghman, an Amsterdam publisher of travel collections, and this served as the basis numerous further editions, also in French and English. Saeghman's variant of the work included several incongruously selected illustrations taken from the publisher's stock (which was itself inherited from the stock of another bookman, Joost Hartgers), and these blithely set before the reader a menagerie of exotic crocodiles and elephants. While the former does inhabit the peninsula, the latter is wholly alien to Korea, and neither, certainly, is mentioned in Hamel's account, an oversight that Saeghman addressed with an added section of text. This version of the book notably did not include an author's name on the title page. It was the work of Gillis Saeghman rather than Hendrick Hamel.[53]

The apparent omission of an author's name from a title page may be less an oversight than, at first blush, might seem to be the case. The practice of obscuring an author's identity in print was, once again, not an unusual practice in this period, although it occurred more frequently in less established and more elastic genres—such as geography—than was otherwise the case.[54] Furthermore, the practice entailed less a matter of omission than obfuscation or perhaps conflation. Authors were not necessarily scuttled altogether so much as they were embedded elsewhere in the narrative, replaced in key prefatory devices, or simply skipped over on the title page (even while mentioned elsewhere in the text), which might defer on this matter to the printer-publisher. Cartographic materials—to take a slightly different example—typically bore the name of a printer-publisher, even when the sketching, drafting, and engraving had plainly been done by other specialists, a fact that was sometimes specified subtly in the lower corner of a sheet map (as opposed to the more central cartouche). The publisher thereby claimed authorship of and responsibility for the material, a well-established tradition in the field of cartographic printing—Blaeu, Janssonius, and van der Aa all gained their reputations this way. In the case of printed geography texts, however, the role of the ostensible "author" was less obvious, not least insofar as the narrative was rarely composed by a single writer; and this may have permitted the conflation of author and editor—and, accordingly, the dilution of the authorial role.

This blurring occurs in several van Meurs publications, the authorial attributions of which have long been murky. The well-known volume *America*, published originally in 1671 and in many later editions, was composed chiefly by Arnoldus Montanus, yet it is often attributed to the English printer John Ogilby, who left his own name, and the presumption of his personal authorship, on the title page of the English edition (a great irony, since Ogilby relied so heavily on van Meurs for the book's layout and production).[55] A van Meurs–produced description of Japan, also undertaken principally by Montanus, receives the same sleight-of-hand treatment in its French edition, which omits the name of an author on its title page and thus allows its readers to affiliate the volume with the only name available: Jacob van Meurs. A seeming slip of the pen in the dedication of Dapper's geography of China makes reference to other van Meurs–published books, including several that are not at all associated with Dapper. The publisher, in other words, has slipped himself into the place of the author, from whom he can, in this case, barely be distinguished. The two roles, for all intents and purposes, have been utterly conflated.[56]

The same process of managing, if not quite manipulating, textual copy also applies, in numerous ways, to the visual matter of printed geographies. Again, the key figure is the editor-printer-bookseller, who acquired or commissioned sketches to illustrate publications and then steered these into production, sometimes even engraving the plates himself (as was the case with van Meurs, who likely did many of the prints in his books). Early modern printed images, like printed texts, were rarely the work of a single "author"—certainly not the putative author of the text—let alone a single "artist." Rather, they traveled a long and meandering road from their original conception to their eventual publication—or, likely, *publications*, since a printer's store of images was routinely recycled, reworked, and reissued in copious forms.[57] This is not to say that these images were of any lesser quality; one of the great selling points of early modern Dutch geography was precisely its superior and often expressly made etchings and engravings.[58] Yet well-produced illustrations were valuable commodities and therefore worth reprinting. Hard-to-obtain cityscapes, scenes of global "wonders," vignettes of foreign peoples, pictures of exotic *naturalia*—all of these sold books, and all of these enjoyed an extensive afterlife in the world of print. Thus Saeghman's edition of Hamel's Korean "journal" bears illustrations of ostentatiously exotic fauna, which he inherited from an altogether different printer, Joost Hartgers, who had been active in the first half of the century (see figure 16). Pieter van der Aa deployed twice, at least, virtually every plate that came into his possession, almost as a matter of policy. After acquiring Romeyn de Hooghe's superb etchings for Simon de Vries's *Curieuse aenmerckingen*, a collation of exotic "curiosities" printed in Utrecht in 1682, van der Aa published these separately in an oblong picture book, titled simply *Les Indes Orientales et Occidentales et autres lieux* (circa 1700).[59] The work evidently enjoyed commercial success, and the plates subsequently had more than a few further showings—including ultimately in the *Galerie agreable*.

Pictures also circulated in various *forms* of print, demonstrating not only the versatility of the images but also of the image-makers—the impresarios of print. Hendrick Doncker converted the frontispiece from Philip Baldaeus's book on religion in Malabar (1672) into a cartouche for a maritime map of South Asia (circa 1680; see figures 106 and 107)—an egregious, yet hardly exceptional case of iconic borrowing (or "iconic circuits," to adopt Craig Clunas's critical vocabulary).[60] Pictures, more generally, had an impressively prolonged existence in print, as they zigged and zagged from one source to another. Among the longest-lived exotic images, famously reproduced in scores of prints and material objects, was Albrecht Dürer's armor-plated rhinoceros (1515), whose checkered history—including an appearance in a van Meurs publication—exceeded two centuries.[61] (It was supplanted only in the eighteenth century by a Dutch-designed engraving of "Clara," the nearly-as-legendary Indian rhinoceros who toured Europe from the 1740s with a Leiden sea captain.)[62] These sorts of elaborate itineraries also guided the lives of geography illustrations of this period. Among the most intricately traveled exotica were the Jesuit manuscripts—including pictures—of Adriano de las Cortes (1578–1629), composed during the author's early seventeenth-century sojourn in China. These fell into the hands of Jacob van Meurs about a half-century later, and the Holland publisher integrated the Spanish missionary's sketches into Dapper's geography of China—an irony of sorts, since Dapper's text narrated the failure of a Dutch embassy to the imperial court, foiled largely by Jesuit interventions. Several of the pictorial motifs from the van Meurs publication appeared in subsequent years in the decorative arts—herein lies a primary source of eighteenth-century chinoiserie—and many of the plates were reworked for other publications, including, well over a half-century later, a lavish volume on global religion, the *Ceremonies et coutumes religieuses*, produced by the Huguenot printer-engraver team of Jean-Frédéric Bernard and Bernard Picart. The stunning graphic work of Picart became the most influential depiction of religious customs in the early Enlightenment, a Huguenot-produced set of images derived (partly) from Jesuit-made sketches, as mediated, orchestrated, processed, and disseminated by the Amsterdam impresario of print Jacob van Meurs.[63]

Book Appeal

Did the fabulousness of the pictures, the framing of the narratives, the processing of the texts, and the assorted other clever mechanisms of Dutch-made geography contribute to its broad appeal? There can be no doubt that the architecture of these books contributed significantly to their popularity, that form influenced function in the way it induced and shaped manners of reading and consumption. As much by construction as by narrative content, volumes of exotic geography were designed to entice customers; they traded on a well-honed typographic "look," which may have been their most distinctive quality. Books were typically large, bulky, textually disheveled, and visually opulent—they were hodgepodges. Yet they came with several devices to navigate their typographic and visual exuberance. To this jumble of texts, tables, charts, maps, pictures, and more, Dutch volumes of geography delivered—and often announced as much on the title page—a profusion of paratexts. These were meant to help the consumer navigate this cunningly constructed printed form of the world. To begin with, volumes of geography were habitually large—folio was the all but default size (books originally published in folio, however, often came out subsequently in smaller-format editions)—and they asserted their ample girth and bulk directly on their title pages, which boasted of the cornucopia to come. To make this amplitude easier to manage, many volumes were printed in the easy-to-navigate double-columned format—which, as a bonus, allowed for twice the marginalia to guide the potentially overstimulated reader through the text. The look of a single volume, moreover, might carry over to other, similarly manufactured books. For even when volumes of geography were not explicitly serialized, as was the case with so many of van der Aa's products, this could be implicitly done by printers who published their books according to a regular bibliographic rhythm and in matching typographic proportions.

This might be thought of as the "atlas" approach to publishing: standardize the product and then present it as an ensemble, which is how the multivolume atlas developed from the tradition of single-sheet map printing. Johannes van Someren produced a series of practically identical publications that combined shipwreck narratives with ethnographic descriptions, in the latter case mimicking the prose and picture style of van Meurs, with whom van Someren sometimes collaborated. Three volumes appeared in rapid succession in the 1670s, two narrowly focused on the coasts of Malabar and Coromandel and on Bengal, respectively, and a third more expansively covering Asia. They shared similar dimensions and layouts, and in their graphic content they broadly resembled one another: engraved frontispieces, full-page illustrations, sprawling city and port views, and so on (compare figures 60 and 106).[64] Van Meurs's geographies also carried a consistent look, so much so that they were often packaged together—most tellingly in their English-language editions, which appeared collectively under the name of John Ogilby. Ogilby made several of the Montanus and Dapper books available per subscription and then published them under generic titles: *Africa* (1670), *America* (1671), and *Asia* (1673).[65] He printed others under the equally broad titles *Atlas Japannensis* (1670) and *Atlas Chinensis* (1671), and he promoted the entire lot as his "Great Atlas" series.[66] That these volumes conveyed parochial, "local" narratives—of Dutch-directed embassies to the courts of Beijing and Edo, for example—was shrewdly disguised by their purposefully broad, "universal" titles, which advertised generic (that is, non-Dutch) geographies. They were offered simply and unassertively as the latest and finest descriptions of the world.[67]

Paratexts were a great part of Dutch geography's appeal. Paratexts could be a large part of the appeal of *any* book printed in this period, yet for geography in particular, and for the large and baggy variant of the genre produced in the Netherlands around 1700, they were especially fundamental.[68] Volumes of exotic geography carried so much stuff—they blended disparate narratives, recycled far-fetched images, introduced unfamiliar locales—that they all but required some form of special assistance. Their carefully laid-out architecture, accordingly, was designed for easy access and the ready negotiation of their textual and graphic space. Volumes were assembled to usher the reader—better, consumer—through their complex structures and to offer an appealing way to sample the "morsels" of exotica (to invoke a different metaphor, which was employed in one prefatory note) housed within.[69] Prefaces were de rigueur—"a book without a preface is like a body without [a] soul" accord-

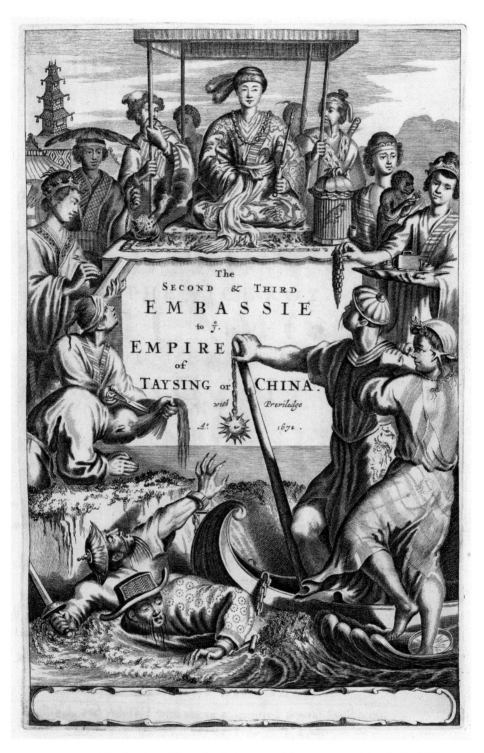

The
SECOND & THIRD
EMBASSIE
to y̆.
EMPIRE
of
TAYSING or CHINA.
with Previledge
A°. 1671.

FIGURE 17. After Jacob van Meurs (atelier), engraved frontispiece to John Ogilby [Olfert Dapper], *Atlas Chinensis* (London, 1671). By permission of the Huntington Library, San Marino, California.

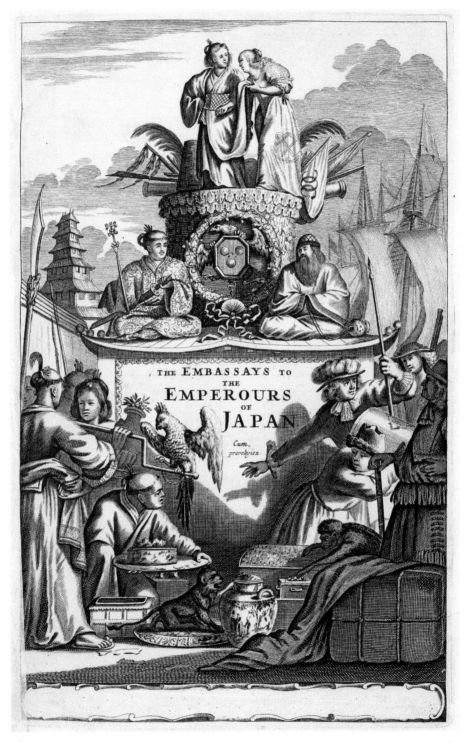

THE EMBASSAYS TO
THE
EMPEROURS
OF
JAPAN

Cum,
prœvlegien.

FIGURE 18. After Jacob van Meurs (atelier), engraved frontispiece to John Ogilby [Arnoldus Montanus], *Atlas Japannensis* (London, 1670). By permission of the Huntington Library, San Marino, California.

ing to one[70]—and they served to call attention to the rich features of their book's well-stocked pages. Yet prefaces also invited what book historians call "extensive" (rather than "intensive") reading: brief forays into the volume, cursory nibbles of various selections, rather than a more thorough absorption of the entire, inherently convoluted contents of a book. To help the reader along, tables of contents could themselves be fairly extensive; they did the job of counseling the reader on what needed attention and punctuating particular chapter highlights. And the chapters themselves often included their own detailed summaries. They were, moreover, exquisitely subdivided into smaller, bite-size portions—again, with the goal of encouraging easy textual digestion. Generous marginalia allowed browsers to alight on this or that pivotal point—as determined by the printer, to be sure—and the liberal use of indices, occupying dozens of pages at the end of the book, gave the reader still further direction. Paratexts had the effect of reconfiguring the textual tangle of Dutch geography by transforming it into easily navigable terrain.

All of these devices helped shape a *literary* approach to exotic geography, yet it was left to the considerable visual apparatus to dictate how "readers" actually looked at these volumes. And *looking* is the appropriate response to a work of Dutch geography and surely a central part of its appeal. "Cuts [engravings]," wrote another observer of the print world circa 1700, with Dutch geography specifically in mind, are "the Soul of performances of this kind."[71] The performance began at once with the engraved frontispiece, which, in the case of Dutch-made products—just as was the case with the preface—was well-nigh obligatory.[72] The frontispiece established the aesthetic style for the volume; it offered a window onto the bookmaker's slant on the material and his or her strategy of pictorial presentation. It also invited the viewer in. Handsomely engraved (or etched) and often signed by a known artist—not at all standard practice for book illustrations—the frontispiece characteristically depicted an allegorical figure associated with the region, or perhaps a more generic representation of History (*Clio*) or Geography. This central figure was typically surrounded by a mass of swirling artifacts, commercial products, ethnographic "types," exotic flora and fauna—all meant to convey the richness of the region. The frontispiece, in other words, replicated in visual terms the textual hodgepodge housed within. It also hinted at the plentiful engravings of the volume, which normally covered full-page folios, not uncommonly spread out over two pages, and sometimes, as in de Bruijn's books, stretched more ambitiously over multiple folio pages, which folded out (pages were expressly glued together for this). These were the star attractions of this brand of performance, and they tended to be advertised as such on the title page, which invariably spotlighted the quantity and quality of pictures: executed in loco, drafted directly by the author (in both instances, implying the act of eyewitness sketching), or simply done "expertly." Dutch geography was renowned for its superior illustrations, a feature noted by the English publishers Awnsham and John Churchill, who

FIGURE 19. Jacob van Meurs (atelier), "Africa" (engraved frontispiece), in Olfert Dapper, *Africa* (Amsterdam, 1668). Special Collections, University of Amsterdam (KF 61-3999).

incorporated several Dutch accounts into their *Collection of voyages and travels* (1704–1732), and who marveled that Dutch-made products "so plainly [represent] all things observable or strange there [in the Indies], that with the help of the Cuts we seem to be conversing with the People of those parts, to see all their Towns and living Creatures, and to be thoroughly acquainted with their Habits, Customs, and Superstitions."[73] These cuts could be professionally colored, likewise a service of the Dutch bookmaking industry, or they could be augmented with additional engravings— throw-ins, as it were, of maps, cityscapes, illustrated *naturalia*, and the like, which printers regularly inserted into their final products.[74]

That final product ultimately obtained a distinctive appearance, and this perhaps more than anything made books of this ilk stand out. There was a characteristic look to volumes of exotic geography produced in, or derived from, the Netherlands, an identifiable, brand-like quality that pointed at once to their typographic origins and their method of manufacture. This quality, at the same time, indicated another form of value: it marked these volumes as possessing those particular traits of the genre, and those critical measures of "credit," that rendered them worth having.[75] Dutch products, in short, achieved a well-defined, broadly admired brand identity. This identity resulted as much from Chartier's "editorial practices" as from anything else—and certainly more from the bookmakers' input than from

FIGURE 20. Jacob van Meurs (atelier), "Vogel Louwa" (engraving), in Johan Nieuhof, *Gezantschap der Neêrlandtsche Oost-Indische Compagnie* (Amsterdam, 1665). Special Collections, University of Amsterdam (OM 63-116).

authorial habits, textual content, or even that time-tested selling point of exotic fare, "novelty" and originality. The *construction* of Dutch geography books sold Dutch geography books. And the corollary is also apt: the same narrative and even the same text tended to look different when handled by different ateliers; and Dutch bookmakers, who well understood this fundamental point of their trade, designed books that appealed. Theirs was the brand to beat. Nieuhof's China narrative circulated, in fact, in various distinct manuscript sources, one of which landed in the hands of the Parisian publisher Melchisédech Thévenot, who specialized in travel literature. Eager to realize a profit, Thévenot promptly put out a different version of the work intended to rival van Meurs's. It failed. It was a mere sixth of the length of the original Dutch-made version (Thévenot added fewer supplementary texts), with nowhere near the level of typographic detail (the paratexts were meager and inexpertly done), and, most vitally, with a vastly inferior visual program (the engravers made a hash of the illustrations, cramming multiple pictures and ethnographic vignettes onto a single plate). The result compared poorly to the French translation that van Meurs himself produced in 1665, a book to which Thévenot's volume likely ceded place on most collectors' bookshelves.[76] Taking their cue from van Meurs, Dutch printers adhered to this winning commercial formula when it came to manufacturing geography. They highlighted precisely their workshop interventions and their *printerly* mode of production. Dutch bookmakers, in this way, commodified exotic geography.

Why Dutch bookmakers, and why exotic geography? The second question may be more quickly dispensed with than the first. The high cost of producing this brand of book—printed on large paper, adorned with abundant illustrations, incorporating disparate texts—encouraged a sound, market-focused strategy of publication. These were user-friendly products that addressed consumer desiderata. Of course, many early modern books had high production costs, and many genres produced in the printing hub of Holland reached out to large, European audiences. In the broader scheme of things, Dutch geography books were not unique in their wide appeal and commercial success. Yet volumes of geography tended to be more costly to produce than others—their size alone dictated as much—and this necessitated a more market-savvy approach. The considerable initial investment meant that deluxe geography books *had* to sell—hence also the use of subscription.

More generally, the field of geography, in print and otherwise, was far more commercially oriented in the Netherlands than elsewhere. This had to do in part with social rather than purely economic causes—and this points to the Dutch-specific factors of publication. The production of geography in the Netherlands was controlled not by the crown (the relatively marginal house of Orange), learned academies (typically established under the auspices of a prince or high-born sponsor), or even overseas trading companies—all of which was the case, to varying

FIGURE 21. Triumph arch (engraving), in Melchisédech Thévenot, *Relations de divers voyages curieux* (Paris, 1666). Special Collections, University of Amsterdam (KF 62-4220).

degrees, in Spain, Portugal, England, France, and Italy.[77] Nor were publications particularly patron-orchestrated—even if there were some conspicuous instances of patron-author collaborations (many involving the Amsterdam regent Nicolaes Witsen, who avidly supported Dapper's researches, de Bruijn's sojourns, and Rumphius's and Kaempfer's natural history writings).[78] Rather, Dutch geography hewed to a more plainly entrepreneurial path than elsewhere. Printers and map-makers pitched to the open market and therefore had no need to abide by royal or patron demands. Pieter van der Aa exemplified this modus operandi, assiduously establishing his own brand of geography, and he profited handsomely from his enterprise. His books, moreover, received their "credit" directly from the market-place and from their brand identification—a fact that may undermine historio-graphic assumptions about early modern science and its presumed reliance on learned and aristocratic sponsors (as opposed to market factors) for its validation.[79] Dutch exotic geography, in all events, rested on a more sturdy typographic, print-erly, and entrepreneurial foundation than was the case elsewhere in Europe.

For these and other reasons, Dutch geography stood apart from the competi-tion. It took an innovative approach, it had a distinctive look, and it cultivated a broadly European audience. In a paradoxical way, however, this brand of geogra-phy sold well by being at once Dutch, yet not Dutch: by having a recognizable form that could be readily affiliated with Holland bookmaking, yet by also blur-ring, or effacing, from its content any parochially Dutch focus or any vestiges of a Dutch colonial agenda. This allowed for narratives of VOC embassies to China and Japan to pass as generic "atlases" and for personal journals of Dutch East India Company and Dutch West India Company employees to be repackaged as anony-mous "descriptions" of indeterminately exotic locales. It also led to the consistent publication of translations of texts and of captioned illustrations—undertaken al-most invariably in the Netherlands, under the auspices of a Dutch atelier—in forms that were plainly meant to reach non-Dutch audiences. These were "European" books: they were not entirely without an agenda—hardly feasible for the genre of geography—yet their angle and perspective was generically "European," and their scope and ideology were pan-colonial and hyper-imperial. Dutch geography pitched broadly, and, consequently, its influence was extensive.

The European profile of these volumes is significant. It is also highly unchar-acteristic and strikingly innovative, if not groundbreaking, for the field of early mod-ern geography. A glance backward to some of the more ambitious projects of the earlier seventeenth century, or even the sixteenth century, reveals a wholly different, decidedly provincial, and palpably patriotic approach to the textual (and visual) description of exotic lands. Richard Hakluyt famously compiled in the 1580s and 1590s "the Prose Epic of the modern English nation," a collection of texts that of-fered Elizabethans an imperial-minded survey of the age of discovery.[80] While it comprised materials taken from both English and non-English sources, Hakluyt's *Principal navigations* (1598–1600) was itself never translated—it remained an ex-clusively British saga.[81] Hakluyt's near contemporary and counterpart in France, André Thevet, who served as France's royal cosmographer for much of the latter half of the sixteenth century, composed a sprawling account of the French colonial enterprise in the West, the very title of which betrays its Gallic perspective: *Les singularitez de la France antarctique, autrement nommée Amerique* (1557).[82] Spanish volumes gave, if anything, a less coy—which is to say, less disinterested and more bluntly imperial—account of the *Conquista* in the several histories and descriptions of exotic lands composed in the wake of Castilian expansion. The first major account of the American natural world, Gonzalo Fernández de Oviedo's *De la natural hystoria de las Indias* (1526), was conceived "as imperial propaganda" (as one critic recently described it), a point plainly emblazoned on its frontispiece in the form of a Habsburg coat of arms.[83] Several other volumes of Spanish history, in a similar fashion, were stamped on their covers with imperial marks of approval—for example, Francisco López de Gómara's vigorous *Historia general de las Indias* (1552), a work that came to be known, none too bashfully, as "Hispania Victrix" (figures 22 and 23).[84] While these works may have been translated in various forms, they flourished primarily in Spanish-language editions and for parochially Spanish-identifying consumers. Neither they nor most other books on the sixteenth- and early seventeenth-century market appeared in anything approaching the quantity of Dutch-made products of the second half of the seventeenth century.[85]

A glance sideways, toward other geography projects printed more or less contemporaneously with the van Meurs and van der Aa–era ones, reveals, once again, the distinctiveness of the Dutch brand of print geography. The difference between the van Meurs (Amsterdam) and Thévenot (Paris) variations of Nieuhof's China book has already been noted. In London, Ogilby's publications could match Dutch ones only because they were manufactured, more or less, under the auspices of van Meurs himself, who shipped the plates and sometimes even the engraved pages directly to his less well-outfitted (and less typographically adept) English colleague. De Bruijn's volume on the Levant underwent a similar process of translation and transition—once he completed the Dutch and French editions (printed in Delft), the artist shipped the plates to a London printer—and this accounts for the near identical look of the English editions of de Bruijn's publications. By contrast, when a book originated in another market, it gained in quality once it was appropriated—the modern publishing term "acquired" seems too mild for the early modern practice—by Dutch bookmakers, who added, embellished, and produced, more often than not, what would soon become the most sought-after edition available. This was the trajectory of Charles de Rochefort's description of the Caribbean, Jacob Spon and George Wheler's explorations of the Levant (the Dutch edition of which included engravings by the masterful Jan Luyken), Louis Hennepin's patchwork accounts of French territories in North America, and even some of the Jesuit narratives of the Far East. Martino Martini's map of China circulated most prominently in the form given to it by Joan Blaeu, while Athanasius Kircher's *China illustrata* gained its fame once printed in two Amsterdam editions

FIGURE 22. Frontispiece (woodblock print) to Gonzalo Fernández de Oviedo, *De la natural hystoria de las Indias* (Toledo, 1526). Courtesy of the John Carter Brown Library at Brown University.

FIGURE 23. Frontispiece (woodblock print) to Francisco López de Gómara, *Historia general de las Indias* (Zaragoza, 1552). Courtesy of the John Carter Brown Library at Brown University.

(both 1667), the first by Janssonius van Waesberge and the second by van Meurs—who, in this case, played the part of pirate.[86]

All of this points to the simple fact that the Dutch graphic and print juggernaut was both unsurpassed and insuperable when it came to geography, and that the market for Dutch-made volumes was the most competitive, far-reaching, and consumer-driven of its day. Holland bookmakers possessed print resources unmatched in Europe. Richly endowed with paper makers, typesetters, copper engravers, and map makers, Dutch ateliers developed additional techniques—sale by subscription, in-house translation, serial publication—that sustained the industry and enabled the output of geography products keenly sought across Europe. Dutch bookmakers, furthermore, had relative independence in terms of production: no learned academies with which to contend, limited royal entanglements or intrusive patronage to worry about, weak government control (and thus minimal censorship) from the decentralized States General, and so on. Book manufacturers in the Dutch Republic, more than anywhere else in Europe, could operate according to market conditions. They made, in turn, books that appealed.

The "Interest" and "Credit" of Geography

Making books of this nature surely changed the way the exotic world was perceived. Large, rambling, visually opulent compendia of geography, printed in several formats and translated into multiple languages: Dutch geography books shaped the way European consumers saw the world. It also changed the way geography functioned in early modern Europe and how knowledge of the world came to be processed at this critical juncture in global history. The very style and novelty of the Dutch brand of geography and its extensive market reach, moreover, could not help but affect practices of *engaging* with the world. Form influenced function, function instigated attitudes, and attitudes, one presumes, inspired actions. This is not to say that Dutch editorial practices of the later seventeenth century on their own cast a pall over European expansion and policies in the colonial world: neither metropolitan schemers nor imperial agents needed much prodding. Nor is it particularly surprising or groundbreaking that texts were massaged, collated, and detached from their original contexts, or that engravers let their imaginations run wild as they shrewdly redesigned original, on-site sketches—all common enough practices in early modern printing. The significance of this moment rests, rather, in the *effect* to which these practices were put in the production of geography and, additionally, the effect these carefully constructed books may have had on their target audience. The very success of Dutch-made geography at this particular moment in the history of overseas expansion prompts the fundamental question of intent or design—what might be called *ideology*, were the answer that simple.

The questions, in all events, are basic. To what purpose were these works edited, for what readership were they geared, and to what end were they produced? The bookmaking strategies pursued by the Dutch impresarios of print around 1700 force us to rethink the presupposed ideologies of their final products—of the processed texts, manipulated pictures, and alleged discourses embedded in tomes of geography. They complicate, furthermore, efforts to gauge how sources of exotic geography, even those plainly dedicated to sites of imperial importance, may have served their makers' agenda. Who, in the end, can claim authorship of, and authority over, a *text* once it has undergone the inevitable transformations that render it a *book*? How can colonial or imperial ideologies be extracted from geographic texts when the books that bear them are manufactured by much messier, less straightforward, and more "printerly" processes than critics have generally recognized? Rather than on the author's ideology, more light should be shed on the printer's imperatives—which may, too, have pertained to empire and expansion, yet in more subtle ways. The relatively innovative approach taken by Dutch bookmakers in the second half of the seventeenth century marks an important shift in terms of not only printing exotic geography but also engaging with the exotic world. Their methods of production invite us to reassess works of geography in terms of the narrative's authorial role, its truth claims and expression of "interest," the value accorded to eyewitness reports, and the ultimate "credit" granted to the Dutch brand of printed geography. Their methods encourage us, in short, to reconsider the relationship between exotic geography and colonial action—between knowledge and power.

The starting point for such an inquiry would be the indispensable question of authorship. Among the most striking shifts in Dutch-made products was the displacement of the titular author of these volumes and, correspondingly, a reallocation of "authority" in the genre of geography. During the Renaissance, geography and travel literature, in particular, had been grounded in the first-person narrative, by which the author (or putative author) provided a personal report of events experienced or witnessed overseas. The allegedly bona fide encounters and firsthand observations of an individual traveler validated the account, and post-1492 authors were especially at pains to advertise this.[87] Authors (along with their editors) routinely made note of their singular role in creating their account: of their personal exertions to visit newly discovered lands and record exotic wonders. Christopher Columbus opens his 1493 letter to the Spanish monarchs—a document intended for public consumption and quickly ushered into print—by accentuating his own, hard-won efforts in this unprecedented voyage to the Indies, and this is also the tack taken by Amerigo Vespucci in his famous letters describing what was now identified as "the new world" (*mundus novus*). The latter case is especially instructive, since the Vespucci texts make so much of their author's personal role in both journeying overseas and compiling an account of his experience—a terrific irony, it turns out, insofar as these texts are now understood to be "fraudulent," substantially composed by stay-at-home humanists in Florence rather than by the "author" himself.[88] For the next century or two, in any case, the function of the author in authenticating accounts of exotic geography and verifying the veracity of far-fetched "facts" was vital and invariable—so much so, that by 1726 the habit would be satirized by Jonathan Swift in *Gulliver's Travels*.[89] Yet Dutch geography in the second half of the seventeenth century subverted this convention in many ways, as the author-function came to be appropriated by the editor-bookmaker, who increasingly assumed for him- or herself narrative authority.

This innovative maneuver could occur in several ways. The casual manner in which Jacob van Meurs tossed around the names of his writers, conflating Dapper's work with Montanus's (as he did in a dedicatory note to Dapper's China volume), hints at the pecking order in the geography-book business: printers could slight authors, who worked on their behalf. (Van Meurs would omit Montanus altogether from the title page of the French edition of *Japan*.) It also indicates the subtle deterioration of the author's place in a book's mode of production—at least in the atelier of van Meurs and other bookmakers of his ilk. Van Meurs tended to publish "descriptions" (*beschrijvingen*), as opposed to "journals" (*journalen*): the first endeavored to provide an overview of a region and its attractions, while the second gave a particular perspective based on a singular journey (compare the medieval itinerary).[90] Yet even as the van Meurs brand of geography advertised itself as *description*, it slyly inserted manuscript materials compiled originally in journals—perhaps by a VOC employee, although not unlikely by a Jesuit author, a Spanish agent, or a Portuguese trader whose orphaned manuscript somehow came on the market. In this way, volumes of exotic geography declined to clarify, or simply avoided acknowledging, the true authorship of their texts.

The very format of a van Meurs product and the many other books produced in a similar vein may also have had the effect of diminishing, or blurring, the authorial function. Digressive, meandering, often unspecific, and generally impersonal descriptions of exotic locales meant that the consumer obtained a book about a *place* rather than by a *person*. It demonstrates, further, the demotion of the author in deference to the bookmaker-publisher, who would have had a hand in compiling the text, perhaps even providing the titular author with the raw materials needed to draft these volumes. Even the ample use of pictures contributed to this end: by diluting the place of the text in a volume, the bookmaker weakened the role of the putative author of that text. The author became decentered, one of several contributors to a printed product, and had to yield a portion of the title-page credit to the graphic artists, mapmakers, and so on, some of whom would have been named if their reputations merited this.[91] Finally, the process of "branding" geography had a similarly diminishing effect on authorship. While Dutch bookmakers may have published proper (that is, ascribed) travel journals—as van der Aa regularly and successfully did in his *Naaukeurige versameling*, a series that reproduced the greatest hits of early modern travel literature—they would have printed these in consistent and serialized forms. This left the bookmaker's distinctive mark, as opposed to the author's personal style, front and center on the book. The consumer ordered the latest installment of a van der Aa product—it was the latter's name, after all, that reliably appeared on the title page—rather than a specific narrative by a particular traveler. The "credit" of the volume, consequently, derived less from the author's reputation than from the printer's.

The brand of exotic geography produced in the Netherlands in this period is notably impersonal, and it is precisely this quality that allowed it to slip so effortlessly across national and even confessional lines. The author and his or her personal narrative rarely receive close scrutiny or become the focus of the text. These are not spiritual "itineraries" in the medieval tradition or the heroic voyages of discovery popularized in the sixteenth century. Indeed, the reader learns very little about Olfert Dapper and Arnoldus Montanus from their books. (We know next to nothing about the former and only a smattering about the latter, gleaned from a polemical exchange Montanus carried on with a Jesuit antagonist—in Dutch, in unadorned pamphlets, and in limited circulation.) And if we do have a better sense of certain other authors of geography texts, such as Wouter Schouten or François Valentyn— the first wrote a hugely popular "voyage" covering South and Southeast Asia, while the second composed a massive, full-service description of the East Indies—the facts of their lives are of secondary importance to the rambling narratives of their books (which happened to incorporate, inter alia, material taken from other unidentified travelers in the region). Moreover, what biographical details do exist tend to be embedded in the text, deposited deep in the narrative rather than highlighted in an opening chapter; and these data, accordingly, would only vaguely have framed the readers' perspective. Tucked away in the fourth of Valentyn's five thick volumes on the Orient is a brief recitation of the author's trips to the Indies and a pithy review of his employment with the VOC; he is otherwise barely present.[92] In Schouten's book, which presents itself as a personal journey to the Indies—an overtly subjective narrative, in other words—the author does insert himself into some of the action, yet his service for the VOC is barely touched upon. He offers, instead, a generically *European* story about the wonders of the East. In both cases, the author as a Dutch colonial actor is all but expunged from the narrative, and this allowed the two books, Schouten's in particular, to enjoy broad success.[93]

If the author's role had been diminished in these works, and in some cases effectively effaced, the role of the bookmaker took a turn in the opposite direction. In the absence of a prominent, robust author-figure to lead the reader personally through the volume, the editor-figure filled this absence and occupied an enhanced position. In fact, the argument could be made, as it was in the preface to one Dutch-designed geography-cum-ethnography on global religions, that stay-at-home bookmen were better situated than overseas travelers when it came to creating works of geography. In the English edition of the *Ceremonies et coutumes religieuses de tous les peuples du monde* (1733), an extensive prefatory note by the translator-editor considers a hypothetical global traveler who visits all the lands of the world and then makes an account of what he sees. "But such a Man as this has never yet existed," he submits, "and in all human Probability never will." Such grand travel combined with ambitious travel writing is "esteemed little better than Knight-Errantry"—a fool's errand and impractical. A better proposition would be to combine a wise reader of travel narratives with an intelligent redactor, who could bring together in a single volume several scattered accounts and then embellish these with expert engravings, "set off with . . . Truth and Advantage," as had been done with the superbly illustrated volumes of the *Ceremonies*. The preface goes on to celebrate not the intrepid globetrotter but the "Persons of true Taste" who consumed print geography, which, if "methodically digested, and drawn up with a strict Regard to Truth," was most advantageous. The editor thus inverts the normal privileging of the eyewitness traveler by esteeming instead the stay-at-home reader, the avid collector, the expert collator, and the learned consumer of exotic geography: "Men of Penetration and Judgment," as the prefatory note puts it, who know what brand of book to buy and what sort of bookmaker to rely on.[94]

At stake, as these comments make clear, is nothing less than the truth. "Truth and advantage," "strict regard to truth," "true taste": volumes of geography served a vital role in conveying the "truth" about the world, and the very popular volumes of exotic geography made in the Netherlands at this time played an ever more central part in this process. "Truth," of course, was an unfixed currency in this period (as in other periods, to be sure). It was a currency, moreover, frantically traded on the open market, with books of geography but one of the many commodities that established its value. But geography was an especially important commodity at this late seventeenth-century moment, when European notions of truth increasingly impinged on the rest of the globe. And as forms of exotic geography evolved, so did notions of "truth." In the years that Nieuhof's China manuscript circulated—the period following his return to Europe and brief respite from travel, yet before van Meurs converted his account into a book—Melchisédech Thévenot noted that, in this age of intense curiosity, Dutch merchants furnished the finest accounts of exotic lands. Their descriptions were "truthful" and "unvarnished" ("*véritables . . . sans déguisement*"), he asserted; "they report only what they see."[95] This express desire for eyewitness reporting from on-site merchant-travelers may seem self-evident, yet

Thévenot's comments contrast tellingly to the approach taken just a few years later by Jacob van Meurs himself, once he had printed the Nieuhof manuscript and so launched the brand of exotic geography that would dominate the market over the coming decades. When pitching a volume of geography just a few years later, in this case a book on Japan by Montanus—compiled, however, with the support of several unattributed accounts—van Meurs homed in precisely on the *distance* that the book's titular author had from his subject and on the value of geography when composed by stay-at-home scribes.[96] Montanus had the accomplished style and evident advantages of a seasoned *veelschrijver*, contended van Meurs, "from whom a more polished historical *truth* will be presented than could ever be composed by the quills of East Indies merchants."[97] Van Meurs reverses the order of things: better a well-penned book (which, incidentally, Montanus's *Japan* decidedly was not) by an arm-chair scribbler than a first-person narrative from an East Indies trader. And further: "truth" from a *veelschrijver*, particularly when packaged with an impressive battery of pictures and paratexts (as any van Meurs product would have been), trumps a wind-and-weather report from a product-and-profit-minded merchant.

Did van Meurs intend with his comments to make a larger epistemological point about the nature of truth and the limited value of eyewitness reports and thereby to challenge the Renaissance, indeed Baconian, paradigm shift in terms of knowledge production—which, at its core, demanded a more vigorous process of observing and validating that which had passed, as far back as the days of Sir John Mandeville, simply as a "wonder"?[98] Perhaps, but one editor's prefatory come-on—van Meurs's shilling of Montanus's book and the several others on the printer's list that bore the same traits—hardly counts as a seismic shift in debates on knowledge making. It does hint, however, at a notable shift in geography making, especially in the market-oriented, consumer-friendly format that van Meurs promoted. Van Meurs's riff on geography comes at the close of a digressive, dedicatory essay that reviews the state of the field and the publisher's own contributions to it; it strikes both a professional and a commercial note. Van Meurs opens with boilerplate about the expansion of the known world since the time of Columbus (offering a sly advertisement for Montanus's other van Meurs–made volume, *America*); next, he invokes the lately revealed wonders of the Far East (which has the effect of bringing attention to Nieuhof's China book); and finally, he promises in the publication at hand a marvelous read on the faraway kingdom of Japan. In underscoring the author's stay-at-home perspective and the advantages of this approach, van Meurs makes two points, one explicitly and the other implicitly. First, he preemptively discards the time-honored credit granted to firsthand observation; this point is made plainly, if idiosyncratically. Second, he neglects to highlight the fairly significant fact that Montanus, as a Dutch-based writer, had direct access to those colonial archives that would have accumulated in the Netherlands. Indeed, there is no mention at all that the Dutch by this time (and for the past three decades) were the only Europeans with commercial access to Japan, which they enjoyed by way of their exclusive factory and warehouse in Dejima.

This highly conspicuous omission is directly and strategically linked to van Meurs's innovative style of geography. Both points pertain to the question of "interest." In the case of Montanus's reporting on Japan from afar, van Meurs made a virtue of the author's observational distance. His account is deemed *preferable* for its impersonal point of view; it gains value not so much despite, but because of, its genesis with a stay-at-home author, who appears unencumbered by the concerns of overseas merchants and their pursuit of profit and advantage. It is meant to be disinterested. The same quality, by extension, would have applied to the other publications that emanated from van Meurs's in-house writers—books penned by Dapper, for example. Yet pointing this out in a volume on Japan made extra sense. For the exclusive presence of Dutch merchants in Japan may have implied, by contrast, their potential "interest": their biases, their agendas, their commercial and colonial prerogatives. Van Meurs is at pains to dispel any concern the reader might have that Montanus was offering a *Dutch* perspective—he avoids any mention even of the Dutch in the Far East, let alone their exclusive control of the Japan trade—and his brand of geography functioned in a similar manner. Despite their titular authors, his books endeavor to affect an impersonal style; they play down, or even disguise, any overt Dutchness or Dutch colonial success that may prevail in the places they describe. Whatever their textual origins, they strive for disinterested narratives. For these and other reasons, van Meurs's publications enjoyed remarkable success well beyond the borders of the Netherlands.

The New Geography

In an essay on travel literature and ethnography, the sociologist Justin Stagl and anthropologist Christopher Pinney identify an important distinction between the prose of travelers and the work of ethnographers. "Travel reports proceed more or less *narratively*," they observe, "whereas [modern] ethnographic monographs proceed more or less *descriptively*." Stagl and Pinney go on to highlight certain textual shifts that are said to have taken place over time (they also express some reservations about this line of analysis), which distinguish newer forms of anthropological prose from older ones in terms of how they position the author's engagement with the places and peoples described: "Ethnographic monographs tend to mask the concrete person of the traveler as well as the exact temporal and local circumstances under which the experience of alterity occurred. Ethnographic knowledge is thus not offered in its 'raw' form, but semi-processed in a form that makes it amenable to the generalizations of the discipline of anthropology."[99] Although addressing the advent of the modern ethnographic study, Stagl and Pinney's comments speak, as well, to developments that took place in the relatively new genre of travel literature and in other early attempts to describe, in printed form, exotic constituencies—geography, that is, by another name. Travel literature and geography are certainly not identical, yet they commonly intersected in this earlier, predisciplinary era, and they both underwent critical revisions in terms of their mode of production and manner of presentation—changes that are often obscured in the rush to identify any potentially "modern" qualities.

The transformations in print geography that took place in the later decades of the seventeenth century and first few of the eighteenth came about, in part, by bookmakers' shrewd appropriation of travel materials—drawings as well as texts—which they put to new uses. Their innovations had to do precisely with the distinctions Stagl and Pinney point to between personal narration and impersonal description, the latter mode increasingly used in products made by van Meurs and his colleagues. European exposure to the world, it hardly needs emphasizing, expanded vastly in the Renaissance, when more and more geographic information became available. The production of travel journals flourished from the late fifteenth century, following the voyages of Columbus and Vasco da Gama, and the "enterprise of the Indies" gave rise also to the official travel report, a document prepared for the patrons of overseas projects for the purpose of colonial planning. Instructions for travelers, expressly designed to guide patterns of overseas description, served in the context of the Spanish and Portuguese imperial programs—the *Casa de la Contratación* (Seville) and the *Armazém da Guiné e Índia* (Lisbon) collected and collated this sort of data—and there exist VOC variants of these travelers' directives, as well.[100] European expansion gave rise, in short, to European narratives of expansion. Yet the abundance of manuscript material did not necessarily translate into an abundance of printed books—nor did it ultimately shape the *kind* of books derived from these sources. Leaving aside questions of access—the Dutch and English trading companies, no less than the Iberian crowns, tried to restrict the circulation of valuable trade secrets, albeit with limited success[101]—there was also the basic issue of how materials were handled, by whom, and to what end.

And *for* whom: for whom were these materials designed? This is to ask about the intended consumers of these volumes and to think about their European dimensions. Joan-Pau Rubiés has argued that, in post-Reformation Europe, travelers required a common language to communicate beyond religious divides; they needed to devise forms of description that readers of all confessional stripes could trust.[102] And this may hold true for manuscript sources, whose authors tended to follow specified conventions of narrative, often codified in colonial questionnaires: the lay of the land, potential for commerce, advantages of colonization, and so on.

Yet for *printed* books, which were necessarily the product of publishers, it was almost certainly the opposite. Over the course of the "cold war" of the Reformation, which endured at least through the mid-seventeenth century, travel accounts dedicated to contested territories overseas were decidedly "hot" documents—provocative and even divisive. They typically offered Spanish, English, or French perspectives of those lands coveted by these rival powers. They pitched locally, in other words, and no recourse to eyewitness reports, assertions of "fact," or demonstrations of "truth" could change this.

This is where Stagl and Pinney's observation becomes useful. In the form of *personal narration*, travel accounts could not help but reveal their "interest"; there is something inherently partisan about serving overseas for one or another imperial regime or commercial trading company. As a generic *description*, however, that affects an impersonal tone and perspective, a work of geography could shed its original context as a travel account. Bookmakers in the Netherlands acquired manuscripts that may have originally been composed *narratively* (to adopt Stagl and Pinney's term), yet they assiduously stripped these materials of all personal, parochial traces. The engagement of an armchair traveler to assemble these books only abetted this process: Dapper channeling Adriano de las Cortes on China or the many Italian and Portuguese authors he used for *Africa*, or Montanus appropriating Spanish and English sources for *America* or the multilingual menu of materials he worked into *Japan*.[103] The case of *Japan* is particularly instructive. Reinier Hesselink has noted the "extremely odd construction of this book," pointing to a haphazard narrative that defies any chronological or historical logic. This results from the intermingling of three separate narrative threads, which are woven together in no obvious order and with several unrelated patches of interlaced geographic material—mostly, yet not entirely, related to the Far East.[104] The resulting geographic "narrative" so fully subverts that generic form that it can hardly be placed under the same rubric. Rather than *narratively*, it proceeds *descriptively*, and it offers something neither journal-like nor in the manner of ethnography, but follows a style all its own: exotic geography. Even books penned by bona fide Dutch travelers and drawn from on-site reports—Nieuhof's *China*, Baldaeus's *Malabar*, Schouten's *Voyage*, Valentyn's *East Indies*—were cleverly and adeptly revised by bookmakers and typically augmented with other manuscript sources, quite a few of these originating with Jesuit writers (as was the case, ironically, with Baldaeus's account of Indian religion). Narratives were so thoroughly refashioned that the final product barely betrayed a trace of the original, contextualized travel report.[105]

In a sense, exotic geography might almost be defined by what it was not, yet this very absence constitutes an important set of qualities that finally add up to the brand's success. Printed volumes of geography produced in the Netherlands, even when attributed to on-site reporters, tended to *deemphasize* the travelers' presence in the exotic locales they described. The personal, authorial role was effaced whenever possible, and it certainly was not made the focus of the narrative. Texts in this descriptive mode rarely tracked an individual's daily progress; they followed a non-prosaic, non-journal-like trajectory that was, by contrast, markedly impersonal. They offered anything but an eyewitness perspective on overseas events. As a consequence, these works were nonhistorical in the sense that they focused on exotic *spaces* in preference to individual *experiences*. And this had further implications: an impersonal style meant a relative absence of personal encounters, of interpersonal engagements, of intercolonial interactions. Works of geography presented in this manner eschewed the sort of political and imperial approach that had otherwise characterized so much early modern writing on the extra-European world. They were nonconfessional in their avoidance of Catholic-Protestant polemics, they were apolitical in the way they skirted the history of past colonial rivalries, and they were ultimately noncommittal, meaning non-imperial, in their disinclination to promote competing claims for this or that territory abroad.[106] All of these absences gave these volumes their most beguiling quality. From a broadly European perspective, they were blandly neutral. This is not to suggest that these works lacked an ideological bent, but rather that they approached their subject from a scrupulously "universal" perspective—stripped of personal, historical, confessional, and local particulars—to suit the demands of their Europe-wide audience. They did not adhere to the traveler-author's course so much as to the editor-bookmaker's, and this underscores the commercial imperative of their makers. Holland-made geography was designed to sell.

In arguing that a series of negatives could produce a positive, it may be worth casting a quick glance at the reverse: the way an author's *presence* in a volume and a bluntly polemical narrative could have the effect of nullifying a reader's access to a world of geography. Compare the works of geography that competed with Amsterdam's—in this case, ones produced in Antwerp, where bookmakers had possibly even better access to far-fetched manuscripts, which would have poured into this Catholic stronghold with the steady stream of Jesuit travelers who passed through town. There are several examples to choose from, yet the ones that may offer the sharpest contrast are those by Cornelius Hazart (1617–1690), a prolific author who set himself up as the great antagonist to the empire of Dutch geography. A Flemish-born priest who penned some ninety books and pamphlets, most of them addressing matters of religion, Hazart also composed a world history of the church that appeared around 1670 and, in its global concerns, can be seen as a competitor to Dutch publications of the period. In fact, Hazart explicitly criticized Dutch-made works of geography, not least for their shabby treatment (he imagined) of the Jesuit mission abroad, particularly in Asia. He singled out for abuse the work (and person) of Arnoldus Montanus, and the two men engaged in a nasty pamphlet exchange after Montanus's *Japan* debuted in 1669. Their differences came down to both substance and style. First, Hazart, who considered himself something of an expert on the Far East based on work he did for his *Kerckelycke historie van de ghe-heele wereldt* (Ecclesiastical history of the whole world, 1667), objected to Monta-nus's narrative of Christian history in Japan—or rather, his lack of narrative and loosely told story of the Catholic persecution in Japan in the early years of the seventeenth century. Second, he complained about the poor prose style and slap-dash organization of Montanus's book, which pertained to the inchoate narrative: the author was barely focused on the topic at hand, and *Japan* was literally all over the map. Hazart and his publisher, Michiel Cnobbaert, took by contrast a more pointedly polemical stance. Their global religious history—like Amsterdam publi-cations, a fairly well illustrated volume—highlighted "*especially* the expansion of the Holy Faith, martyrdoms, and other courageous [*cloecke*] Roman Catholic deeds accomplished in the four corners of the world."[107] Theirs was an unapologet-ically Catholic narrative, filled with authorial interventions on the progress of the church, the success of the Jesuits, and the like. It was also, though, a conspicuously parochial narrative that never achieved the success of Montanus's geography: it was printed only in Dutch and German. Meanwhile, the ever entrepreneurial van Meurs, noting Hazart's critique, edited out the portions of *Japan* that may have caused offense. He then promptly published translations of Montanus's book in German and French (for Catholic readers, in other words), and supervised the En-glish edition published by Ogilby.[108]

Hazart's geography was Jesuit geography, which was sacred geography and thus the opposite of exotic geography. Narrated by the members of the Jesuit order who generally labored overseas, these works offered eyewitness accounts of the events they recorded and provided an invariably disciplined, missionary's perspective on the world. They took sides. In this, geographic accounts such as Hazart's differ ap-preciably from the Dutch variations of the genre, which decline precisely to make statements that would offend this or that community of readers. The difference here is not so much the confessional divide between the Northern and Southern Netherlands—to reiterate, van Meurs marketed his books to French, German, and English readers, many of whom presumably were Catholic—but rather the matter of "interest," a quality that Hazart's volume indubitably possessed. So did Monta-nus's, of course, yet this may have reflected the publisher's—van Meurs's—com-mercial interests more than the author's religious perspective. By downgrading the author and his or her concerns, Dutch-made books elevated the place of the pub-lisher in the production of knowledge and hence underscored the commercial im-perative of the business of geography.

The blend of Jesuit narrative and authorial "interest" comes into play once more in the great study of China that appeared at the close of this Dutch era of

FIGURE 24. Quirijn Fonbonne after Antoine Humblot, "Habillemens des Chinois" (engraving), in Jean-Baptiste Du Halde, *Description geographique, historique, chronologique, politique, et physique de l'empire de la Chine* (Paris, 1735). Special Collections, University of Hawaii Library.

bookmaking, Jean-Baptiste Du Halde's *Description geographique, historique, chronologique, politique, et physique de l'empire de la Chine* (1735), a stunning production that marks in many ways the ascendancy of French-made geography.[109] Du Halde's book compares well to earlier samples of Dutch geography: it presents a lavish, four-volume set, beautifully printed and expertly illustrated. And the editor himself was well positioned to orchestrate a vast geographic enterprise. Du Halde (1674–1743), who entered the Company of Jesus as a young man and soon took over the editing responsibilities for the *Lettres édifiantes et curieuses*—regularly published accounts of Jesuit missionaries, based on their sojourns abroad—never journeyed to China himself, yet he based his *Description geographique* on the reports of seventeen colleagues who did. The sum of these parts is a rather grand whole: a sweeping overview of China, the land, and its people; an analysis of China's imperial regimes, religious customs, and artistic traditions; and a history of European interventions in the Far East. It differs from Dutch geographies of the Middle Kingdom—the reigning studies up until then would have been Nieuhof's and Dapper's—chiefly in the way it foregrounds the Jesuit efforts to evangelize in China and, more generally, the progress of Catholicism in the East. This perspective would naturally have limited Du Halde's appeal to a pan-European audience, yet his book did experience a certain success: a second French edition appeared almost at once (printed in the Dutch Republic, to be sure), as did an English translation. The latter volume, however, strenuously took issue in a translator's preface with Du Halde's approach, questioning both the "accuracy" of the work and its overall "credit." And the problem lay precisely with the religious orientation of Du Halde and his Jesuit sources—a perspective plainly advertised in the paratexts and consistently invoked in the text—and with the partisan viewpoint that resulted. Du Halde may have anticipated this predicament in his own preface, where he praises Jesuit reports as superior to others and notes particularly the "disinterestedness" (*désintéressement*) of his coreligionists. Not so, claimed the London translator, who felt obliged to sanitize Du Halde's work of its devotional excesses and to alert English readers to the problem: "If at any time I appear in Opposition to the Missionaries['] religious Notions," he averred, "it is because I judged it not honest to spread their Poison in a Protestant Country without the Antidote along with it."[110] And herein lay the dilemma: When geography takes an obvious perspective, it alienates certain readers. When geography fails the test of "disinterest," it fails to cross borders, be these confessional or national. And when geography earns the label of "poison," it is unlikely to have many takers.

Du Halde's imposing description of China sits, literally and figuratively, at the opposite end of the early modern geography bookshelf from van Meurs's publications, including those authored by Nieuhof and Dapper. Du Halde's work appeared nearly three-quarters of a century after van Meurs's splashy debut in geography—Nieuhof's phenomenal 1665 best seller on China—and it affects a markedly different voice and style. It brings into sharp relief, by comparative example, those qualities of exotic geography that had developed in Dutch ateliers over the previous decades. An Englishman's resistance to a Frenchman's view of the world—for this, in essence, is the translator's objection to Du Halde's magnum opus—is not unusual in and of itself. This is the general course of geography, which generates a highly parochial mode of knowledge and hence induces a highly partisan reaction. The resistance to Du Halde illustrates, most essentially, the stumbling blocks for *any* hegemonic brand of geography, be that a French or English brand, Spanish or Dutch, Catholic or Protestant, and so on. It neatly demonstrates the dilemma of geography: to be interesting without being interested, to gain the trust (and attention) of the reader without alienating him or her. What is more unusual than Du Halde's provocation of his English translator, by contrast, is van Meurs's success among his broadly European audience and the *absence* of much controversy surrounding his publications—at least in the late seventeenth and early eighteenth centuries. This suggests the commercial, rather than religious or imperial, imperatives driving Dutch geography, and this points, in turn, to the pivotal role of the editor in making exotic geography.

What constitutes "exotic geography"? Perhaps this question can be better reformulated to highlight the consumption of these products—by their largely European audiences—rather than their subject matter, and the distinctive form they took upon publication, which contributed so palpably to their wide appeal. Pictures, paratexts, page upon page of rambling "descriptions" compiled by impersonal authors and directed at disparate topics that could be situated outside of Europe (the Greek-derived *exoticos* meaning merely "outside of"): exotic geography in its printed form was a mode of production as much as anything else. It was a style rather than a space. That this style induced certain conventions of presentation, habits of production (and of reproduction of consistently successful texts and images), and generic devices is highly significant: the medium in many ways was the message.[111] The medium also induced conventions of reception: exotic geography, which circulated across a wide swath of Europe, was surely not "read" in the commonly understood sense of that word. It was more accurately looked at, skimmed, or picked over for sundry appealing bric-a-brac. When James Boswell asked that Enlightened bibliophile Samuel Johnson whether he should read the immense works of geography so prevalent in his day—it was in fact the English edition of Du Halde's tome that prompted Boswell's query—Johnson is reported to have replied, "Why yes, as one reads such a book; that is to say, consult it."[112]

"Such a book" by Dr. Johnson's day—thriving, imperial, Georgian London—was a known commodity. The form and style of exotic geography, its generous proportions and typographic layout, were easily identified. It had a "pleasing" presentation, engaging features, and readily accessible contents. It was a winning brand. This brand had attracted, by this time, an extensive audience and accrued considerable "credit." If not quite read, volumes of Dutch-made and Dutch-inspired geography were consulted—and very widely so. Judging by the evidence of production runs, reprinted and pirated editions, multilingual translations, and the anecdotal evidence of the likes of Johnson, exotic geography in its smartly packaged forms was ubiquitous. It shaped Europe's conception of the world well into the age of Johnson and beyond.

Let observation with extensive view,
Survey mankind from China *to* Peru.

—SAMUEL JOHNSON, *The Vanity of Human Wishes*

Now I shall open this body, as it were, to offer you a view of the interior.

—CORNELIS DE BRUIJN (on Persepolis), *Reizen over Moskovie,*
door Persie en Indie

[CHAPTER TWO]

SEEING THE WORLD

Visuality and Exoticism

Viewing the World

By the turn of the eighteenth century, Europeans enjoyed an unprecedented ability to view the world. Habits of travel had not so drastically changed—overseas voyages were still the unhappy lot of sailors and soldiers, by and large, made to staff the dangerous and commonly fatal expeditions of conquest and trade abroad. Yet to see the world in mimetic form—to view it in the wide range of devices dedicated to the replication of the exotic world—had become remarkably easy by this time, especially in the abundantly produced and widely circulated sources of Dutch geography. These sources delivered the things of the world, increasingly, in a strikingly visual, readily viewable, and pronouncedly pictorial form. Maps, atlases, and hand-colored topographic views; picture books displaying the ethnography and history of foreign lands; plentifully illustrated travel accounts and natural histories; landscape and still-life paintings, and copper engravings of exotic peoples, flora, and fauna; a vast range of material arts, ornately embellished with exotic motifs: all of these furnished images of the world, and never had these images been more effortlessly obtainable than in the decades surrounding 1700. Indeed, volumes of print geography—by tradition, a textual genre—had become intensely reliant on illustrations and emphatic about the place of images in their presentation of the world. Geography, in short, had taken a "pictorial turn."[1]

Why geography, and why pictures? One simple answer points to the basic desire of early modern Europeans to view the world, especially those so-called new worlds that, over the previous two centuries, had been spectacularly "discovered." The very word *discovery* implied an act of revelation or seeing, a process of making visible and viewable that which had been hitherto unseen, and exotic places in particular enticed viewers and lured inquisitive eyes.[2] Seeing was inherent to the discovery of the early modern world, and knowing the world—a noble pursuit in the wake not just of Columbus, but also of the telescopic tinkering of Galileo Galilei and the microscopy of Antonie van Leeuwenhoek—came via processes of observation. This proposition was a standard leitmotif of a certain brand of geography. "All who are curious," wrote Jean de Thévenot in the account of his travels through large portions of Asia in the 1650s and 1660s, "delight in the Rarities they *see*; and there are but few, who, if they were not otherwise engaged, would not willingly be themselves the *witnesses* and *spectatours* of them." Thévenot highlights a visual approach to the world and the would-be traveler's ocular engagement with global wonders. Like Samuel Johnson in his famously redundant exhortation to view exotic knowledge (see chapter epigraph)—"observation" is augmented by "view" and the further desire to "survey"[3]—Thévenot prescribes a process of *seeing* the world. For those without opportunity to see for themselves ("otherwise engaged"), moreover, Thévenot recommends pictures of the world—such as those that illustrate his much embellished, oft-printed *Travels into the Levant*. By pictorial means, "all who are curious" could observe and enjoy the world—note, too, the emphasis on the "delight" or pleasure in exotic things—albeit at a distance.[4]

Pictures provided a distinct pleasure to the armchair traveler, yet they served other, potentially more critical needs, as well. Distance demanded a more productive regime of representation, a more reliable means of communicating faraway rarities to stay-at-home consumers of geographic literature, and visual forms offered a ready solution to this essentially epistemological problem. By employing graphic forms to describe distant phenomena, illustrations allowed the learned of Europe to process exotic knowledge more effectively. Pictures delivered data from a distance.[5] This conception of geography's visual agenda was not entirely new. Abraham Ortelius had recognized geography's ocular purpose in an oft-cited epigraph inscribed onto the frontispiece of his *Parergon*, the supplemental volume of ancient geography added to the *Theatrum orbis terrarum* (Theater of the whole world): "Historiae oculus geographia" (Geography [is] the eye of history).[6] By this Ortelius meant to assert geography's role in providing a visual compendium for the discipline of history. Geography allowed historical knowledge to be visualized. Geography, by definition, took an intrinsically visual, or *graphic*, approach to its data, and Ortelius (following, among others, the Renaissance polymath Petrus Apianus) codified the epistemological value of this function.[7] The implications for *exotic* geography, more particularly, could not have been missed. If history, especially its ancient variant, needed assistance to visualize a distant past— the *Parergon* mapped out, or graphed, the ancient world—then the geography, especially of exotic lands, confronted a similar problem in presenting a distant present. Exotic reporting necessitated some form of visual apparatus, and this was a point regularly raised in the richly illustrated volumes of geography produced circa 1700. "Copper engravings also needed to be made," explained Engelbert Kaempfer regarding his conspicuously visual study of the natural and human phenomena he encountered in Asia, "since exotica are very difficult to comprehend without the help of clarifying illustrations."[8] Pictures "clarified" and "surveyed"; they enabled the "discovery" of foreign places and the virtual witnessing of exotic wonders. And pictures, accordingly, were ubiquitous in sources of geography circa 1700.

Or rather, pictures proliferated in Dutch-made and Dutch-derived sources. Pictures were associated with the Dutch style of geography—with certain paintings, to be sure, and decorative arts and ornate maps, yet also and preeminently with printed books depicting exotic lands—and pictures largely characterized the Dutch "brand." Pictures gave Dutch geography its distinctive look, and consumers across Europe in the decades surrounding 1700 recognized and even anticipated Dutch products for their vibrant visuality. Johan Nieuhof's popular description of China gained its high reputation, according to a London publisher, for its fabulous "cuts" or engravings. This illustration-rich, van Meurs–produced volume (even in the form pirated by English printers in 1704) "so plainly represent[ed] all things *observable* . . . that with the help of the Cuts we seem to be conversing with the People of those parts, to *see* all their Towns and living Creatures, and to be thoroughly acquainted with their Habits, Customs, and Superstitions."[9] Pictures were the thing. They served as the chief attraction of Dutch books, "the Soul of performances of this kind," as another printer phrased it, in this case with reference to the "embellishments" of an Amsterdam-manufactured account of Japan.[10] Melchisédech Thévenot, uncle of the well-known traveler Jean and a leading Parisian producer of travel literature, remarked on the keen anticipation among his fellow bookmen of Dutch-made volumes, since "they describe things as they are . . . they report only what they *see*."[11] Again, the emphasis lies on the visual and on Dutch expertise, and Thévenot himself was quick to adopt the illustrations of Dutch publications into his own, whenever he could. (It scarcely helped: Dutch printers produced French-language editions with superior and superfluous prints.) Indeed, the well-made, richly illustrated books crafted in Holland were the envy of the industry. There was little to compare to them—Theodor de Bry's folios from earlier in the century came closest, yet contemporary English-, French-, and Spanish-produced volumes hardly approached the visual quality of Dutch imprints—and this accounts, more than anything, for their remarkable success. When Europeans "looked" abroad, they turned to Dutch pictures, and this rendered Dutch producers not only the geographers, but also the eyes of Europe: they observed, surveyed, and made viewable the exotic world.

To recalibrate our previous questions: Why geography *then*—why a conspicuously pictorial turn in products of Dutch geography beginning in the final decades of the seventeenth century and continuing into the early eighteenth? And why pictures *there*—why the emphatically graphic approach taken by Dutch manufacturers, in particular, when it came to global materials? The answers to these questions entail an analysis of processes of viewing the world in the period around 1700 and an exploration, more particularly, of those visually rich sources of geography that, even while consumed across much of Europe, came most commonly from the ateliers of the Netherlands. Dutch-made books described the world in word and fabulous image; they contained the most abundant, most splendid, and ultimately most popular illustrations. This pictorial approach to geography gained Dutch products a wide following—Dutch-illustrated books and illustrations derived from Dutch books were reprinted and otherwise replicated deep into the eighteenth century. And it established a look and mode of presentation for exotic geography that remains the standard, arguably, to this day: think *National Geographic*. Yet this visually oriented strategy was highly innovative at the time. Its inherent cartographic content notwithstanding, geography had traditionally taken a textual approach to its subject; narratives of overseas voyages and histories of extra-European polities drove most accounts, which tended to rely on classical sources (for history) and navigators' journals (for prosaic description). None of the leading volumes of the sixteenth and early seventeenth centuries—Giovanni Battista Ramusio's *Navigationi et viaggi* (1550–1559), André Thevet's *Cosmographie universelle* (1575), Richard Hakluyt's *Principal navigations* (1589–1600), Antonio de Herrera's *Historia general de los hechos de los Castellanos* (1601–1615)—had anywhere near the pictorial impact of a typical van Meurs product (granting, again, de Bry's publications as something of an exception and precursor).[12] None advertised their (often scant) images, as would become regular practice among the entrepreneurial publishers of the Netherlands, and none established a "brand" of visually rich geography. Dutch-made volumes, by contrast, rather than merely narrating events, sought to observe them, illustrate them, and veritably anatomize them—which was precisely the tack taken by the artist-turned-traveler Cornelis de Bruijn in his spectacularly illustrated books on the Levant, Muscovy, and Persia. De Bruijn's choice of metaphor—"Now I shall open this body, as it were, to offer you a view of the interior"—is apt. Dutch geography, in its relentless recourse to pictures and forms of mimetic representation, provided a visual spectacle as well as a lesson in observation, and it resembled in this way both the popular spectacle of the anatomy theater and the graphic illustrations of the post-Vesalian anatomy book. It offered, in short, the chance for *autopsia*. It thereby opened up the globe and rendered the world astonishingly viewable to early modern Europe.

How: Making Pictures and Making Exotic Geography

The world opened up on the opening page of a typical volume of Dutch-made geography: the frontispiece. The frontispiece served as the entrée to the book at hand, ushering in the reader and offering a pictorial synopsis, or at least a substantial visual hint, of the content to come. It set the tone for the volume and, in its very form—an elaborately designed and, more often than not, excellently etched or engraved illustration—underscored the visual character of the product. This recourse to the frontispiece as a visual cue was not new. The Jesuits and their printers had pioneered its use in books produced from the 1620s (many of them made in Antwerp), employing a graphic strategy that dovetailed neatly with the Order's preoccupation with the visual.[13] In Jesuit-designed volumes, the frontispiece had a plainly religious and didactic purpose—to see was to comprehend, in a most basic sense, and to comprehend was to believe. Yet the frontispiece also lent a theatrical aspect to the formal opening of a book (figure 25). This feature can be found, as well, in volumes of late seventeenth- and early eighteenth-century geography, where the frontispiece functioned as a prologue to the drama of geography. (And the affiliation of geography and theater—the theatrical conceit of geography—had a long pedigree, going back at least to Ortelius's *Theatrum orbis terrarum*, published with a strikingly staged frontispiece in 1570 [figure 26].)[14] In some cases, the frontispiece might even make the case for the "art" of geography, underscoring the visual approach to be pursued in the volume at hand. Cornelis de Bruijn's richly illustrated account of the Levant (1698) alludes to the elevated status of picture-making—de Bruijn himself was an accomplished draftsman and painter—in an allegorical frontispiece that features the figure of Fame crowning Hercules (denoting perhaps the artist-author's massive labors), both of whom hover above the arts of painting, sculpture, and architecture (figure 27). De Bruijn announces his intentions, as well, on the title page, which promotes a product "enriched with more than two hundred copper plates, illustrating the most famous landscapes, cities, etc., all done by the author himself and drawn after life." The pictures were the selling point.[15]

In the case of de Bruijn's publications, it is unusually clear how books got their pictures. The author himself was the traveler, draftsman, and publisher all rolled up in one, as he proudly broadcast on the title page. Yet de Bruijn's was not the typical pattern of publication, nor was the production of book illustrations ever quite so transparent. How did exotic pictures get made? Rather than looking to the "author" or the name placed most prominently in the book's title, the point of departure should be lower on the page, at the address of the printer or bookmaker (whose roles were typically combined in Holland's book industry; in London and Paris, by contrast, they might remain separate). Indeed, there was a critical division of labor between the author of the narrative—and even this function might have been up

FIGURE 25. Cornelis Bloemaert, frontispiece (engraving) to Daniello Bartoli, *Historia della Compagnia di Giesu* (Rome, 1659). Saint Louis University Libraries Special Collections.

for grabs—and the author of the illustrations, the latter role commonly filled by multiple, unheralded residents of the printer's atelier. To produce the lavishly "enriched" volumes of Dutch geography required, above all, the direction of the printer, who took charge of the illustration program and managed this facet of

FIGURE 26. Frontispiece (engraving) to Abraham Ortelius, *Theatrum orbis terrarum* (Antwerp, 1570). Special Collections, University of Amsterdam (OF 72-30).

production with the same entrepreneurial energy as any other. The printer shopped for fresh (or sometimes not so fresh) manuscript material, an increasingly valuable commodity as the market for geography and travel literature expanded in the second half of the seventeenth century. Original sketchbooks were especially prized,

FIGURE 27. J. Mulder after R. du Val, frontispiece (engraving) to *Reizen van Cornelis de Bruyn, door de vermaardste deelen van Klein Asia* (Delft, 1698). Utrecht University Library.

and these derived from several sources. They came directly off ships returning from the Indies, a by-product of the Dutch East India Company's policy of sending draftsmen overseas to describe, in pictures as well as words, the lay of the land, its peoples, and its products; this was the origin of Johan Nieuhof's manuscript.[16] Alternatively, drawings and paintings could be personally commissioned and collected by private patrons in the Netherlands, who might have had connections with an overseas trading company, yet also had a special interest in early modern *materia exotica*. This accounts for the large corpus of visual material amassed by Nicolaes Witsen, an Amsterdam regent and avid collector, and for the Brazilian compositions of Albert Eckhout, Frans Post, and Georg Marcgraf, which were done under the direction of Johan Maurits of Nassau-Siegen.[17] And while these rich materials, highly coveted by elite collectors, were less likely to end up in the hands of profit-minded printers, other sketchbooks, sometimes undertaken by the same artist or copied after the commissioned originals, did make their way into the open market.[18] Rarer were the instances of independent artists traveling abroad, such as de Bruijn, yet this was not so unusual in the field of natural history, where the naturalist him- or herself might carry out the task of careful draftsmanship. (Maria Sibylla Merian is a fine example.)[19]

FIGURE 28. "Een mallabaars pelgrim. Een pappoe met een staartje" (ca. 1685–1710); watercolor and wash. Special Collections (Nicolaes Witsen Collection, ms. Bf 58b), University of Amsterdam.

In a strong market for illustrated geography books, printers availed themselves of whatever materials became available, be they "new" and "original," as so many title pages dubiously advertised, or not. Bookmakers had always purchased stock from one another, especially used but still valuable copper plates and unused but readily adoptable engraved prints, and this was the case, as well, for the genre of geography. Images, in this way, were recycled from earlier publications and refurbished, as older prints underwent subtle revisions and practical renovations to make them more suitable for their second (or even third or fourth) iteration. This holds true particularly for cartographic materials, where cost-saving tactics trumped the desire for up-to-date accuracy. Printers also reused stock from their own publications, converting North American Indians, for example, into (feathered) South Asian warriors—again, a fairly routine trick of the trade, practiced most pervasively perhaps by the prolific Pieter van der Aa, who mined his massive archive of images to produce the massive, late-career picture books that established his reputation.[20] Savvy bookmakers, in addition, produced translations of their volumes (here the case of Jacob van Meurs stands out), not only as means to circulate their images to a wider audience but also as a cost-effective way to squeeze maximum profit out of their investment in copper plates. In certain cases, the plates themselves or the prints created from those plates shipped directly to a foreign printer, who could then publish editions of Dutch-made books with Dutch-made pictures under his own name and address (as was the practice of the Royal Geographer John Ogilby).[21]

Pulling the strings through these processes was the printer. As meandering and lengthy as the path might have been from the original sketch of an exotic subject to its final form as a book illustration, this progression was orchestrated throughout by the resolute (and canny) figure of the printer. The printer-cum-bookmaker—who might combine the activities of book selling, copper-plate engraving, art dealing, and of course printing[22]—acquired the image from the artist or on the open market; employed a draftsman, when necessary, to transform raw sketches into finished compositions; and engaged a skilled engraver or etcher to prepare copper plates for printing. At the end of the day, however, it was the printer's product as much as anyone else's. In fact, in several instances the printer undertook much of the work of "embellishment" him- or herself, doing the final design or even the engravings based on rough sketches. Van Meurs was instrumental in illustrating those books published under his name. He trained as a graphic artist and identified with that vocation (*plaatsnijder*, or plate engraver), and he did many book engravings himself. He moved over the course of his career from maker of prints to merchant of prints—and ultimately to merchant of the sumptuously illustrated books that bore his and others' rich graphic work. (He signed off on his edition of Nieuhof as "Bookseller and Engraver.") And while van Meurs may have worked with well-developed manu-

Tymorese Soldaten.

FIGURE 29. Jacob van Meurs (atelier), "Tymorese Soldaten" (engraving), in Johan Nieuhof, *Gedenkwaerdige zee en lantreize door de voornaemste landschappen van West en Oostindien* (Amsterdam, 1682). Special Collections, University of Amsterdam (KF 61-4601).

scripts, such as Nieuhof's description of China, he more often than not assembled
and developed texts from scattered sources, revised and enhanced rough sketches to
generate detailed engravings, and generally pursued whatever opportunities presented themselves to create his trademark illustrated books.

Consider the geography of China, a cause to which van Meurs contributed considerably: two separate, handsomely illustrated folio volumes in the space of five years, which were regularly reprinted and widely translated into Latin, English, French, and German. For the first of these publications, Johan Nieuhof's report of the Dutch embassy to Beijing, van Meurs had excellent material to work with in the form of a first-hand narrative obtained directly from the author's brother Hendrik. The manuscript included ample illustrations done by a reasonably accomplished draftsman: something in the order of eighty watercolored pen drawings, which are generally attributed to Nieuhof. Yet the published book boasted close to 150 engravings, and to make up the difference, van Meurs would have necessarily augmented Nieuhof's original drawings with other images of less certain provenance.[23] Nieuhof's pictures comprised mostly cityscapes and topographic views, and while they clearly derived from his journey, they are not drafted entirely in situ; some appear to be based on summary sketches done over the course of his travels, which were worked up after the fact. A drawing of Guangzhou ("Canton") in the so-called Paris manuscript (one of two ascribed to Nieuhof or a copyist), for example, has a mountain and a hilltop structure that are plainly inserted by a later artist.[24] Whatever the case, the illustrations fully *added* by van Meurs are of a wholly different category. They consist largely of ethnographic vignettes, showing the "races," "habits," and "mores" of the land, along with miscellaneous Asian (if not necessarily Chinese) flora and fauna. These almost certainly came from another hand or perhaps the same hand that revised Nieuhof's drawings in preparation for their publication.[25] Some of these additional illustrations are simply atelier copies of earlier works—Dürer's famous Indian rhinoceros makes an appearance in one print, now showcased as a Chinese species.[26] Yet several others point to a far more creative process of revision and adaptation. These indicate the efforts of an artist-designer who would have worked in van Meurs's atelier and adorned the engravings, whatever their origins, with the parasol-shaded *staffage* and leafy palm trees that fill the foreground; with the elegant pagodas and rustic temples on the horizon; and with the many other exotic props that, while spread liberally throughout these images, make nary an appearance in the original sketches (compare figures 32 and 33).[27] In all events, it is the ethnographic illustrations more than any others that recur in later publications. Melchisédech Thévenot's French edition (1666) effectively skips the Nieuhof-derived cityscapes—"seen one, seen them all," Thévenot quipped bluntly[28]—opting instead for a collage of Chinese "types" and other exotic fare derived from the van Meurs–generated pictures (see, for example, figures 157 and 158 and compare figure 21).

For his second book on China, also based on an embassy to the imperial court (by Pieter van Hoorn to Beijing in 1665–1666, following separate trade expeditions along the coast of Fujian in 1663–1664), van Meurs had no bona fide original images to work with, in the sense that the named author of the volume, Olfert Dapper, was neither in China nor a trained draftsman.[29] The volume's rich visual program—

FIGURE 30. Johan Nieuhof (?), View of Guangzhou, in Nieuhof, "Iournaal" (1658); pen and wash. Société de Géographie (coll. Muller 14-IV-1984), Bibliothèque Nationale, Paris.

FIGURE 31. Jacob van Meurs (atelier), "Reinoceros" (engraving), in Johan Nieuhof, *Gezantschap der Neêrlandtsche Oost-Indische Compagnie* (Amsterdam, 1665). Special Collections, University of Amsterdam (OM 63 116).

FIGURE 32. Johan Nieuhof (?), View of Linqing, in Nieuhof, "Iournaal" (1658); pen and wash. Société de Géographie (coll. Muller 14-IV-1984), Bibliothèque Nationale, Paris.

FIGURE 33. Jacob van Meurs (atelier), "Lincing [Linqing]" (engraving), in Johan Nieuhof, *Gezantschap der Neêrlandtsche Oost-Indische Compagnie* (Amsterdam, 1665). Special Collections, University of Amsterdam (OM 63-116).

thirty-nine full-page copper engravings and fifty-six text illustrations—derives, rather, from the bookmaker's enterprise and his atelier's hard work; and in this instance, the tricks of the trade are not so easily detected.[30] Not unusually, the engravings lack signatures. They bear a distinct resemblance, in several cases, to illustrations in the Nieuhof volume—the cityscapes, especially, with their foreground harbors and background pagodas, share a comparable pattern of composition. Yet this may underscore the steady team of draftsmen in van Meurs's employ, the house style of his atelier, and the broader Dutch tradition in topographic views more than it does any overlap of on-site artists. As for the latter, draftsmen may have come from the ranks of the VOC, which commissioned some of the material that made its way into Dapper's text; here, too, there may have been a company style when it came to illustration, reflecting standard VOC instructions to their overseas servants. But much of the visual material came from other, non-Dutch sources, conspicuously from Jesuit travelers who arrived in China far earlier than the Dutch, and particularly from Adriano de las Cortes, who visited China for the Society of Jesus in the 1620s and whose half-century-old description of that experience somehow fell into the hands of Jacob van Meurs. Numerous engravings in Dapper's China volume incorporate drawings from the de las Cortes manuscript, especially those pertaining to ethnographic subjects—yet they do so in a distinctively van Meurs fashion. A series of miscellaneous sketches that show Chinese attire and what might be called status accessories—hats, belts, boots, and so on—is organized by van Meurs into two taxonomic prints, featuring mostly headwear and bearing the caption "Diverse Sorts of Bonnets." The emphasis in the van Meurs plate lies in the curious shapes of Chinese fashion, which has been conveniently collected and, by consequence, decontextualized (see figure 34 and plate 3). Several more scattered vignettes by de las Cortes illustrating imperial justice are worked up by the van Meurs atelier into a sensational set of engravings on the "torture" meted out by the all-powerful Chinese ruler: here it is the cumulative effect of pictures (spread out in de las Cortes's manuscript) that makes an impact (see plate 10 and figures 173 and 174). The Dapper book also includes some exceptional Buddhist devotional prints, based very likely on Chinese originals (these would have been copied: figure 35). Yet as with the Nieuhof volume, it is the ethnographic illustrations fabricated by the van Meurs atelier—images that mostly derive from the unidentified de las Cortes manuscript—that get the most play in the extracted and pirated editions that appeared over the coming decades.[31]

If the originality of these prints was not their most salient quality—the pretense of on-site witnessing and the semblance of veritable mimesis is easily dismissed—this suggests all the more reason to highlight the bookmaker's supervision of geography's production and the role of the mostly anonymous atelier figures who ultimately made geography's pictures. Books were assertively assigned authors on the title page, yet pictures generally came without any clear authority—even

FIGURE 34. Adriano de las Cortes, Types of bonnets, in *Relación del viaje* (ca. 1625);
pen drawing (Sloane 1005). © The British Library Board. All Rights Reserved.

when those pictures were announced more volubly than anything else, both on
those very title pages and in volumes' prefatory apparatuses. There existed, in other
words, an authorial lacuna between the text and the images, between the presumed
author of the narrative and the unnamed maker of the illustrations, and the task of
filling this gap typically fell to the bookmaker's workshop.

The workshop's first line of duty may have been precisely to disguise the fact of this
disconnect—to minimize all signs of this bibliogonic breach. Rarely is there mention
on the title page of a book's illustrator, the exception of de Bruijn proving the general
rule.[32] There is by contrast, and far more commonly, ample discussion of *illustrations*
and the distinct implication that the "author" of the text bears responsibility, as well,
for the images that accompany it. Dapper's volume on Africa (1668) touted pictures
"drawn from life [*na 't leven getekent*] and engraved in copper"—thus implying authorial presence—while Montanus's *America* (1671) claimed to be "embellished with il-

FIGURE 35. Jacob van Meurs (atelier), Guanyin Pusa ["Pussa"] (engraving), in Olfert Dapper, *Gedenkwaerdig bedryf der Nederlandsche Oost-Indische Maetschappye, op de kuste en in het keizerrijk van Taising of Sina* (Amsterdam, 1670). University Library, Vrije Universiteit, Amsterdam.

lustrations done in America after life [*na 't leven in America gemaekt*]."[33] Yet neither of these stay-at-home authors had witnessed anything even remotely outside of Europe (let alone outside the province of Holland); both volumes emanate, of course, from van Meurs's enterprising atelier.[34] More convoluted claims came from writers who had actually journeyed abroad—Philip Baldaeus in Malabar, Jan Struys in Muscovy and Persia, Wouter Schouten in the East Indies—yet whose title-page claims nonetheless carry little weight. Several of the illustrations in Baldaeus's prose description of Malabar ("drawn to life and cut in copper plates") came from the hand of Philips Angel, the unnamed source of a fascinating description of Hindu religion (the highlight of Baldaeus's book), which Angel himself lifted from an Italian Jesuit who had covered the same ground decades earlier (see figure 141).[35] The images in Struys's popular book— the author was a sailmaker with no formal training in draftsmanship—are largely the labor of the bookmakers, Johannes van Someren and Jacob van Meurs, and their workshop assistants.[36] They bear a striking resemblance to pictures in another "eyewitness" account produced by the same publishing team, the *Oost-Indische voyagie* (East Indian voyage) of Wouter Schouten (1676), and one presumes that the alleged witnessing took place in the same atelier and at the same moment: September 1675, when the two printers obtained exclusive privileges for the publication of both books. These state-issued privileges refer explicitly to engravings and illustrations, which were understood to impart considerable added value to the product. No mention is made of the authors of these illustrations, however. It is the publishers who get "credit" and gain ownership in the form of legal protection or copyright.[37]

If no mention is made of the illustrations' "author," or what modern critics might think of as the artist, certainly no mention is made of the draftsmen, engravers, and workshop apprentices who are the anonymous contributors to these productions. Anonymous does not mean wholly neglected, however, and in certain cases, these unheralded craftsmen—what historians of science refer to as "invisible technicians"[38]—do leave their traces. An intriguing notarial record from the Amsterdam archives hints at the fascinating underworld of picture-making at the height of the late seventeenth-century craze for illustrated geography. It records an agreement reached in March 1672 between the publishing tandem of Johannes van Someren and Johannes Janssonius van Waesberge and the engraver Coenraet Decker. Decker agreed to supply the two bookmakers, who specialized in travel and geographic literature, one large copper plate per week and one smaller plate every three days. The contract laid out a sliding pay scale for plates designed by Decker (as opposed to those merely engraved), the "drawn" plates fetching higher compensation. Jacob van Meurs also makes an appearance in this transaction. The two bookmakers, who had hired Decker with a particular project in mind, specified further that the young engraver was forbidden to work for other publishers, particularly van Meurs. Good thing: Van Meurs had actively solicited Decker for other projects (he likely used him for some of the Nieuhof prints), and he later poached the much-sought-after Decker for the Struys volume—yet did so, this time, in collaboration with his onetime rival van Someren. The 1672 notarial document, apart from offering a fascinating glimpse into the inner workings of printmaking—the status of the engraver, rate of production, role of design—vividly showcases the overheated market for professional printmakers. Draftsmen, designers, and engravers, over whom bookmakers vigorously competed, made pictures possible. If most toiled in anonymity, all were vital to the illustration of exotic geography.[39]

In a certain sense, this very anonymity may partly explain the success of these pictures—and, by extension, of Dutch-made volumes of illustrated geography. The more complicated and concealed the path that an image followed to publication, the less easily and directly it could be affixed to a specific author or a distinct narrative. The less attached illustrations were, moreover, the more flexible they could be. This conferred on pictures, sometimes more than authors or their site-specific histories, considerable value. Pictures in their own right sold books, and the origin of an image with this or that embassy or traveler assumed less importance than the inherent interest and seductiveness of the images themselves. Visual appeal, rather than narrative relevance (let alone descriptive accuracy) prevailed. This meant sketches could be enhanced and augmented, as occurred in the case of Nieuhof's and Dapper's volumes: in the one case, original manuscript material was massaged and supplemented by workshop-produced illustrations; in the other, loosely affiliated material from an altogether different traveler (Adriano de las Cortes) was seamlessly inserted into the narrative flow. It meant, as well, that wholly unrelated pictures could be used to "embellish" a weakly illustrated text. This added to a book's worth, needless to say; it also gave the final product the look of Dutch-made geography. Hendrik Hamel's narrative of shipwreck, capture, and enslavement in Korea came out in three different forms. One was "decorated with diverse figures": eight newly made woodblock prints, which had nothing to do with Hamel and precious little to do with his journey, but added immeasurably to the volume's success. A second had pictures appended from the printer's stock, in this case an elephant, crocodiles, and other marvelous beasts intended to lend an appropriately exotic flavor to the narrative (see figures 16 and 36). And a third lacked all manner of illustration—and was, predictably, the least successful edition in terms of print runs.[40]

Whether a book was "Dutch" or not made little difference, in fact, for it could always receive the Dutch-atelier treatment: illustrations, above all, along with the assorted paratexts that became the stock and trade of the Dutch geography business. When Louis Hennepin, a Franciscan of the order of Récollets, journeyed into the western reaches of New France in North America (he took part in La Salle's explor-

FIGURE 36. Korean fauna (woodblock print), in Hendrick Hamel, 't Oprechte journael, van de ongeluckige reyse van 't jacht de Sperwer (Amsterdam, ca. 1670). Koninklijke Bibliotheek, The Hague.

atory mission though the Great Lakes), he lamented a lack of able draftsmen to illustrate his adventure. "I wish'd an [*sic*] hundred times that somebody had been with
us, who could have describ'd [i.e., drawn] the Wonders of this prodigious frightful
Fall," he wrote of the thundering waters of the Niagara River, "so as to give the
Reader a just and natural Idea of it."[41] He returned to Europe, accordingly, with a
manuscript, yet without pictures. When his *Nouvelle decouverte* appeared in print
some years later, however, at the address of Dutch-based bookmakers—first in
Utrecht with Guillaume Broedelet, and then in Leiden with Pieter van der Aa—it
was "adorned" with workshop-produced engravings of the "terrifying" Niagara
Falls; a nude male "sauvage," standing elegantly *contrapposto* before a massive river;
and a fearsome buffalo, who meanders through an incongruously tropical landscape
(an opossum hangs on a nearby tree). A prefatory note in the form of an "Advice to
the Reader" commends the publisher precisely for adding agreeable illustrations
and useful maps to the text. These were particularly advantageous, the reader is assured, since they "give a clear idea of certain things that are better understood when
there is some *visual representation*."[42] This was by now a truism, surely, yet one born
out exceptionally by illustrated volumes made in the Netherlands.

FIGURE 37. Casper Luyken or Jan van Vianen (?), Niagara Falls (engraving), in Louis
Hennepin, *Nouvelle decouverte d'un tres grand pays situé dans l'Amerique* (Utrecht,
1697). Wisconsin Historical Society (WHi-103152).

CHAPTER TWO

The advice to the reader in certain Dutch editions of the *Nouvelle decouverte* may not come from the pen of Hennepin himself. It is more likely the intervention of the Leiden publisher van der Aa, who sensibly wished to bring attention to the illustrations that had been added to Hennepin's text.[43] The author, after all, admits to his lack of picture-making abilities and confesses, by inference, that any images included in his book are not his own—not done in situ, not "drawn from life." They belonged, rather, to the bookmaker, who had invested financial resources in their production, obtained official privileges for their publication, and owned them in any true legal sense. It is to the bookmaker, as well, that "credit" must be granted for a volume's illustrations, which invariably would have been "improved" in the printer's workshop, manipulated by his draftsmen, enhanced by his engravers, or just plain made up or recycled by his team of graphic artists. Nonetheless, assertions were habitually made otherwise, and the matter of the illustrations' authorship was cleverly finessed. Title-page claims boldly insinuated an author's role in the production of images, with claims of picture-making done "after life." Pictures allegedly sketched in situ—as publishers consistently promoted them—might conceivably have been done by another on-site artist, as opposed to the named author, yet that is not the first assump-

FIGURE 38. Casper Luyken (?), North American fauna (engraving), in Louis Hennepin, *Nouvelle decouverte d'un tres grand pays situé dans l'Amerique* (Utrecht, 1697). Wisconsin Historical Society (WHi-103154).

FIGURE 39. Jacob van Meurs (atelier), Sjurpurama volcano (engraving), in Arnoldus Montanus, *Gedenkwaerdige gesantschappen der Oost-Indische Maetschappy in 't Vereenigde Nederland, aen de Kaisaren van Japan* (Amsterdam, 1669). Special Collections, University of Amsterdam (OM 63-363).

tion a reader would make. And pictures themselves could imply authorial presence—as when European-looking draftsmen make their appearance in engraved tropical scenes, thereby implying purported ad vivum production. A roving artist shows up in the foreground of a massive volcanic eruption depicted in Montanus's armchair description of Japan, and similar characters appear in several engravings in Wouter Schouten's *Oost-Indische voyagie*, which was published by the van Meurs–van Someren tandem.[44] Wayfaring draftsmen, more generally, find their way into the many Dutch publications that used this visual rhetoric, and this creates the illusion of eyewitness accounting from the exotic world. And witnessing, in the context of exotic geography, made a basic point. By inserting images of on-site draftsmen into their prints—or by carefully inserting themselves, as de Bruijn proudly did in his own compositions—bookmakers deployed a pictorial device meant coyly to suggest personal narrative: the presence of an author-figure amid those overseas happenings that he or she describes.

Narrative presence was undoubtedly a selling point in volumes of exotic geography—it was underscored particularly in books that derived from individual travel journals. Yet it was not an especially important outcome in the illustration programs that rendered Dutch-made books so popular. In fact, prints tended to *deemphasize* narrative in the sense that, even while depicting exotic scenes and exotic things, pictures paid relatively meager attention to foreign events and overseas transactions—to actual Europeans taking identifiable actions overseas. Place, that is to say, took precedence over time; "description" trumped "narrative" (as demonstrated in the previous chapter). Exotic locales per se showed up more predictably in illustrations than did the deeds of European actors that occurred in those locales, especially episodes of colonial contact and conflict. This approach lent a timeless quality to many of the illustrations—Dutch geography adopted what the critic Johannes Fabian terms an "allochronic" strategy of representation[45]—in which actual events, as such, were minimized. Furthermore, it allowed printers to recycle and reprint engravings long after their original appearance, since they rarely showed historical happenings. It also established a distinct, almost dioramic view of the exotic world, in which illustrators staged timeless scenes of exotic peoples and strange customs, showcased foreign flora and curious fauna—yet carefully avoided narrating recent (and potentially conflicting) histories of Europeans overseas.

What: The Form and the Style of Exotic Geography

There were, in truth, a great variety of ways to picture the world and, consequently, a great range of graphic genres dedicated to exotic illustration. The most common of these genres was cartographic—the depiction of "place" in its most essentialized form—with maps of all types serving as the obligatory component of Dutch print geography: maps of continents, countries, provinces, cities, and so on. Next, and nearly as common, were topographic materials, which typically took the form (as Melchisédech Thévenot wryly noted) of unexceptional cityscapes—less full-blown *vedute* than matter-of-fact delineations of a city's harbor or skyline, as these might have appeared to an approaching ship or an overland caravan. A related form of illustration comprised important buildings and structures: views of palaces, fortresses, courtyards, temples, pagodas, town squares, bridges, and other architectural attractions, which were intended to reveal the political, religious, and social life of foreign lands. Of a somewhat different nature were the depictions of exotic plants and animals—still lifes, as it were. These featured curious creatures and strange specimens (the sort of items collected in a *Wunderkammer*), yet also included more readily procurable *naturalia* of obvious commercial value—nutmeg trees, cinnamon plants, pepper vines, specimens of cotton, ginger, tea, and so on—which were often honored with full-page engravings. There were also ethnographic and social vignettes, which incorporated images of global "races" shown in their various public settings. This entailed quasi-taxonomic pictures of the peoples of the world; their religious, political, and social classes; and the myriad "habits" by which they (purportedly) distinguished themselves. (This genre grew directly out of the popular costume books of the sixteenth century.) While no simple rule applies to the catch-as-catch-can business of illustrated geography books, a pattern of pictures does emerge from the rich chaos of these volumes: a progression from cartographic and topographic prints (far and away the most common) to ethnographic and natural history prints (slightly less ubiquitous, yet popular all the same).

History prints constitute a final, perhaps less pervasive, yet no less significant genre. History prints—this is how narrative prints would be characterized according to the conventions of painting—illustrated events that occurred overseas, and they circulated less commonly in early modern geography, whether in Dutch-produced books or otherwise. They sometimes featured the deeds of a narrator or the European protagonists of a volume, and they may have followed the development of actual "plot"—acts of commerce, feats of conquest, or moments of diplomacy in the region that was being surveyed. Yet this was not always the case, and, as often as not, history prints depicted events that were not necessarily germane to the textual narrative: they described in pictorial terms things or happenings that often were not even included in the accompanying prose account. This narrative disjuncture grew out of the very structure of Dutch-made volumes and their manner of production. If van Meurs used the sketchbook of the early seventeenth-century Jesuit Adriano de las Cortes to illustrate the narrative of the late seventeenth-century stay-at-home scribe Olfert Dapper, certain incongruities were bound to creep in. This was the case with the Dapper volume's torture vignettes. Engravings meant to illustrate harsh episodes of Chinese justice do not readily correlate to Dapper's account, since they inevitably grow out of de las Cortes's personal experience.

This brand of pictorial extravagance—the blithe incompatibility of pictures and words—contributed to the "look" of Dutch-made books: their visual richness and, according to their detractors, their ostensible incoherence. When competing geography publishers criticized the work of their Dutch rivals, they homed in precisely on this substantive disconnect and the "counterfeit" role of pictures. A preface to one edition of Jean-Baptiste Du Halde's *Description of the Empire of China*—a 1735 publication seen as a challenger to the long dominance of van Meurs's volumes on the Far East—takes a well-aimed swipe at "those spurious Compositions which are daily obtruded on the Public by ignorant or mercenary Hands." The preface goes on to decry the "danger" of false pictures and the "credit [geography] has lost" by its recourse to illustrations that lack "certainty" and integrity.[46] "Credit" in this context may be taken to mean narrative truth, and Du Halde's prefatory complaint underscores, once again, the dubious claims of authorial presence made by Dutch book-makers. It misses, however, the larger purpose of exotic pictures: they are ahistorical by design. Rather than historical narratives, they offer timeless (thus ahistorical) images of the exotic world. Rather than illustrating the history of an author's experience (as commonly advertised on the title page), they provide ethnographic and topographic views of an exotic place. Rather than narrating the history of European encounters overseas, they present a diorama of the exotic world.

Pictures in Dutch-made geography, particularly in those volumes that circulated most widely, bear a readily identifiable style. Even while describing disparate regions of the globe and even when recounting wholly distinct voyages, volumes take a remarkably similar approach to illustrating their subject. Exotic pictures share an aesthetic, and this reflects a common strategy taken by publishers regarding the process of picture making and the method of depicting the non-European world. Images tend to illustrate identical themes, irrespective of region. Cartographic, topographic, and ethnographic pictures turn up fairly predictably, sometimes even in that reliable order. Pictures share common formats. Maps invariably flaunt ethnographic cartouches (often two per map); while topographic views, whatever their terrain, zero in on urban (rather than the more common rural) centers and commercial points of entry (in this, they loosely followed generic conventions established in Georg Braun and Frans Hogenberg's *Civitates orbis terrarum*).[47] Nature prints tend to converge on the most curious and commercially viable products; whereas ethnographic vignettes display their subjects typically in pairs, dressed in appropriate costume, bearing apposite accessories, and set in a suitable landscape. No matter what their subject, illustrations are adorned with exotic "extras," and these, too, lend the prints a semblance of standardization: parrots and exotic feathers, the latter ubiquitous in skirts and headdresses; pagodas and immense "idols" (religious statuary) scattered throughout the East; and, above all, the omnipresent palm tree. Uniformity in size also gives prints a coherent look. Most volumes carried plentiful, full-folio engravings; quite a few had double-page plates; and some included fold-out spreads, for which extra leaves needed to be glued in, so as to allow cityscapes and other panoramic views to extend the width of several pages. All of this had the effect of drawing attention to the rich visual program of these books.

Exotic geography also displays a keen awareness of visual presentation and a conspicuous concern with visuality in and of itself. Bookmakers and draftsmen went out of their way to accentuate the pictorial content of their product—some books boasted having *only* pictures—and engravers used various formal devices to enhance the visual effect of their work. In the stunning *Les Indes Orientales et Occidentales et autres lieux* (circa 1700), produced by the much admired etcher Romeyn de Hooghe and the indefatigable printer Pieter van der Aa, pictures emphatically prevail.[48] An illustrated anthology of global geography, the volume comprised

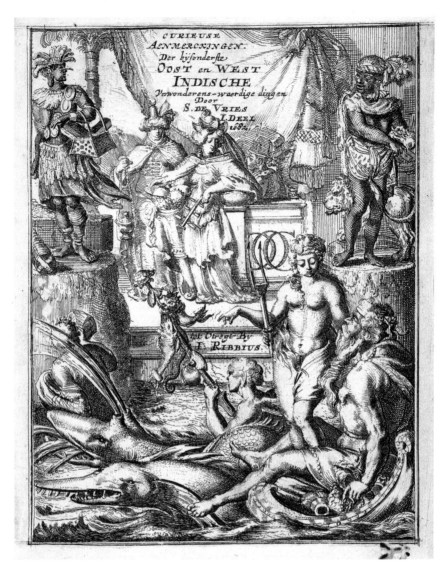

FIGURE 40. Romeyn de Hooghe, etched frontispiece to first volume of Simon de Vries, *Curieuse aenmerckingen der bysonderste Oost en West-Indische verwonderens-waerdige dingen* (Utrecht, 1682). Princeton University Library.

exotic scenes designed by de Hooghe and maps of the continents ascribed to van der Aa. Apart from the cartouches, captions, and labels, however, the book lacked any substantive text: it was a bona fide picture book. It was also printed in oblong, a distinctive format that allowed for broader, more generously drawn compositions, and these were brought into further relief by a form of trompe l'oeil frame engraved into the illustration (see figures 1 and 44). This device—a picture book with framed pictures: "metapicture" is the term used by the critic Wu Hung and later adopted by W. J. T. Mitchell—drew attention to the preeminently visual

FIGURE 41. Romeyn de Hooghe, etched frontispiece to second volume of Simon de Vries, *Curieuse aenmerckingen der bysonderste Oost en West-Indische verwonderens-waerdige dingen* (Utrecht, 1682). Princeton University Library.

quality of the volume.[49] Van der Aa used this strategy (and de Hooghe's etchings) to good effect in several other publications, as well, most notably in his mother of all illustrated books, *La galerie agreable du monde*: a sumptuous, sixty-six-tome magnum opus, which presented a visual grand tour of the world guided by some four thousand pictures.

Along with the format and content of their illustrations, de Hooghe and other draftsmen adopted similar stylistic strategies when it came to representing exotic subjects. De Hooghe himself specialized in dynamic, swirling compositions that

FIGURE 42. Romeyn de Hooghe, etched frontispiece to third volume of Simon de Vries, *Curieuse aenmerckingen der bysonderste Oost en West-Indische verwonderens-waerdige dingen* (Utrecht, 1682). Princeton University Library.

mixed and matched scattered vignettes from numerous extra-European locales to create a single mélange of exotica. Several de Hooghe frontispieces etched for a Simon de Vries series on the exotic world (anthologies of "curious observations," as one volume calls them) follow this pattern in their blend of "Oriental" and "Occidental" peoples, of far-fetched objects, and of exotic natural specimens (figures 40–43).[50] This baroque aesthetic also characterizes the look of a typical van Meurs frontispiece (most of these were anonymously designed) and of the many Dutch-made

FIGURE 43. Romeyn de Hooghe, etched frontispiece to fourth volume of Simon de Vries, *Curieuse aenmerckingen der bysonderste Oost en West-Indische verwonderens-waerdige dingen* (Utrecht, 1682). Princeton University Library.

volumes on natural history, which typically displayed the riches of exotic nature spilling into the composition's central vortex—into the reader's lap, as it were. In *Les Indes Orientales et Occidentales*, an absolute hodgepodge of all things global, de Hooghe and van der Aa offer a series of composite illustrations that are meant to demonstrate exotic life—social customs, religious routines, artistic traditions—by marrying disparate Eastern and Western cultures into single, amalgamated tableaux of exotica. "Musical Instruments of Different Peoples," for example, mingles Turkish, Persian,

FIGURE 44. Romeyn de Hooghe, "Konst Vyeren" and "Musick en Speel Instrumenten" (etching), in *Les Indes Orientales et Occidentales et autres lieux* (Leiden, ca. 1700). Special Collections, University of Amsterdam (OL 76).

1. Instrument de musique formé par un animal de terre. 2. Orgues faites de roseau. 3. Orgues de bois 4. Clavessin Chinois.
5. Tambours des Persans et des Turcs. 6. Timbales des Turcs. 7. Trompettes et autres instrumens des Persans. 8. Flûtes d'os
humains. 9. Musique par le moyen de l'eau. 10. avec des bassins par le Javans. 11. Tours de musique Chinoise.

1. Musik instrument door Aerde beelden. 2. Orgels van Riet. 3. Orgels van Hout. 4. Cineese Clave
cimbel. 5. Persiaense en Turckse Trommels. 6. Turkse Keeteltrom. 7. Trompetton en speeltuig der Persiae
nen. 8. Fluijten op menfen beenen. 9. Water kommen Musijk. 10. Javaense beckens hermonije. 11. Sineese Musijk Toorens

MUSICK en SPEEL INSTRUMENTEN

Instrumens de Musique de differens Peuples.

à Leide, Chez Pierre vander Aa.

23

Javanese, Brazilian, and Peruvian samples. And, to spin heads even faster, this musical image shares the page with a chock-a-block illustration of pyrotechnics from across the whole of Asia (diffidently titled "Artificial Fires of the Tartars").[51]

Another engraver's standby was the "portrait" of monumental *naturalia*: full-blown, full-page illustrations of the outstanding natural products of the exotic world. Ginseng, or "China Root"—"a great enliver [*sic*] of the spirits of a man" with the power to revive souls, even on death's door, and with a market value reportedly three times its weight in silver—filled a full-page composition in Johan Nieuhof's China book; the background of the engraving features an atmospheric pagoda and a few scattered cedars.[52] Similar graphic respect is bestowed upon ginger, tea, cotton, pepper, sugarcane, bamboo, cinnamon, nutmeg, and other notable natural products—and valuable crops—of the tropics. A clove tree rests literally on a pedestal in Nieuhof's *Gedenkwaerdige zee en lantreize door de voornaemste landschappen van West en Oostindien*: a monumental plant, in all senses of the word.[53] Likewise, in Dapper's accounts of Asia the pineapple and the rhubarb (the latter christened "Rhabarbarum Witsoniarum" after the patron and collector Nicolaes Witsen) each get the royal treatment: sumptuous, full-folio engravings of their own.[54] In almost all of these cases, the visual offering far outweighs the relatively modest verbal cue, the meager textual description dwarfed by the supersized illustrations. Pictures, in short, prevail.

FIGURE 45. Jacob van Meurs (atelier), "Wortel China / Racine de la Sine" (engraving), in Johan Nieuhof, *Gezantschap der Neêrlandtsche Oost-Indische Compagnie* (Amsterdam, 1665). Special Collections, University of Amsterdam (OM 63-116).

CHAPTER TWO

FIGURE 46. Jacob van Meurs (atelier), "Nagel-Boom" (engraving), in Johan Nieuhof, *Gedenkwaerdige zee en lantreize door de voornaemste landschappen van West en Oostindien* (Amsterdam, 1682). Special Collections, University of Amsterdam (KF 61-4601).

One more visual tactic underscores what might be construed, in a more straightforwardly commercial context, as the product-oriented approach of Dutch geography. In both the swirling designs of de Hooghe and the aggrandized *naturalia* of a typical van Meurs volume, draftsmen spotlighted the consumable commodities of the non-European world. These clearly fascinated a variety of constituencies, ranging from the merchant and collector to the scholar and merely curious, and these commodities therefore merited full attention. A focus on exotic products per se—on exotica as consumable things—is most strikingly evident in the catalogue-style presentation of certain engravings, in which items are laid out in a serial fashion that suggests a more or less commercial agenda. The "Diverse Sorts of

Bonnets" of Dapper's China publication efficiently collects the scattered drawings of de las Cortes's manuscript, yet it also allows the reader—or better, viewer—to take in the various eye-pleasing hat styles of the Orient (see plate 3). In Witsen's own contribution to geography, a scholarly study of "North and East Tartary" pub-

FIGURE 47. "Goude cieraeden, opgedolven uit aloude Tartersche [*sic*] graven in Siberien" (etching), in Nicolaes Witsen, *Noord en Oost Tartarye, ofte bondig ontwerp van eenige dier landen en volken, welke voormaels bekent zijn geweest*, 2nd ed. (Amsterdam, 1705; 1st ed. 1692). Special Collections, University of Amsterdam (KF 61-1504-05).

lished originally in 1692, an illustration of "Golden Ornaments Excavated from Ancient Tartary Graves in Siberia" not only exhibits these exotic curiosities, but it also displays the brand of collectible that Witsen himself might have ordered from his many overseas agents.[55] This commercial imperative is even more blunt in illustrations of exotic shells—good examples appear in Engelbert Kaempfer's book on Japan, Georg Rumphius's study of Ambon, Charles de Rochefort's history of the Caribbean, and several more Dutch-made books—in which case one of the most readily imported and widely available exotic products is spread out on the page in an easy-to-grasp format. The "product," to be sure, was not always obtainable: a page

FIGURE 48. Volutidae and other shells (engraving), in Georgius Everhardus Rumphius, *D'Amboinsche rariteitkamer* (Amsterdam, 1705). Special Collections, University of Amsterdam (KF 62-2427).

of assorted *kirin* (the mythical hoofed beast of the Far East) presented in Kaempfer's *Japan* was clearly not available for import. Yet the style of its presentation suggested merchandise, all the same, and it placed exotica, once again, in the context of commercial display.[56]

All of these pictorial formats added up to a distinct visual approach to the world—a shared strategy of pictorial presentation. This common style of Dutch print geography had several advantages. A uniform aesthetic, or a common "look" for exotic prints, allowed bookmakers to adhere to readily adoptable pictorial conventions, and this greatly simplified atelier routines and print production. Draftsmen could follow models of illustration no matter what or where their subject: "Indian" feathers worked, whether in India or North America. These practices also bestowed graphic sources with valuable market durability. Exotic prints of a similar cast could be used in multiple contexts, especially when the medley of motifs on which they drew had a broad geographic range: if Peru and Japan were collapsed into a single print depicting exotic music, then that the print could be used twice, at least. And rather than inventing fresh and up-to-date compositions, printers could rely on older, recycled, and perhaps refurbished imagery—the look was part of the product and therefore remained unchanged. Printers traded in stereotypes, to invoke the technical argot of the atelier. Graphic materials, as a consequence, were frequently and unapologetically outdated—Pieter van der Aa's stock served him superbly over a sixty-year career—and they tended to be, for this reason too, ahistorical. Finally, to the practical and commercial benefits of this visual strategy can be added a simple aesthetic consideration: draftsmen and engravers who engaged with exotic subjects worked within a distinctive style or idiom, which was recognizable, adaptable, and apparently popular (to judge from the results). Exotic compositions had proven appeal and adhered to their own formal conventions: they conformed to the fashionable style of the day. Of course, aesthetic and commercial considerations are not mutually exclusive, and this was also the case for the exotic style promoted by Dutch ateliers. Prints of exotic subjects developed a look and established a style, and this brand of pictorial geography dominated the field for several decades, spanning the monumental clove trees that inhabited Jacob van Meurs's volumes of the 1660s and 1670s to the monumental "galleries" of the world designed by Pieter van der Aa over the first third of the eighteenth century.

Why: "A Picture Is a Kind of Universal Language"

To return to the heart of the matter: why pictures? As the cases of van Meurs and van der Aa suggest, there were clear commercial advantages to the pictorial strategy of exotic geography; and it is easy enough to point, as well, to technological reasons for the Dutch success in this market. Yet the second of these explanations might be understood as a response to the first—commercial opportunities instigated technological innovations—and the two causes combined still beg the basic questions: Why did the market demand pictures in the first place? Why did this occur specifically in the field of geography? And why was production concentrated so heavily in Holland? The last of these may be the most straightforward, as a quick comparison of two bibliogonic projects easily demonstrates: the production of Cornelis de Bruijn's magnificently illustrated *Voyage to the Levant* (1698) and the making of John Ray's also well illustrated, yet far less happily produced, *Historia piscium* (1686).[57]

If de Bruijn's and Ray's books do not fit so neatly under the single—modern— rubric of "science," they do overlap substantially on closer inspection, albeit with competing emphases and divergent outcomes.[58] Although his book on the Near East included a respectable enough natural history of the region along with other forms of scientific reporting, and although he provided his readers with valuable scholarly data on the pyramids (with marvelous descriptions of their interiors), the sites of the Holy Land, and other important geo-historical matters, Cornelis de Bruijn was chiefly concerned with pictures.[59] An artist by training, he embarked on his extensive journey through the Ottoman Empire with the goal of *seeing* the sites, since autopsy—seeing with one's own eyes, as he explained with great insistence— always trumped the practice of hearing and reading from others. Scholars had hitherto "let their ears be filled with embellished stories [*verzierde vertellingen*]," yet de Bruijn would witness with his own eyes and record in his own sketchpad, in the best Baconian fashion, in order to "show" his readers the Levant.[60] He therefore traveled himself, drafted himself, and produced himself, more or less, two superbly illustrated books on the East (the second, published in 1711, covers Muscovy and Persia). The *Voyage to the Levant* was printed "for the author," a relatively unusual arrangement in the context of Dutch publishing—printers, rather than authors, typically controlled the publication process. And de Bruijn also initiated a subscription campaign, which reaped prepublication orders for some 1,330 copies (and reduced his personal financial risk). The book ultimately appeared in an edition of three to four thousand copies—a hugely impressive print run for a large folio volume, which far exceeded the typical number for that period: a thousand or so, somewhat less for pricier *pronk* (sumptuous) volumes—and it was quickly translated into French and English.[61] As for the illustrations, de Bruijn fully orchestrated their production, designing and drafting the compositions himself, employing a roster of excellent engravers to make his plates, and—not least—self-financing the cost of publication. More to the point, he made pictures the priority by engraving and printing them first, and only after that turning to the text. In a reversal of the normal pattern of production, in other words, the printer set the text on pages that had already been pressed to the engraved plates. In de Bruijn's books, then, pictures literally took pre-

FIGURE 49. Cornelis de Bruijn, Chameleons (engraving), in *Reizen van Cornelis de Bruyn, door de vermaardste deelen van Klein Asia* (Delft, 1698). Special Collections, University of Amsterdam (KF 61-1401).

cedence, and words were made to accommodate the visual apparatus—the latter, after all, being the raison d'être of de Bruijn's publishing project.[62]

Pictures caused major headaches, by contrast, in the making of the *Historia piscium*, a fish book begun by Francis Willughby, completed by John Ray, and published under the auspices of the Royal Society. The *Historia piscium*, not unlike the *Voyage to the Levant*, grew out of an overseas venture, in this case one that took place in the 1660s: John Ray and his gifted pupil, Francis Willughby, embarked on an extensive journey through continental Europe to study exotic (to these two English-born scholars) species of birds, fish, insects, and plants—a naturalist's Grand Tour through the Netherlands, Germany, Switzerland, Italy, and so on.[63] The traveling naturalists naturally sketched, and on their return to England they made plans to publish their work. After making substantial progress on a bird book, however, Willughby died before its completion, and the publication of his *Ornithologiae* (1676) ultimately fell to Ray, who received financial help for this purpose from Willughby's widow.[64] Ray also undertook the publication of an ich-thyological study, yet here he ran into greater difficulties: namely, the matter of pictures. It is not that Ray eschewed illustration. On the contrary, he highly valued the visual presentation of data, which he believed superseded, in many ways, mere textual descriptions of nature: "Now a good *Figure* having this advantage of [i.e., over] a verbal description," he submitted, "that it conveys speedily to the mind

FIGURE 50. Cornelis de Bruijn, "Areek-vrugt en Betelblat" and "Filander" (engraving), in *Cornelis de Bruins Reizen over Moskovie, door Persie en Indie* (Amsterdam, 1711). Special Collections, University of Amsterdam (OG 77-18).

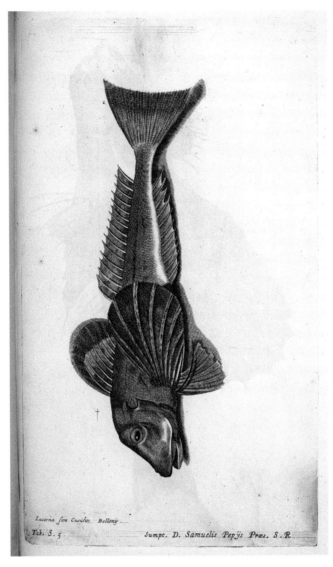

FIGURE 51. "Lucerna" (engraving), in Francis Willughby and John Ray, *De historia piscium libri quatuor* (Oxford, 1686) (shelf mark 445.g.18). © The British Library Board. All Rights Reserved.

with ease & pleasure a clearer & truer *Idea* of the thing delineated, then the understanding can with much labour & in a long time form to itself in a description, be it never so exact." Ray, however, did not have the wherewithal to make good pictures—the financial means, the technical ability, the professional support, and so on. He was therefore compelled to enlist the assistance of the Royal Society, which financed the book's engravings by inviting its members to "sponsor" any number of plates; the London diarist Samuel Pepys, for example, put himself down for sixty. And rather than an arrangement in which pictures took precedence—the intention of Ray, after all, who favored a morphological approach to natural history by which visual data assumed the explanatory lead—the publishers presented the pictures secondarily, almost as an afterthought. The text was printed first in Oxford (by the printer John Hall, with the assistance of John Fell, the Bishop of Oxford), and the plates were done only later in London, under the direction of the Royal Society, and bound *separately* from the textual apparatus.[65]

This odd division of labor (and of printers' versus engravers' ateliers) placed a built-in obstacle to the success of the *Historia piscium*. Although the engravings were relatively plentiful and well done (we know very little, however, about the anonymous draftsmen who made them), the book itself did poorly on the market, and Ray thought that this substantive split was the problem. Of the five hundred copies printed—a fraction of the number of copies printed of the *Voyage to the Levant*—very few sold. Many were ultimately given away in exchange for service, often to members of the Royal Society, or bartered for other books. Indeed, shortly after the book's publication, Robert Hooke, the curator of experiments at the Royal Society and its jack-of-all-trades (and the esteemed Gresham Professor of Geometry), tried to offload copies of the book to other booksellers. He pitched this relatively lavishly illustrated product—for English book publishing, this was an exception to the rule of comparatively less well illustrated natural histories—to an *Amsterdam* book dealer, who was invited to purchase four hundred copies. This transaction was never completed. The offer indicates, nonetheless, not only the poor sales of the book, but also the difficulties and complexities of accomplishing this sort of project in the context of London publishing. Unlike de Bruijn's magnificently illustrated publications, seemingly effortlessly pulled off, Ray's *Historia piscium* was a flop. And while de Bruijn followed up his Levant book with the equally fabulous *Reizen over Moskovie* (Travels into Muscovy), Ray's next installment of natural history, the *Historia plantarum*, was printed without pictures: this time around, he could find no one to finance it.[66]

Cornelis de Bruijn's splendidly rich picture books were but a few in a very impressive Dutch stack: a staggering pile of visually opulent volumes printed in the Netherlands, above all in the final decades of the seventeenth century and first few of the eighteenth. The *Voyage to the Levant* speaks to the enormous production advantages that de Bruijn had over Ray and his English colleagues and, more generally, to the ease with which Dutch ateliers could manufacture graphically sophisticated products that outpaced those of their rivals. De Bruijn's publications, while falling under the rubric of geography (rather than natural history), happen also to fall in the middle of the so-called *decennium mirabilis* of pre-Linnaean natural history: the period from roughly 1695 to 1705, when some of the most superlative and graphically impressive samples of early modern natural history rolled off the printing presses, chiefly of the Netherlands.[67] Ray's travails might also have been compared to the far easier path to publication taken by Maria Sibylla Merian, who compiled a dazzling picture book on butterflies and caterpillars and the plants they habituated in tropical South America (and, like de Bruijn, was self-published) (see figures 13 and 56); by Georg Rumphius, who prepared two visually stunning volumes on the flora and fauna of the East Indies (see figures 48 and 59); or by Hendrik Adriaan van Reede tot Drakenstein, whose massive, twelve-volume, multilingual investigation of the natural world of Malabar consisted overwhelmingly of pictures (see plate 5).[68] All of these authors published (or were published by enterprising bookmakers) within a few years of 1700. In their wake followed Albert Seba, whose gorgeously engraved volumes illustrated chiefly reptiles and birds, and Louis Renard, who published a sumptuous picture book on tropical fish (see plates 4 and 6). (And paving the way for these projects was Willem Piso's *De Indiae utriusque re naturali et medica* of 1658, which covered the East and West Indies, the latter mostly in the form of Brazil.) All of these volumes depicted *exotic* natural history; all of them, as well, consisted disproportionately of pictures. Pictures overwhelmed everything else in these books, and this had the effect of taking over the publication, of decentering the text and its author.[69] Pictures, by purpose, predominated. Yet for all the production advantages of Dutch bookmen, which might explain *how* illustrations got made, the question persists: *why* the visual approach?

Genre may play a role here. Geography and natural history shared, over parts of the early modern period, a disciplinary proclivity for visual presentation, as both de Bruijn and Ray expressly commented, and this points to mutual epistemological concerns—although not necessarily for the obvious reason, voiced by authors and printers alike, that their work was somehow designed to "show" things at a distance, or to serve as an "eye" (as Ortelius put it) for their stay-at-home readers.[70] Pictures also functioned in the more basic sense of giving graphic, and putatively "simple," expression to complex texts; they were understood to clarify hard-to-grasp concepts and to give access to ideas or things that were otherwise inaccessible or difficult to comprehend, which was especially useful when it came to matters exotic. This concern with clarity and the conflation of visuality and lucidity—of pictures and "plainness"—is broached in Robert Beverley's *History of Virginia* (1705), a volume that offered a fairly typical blend of geography, natural history, and what might be called the anthropology of religion, which comprised, in Beverley's case, a wide-ranging exploration of the religious practices of the Virginia Algonquians.[71] Beverley's work foreshadowed by just a few years the still wider-ranging *Ceremonies et coutumes religieuses des tous les peuples du monde* (1723) of Jean-Frédéric Bernard and the engraver Bernard Picart, both Huguenots, who produced a tour de force of "religious" geography with—needless to say for this Amsterdam publication—copious pictures. And in that work, too, pictures were part of the argument.[72] The *History of Virginia*, like *Ceremonies et coutumes*, had something of a Protestant complexion—Beverley came from an Anglican background, and his engraver, Simon Gribelin, was a Huguenot—and this may have prompted the preemptive defense it offered for the deployment of images in a religious context. Beverley rationalized his use of images, since pictures could help "the vulgar and abject Souls" who otherwise might not easily comprehend the "sublime and mysterious in Religion" (he had in mind the "idolatrous" religions of the Indians rather than the Christian faith of his readers) and who therefore would need more "sensual notions."[73] A similar remark crops up in the English edition of the *Ceremonies*, where the volume's editor posited that "no subjects stand more in Need of Illustration than these"—namely, geography and comparative religious history.[74] In both cases, once again, the supposition was that pictures helped elucidate complex matters.

In this understanding of the efficacy of visual sources, pictures provide clarity for the benighted. They make things more accessible for those who cannot travel, certainly, yet they also serve the basic function of making things more lucid for the "vulgar": those consumers of printed books who may not comprehend difficult subjects with mere text. The notion that religion, a "sublime" and "mysterious" matter, requires visual props is, of course, cross-confessional: the Jesuits incorporated images into their post-Reform practices, as in their meditations and exercises.[75] It is also a conceptual paradigm affiliated with important shifts from premodern to modern ways of knowing and assimilating knowledge, and with arguments that associate modernity, and specifically Western modernity, with visual culture.[76] Martin Jay has written insightfully on modernity and the "pleasures of the spectacle," by which he and others have linked visuality to the expansion of popular (read: modern) consumer culture that took place from the onset of the twentieth century.[77] And Lorraine Daston and Katharine Park have made a somewhat related argument pertaining to the shift they perceive circa 1700, when a more learned approach to the natural world in its more exotic manifestations distinguished itself from an older, more inherently visual style of presentation, which henceforth became the provenance of the "vulgar." Depictions of natural phenomena, and especially representations of oddities or "wonders," Daston and Park suggest, were presented in a particularly picture-rich format when they were pitched, from around the turn of the eighteenth century, to so-called vulgar consumers.[78]

"Vulgar" in these instances is meant to signify a less literate (or at least less likely to be literate) audience that would presumably be more susceptible to pictures, since it found certain esoteric matters difficult to comprehend by word alone. Images make understanding possible, and they therefore fill the volumes of the vulgar. Yet picture books in the field of geography, especially the richly illustrated variant produced in the Netherlands circa 1700, certainly did not target a "vulgar" audience. While they may have been characterized retrospectively as less than learned—there were several critiques of Dutch geography penned in the later eighteenth century, and these highlighted its "unscientific" approach—in their day Dutch volumes entered the most elite libraries of Europe, of scholars no less than princes. They were greatly sought-after commodities, which obtained for their owners considerable cultural cachet. For this reason, collectors also hoarded printed geography pictures—Laurens van der Hem had a massive library of images, which numbered well into the thousands—and *sketched* pictures (which served as the basis for the prints) were quite literally safeguarded: de Bruijn left his cache with Witsen for safekeeping between the artist's journeys abroad.[79] More to the point, picture books were often expensive—well beyond the means of the "vulgar" consumer. Van der Aa's *Galerie agreable*, de Bruijn's *Levant* and *Muscovy*, the folio volumes of van Meurs: all were priced for the higher end of the market (which is not to say that lower-end products did not exist, too). And—to be technical—these volumes were also translated into several languages, including Latin ("vulgar" appealing to a strictly vernacular readership), which expanded their appeal to elite consumers broadly across Europe. The "scopic regime of modernity" undoubtedly existed in *early* modern sources, particularly the intensely illustrated volumes of Dutch geography from circa 1700, yet this regime cannot so easily be explained by invoking the needs of the "vulgar."[80]

Quite the reverse may be the case. The deployment of images in many of these volumes, particularly in works of natural history and geography (which typically had substantial natural-history content), often claimed a more noble purpose: to establish the truth. "Those things that are presented to the eyes and depicted on panels or paper," wrote the sixteenth-century naturalist Leonhart Fuchs, "become fixed more firmly in the mind than those that are described in bare words." Pictures here take precedence over prose; visual cues establish or solidify—they *fix*—in the mind's eye (in this case) natural historical matters. "[They] can communicate information much more clearly than the words of even the most eloquent man," Fuchs submitted.[81] Pictures can also *verify* in the literal sense of making a textual claim more solidly truthful and therefore more believable. And they can *testify* in the sense of offering witness from afar and confirming the credibility of far-fetched narratives of "wondrous" *naturalia* and other exotic fare. Louis Renard pitched the plates in his *Poissons, ecrevisses et crabes* (1718) as "drawn from life," executed "most truly [*à la vérité*]," and a "true" representation of tropical marine life.[82] To make this point still more emphatically, Renard appended several "testimonials" for his book that "certified" its veracity and the value of its pictures, one of these testimonials quoting the Dutch minister François Valentyn, who had served in the Indies (from where many of the specimens derived). Valentyn affirmed that the images were wholly true: "tout vérité."[83] What Renard did not need to point out to the consumer of his book was that the pictures contained within were not only the whole truth; they were the whole of the book, since the volume consisted almost entirely of engraved plates.

This manner of verifying, both by Valentyn and by those images to which he duly attested, accomplished what the sociologist of science Steven Shapin has called "virtual witnessing"; it provided Renard and his readers with a "technology of proof."[84] The recourse to *visual* proof (as opposed to textual) fits contemporary practices of natural history and geography, both of which embraced a tradition of display and spectacle. Science in early modern Europe—the convenient modern term "science" is, of course, anachronistic[85]—was typically *performed*, and this meant that science was commonly rendered into visual formats or otherwise visualized. In her seminal study of early modern natural history and habits of collecting in this period, Paula Findlen speaks of the "spectacle" of science and the "aesthetic production of knowledge."[86] Unlike the Romantic ideal of isolated genius, Baroque science invoked the model of open discourse, public performance, and courtly presentation, and this meant that the production of knowledge often involved some manner of display. Geography did not function in quite the same way as the natural sciences discussed by Findlen—although geography could be exhibited, it was not typically performed as such.[87] It did, however, have an inherent visuality, or what might be called *spectacularity*. Geography was delivered as spectacle—in spectacular objects, to be sure, yet above all in spectacular pictures (including maps)—and it was, by definition, inherently "graphic." It established the truth for the stay-at-home traveler by means of *autopsia*—the ability to see for oneself via pictures, a process de Bruijn likened to medical autopsy—and it did this most effectively in the plentiful, prominent, well-produced prints of Dutch-made geography.[88]

Seeing is believing. The proverb in praise of *autopsia* was invoked frequently in early modern Europe, particularly in the post-Vesalian world, where "autopsy" took the form not only of the increased practice of postmortem examination, but also the phenomenally popular picture book published in Vesalius's name and graphically illustrating the human body, *De humani corporis fabrica* (1543).[89] The merits of vision were even more intensely embraced in the post-Baconian world, which placed high trust in the efficacy of *observing* the so-called advancements of learning—and of recording these observations in pictorial form. Among the reasons for this faith in the visual was a belief that pictures functioned as a type of universal language, and they served particularly well for material description. Pictures provided a direct, unmediated knowledge of the world that transcended the cacophony of the post-Babylon universe. This almost fundamental confidence in images stood behind the bibliographic projects of Vesalius and Fuchs—the two were roughly contemporaries—in which pictures "formed a vital part of their effort to make their . . . subjects as universal as possible," as Sachiko Kusukawa has commented.[90] Fuchs clarified this point in the preface to his meticulously illustrated *De historia stirpium* (History of plants): "Indeed, nature was fashioned in such a way that everything may be grasped

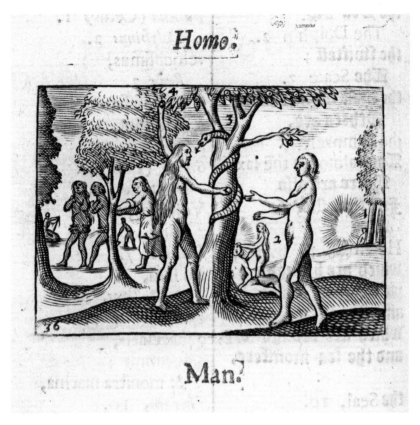

FIGURE 52. "Homo / Man" (engraving), in Johann Amos Comenius, *Orbis sensualium pictus, hoc est, Omnium fundamentalium in mundo rerum, & in vita actionum, pictura & nomenclatura* (London, 1659). By permission of the Folger Shakespeare Library.

by us in a *picture.*" Everything material, he argued, could be readily comprehended by the generic "us" if rendered in graphic form.[91] This tack was similarly taken by Sir Francis Bacon, who called on his adherents to "dissect" the natural world: to lay it open for all to see.[92] And it thrived also in the Netherlands from at least the early seventeenth century, finding among its most vocal proponents the Czech educator and Amsterdam expatriate Johann Amos Comenius (1592–1670), who became a strong advocate of teaching through pictures. A member of the Unity of the Brethren Church (an offshoot of the Hussite movement) and a refugee from the Bohemian wars of religion, Comenius nurtured distinctly irenicist aspirations for Christian Europe, and he championed an educational system that, as a consequence, might reach out to the broadest possible constituencies (he advocated what today might be called universal education). Toward this end, he designed a classroom textbook that would teach through pictures. The aptly titled *Orbis pictus* (World in pictures) was a picture book, plain and simple, with large woodblocks captioned by relatively meager text.[93] Its motivating principle was straightforward: to instruct directly through the eye, with visual prompts, rather than through the ear, with intricate texts (intricate Latin would have been the classroom norm). Pictures had the ability to transcend parochial boundaries, Comenius proposed; visual language was common to all. His approach was neatly epitomized in the remarks of John Evelyn, the English diarist and a founding member of the Royal Society, who greatly admired the Comenius textbook and commented simply that "[a] picture is a kind of Universal Language."[94]

The *Orbis pictus*—or *Orbis sensualium pictus* (The visible world in pictures), to use its full and perfectly fitting title—placed enormous trust in the explanatory power of pictures. Comenius imagined in pictures a most perfect means of communication—a cross-cultural, cross-confessional, transnational medium that conveyed the essence of things. He deemed pictures, consequently, as *preferable* to words—as did most producers of Dutch-made geography.[95] Pictures made it easier to convey the most rudimentary elements of a child's education, according to Comenius, just as pictures might translate (as the Jesuits had also theorized) the most basic, unmediated truths of the Christian faith. They made matters "clearer and truer," as John Ray put it, in his case in reference to illustrated natural history. Pictures, it was further understood, offered the surest and truest means to present the expanding and complex world, and in this sense Comenius's *Orbis sensualium pictus* might be seen as a pedagogic partner to the geography "text" of Pieter van der Aa, the picture-rich *Galerie agreable du monde*: both rendered their global subjects into visual forms that (their authors imagined) could be easily "read," and both pitched their products to a broad-minded audience that transcended parochial interests. Van der Aa, that is to say, designed his books as did Comenius with a European consumer in mind; the world that he and Comenius endeavored to describe was the non-European world, displayed for a European audience. This loosely ecumenical approach further encouraged the use of pictures, which were understood to offer not only an appealing medium, but also an accessible one (if not realistically accessible to the "vulgar" when offered in the luxurious form of the *Galerie agreable*).[96]

The arguments for visuality and for the "universality" of pictures pertain, as well, to arguments for "truth": pictures were assumed to present their subjects with minimal mediation and in an unvarnished, more direct, and therefore more accurate—more *true*—form than would otherwise be possible through words. Pictures promised mimesis, and mimesis implied truth. Again and again, the paratexts in volumes of Dutch geography—the prefatory notes, title-page descriptions, editorial addenda—return to two basic points: that they offer the best illustrated books available, and that they provide the most "true" replications of their exotic subjects. Yet the actual production of these pictures demonstrates, just as consistently, the considerable gap between the promise and product of Dutch geography: the claims of eyewitness "truth" and direct replication of exotica, and the facts of atelier interventions and reproduction by committee.

This discrepancy is particularly glaring in the field of exotic natural history, where firsthand observation and on-site draftsmanship were most prized—yet rarely the mode of production.[97] To start with, it was standard practice to sketch from dead species. In certain cases—for some mammals and birds that could be easily and expertly preserved—this made relatively little difference, since artists could work from well-maintained specimens: hardly drawing "from life" (ad vivem or *na het leven*), as invariably claimed on the title page, yet fairly close to the real thing. For other flora and fauna, however, more serious problems would have obtained. Louis Renard's adamantly "true" pictures of the tropical species in his *Poissons, ecrevisses et crabes* were done, in most cases, from dead, rotting specimens. Renard, who never visited the Indies, was not himself involved in drawing the vibrant images of marine life in "his" book—he clarified as much in his preface, where he explained the origins of the book's illustrations from "reputable" VOC employees, including Frederic Julius Coyett, son of the governor of Ambon, Baltazar Coyett; and Samuel Fallours, a VOC-employed "artist painter," who had been stationed on Ambon. Yet Renard neglected to mention the many other contributors, including indigenous artists, who would have done much (if not most) of the field work, especially the initial sketching. The named VOC figures turn out to be "responsible" for the art work, as Renard delicately puts it, yet not fully authors of it; final drafts were often third- or fourth-hand renderings of an original, anonymous drawing. Nor did Renard reveal how the brilliant coloring was achieved. In fact, the "diverse coloration" (as the title page phrased it) was the chief selling point of the book, and all known copies of the *Poissons, ecrevisses et crabes* possess stunning, hand-colored illustrations, which are meant to be uniform from copy to copy in their shading (see plate 4). This consistency strongly implies that the coloring was directed by the publisher, in the atelier, rather than by the individual owners, who would have otherwise used independent colorists (as was commonly the case). This also means that the publisher's affirmation of "truthfulness" would have extended, as well, to the vividly tinted species, done under his auspices. Yet this coloring would have necessarily been applied in Renard's workshop long after the fish had lost their natural hues, a fact that accounts for the "almost surrealistic renderings" (as one specialist calls it) that result. Colors, as modern ichthyologists have commented apropos Renard's fish book, were assigned to particular species "in a totally arbitrary fashion and have no similarity whatsoever to those of the living" animals. They are mostly fanciful.[98]

A similar pattern of production characterized several other well-known works of exotic natural history that streamed out of Dutch workshops. The nearly eight hundred plates in Hendrik van Reede tot Drakenstein's *Hortus Indicus Malabaricus* (1678–1693) were most certainly not drawn ad vivum by the titular author, a noble-born Dutch governor of Cochin who functioned more as director and patron for the project than draftsman (see plate 5).[99] Baron van Reede, a lifelong military man with an eminent Utrecht lineage and no training in natural history (or Latin), declared that he "gathered" the exotic flora exhibited in his book, yet he left it to others, including certain local scholars and physicians of Malabar (Kerala), to sketch and describe them.[100] The *Hortus Malabaricus*, with its ample illustrations captioned in multiple languages—Malayalam (common in Kerala), Konkani (spoken in Goa), Malay (transcribed in Arabic script), Latin (indicating the script; the nomenclature tends to be Portuguese or Dutch)—was a thoroughly collaborative effort. Yet even this characterization fails to recognize the less-than-visible technicians who did the legwork for this major publication: a certain Carmelite missionary, Matteo di San Giuseppe, who likely instigated the project when he furnished van Reede with field notes and sketches (reminiscent of the Jesuit labors that stood behind Philip Baldaeus's *Naauwkeurige beschryvinge van Malabar en Choromandel*); the VOC soldiers, trained in surveying and draftsmanship, who worked up these drawings and others by indigenous draftsmen employed in the field; and, not least, the Leiden professor of botany Arnold Seyen, the Utrecht professor of anatomy Johannes Munnicks, the Amsterdam botanist Jan Commelin (who also served as director of the city's botanic gardens), and the several others who "edited" the volumes in the Netherlands and organized their publication. All of this amounted to a truly impressive line of production and made for a stunning final product—yet hardly unmediated truth.[101]

In the case of Albert Seba's magnificent "treasury" of natural specimens—the massive collection of engraved plates, many of them double folio, that bore the title *Locupletissimi rerum naturalium thesauri accurata descriptio* (1734–1735)—the issue was not so much on-site replication, since Seba's volumes illustrated the contents of his own cabinet, amassed over decades of steady labor as a professional apothecary and amateur collector. Although the prospectus for the multivolume set advertised pictures "drawn from nature," this was understood to denote reproduction directly from the specimens in Seba's collection—snakes, reptiles, birds, insects, plants, shells, minerals, and other *naturalia*—rather than from on-site draftsmanship or from the artist's imagination. It was scarcely ad vivem fare, yet "natural" in the sense of directly observed.[102] Yet even this implicit concession to "truth" fails to explain many of the forms in Seba's *Thesaurus*, which belie the title-page promise of "accurate" replication. There are, for example, several fantasy creatures that surface throughout the volumes—a seven-headed hydra joins two prosaic "American" birds and a flying lizard on one plate (figure 53)—and there are other specimens that barely rise to the level of credibility.[103] Such fabulous species may have reflected a persistent penchant of premodern natural history, which, even in the age of Linnaeus (who visited Seba's cabinet), was hard to quit. Renard, for his part, could not resist inserting a mermaid ("Sirenne") into his fish book.[104] But Seba added other embellishments, as well, and his illustrations, especially for the first two volumes—these were the ones printed in 1734–1735, while the author was still living and able to direct

FIGURE 53. "Tab. CII [Hydra, flying dragon, birds]" (engraving), in Albertus Seba, *Locupletissimi rerum naturalium thesauri accurata descriptio* (Amsterdam, 1734–1735). Special Collections, University of Amsterdam (OL 63-1941).

FIGURE 54. "Tab. LXVI [Serpents]" (engraving), in Albertus Seba, *Locupletissimi rerum naturalium thesauri accurata descriptio* (Amsterdam, 1734–1735). Special Collections, University of Amsterdam (OL 63-1942).

their publication—were presented in a conspicuously stylized manner that would seem more decorative than "natural." Snakes coil in exquisite calligraphic twists and curls, and lizards march in tight, symmetrical formation. Some plates illustrated live-action shots: gatherings of reptiles, birds, insects, and plants, interacting in a living habitat that offered the viewer a tableau of the natural world. These montages imply narrative. Species nourish, pollinate, procreate, and prey on one another in a manner that intimates a slice of natural life. Yet a single sheet might mix and match within such a montage specimens that hail from different geographic regions and

FIGURE 55. "Tab. XLI [Serpents, lizard, bird, spider, guava tree]" (engraving), in Albertus Seba, *Locupletissimi rerum naturalium thesauri accurata descriptio* (Amsterdam, 1734–1735). Special Collections, University of Amsterdam (OL 63-1942).

FIGURE 56. J. Mulder after Maria Sibylla Merian, Pineapple and cockroaches (engraving), in *Metamorphosis insectorum Surinamensium* (Amsterdam, 1705). Special Collections, University of Amsterdam (OL 63-1090).

even different continents—an African royal python with an American scarlet ibis, joined by a rufous-tailed shama from Southeast Asia (see plate 6)—and this mélange gives the lie to the impression of a bona fide "natural" environment. More to the point, the carefully crafted plates entail combinations and arrangements that would have been impossible in the real world of nature, let alone in the quiet confines of Seba's cabinet, where lifeless lizards and stilled snakes inhabited, in actual fact, the narrow boundaries of a specimen jar.[105]

Not all exotic natural history followed the same procedures and manipulations. Maria Sibylla Merian also assembled and animated natural species to show, in her case, the miraculous metamorphosis of sturdy caterpillars into the delicate butter-

CHAPTER TWO

flies of Suriname. Yet Merian, like the itinerant artist Cornelis de Bruijn, famously traveled to the tropical habitat of her subjects to sketch them in situ, and these drawings fairly directly formed the basis for the copper engravings made back in Amsterdam. In this case, claims of personal observation, on-site drawing, and ad vivem representation mostly do match modes of reproduction.[106] Merian and de Bruijn, however, may be the exceptions that prove the rule of a typically more flexible approach to the "truthful" recreation, in printed form, of exotic nature: to the idea of ad vivem mimesis, of "accurate" observation, of bona fide sketching, and so on. The distinction here is not quite between the genuine travelers and peripatetic draftsmen, on the one hand, and the less-than-trustworthy patrons and atelier-based bookmakers, on the other, who orchestrated the process of picture-making and published the results. Even in the case of well-known eyewitness observers, who journeyed at great length and expense to sketch overseas, the reproduction of exotic *nature*, in particular—more so than the reproduction of other exotic subjects—could still be convoluted. Johan Nieuhof traveled, sketched, and personally delivered his manuscript back in Amsterdam, where his brother Hendrik shopped it among publishers eager to produce a fresh book on China. The images of the natural world, however, were often egregiously stale (unlike the comparatively novel city views). A series of engravings depicting outsized flora—cinnamon, ginger, tea, and other high-value Asian crops, each placed prominently in the picture frame's foreground—borrowed liberally from Michael Boym's *Flora Sinensis* (1656), although the compositions now incorporated background scenes with Chinese *staffage* and decorative pagodas and palms (see figure 45).[107] As for fauna, not only did Dürer's renowned rhinoceros (1515) fill one plate (see figure 31)—a majestic species, no doubt, yet by this point a century and a half old—but so too did a nearly as popular sperm whale (figure 57), derived from a widely reprinted engraving by Jan Saenredam (1602), which was itself a variation of a famous print designed by Hendrick Goltzius (1598).[108]

Rather than bona fide travel or on-site witnessing, which were simply stages in the process of production, or direct observation, which could take place ostensibly in the tropics or in the *Kunstkammer* alike, what sets these volumes of geography and natural history apart is their outstanding presentation of pictures: their look and quality of visual presentation, and their endorsement of a pictorial program that unambiguously invoked the act of "true" seeing, on-site drafting, expert engraving, and so on. In effect, these volumes often traded on a rhetoric of truth and a *semblance* of seeing. Seeing per se could be less important than *seeming* to see, and the gap between semblance and true sight could be profound.[109] Georg Rumphius (1627–1702), who gained high repute as the "Pliny of the Indies" for his splendidly illustrated studies of tropical nature and exotic geography—*Plinius Indicus*, as one book crowned him, or *Plinii Indici celebris,* according to another (even while some of the celebration may have been orchestrated by the author himself, not to men-

FIGURE 57. Jacob van Meurs (atelier), Sperm whale, in Johan Nieuhof, *Gezantschap der Neêrlandtsche Oost-Indische Compagnie* (Amsterdam, 1665). Special Collections, University of Amsterdam (OM 63-116).

tion his publishers)—earned his scholarly accolades almost by the negation of sight: he was blind. Rumphius, who arrived in the Indies as a young soldier and suffered from progressive and debilitating glaucoma, lost sight completely at age forty-two— he would live another thirty-three years—and even in his earliest months stationed abroad, he complained of the "fierce" and blinding sun of the tropics, which weakened his vision.[110] This did not, however, register as an impediment to his work of close observation: first, the *D'Amboinsche rariteitkamer* (The Ambonese curiosity cabinet, 1705), a study of crustaceans, shells, and minerals of the East Indies; and next, the *Herbarium Amboinense* (1741–1750), a posthumous publication, which, like his earlier book, was suffused with engravings purportedly "drawn from life" by the author.[111] Although a closer reading of the text and of Rumphius's official correspondence with the VOC (for whom he worked in a commercial capacity) reveal the obvious obstacles posed by the loss of sight to a project predicated on meticulous scrutiny—he labored in "sad darkness," he laments, and "with borrowed pen and eyes"—this fact does not at all hinder the high regard achieved by the volumes. They were esteemed as feats of visual recording, personal description, on-site field work (*in locis reperta*), and, not least, impeccable illustration.[112] Indeed, the author practically calls attention to this paradox by his use of ocular metaphors (his work may be seen "by all eyes"); by his saga of the volume's ill-fated production (what few drawings he made before going fully blind were lost in a fire); by his style of writing (he concentrates on a level of detail so fine as to challenge even a full-sighted naturalist); and, not least, by his mode of self-presentation or self-fashioning. The wonderful frontispiece designed for the manuscript of the *Herbarium* shows a stylishly dressed Rumphius in the field, ostensibly sketching a tropical banyan tree (see plate 7). He is

FIGURE 58. J. de Later after P. A. Rumphius, "Effigies Georgii Everhardi Rumphii" (1695) (engraving and etching), in Georgius Everhardus Rumphius, *D'Amboinsche rariteitkamer* (Amsterdam, 1705). Special Collections, University of Amsterdam (KF 62-2427).

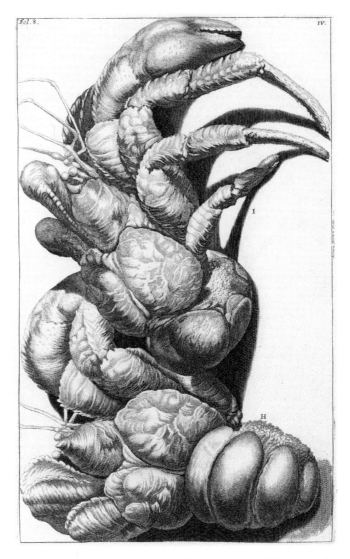

FIGURE 59. Cancer crumenatus [*Birgus latro*] or Coconut crab (engraving), in Georgius Everhardus Rumphius, *D'Amboinsche rariteitkamer* (Amsterdam, 1705). Special Collections, University of Amsterdam (KF 62-2427).

a model of keen observation, his eyes fixed intently on his subject. A sharp eye might note, however, that the European naturalist is joined by an indigenous assistant, whose deep-brown skin blends almost imperceptibly into the dark-hued bark of the tree; and that he may receive help, as well, from a second aide, whose dusky coloring allows him to fade easily into the shaded brush in the background. But the author-as-observer is central: he is an archetype of scientific vision.[113]

Rumphius's mirage of sight—what might be thought of as a carefully staged regime of observation and of visual production—fit into a by now standard mode of geography. It followed a protocol of "seeing" the exotic world by deploying the operative tropes of observation. That Rumphius was blind—that he had to rely on others for his allegedly ad vivem illustrations and that his publishers therefore resorted to copying images when this proved necessary: not an uncommon practice, in fact[114]—did not make much of a difference. He was not alone, even, in his oxymoronic status as a blind observer. Peter Kolb (1675–1726), a German naturalist and astronomer who lived for several years in the Dutch colony of Cape Town, conducted astronomical and meteorological observations and made recordings, otherwise, of the natural world of South Africa. These formed the basis of an extensive description of the region and its inhabitants, all of which was "closely" observed, "according to the truth," and augmented with liberal illustrations in the Dutch-made edition of his work that became the standard—all of this notwithstanding the crippling deterioration of the author's vision. Like Rumphius, that is, Kolb lost his sight while overseas; he portrays himself as "blind" in the volume's preface.[115] The Swiss naturalist François Huber (1750–1831) began to lose his vision already from age fifteen, yet this was no impediment to his work on—of all God's creatures!—the bee, which he described in exquisite detail in his *Nouvelles observations sur les abeilles*, published in Geneva in 1792. Huber also makes a starring appearance in his close colleague Jean Senebier's aptly titled *L'art d'observer* (Geneva, 1775), where he is cited—without apparent irony—as an outstanding model of observation, someone who "saw way beyond anything his predecessors thought they had observed."[116] Although Huber and Senebier's work appeared a few decades after Rumphius's (whose final, posthumous study on tropical flora appeared in 1755), it still subscribed to the same strategic trope of close observation. It enlists the same regimen of sight, and it offers the same semblance of visual engagement: a keenly observant "author" whose labors result in an abundant supply of "true" pictures.

The Performance, Problem, and Paradox of Pictures

Dutch exotic geography of these years not only adhered to this regimen of observation; it pioneered and perfected many of its techniques, and it came to be branded, accordingly, as a distinctly visual genre. What might be termed the semblance of sight was instrumental, as was the profile of the author as a keenly observant informant. This combination of sight and on-site observation led unswervingly—or so it was insinuated by the publishers—to the production of highly valuable pictures: "the Soul of performances of this kind." And it was, in many ways, a *performance*. Bookmakers assiduously promoted the author-figure of their products as a profile of observation: not merely an on-site spectator of exotica, but also a meticulous surveyor and draftsman of all that was observed. This conceit often demanded a certain willful suspension of the readers' belief. Wouter Schouten's *Oost-Indische voyagie*—Schouten is the titular author of an all-embracing description of the "Indies," which ranges over the near entirety of Europe's exotic world and well beyond the abilities of even the most prodigious wanderlust—invokes the trope of authorial witnessing right from the get-go. The volume's frontispiece includes—beside its swirling anthology of exotic peoples and products, flora and fauna, all of which envelops a turbaned "Oriental" prince who sits under an iconic parasol and atop a comically misplaced rhinoceros—a single "European" attendant, who is readily identifiable from his costume. This male figure stands off to the side (on the left), and he casts his glance outside of the picture frame, as if to promise the viewer that his gaze will take in even more wonders than those encapsulated by the frontispiece. Throughout the volume, furthermore, engravings incorporate a lone European figure standing or sitting on the margins of a composition, intently observing or sometimes sketching the scene before him. This figure is plainly meant to stand for Schouten himself, who boasts that the book's illustrations are "drawn by the author himself in the Indies"; the text also alludes repeatedly to this or that "wonder" personally "seen" by the narrator.[117] Yet elsewhere the narrator admits that he did not observe all of the exotica he describes—reports of Japan and the Far East are conveyed from other credible and "praiseworthy eye and ear witnesses."[118] And the standout illustrations of some editions of the book—double-folio plates that blend a fascinating potpourri of global exotica—also give the lie to the trope of eye-witnessing: these etchings turn out to be the work of the prolific Romeyn de Hooghe.[119]

Bona fide or not, pictures nevertheless bore a substantial burden in these volumes. They were—it bears repeating—"the Soul of performances of this kind." This extraordinarily revealing insight into Dutch exotic geography in its printed form comes not from a Dutch-made text but an expressly competing volume—Kaempfer's *History of Japan*, published in London in 1727—which, despite its several attractive illustrations, took issue with the still more plentiful illustrations of a rival publication. The latter volume—printed more than half a century earlier yet still in demand and by now in its ninth edition—was, invariably, the product of Dutch publishing: in this case, the so-called *Atlas Japannensis*, which, if nominally authored by Arnoldus Montanus, is more fittingly understood as a creation of the van Meurs atelier, which furnished the volume's copious engravings.[120] At issue, to be sure, was also the poor quality of Montanus's narrative: a pastiche of meandering texts and exotic "observations," roundly criticized as "full of large digressions,

Opposite page FIGURE 60. Jacob van Meurs (atelier), engraved frontispiece to Wouter Schouten, *Oost-Indische voyagie* (Amsterdam, 1676). Special Collections, University of Amsterdam (OG 77-17).

Aanmercklijke
VOYAGIE
Gedaan door
Wouter Schouten
Naar
OOST-INDIEN
1676.

t'AMSTERDAM By
Jacob van Meurs *en* Johannes van Someren
Boeckverkoopers in Compagnie
Met Previlegie.

often altogether foreign to the purpose." "But what is most material," complained the author of these charges, the Swiss naturalist and Fellow of the Royal Society Johann Gaspar Scheuchzer—Scheuchzer was responsible for the English translation of Kaempfer's manuscript from the original German, which he did on command of Sir Hans Sloane—"[is that] most of the Cuts, which are the greatest embellishments, and, as it were, the Soul of performances of this kind, *do greatly deviate from truth*, representing things not as they were, but as the Painter *fancied* them to be."[121] At issue, then, is the matter of credibility and veracity—and the efficacy of exotic pictures. This challenge goes directly to the author, Montanus, who had boasted on the title page of "the great number of pictures drawn in Japan"; yet it also assails van Meurs, who staked much the same claim of authentic replication and *na het leven* sketching in the official privileges for printing the book obtained from the States of Holland.[122] Somewhat curiously, this matter of pictorial authenticity and directly observed illustration crops up in nineteenth-century assessments of Dutch geography, as well, when the understood lack of "fidelity" renders the books of Montanus and company highly suspect. The volume on Japan, and particularly its pictures, was judged "inauthentic" by the Japanologist A. J. C. Geerts, whose modernist critique may have been launched already by the second quarter of the eighteenth century, when the problem of representation was originally broached by Scheuchzer: Dutch exotic geography relied too heavily on pictures, which were fanciful embellishments, deviated from the truth, and offered anything but genuine observation.[123]

There is a backstory to these critiques. Montanus (as was briefly summarized in the previous chapter) had a knack for controversy and, in the wake of the Japan book's publication, became quickly mired in a nasty polemical exchange with an Antwerp Jesuit, Cornelis Hazart. A geographer and chronicler of global church history and an ardent controversialist himself, Hazart took issue both with the form and content of the Montanus book. The content, which included a history of Europeans in Japan, seemed to Hazart inadequately reverential of the fate of those Catholic missionaries to the islands who had been violently persecuted by the Tokugawa shogunate. Hazart criticized Montanus—a Calvinist minister by vocation—for his inaccurate history of Japan and his disrespectful interpretation of Catholic-reported miracles said to have occurred there. But Hazart also launched a broadside over the book's form, specifically its pictures, which he likewise deemed inaccurate, impertinent, and even salacious. Some images depicted "naked" women (he refers, presumably, to the "Description of a Japan Whore," likely the *oiran* [courtesan], and the accompanying illustration), which was highly indecent, not to mention immaterial to the narrative of Japan. The images, Hazart averred, were simultaneously irreverent and irrelevant.[124] This was not quite the same as the Kaempfer–Scheuchzer attack, which lacks any confessional rancor. Yet

FIGURE 61. Jacob van Meurs (atelier), Japanese prostitute (engraving), in Arnoldus Montanus, *Gedenkwaerdige gesantschappen der Oost-Indische Maetschappy in 't Vereenigde Nederland, aen de Kaisaren van Japan* (Amsterdam). Special Collections, University of Amsterdam (OM 63 363).

it does spotlight the growing backlash against Dutch geography for its "looseness"—and for its inappropriate recourse to pictures.

And these complaints multiplied. Willem Bosman, introducing his 1704 description of Guinea, derided the "fabulous author" of a prior account who played loosely with the "truth"—he was fingering the prolific Olfert Dapper, who together with van Meurs produced the reigning best-selling account of Africa—and Bosman scoffed more generally at the mendacious genre of geography as published over the previous years. He singled out the Dutch: "In this Country of Holland"—Bosman himself was Dutch—"we have . . . writers in the last [seventeenth] Century, who set forth many books, and are now so well known by the bulkyness of their Writings, and the manner of their *performances*, that 'tis needless to say more of them than this." Again, the matter is the "performance" of geography, or its presentation of data, and the predicament pertains both to the putative presence of the author (about which Bosman does in fact does go on "to say more") and to the problem of pictures.[125]

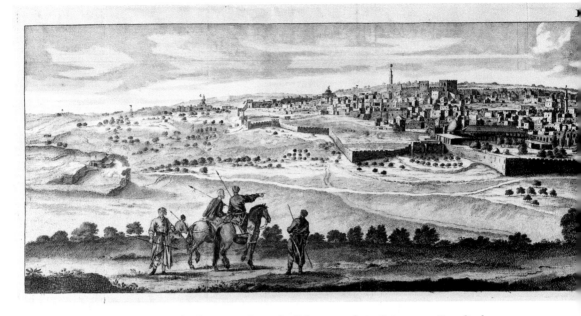

FIGURE 62. Cornelis de Bruijn, "Ierusalem" (engraving), in *Reizen van Cornelis de Bruyn, door de vermaardste deelen van Klein Asia* (Delft, 1698), 28 × 124 cm. The National Library of Israel, Eran Laor Cartographic Collection, Shapell Family Digitization Project and the Hebrew University of Jerusalem.

The problem of pictures may also be understood as the *paradox* of pictures and the complicated—indeed contradictory—claims made on their behalf to be trustworthy vehicles for presenting exotic knowledge. Despite Johann Gaspar Scheuchzer's contemptuous comments regarding the "embellishments" of a competing volume on Japan, he (along with his collaborating publisher) had his own problems with authenticity. For although Kaempfer produced original sketches for the book that ultimately became "his" *History of Japan*, these images followed a typically circuitous path to publication. Original drawings "by my own hand," as Kaempfer wrote, often required the assistance of a "discreet young man," who apparently undertook the actual field work (thus a quasi-invisible, indigenous technician); manuscript sketches invariably underwent alterations in European ateliers; several illustrations that made it into the book derived from altogether different sources (including Japanese woodcuts); and so on.[126] The convoluted lineage of Kaempfer's images, in other words, still admitted several layers of intervention, not terribly unlike a typical van Meurs product. Scheuchzer's disparaging remarks may simply have been a marketing ploy.

Perhaps nowhere did the paradox of exotic pictures come into sharper relief than the case of Cornelis de Bruijn (1652–1727), who structured his books and built his reputation on the very basis of his meticulously made illustrations, done over the course of his extensive Asian travels; yet who was attacked by his critics and embroiled in controversy precisely on this matter: on the role of artistic sight

CHAPTER TWO

and on-site observation and, by extension, on the production and heuristic value of exotic illustrations. Indeed, among the many exceptionally illustrated volumes of early modern geography produced in the Netherlands, de Bruijn's stand out for the high quality of their pictures. And among the many claims of on-site visual recording, de Bruijn is the most emphatic: his entire career was predicated on his personal travel and on-site draftsmanship and the subsequent production of illustrated books from his labors. De Bruijn and his books epitomize both the pictorial turn and pictorial paradox of exotic geography.

Cornelis de Bruijn—whose circumstances were briefly touched upon in the context of John Ray's far less fortuitous history of picture production—was born in 1652 in the Hague, where he trained as a painter.[127] In 1674 he left the Netherlands for Rome, where he joined the society of Dutch and Flemish artists, the Bentvueghels (also known as the Schildersbent, or painters' clique), and dedicated his time particularly to the sketching of antiquities—a skill that would serve him well for the rest of his career. De Bruijn, who professed a keen and lifelong "inclination for traveling," next embarked on an extended journey (1677–1684) through the eastern Mediterranean—Turkey, Syria, Palestine, Egypt, Cyprus, and several Greek islands—sketching as he went.[128] He returned to Italy in 1684, where he worked for some eight years in the Venetian studio of Johann Carl Loth (or Carlotto), and finally landed back in The Hague in 1693. At this point, de Bruijn launched his great geographic enterprise, rendering his notes and sketches into *Voyage to the Levant*. This luxurious folio, printed in 1698, contained over two hundred plates and numerous "jumbo" views, including an astonishing two-meter cityscape of Constantinople and a massive panorama of Jerusalem (both of which folded out: see figure 62). The Levant book went through multiple editions and translations, and the suc-

FIGURE 63. Cornelis de Bruijn, "Grafstede der Koningen" (engraving), in *Cornelis de Bruins Reizen over Moskovie, door Persie en Indie* (Amsterdam, 1711). Special Collections, University of Amsterdam (OG 77-18).

CHAPTER TWO

cess of this project begat another. This time the materials derived from a lengthy stay in Moscow (via Archangelsk), where de Bruijn painted for (and apparently befriended) Peter the Great; and a more than two-year journey through Persia, which included a three-month stint in Persepolis, the site of the ancient Achaemenid palace complex, where de Bruijn methodically sketched the famous ruins.[129] The result of these labors appeared in print as *Travels into Muscovy, Through Persia and India*, published originally in 1711 (and in several subsequent editions), with well over three hundred plates, including more of de Bruijn's trademark gargantuan panoramas, copious illustrations dedicated to the ruins of Persepolis, and so on. The success of the Muscovy volume is mildly debatable—it enjoyed further editions and translations, yet not all of these sold out—but the broader impact of de Bruijn's descriptive tours de force is incontrovertible: his volumes were broadly admired, above all for their remarkable pictures.[130]

De Bruijn's pictures, along with the strikingly pictorial—or better, *painterly*—approach he took to his publications, merited this admiration. Pictures were the central feature, the raison d'être of these volumes; and de Bruijn made himself, as the on-the-spot artist, likewise a central point of focus. This was not merely a matter of quantity—the terrific number of engravings prompted the great bibliographer of travel literature Edward Cox to call de Bruijn's first book simply "one of the best illustrated works on the Levant," and Cox noted how de Bruijn's second effort (*Muscovy*) surpassed even his first.[131] It was also the structure of the books, the quality and novelty of the illustration program, and, not least, the way the author insinuated himself and the very act of picture-making into the narrative. De Bruijn took a determinately and self-consciously visual path to the construction of exotic fare, and this garnered attention. To a degree, he culled many of his techniques from his predecessors, distilling what had by this point (circa 1700) become an established pattern of illustrated geography publications. He devised helpful chapter summaries at the head of the many brief and readable chapters (*Levant* incorporated seventy-nine chapters into a 288-page book); he sprinkled his folio pages with liberal, descriptive marginalia that guide the reader through the double-columned text (a double-columned layout made large-format folios that much more readable) and he included a lengthy, and typically comprehensive, index. All of this rendered de Bruijn's books, despite their somewhat bulky dimensions, eminently manageable: browsable and user-friendly instruments that function much like the modern coffee-table book.

Yet de Bruijn also adjusted many of the formulae of Dutch geography by injecting a distinctly painterly perspective into his endeavors—he was, after all, a painter—which is evident in the innovative ways he composed his pictures. De Bruijn not only sketched; he sketched vistas and scenes multiple times and from multiple perspectives. He produced both pen drawings and watercolors, and he

FIGURE 64. Cornelis de Bruijn, "Alexandria" (engraving), in *Reizen van Cornelis de Bruyn, door de vermaardste deelen van Klein Asia* (Delft, 1698). Special Collections, University of Amsterdam (KF 61-1401).

Opposite page FIGURE 65. Cornelis de Bruijn, "Pompoentjes en andere vrugten / Petite Citrouïlles et autre Fruits" (engraving), in *Cornelis de Bruins Reizen over Moskovie, door Persie en Indie* (Amsterdam, 1711). Special Collections, University of Amsterdam (OG 77-18).

naturally painted: in some cases for illustrious collectors, such as Peter the Great and Nicolaes Witsen, in other cases for the open market and (presumably) his own use.[132] Through these exercises, he developed a visual vocabulary and pictorial style for the exotic world, and this led to exceptional compositions that show all the hallmarks of an accomplished, well-trained artist. Levantine landscapes spin out romanticized settings, which feature languid shepherds standing amid Near Eastern ruins; these show the influence of de Bruijn's Italian training. City views draw the observer into the composition with highlighted figures on the periphery (often with dogs, flocks of animals, and so on) who point to the main attractions (see figure 62)—this device is common in several Dutch genres—while strategically placed vignettes of social interaction at the center of many architectural scenes an-

POMPOENTJES EN ANDERE VRUGTEN.

SEEING THE WORLD

Left FIGURE 66. Cornelis de Bruijn, "Samojeedse Vrouw" (engraving), in *Cornelis de Bruins Reizen over Moskovie, door Persie en Indie* (Amsterdam, 1711). Special Collections, University of Amsterdam (OG 77-18).

Right FIGURE 67. Cornelis de Bruijn, "Samojeedse Man" (engraving), in *Cornelis de Bruins Reizen over Moskovie, door Persie en Indie* (Amsterdam, 1711). Special Collections, University of Amsterdam (OG 77-18).

imate the depictions of famous sites—again, revealing the traces of de Bruijn's experience sketching in Rome. The remarkably full panoramas of exotic places are made possible by de Bruijn's technically proficient skills in working out perspectives. And when he engraves set pieces of exotic *naturalia*, de Bruijn does this not so much in the catalogue style of a van Meurs illustration, but in the tradition of Dutch still-life painting—as with the fabulous "Pompoentjes en Andere Vrugten / Petite Citrouïlles et Autre Fruits," where he enhances the artfully arranged fruit with superb cross-hatched shadowing and the contrasting texture of the wooden table.[133] Likewise, de Bruijn composes exotic portraits with great feeling and lively presentations. The sympathetically rendered "Samojeedse Vrouw" and "Samojeedse Man" compare favorably to the many pendant portraits of Amsterdam burghers

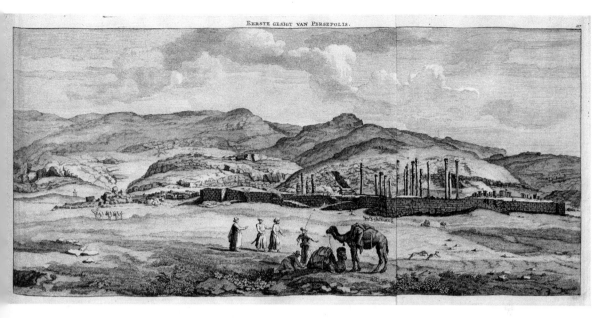

FIGURE 68. Cornelis de Bruijn, "Eerste gesigt van Persepolis" (engraving), in *Cornelis de Bruins Reizen over Moskovie, door Persie en Indie* (Amsterdam, 1711). Utrecht University Library.

FIGURE 69. Cornelis de Bruijn, "Tweede gesigt van Persepolis" (engraving), in *Cornelis de Bruins Reizen over Moskovie, door Persie en Indie* (Amsterdam, 1711). Utrecht University Library.

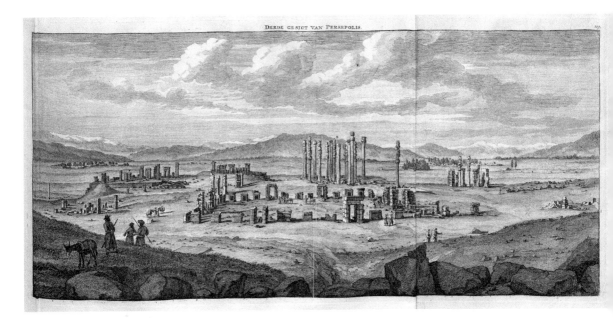

FIGURE 70. Cornelis de Bruijn, "Derde gesigt van Persepolis" (engraving), in *Cornelis de Bruins Reizen over Moskovie, door Persie en Indie* (Amsterdam, 1711). Utrecht University Library.

FIGURE 71. Cornelis de Bruijn, "Vierde gesigt van Persepolis" (engraving), in *Cornelis de Bruins Reizen over Moskovie, door Persie en Indie* (Amsterdam, 1711). Utrecht University Library.

commissioned at the height of the Golden Age.[134] All of these painterly habits serve de Bruijn particularly well in his representation of classical ruins and, above all, in the many engravings of Persepolis, which were at the heart of the Muscovy and Persia volume. The four separate vistas of the Persepolis compound take advantage of the way the mountains surround the ruins; they also allow the reader—or, more properly, the viewer—to circumambulate the site visually, as it were. The monumental engravings of the carved reliefs—on grand staircases, imposing columns, great slabs of ornamented stone, blocks of cuneiform—impart a sense of magnificence, vastness, and grandeur to the antiquities. They also give the viewer the feeling of presence: of being up close to the epic remains of the ancient world.

And this brings up one more quality of de Bruijn's engravings: his ability to make the viewer feel on hand in the exotic world he describes in pictures. This is achieved, in part, by the strong sense of authorial presence skillfully built into de Bruijn's mode of narration and representation, and this brings us back to the matter of on-site observation and picture-making. De Bruijn went to great lengths to establish the "veracity" of that which (as he put it) "I have seen with my own Eyes, and have examined with the utmost Attention and Care."[135] He did so both through the tropes of witnessing and on-site observation, and through the recurrent interventions of the author into the process of making pictures. He was, more than any other author of exotic geography, self-consciously and graphically *present*. He was not only there; he was there to make pictures. During a "charming" (a favorite word of de Bruijn) excursion along the coast of Asia Minor, where the plucky author hoped to locate and sketch the ruins of ancient Troy, de Bruijn asks his party of Greek sailors to steer their vessel toward "Bababarnoüe" (Baba Burnu: "the father's nose"), a promontory just south of the Dardanelles considered to be the westernmost point of Anatolia. On landing, they are met by local fisherman who sell them some fine "Barbonnes," a regional fish resembling perch, which are then prepared for supper. "Our mariners manag'd the Cookery in so Pleasant and Jovial a way," de Bruijn comments, "that we could not forbear smiling; add to this, that the Cook who was troubled with a violent Pain in his Teeth, had bound up his Face with a ragged Dish-Clout [cloth], and so made a pleasant Figure." The use of "figure" is meant literally and figuratively, for the narrative vignette prompts de Bruijn to sketch that "figure" in order to bring the viewer into the scene: "This passage was so diverting, that I could not forbear drawing the Picture of it" (figure 72).[136] De Bruijn inserts himself, moreover, centrally in the scene, where he is shown asking the bandaged cook when the food might be ready. And once one realizes that de Bruijn is dressed after the "native" fashion, one also begins to notice how often the figure of the artist appears in such views. Indeed, de Bruijn qua artist and eyewitness observer pops up all over: in the pyramids of Egypt (negotiating a

FIGURE 72. Cornelis de Bruijn, Baba Burnu ["Bababarnoüe"] (engraving), in *Reizen van Cornelis de Bruyn, door de vermaardste deelen van Klein Asia* (Delft, 1698). Special Collections, University of Amsterdam (KF 61-1401).

cramped interior passage), in the markets of Istanbul (mingling with the crowd), in the tents of the Samoyeds, and—more subtly—in the ruins of Persepolis. This allows de Bruijn to claim, somewhat more vigorously than is done in other volumes of exotic geography—he was surely aware of the operative clichés of the genre—that he offered a "just and accurate description" of things "to be found on the spot," matters to which he had been "an Eye Witness" and could therefore sketch with "Sincerity and Exactness." While others made pictures that "have more the Air of Romance than Reality," on-the-spot de Bruijn offered bona fide sight:

> I have made it an indispensible [*sic*] Law to my self, not to deviate in any respect from the Truth, meerly [*sic*] to give an ornamental Air to this Work, in which there are no facts but what are related with the strictest Veracity. . . . The Reader may judge of my proceeding, by the Number and Beauty of the Plates distributed through the whole Work, and which are executed with all possible Justice and Accuracy. I can affirm too, that I have drawn with my own Hand, and immediately from the Life, all the Plates now presented to the Public.[137]

Thus did de Bruijn stake his claim to Truth, and readers did judge: precisely, it turns out, on the "Accuracy" and quality of de Bruijn's illustrations, and on the merit and "Veracity" of the author's on-site, "own Hand" draftsmanship. Above all,

SAMOJEEDSE TENT VAN BINNEN TE ZIEN.

FIGURE 73. Cornelis de Bruijn, "Samojeedse Tent van Binnen te Zien" (engraving), in *Cornelis de Bruins Reizen over Moskovie, door Persie en Indie* (Amsterdam, 1711). Special Collections, University of Amsterdam (OG 77-18).

verdicts turned on the "celebrated" ruins of Persepolis and their representation—pictures, in other words—which lay, after all, at the heart of de Bruijn's enterprise. In fact, de Bruijn's Persian book made an immediate splash, owing to the doubly great interest in early modern Europe for antiquities *and* exotica; and it attracted attention from several quarters and for various reasons—much of which came down to the question of "seeing," reporting, and replicating exotic subjects. The first round of objections took a fairly typical and relatively rudimentary form: criticism from the author of a competing publication, Abraham Bogaert, who accused

FIGURE 74. Panorama of Persepolis (engraving), in John [Jean] Chardin, *Voyages de monsieur le chevalier Chardin en Perse et autres lieux de l'orient* (Amsterdam, 1711). Princeton University Library.

de Bruijn of using his "eyes"—the metaphor, ironically, was visual—more as a plagiarist than as a bona fide overseas observer.[138] This was a crude accusation, easily disproved by de Bruijn's supporters, and it failed to stick. The next round of allegations, however, while also questioning de Bruijn's integrity, came from a more refined source with a more sophisticated, which is to say "scholarly," strategy of critique. It originated with a former professor of ancient history and rhetoric, rector of the Deventer Athenaeum, and member of the States General, Gijsbert Cuper, who was, as well, an avid collector of antiquities, renowned bibliophile, diligent scholarly correspondent, vital "information broker"—in short, a major player in the early eighteenth-century republic of letters, with broad influence in the Netherlands and across Europe. It represented a major assault on the quality of "seeing" and the problem of pictures in exotic geography.[139]

Significantly, Cuper took his critique not directly to de Bruijn but to Nicolaes Witsen and other men of letters, whom he wrote beginning in the fall of 1711, questioning the merit, accuracy, and authenticity of de Bruijn's Persepolis engravings. Matters had begun more or less cordially, when Cuper visited de Bruijn in Amsterdam to inspect the antiquities that the latter had retrieved (that is, pilfered) from Persia and to look at his sketches of cuneiforms, which the artist then copied for the collector; this was in 1709, prepublication. Cuper later wrote an enthusiastic letter to Witsen in August 1711, immediately after *Muscovy* first appeared in print, to express his delight with the volume. Yet he made an about-face later that year, when another book on Persia appeared, this one from the hand of the French-Huguenot traveler-cum-antiquarian Sir John Chardin (1643–1713), a well-born and well-connected Fellow of the Royal Society (he had settled in London for religious reasons).[140] At this point, Cuper wrote to several more of his scholarly correspondents and ultimately to Witsen—yet not de Bruijn—questioning the veracity of de Bruijn's pictures and, in effect, the entirety of his "observations" on Persepolis: how could they be trusted, if they did not accord with those of the esteemed Chardin? The charges expanded the following year, when Engelbert Kaempfer (1651–1716) published his *Amoenitatum exoticarum* (1712), which also contained pictures of Persepolis and its antiquities and which also demonstrated—at least according to Cuper—the deficiencies of de Bruijn's work. The Persepolis engravings had now become a hot affair, debated among "persons of distinction and great learning"—the antiquarians of Europe—no less than the vendors "in the bookstalls," as de Bruijn would later note when he himself entered the fray in 1714 with a pamphlet that defended his role as a "true" observer and reliable reproducer of exotica.[141]

The problem, once again, came down to pictures and *autopsia*: how to *see* the ancient sites of (in this case) Persepolis; how to engage with exotic ruins in situ;

FIGURE 75. Panorama of Persepolis (engraving), in Engelbert Kaempfer, *Amoenitatum exoticarum politico-physico-medicarum fasciculi V* (Lemgo, 1712). Princeton University Library.

how then to represent and reproduce them in a visual form; and, more globally, how to picture exotica. Cuper's perspective was indubitably that of his scholarly milieu, yet the issue was not simply classical learning versus rudimentary picturing. Despite the persistent reliance of early modern scholars on ancient textual authorities, there was, nevertheless, a competing emphasis on *seeing* antiquities.[142] Chardin and Kaempfer, after all, had seen the ruins themselves, just like de Bruijn. But they offered less accomplished reproductions, and, for Cuper, the sketchier images from their hands were somehow more compelling. De Bruijn's formal reply to Cuper—published in pamphlet form as the *Aanmerkingen over de print-verbeeldingen van de overblyfzelen van het oude Persepolis* (1714) and also translated into English and French—concentrated precisely on this point and the contrasting methods of visual replication. The "hand" of Chardin, as de Bruijn pointed out, turned out to be the hired hand of the draftsman Guillaume-Joseph Grélot; Chardin might have observed, yet he did not draw. Kaempfer did his own sketching, yet the engravings of Persepolis in his book were executed independently (as Kaempfer himself admitted), without direct input from the author. This led to a critical disjuncture: between author and draftsman, in one case (Chardin), and between artist and engraver, in the other (Kaempfer). De Bruijn denounced the "unskillfulness in designing," the "inaccurate sketches," and—perhaps most damning— the "mercenary" draftsmen who had produced these competing illustrations.[143]

Another key factor was time: the duration of de Bruijn's sojourn in Persepolis—a full three months—compared favorably, he argued, to the far briefer stopovers of Chardin (three days) and Kaempfer (five days). Chardin, moreover, not only spent a fleeting few days at the ruins; he also delayed publication of his pictures for decades. His engravings of Persepolis appeared only in the 1711 edition of his *Voyages*, thirty-one years after his return to Europe—and coincident with the appearance of de Bruijn's rival volume. In the case of Kaempfer, the stay was short and the effort was slight, de Bruijn insinuated, and here the trained artist made much of his stamina: three full months on site, in the elements, to render exceptionally precise drawings. Indeed, the *Aanmerkingen* dazzles with details and measurements—de Bruijn's notes and/or memory must have been superb—and overwhelms with data: on these grounds, de Bruijn more than acquitted himself. Yet the main thrust of his argument was a spirited defense of on-site draftsmanship and, by contrast, the "mercenary" quality of his rivals. And herein lay an irony: the entrepreneurial painter challenged his learned rivals over the "truth" of their knowledge and pictures of exotic places by arguing that their wares were tainted by crassly commercial concerns, while his efforts offered more truthful mimesis. "Now I shall open this body," declared the artist-cum-anatomist de Bruijn, choosing his metaphor carefully, "to offer you a view of the interior."[144]

There were other ironies, as well. De Bruijn's section on Persepolis suffered from its own disjuncture, insofar as the text had been written by a certain "H. P.," or Herr Praetorius, a German friend of de Bruijn living in Haarlem.[145] Unusually for the field of exotic geography, the pictures reflected a more conscientious effort at bona fide mimesis than the words; textual narrative serves, if not quite as an afterthought, as a retrospective gloss on illustrations. But a bigger irony may be that the brand of Dutch geography, which had come under assault of late for its unreliable and misleading pictures—mere "embellishments" concocted to lure the eye of the unwary consumer—was in this instance challenging "scholarly" texts for the mantle of truth. Cuper had instinctively trusted what I have called the semblance of sight rather than the real thing—the "mercenary" draftsmen and unsupervised engravers who had produced what was incontrovertibly embellishment, albeit for nominal authors and putative draftsmen of high repute (Chardin and Kaempfer). More generally, Cuper did not fully trust de Bruijn—he enlisted the highborn scholar Witsen to mediate the dispute rather than deal directly with the entrepreneurial painter himself—and his actions suggest an alternative regime of trust. An industrious and ambitious denizen of the largely elite and profoundly textual republic of letters, Cuper operated in the market of early modern scholarly (and political) patronage. He placed his scholarly faith and invested his professional stock in the prestige of the competing authors, Chardin and Kaempfer, and in the cultural capital that he might accrue were he successfully to arbitrate and then circulate the most "correct" descriptions of Persepolis. His reasoning, if circular, made sense within his social and intellectual milieu. Since Chardin and Kaempfer possessed scholarly and social status, their pictures could be trusted; since de Bruijn did not, his visual "performance"—his claims of true and on-site replication, and his hard-won and superbly made illustrations—would have to be challenged as counterfeit, the questionable embellishments of exotic geography.

The market for exotic geography, however, may not quite have followed Cuper's market of patronage or his investment of scholarly capital. For despite the controversy that swirled around them, de Bruijn's illustrations eventually rose to the top of the heap and emerged from the Cuper dust-up more or less triumphant. Chardin's and Kaempfer's pictures of Persepolis languished following their appearance in 1711 and 1712, respectively; meanwhile, de Bruijn's *Muscovy* appeared in a second Dutch edition (1714), a French edition (1718), and a deluxe, two-volume English edition (1737).[146] More to the point, de Bruijn's engravings of Persepolis's ruins appeared on their own in myriad forms and editions that, if not lending themselves so easily to bibliographic record—they appeared, by this time, with engravers and printers who had no connection to de Bruijn's original publishers, often in specially devised "atlases" or narrowly prescribed picture books—

FIGURE 76. "A View of the Ruins of Persepolis as Taken from the Plain" (engraving), in S[amuel] Harding, *Persepolis illustrata, or, The ancient and royal palace of Persepolis in Persia* (London, 1739). The Getty Research Institute, Los Angeles (88-B5354).

do attest to the strong consumer demand for his pictures. One of these editions, published anonymously in 1739, can be traced to a London printer on St. Martins Lane, S. Harding—the printer all but certainly never journeyed to Persia—who produced an exquisite version of *Persepolis illustrata* (as he called it) for the luxury market.[147] It comprised a letterpress title page to introduce eight leaves of engraved text and thirteen finely engraved illustrations, which plainly derive from the *Muscovy* plates. The Harding images are less "pictorial" than de Bruijn's in the sense that they include fewer of the extra, "painterly" devices that so successfully animated the original compositions: local Persians milling about the ruins, domestic animals weaving in and out of the picture frame, strategically placed flora and fauna, and so on. They offer, rather, a cleaner, uncluttered, "classical" style, which highlights the ruins above all else. They are successful, all the same, and present Persepolis as *picture*, following the spirit of de Bruijn's originals. In fact, in all of de Bruijn's and the derivative editions, pictures were the focus, as the many reviews of de Bruijn's work, including several in scholarly journals, were keen to emphasize. The illustrations were simply "magnifique," according to one commentator writing in the *Acta eruditorum*. They were an exemplary model, most agreed, of presenting faraway wonders—of showing what Kaempfer had called in his own volume "exotic pleasures."[148]

These many editions also showed the close correlation of pictures and exotica: of the emphatically visual approach taken by print geography when it came to presenting the extra-European world. In the short term, the engravings of de Bruijn's volumes, in both *Levant* and *Muscovy*, demonstrate the utter success of the Dutch mode of producing exotic geography. Pictures sold, and the abundance and quality of Dutch-made products sold best. With time, however, and as the inquiry into the exotic world began to brush up against the more ostentatiously "learned" study of exotic antiquities—this was the case for much of the Levantine world, for sites in Persia and Iraq, and for the increasingly sought-after inquiries into the "ancient" civilizations of China and Japan—the scholarly world began to push back. The Cuper–de Bruijn affair foreshadowed many of the "learned" Enlightenment engagements of the eighteenth century, in which certain earlier forms of knowledge were dismissed as "vulgar."[149] Indeed, Chardin earned greater admiration in the later decades of the eighteenth century from the likes of Montesquieu, Voltaire, Rousseau, and Gibbon.[150] Chardin as well as Kaempfer, it should be stressed, did include pictures in their publications, and virtually *all* volumes of geography, Dutch or not, had some manner of illustration. Yet the form of these pictures and the mode of their presentation—and the narrative role of the authors in their presentation—differed utterly from de Bruijn's highly self-conscious illustrations. Increasingly, moreover, the "semblance of sight" gained the author greater credit, as occurred most spectacularly in the case of the blind Swiss naturalist—and model of scientific observation—François Huber. And this brings up a final irony of de Bruijn's splendidly illustrated volumes. While the famed "Pliny of the Indies," Georg Rumphius, endured for decades as an authoritative "witness" to the wonders of the exotic world *despite his blindness*, the immensely skilled draftsman Cornelis de Bruijn, who exemplified the qualities of on-site observation and *autopsia*, ultimately did not. In the end, "seeing" may have been believing, yet the genre of exotic geography circa 1700 demanded a special form of both sight and belief.

Those who are Nobly born of that Country, are so delicately Cut and Rac'd [raised—that is, incised] all over the fore-part of the Trunk of their Bodies, that it looks as if it were Japan'd; the Works being raised like high Poynt round the Edges of the Flowers: Some are only Carv'd with a little Flower, or Bird, at the sides of the Temples, as was *Caesar*; and those who are so Carv'd over the Body, resemble our Ancient *Picts*, that are figur'd in the Chronicles, but these Carvings are more delicate.

—APHRA BEHN, *Oroonoko: Or, The Royal Slave. A True History* (1688)

CHAPTER THREE

EXOTIC BODIES

Sex and Violence Abroad

Exotic Bodies and European Mirrors

Looking at and "seeing" exotica was a common enough pastime in early modern Europe, yet the object of European interest was by no means restricted to the mundane and scattered things of the world, to the disparate material objects and natural wonders that could readily be collected, replicated, and circulated within Europe. The exotic body itself also commanded considerable attention, in both word and vivid image, its very flesh exposed and examined, its sundry parts pricked and prodded in myriad and revealing ways. This took place largely by proxy, in widely available descriptive accounts—books, prints, maps, and paintings, most of which purported to offer eyewitness reports (even when plainly fictional, as in Aphra Behn's novel *Oroonoko*). And it took place in relative abundance: the exotic body was ubiquitous for consumers of early modern geography and of the literary and visual arts that incorporated geographic themes. Especially during their most intense period of geographic production—once again, the final decades of the seventeenth century and the first few of the eighteenth—Europeans were invited, in an impressive array of forms and venues, to observe an expressly "exotic" body: a body located explicitly beyond the borders of Europe, and a body meant to remain outside of Europe. This exotic corporality had distinctive qualities, several of which recur often enough to suggest an exotic archetype. Europe's exotic body was a site of sexual "perversion": of titillating sexual practices, typically characterized as "lewd" and obscene, and registering with the narrator of these descriptions (when related in textual sources) equal measures of abhorrence and fascination. The exotic body also endured extravagant and graphic violence, commonly meted out by cruel and ostentatiously sadistic sovereigns—those who would come to be known as "Oriental despots" by Edward

Gibbon's day.[1] And the exotic body was elaborately staged. It was meant to be *seen* by its European audience, indubitably enticed by what they saw, and its presentation was predicated on a presumed voyeurism on the part of this European audience. The latter was encouraged to look at, and simultaneously warned of, the dreadfulness and perversity of that which was witnessed on the exotic stage.

The staging of the exotic could be truly dramatic, sometimes scandalously so. In the *Reysen* (Voyages, 1676) of Jan Struys—a phenomenal best seller that appeared in French, English, German, and Dutch editions—the author describes in exquisite detail the "horrible storms and shipwrecks," "harsh slavery," outrageous "cruelties," and all-around deprivation that he purportedly observed and himself endured during his extensive voyages in the East. This, certainly, is standard fare in a genre that might be called disaster travel: one need think back only to the classic account (which debuted just slightly before Struys's and was endlessly republished) of that hapless seaman Willem Bontekoe.[2] What distinguishes Struys's narrative, however, and the many others of its ilk that appeared in the later seventeenth century are the serial episodes of utterly gothic violence, both sexual and somatic. From Struys's narrative we learn that the noblemen of Siam are tortured with hot coals, then brutally gored to death by elephants (among the many creative means of capital punishment); that the slumbering body of an Indian woman is cast gratuitously into a bonfire; that an inebriated Cossack hurls his poor Persian concubine into the Volga as an offering to the river; that a Madagascar woman is ravished by a strange breed of white ape; that a woman trapped aboard a pirated East Indian junk suffers repeated rape by the crew, after which she is heartlessly executed by her enraged husband for her alleged "sins." All of this culminates in an episode of appalling violence, which the volume's printers (Jacob van Meurs and Johannes van Someren) encapsulate on the engraved frontispiece. Suspecting his wife of adultery, a Persian gentleman crucifies the woman for several hours, we are told—the author claims to have witnessed entirely these bouts of "brutal violence"—after which he meticulously flays her still breathing body. The enraged husband then nails his wife's skin to a wall for all to see—a "monument" or "mirror" of the affair—and casts what remains of her body (the "carcass") to the scavenging dogs on the street. An easily discernible rendition of the victim's flayed skin serves as the ghoulish cartouche for the volume's engraved title, a graphic allusion to this drama of violence. The full-page cover illustration also includes an image of a grossly stripped body stretched across a bench in the foreground as well as other vignettes of corporal punishment, meant to synthesize the narrator's many misadventures: a young man bound and shot through with arrows, his pained body writhing, Saint Sebastian–like, against a tree; the same male figure trussed and dragged off into a wilderness by galloping horses; a turbaned, mustachioed, "Oriental" gentleman, whose gestures and surrounding entourage would suggest that he is the one orchestrating these elaborate dramas of violence.[3]

CHAPTER THREE

FIGURE 77. Jacob van Meurs (atelier), frontispiece (engraving) to Jan Jansz Struys, *Drie aanmerkelijke en seer rampspoedige reysen*, 2nd ed. (Amsterdam, 1677; 1st ed. 1676). Special Collections, University of Amsterdam (O 63-41).

Such harrowing scenes and images recur in numerous prints, texts, paintings, and other engagements with the exotic world that appeared in the late seventeenth and early eighteenth centuries. The most prominent themes in these materials—of adultery and rape, of sensuality and suffering, of violence and torture, of titillating crime and grisly punishment—point toward a world seemingly apart from Europe, where excruciating somatic pain, perverse sexual practices, and all-around bodily torment served as a source of both fascination and "instruction," albeit the sort of voyeuristic instruction that requires reading or seeing acts of sex and violence in order to denounce them. Descriptions of sex and violence, of course, were hardly foreign to early modern Europeans. The Continent had been awash with prints, broadsheets, pamphlets, and chronicles describing the ceaseless European conflicts of the preceding decades, including the pungent and salacious fare that derived from the Reformation, which narrated in highly partisan terms Europe's vicious wars of religion. Dutch ateliers in particular had contributed their share of fodder during the Dutch Revolt. Rebel factions and their opponents were eminently capable of impugning their enemies with sharp, often shocking depictions of the mayhem and violence—"fire and sword"—that was visited by enemy soldiers, reputedly, on Dutch populations, and of the "tyranny" perpetrated by the duke of Alba's men against innocent "women and children." What had changed by the later years of the seventeenth century, however, especially in the wake of the Peace of Westphalia (1648)—Europe was henceforth done, theoretically, with its more-than-century-long civil war of religion—was the location of these offenses. Heinous acts of military and judicial violence, and "lewd" practices of hetero- and homosexuality, now took place outside of Europe, in the "exotic" world—again: from the Greek *exoticos* or "outside of"—and thus beyond the confines of Europe's cultural *oecumene*. Extraordinary sexual behavior and abhorrent violence could still be vicariously "witnessed" by Europeans, yet it had been displaced to an exotic environment and transferred to an exotic body.

If sex and violence may be said to have a geography, their spatial range by the second half of the seventeenth century had increasingly begun to match that of Europe's exotic world. At a moment of expanding colonial ambitions and intensifying engagements, commercial and imperial, with the "outside" world, Europeans imagined sexual "perversions" and located instances of corporal violence—"torture" in contemporary argot—in spaces well beyond their own borders. More to the point, they ascribed these instances and practices chiefly to non-Europeans, and they affiliated them with a broadly extra-European geography. Promiscuous women (and men) could be commonly found in Asia, Africa, and the Americas; excessive violence could be readily witnessed, as Struys's report implies, across large portions of Asia, not to mention the more traditional sites of "tyranny" in America and Africa. It is worth pointing out the particular irony of Struys's testimonials. The putative author of these torments (and the *Reysen* is understood by modern critics to have been ghostwritten) hailed from the village of Wormer in Holland's Northern Quarter, which witnessed itself some of the most ferocious episodes of violence of the Dutch Revolt. The Northern Quarter also served as the setting for several propaganda prints, which grimly illustrated the torture of rebel and loyalist populations alike.[4] Yet by Struys's day, exotic torture and torment had supplanted homegrown variants, at least in its most descriptively lurid forms, as "witnessed" in sources of geography. In a sense, then, Struys's and similar accounts truly did offer a mirror for their European audience, yet a mirror that may not quite have reflected in ways their authors imagined.

Forms of geography from this period—the myriad mirrors of the world produced from around 1670 to 1730—illustrate early modern Europe's imaginative displacement of exceptional sexuality and violence, reflecting their strategic exportation to the non-European world. They highlight—vividly, sensationally, harshly—the exotic body as a site of abuse: of sexual and physical violation, to be sure, yet also of judicial and military maltreatment of a sort that might fall under the rubric of torture. The exotic body was an object of deep fascination for authors, artists, and printers of the period. Aphra Behn all but fetishized the body of the fictional African-born prince (and later slave) whom she deftly sketched out in her 1688 novel *Oroonoko*. She marveled at the "delicately cut" scarification that marked his body as exotic, and she invoked a pointedly exotic simile—the art of "japanning," by which she meant lacquering—to express her fascination with the decorated, if disfigured, flesh of her African-turned-American protagonist. European painters invested similar care in their meticulous renditions of flesh in their portraits of non-European bodies, and images of the exotic body proliferated, as well, in the graphic and material arts. The exotic body could be "curious" as well as sensual, admired as well as abused. It was, in all cases, *looked* upon with keen interest: "witnessed" by travelers and writers, staged by draftsman and engravers, scrutinized by painters and novelists. While no single, definitive way to represent the non-European body developed in sources of this period, several motifs do emerge. The exotic body was characterized by its sensual appeal, capacity for pain, and racial ambiguity. Taken together, these qualities "softened" the exotic body, as it was exposed to the steady gaze of European consumers and would-be colonialists. In an important sense, sources of geography had the effect of priming the exotic body for European control.[5]

Exotic Sex (and Violence)

If there was a prototypical exotic body, a most commonly "witnessed" figure who inhabited the scores of descriptions and illustrations of this Dutch-made brand of geography, it would have been the sensual female form as described, almost invariably, by a male European viewer (Aphra Behn's *Oroonoko* notwithstanding). In his

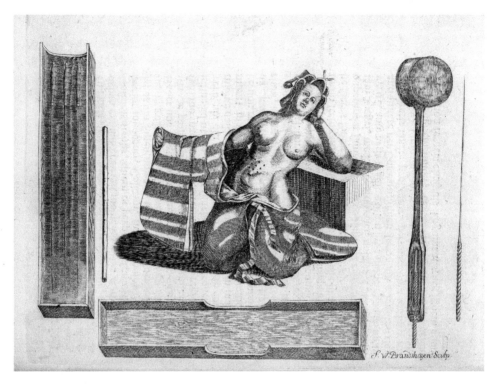

FIGURE 78. F. W. Brandshagen after G. van der Gucht, Acupuncture (engraving), in Engelbert Kaempfer, *Amoenitatum exoticarum politico-physico-medicarum fasciculi V* (Lemgo, 1712). Princeton University Library.

landmark study of Western attitudes toward the Middle East, Edward Said identified the "spectacular" sensuality that characterized much European prose on the Orient from the (chiefly later) nineteenth century. In *Orientalism* and other works, Said cast his critical attention on the heated "sexual promise" and richly "lurid detail" that a reader encounters in such classic texts as Gustave Flaubert's *Salammbô* (1862) and that a viewer confronts in the Oriental paintings of Eugène Delacroix and Jean-Léon Gérôme.[6] In truth, however, the spectacle of exotic sensuality flourished long before Said's moment of Orientalism; alluring and enticing women (and men, as Said also noted) had their bodies routinely exposed to stay-at-home European consumers of the world already in the early modern period. Whether in the fictional seraglios of Behn's Africa or in the excited reports of Asia-seasoned merchants, exotic women occupied a conspicuous place in the early modern geographic imagination. In Turkey, Cornelis de Bruijn noted the "neat" and "cleanly" bodies of the local women, so "that our European women must needs yield to them the pre-eminency." The women of Chios were the most "pleasant" the author had ever met (which would appear to have been many) and had "fine shapes," which lamentably were too often obscured by their modest "habits." De Bruijn spent most of his time on this Aegean island drafting a city-view and landscape, and he expressed his regret that he could not have "enjoyed the Company of the fair Sex" a bit more. By contrast, in Stanchio (Kos) de Bruijn had to struggle to stay out of the clutches of the lewd Greek women who frequented his inn (or so he reports).[7] Engelbert Kaempfer lodged a similar complaint regarding his experiences in Japan, where every public hostel, he grumbled, might double as a "bawdy-house."[8] Despite such expressed squeamishness, Kaempfer opted for a bare-breasted female model to illustrate the East Asian practice of acupuncture in a print that would seem almost gratuitously lascivious.

Kaempfer's ambivalence about Asian sexuality—hypocrisy may be too strong a word—points to one of the more salient qualities of the exotic body: its all but irresistible allure. More than merely "clean" and "pleasant," women who inhabit the world outside of Europe are "charming" and "tempting," and they incite in those who glimpse them equal measures of wonder and desire—a quasi-sensual reaction that borders on what several European observers term "lust." Women in Istanbul are coquettish, de Bruijn asserts based on his personal experience of their charms. The ladies of that cosmopolitan city lay about all day on the "sopha," "idle" and "lascivious," and are "naturally inclin'd to be Le[w]d." More dangerously to the European (male) visitor, they flirt:

> When they meet with any *Franks* [Europeans] in the Street (which is very seldom their Fortune to do, being almost always kept within Doors) and when they are out of Sight of their Husbands and other *Turks*, they make a Stop to Speak to those Strangers, and in their Discourses mix a great many Charming and Passionate Expressions. They tell them that they are very Sorry that they are *Infidels*, that they would Burn for their Sakes, &c. This they express with so moving an Air, that one can hardly forbear being touch'd and affect'd therewith, especially if lifting up their Vail [*sic*] of Black Crape, which usually hangs over their Faces, they dart a Glance or Two of their fine Eyes, and by their amorous Looks add Rhetorick to their Tongues and their passionate Gestures. This is what I have often experienc'd, and therefore can Speak of it with the greater Confidence.

This flirtation—"fine Eyes," "amorous Looks," "passionate Gestures"—plays out still more brazenly in Old Cairo, where lewd women reputedly expose themselves: "I had heard before of those Sort of Women," de Bruijn informs his curious readers with some satisfaction, "and was well enough pleas'd the Experiences confirm'd what was told me of them, but would not take any farther notice."[9] In Amboyna, the local women "are very Lascivious"—additionally, "unchaste" in some translations—"and extremely desirous of the Christians," according to Johan Nieuhof. "If they find themselves disappointed in their Expectation, or that they are left by their Gallants," he adds, "they have a way of infecting them with a certain Poyson." These poisoned gallants "were bewitched," according to Nieuhof, their manhood having been reduced to a state of impotency. "Without their lust, they cannot adequately perform with women"—namely, with dangerously *exotic* women.[10]

The perils for unwary "Christians" (and presumably for indigenous men, as well) came not only from women wielding poisons but also, and more fundamentally, from the corporal temptations that lurked abroad. The exotic body incited lust and it tantalized, and this put the consumer of exotic geography in a position of liminality: aroused, yet from a distance. The beautiful young Jewish boys who danced for their elders in Istanbul, according to de Bruijn, "shew the most shameful Postures that can be Imagin'd; having so accustomed their Limbs from the Childhood to all manner of Movements, that they can shew you a Thousand different Tricks." Perhaps as a consequence of these tricks, "sodomy [is] very common among the Turks." This disposition would not be for lack of counterefforts by Turkish women, however, those wives of "lustful" Muslim men who shamelessly "stroke and caress the members" of their polygamous husbands to lure them to bed. This utterly provocative account comes from the Dutch naval surgeon Wouter Schouten, who informs his readers that in Japan "men can use a whore or concubine without punishment whenever they *lust* for one"; that the "majority" of men in Siam (Thailand) are predisposed to voluptuousness and lewdness ("*wellust*"); and that Muslim men, more generally, incline toward the condition of "lust." Lust was plainly a leitmotif for Schouten, as it was for others reporting from the exotic world, and it also affected the author personally, albeit in a more chaste manner: "Wanderlust," professed Schouten, "is a powerful passion of the soul." Wanderlust, in effect, serves as the lust of choice for narrators of exotic geography, an alternative to the more dangerous variant of this passion.[11]

Perhaps as a way of negotiating the lure and danger of exotic bodies while avoiding the sins that those bodies could provoke, sources typically engaged in a kind of vicarious voyeurism, allowing the reader-viewer to "see" exotic actors without becoming fully ensnared by the inevitable, ensuing "lust." Accordingly, as with most other facets of this brand of geography, pictures played a key role in conveying scenes from abroad, in this case describing the physical appearance and corporality of the non-European. Yet it is striking, all the same, how often pictures function both to expose the "lewdness" that lurks beyond Europe's borders and implicitly to condemn it. They convey a paradoxical attraction to, and simultaneous disavowal of, the exotic body. While de Bruijn often disapproves of the improper sexual practices, "performances," and appearances he witnesses over the course of his Asian travels, he readily pictures these for his reader, in both textual

CHAPTER THREE

descriptions and vivid engravings—the latter often centering on female subjects. "The manner wherein the Ladies of Constantinople are attir'd," he testifies, "hath a particular Air of Grandeur and Magnificence in it," which entails elaborate fabrics, jewelry, headdresses, and the like. The images that illustrate this attire rather delicately portray the local women with—one cannot help but note—indelicate décolletage. De Bruijn was surely attentive to these details. He carefully describes "The Ladies of the Grand Signior's Seraglio," slyly observing the "large Plumes of Black Feathers, which dangle down before their Bosoms." To explain how he could lay

FIGURE 79. Cornelis de Bruijn, Ladies of Constantinople (engraving), in *Reizen van Cornelis de Bruyn, door de vermaardste deelen van Klein Asia* (Delft, 1698). Special Collections, University of Amsterdam (KF 61-1401).

eyes on these ladies, sequestered as they would have been in the Sultan's private chambers, de Bruijn refers just as slyly to "pictures of several [ladies] which they gave me."[12] Whether or not Ottoman-made pictures would have been this revealing—we have no direct evidence for this—European ones, made by de Bruijn and otherwise, commonly were. Thus the "habits" of exotic women, as engraved by European draftsmen, typically exposed more flesh than those of European women. Women posed bare-breasted for the European reader in Makassar (Indonesia), Cochin (India), Fort Dauphin (Madagascar), the Cape of Good Hope, and several other exotic ports of call—or so at least they appeared to in works such as Carel Allard's fairly typical and oft-reprinted costume book, the *Orbis habitabilis oppida et vestitus* (circa 1685).[13]

Exotic voyeurism might take two forms, one more explicit and the other slightly less so. In many instances, the viewing could be done in plain sight, as it were, with

FIGURE 80. Carel Allard, "Mate Calo" (engraving), in *Orbis habitabilis oppida et vestitus, centenario numero complexa / Des bewoonden waerelds steden en dragten, in een honderd-getal begreepen* (Amsterdam, ca. 1685). Special Collections, University of Amsterdam (OM 63-1448).

CHAPTER THREE

minimal subtlety or guesswork. Sources of geography simply bared the exotic body for all to see: Kaempfer's topless female model illustrating the techniques of acupuncture (see figure 78); the glistening, pulsating African bodies depicted in the painter Dirk Valkenburg's so-called *Negroes Dancing* canvas (sometimes titled *Slave Play*) (see plate 8); the series of bare-bosomed female figures (paired with mostly bare-chested men) painted by Albert Eckhout for the governor of Dutch Brazil and reproduced in print media for decades to follow (see plate 9 and figures 139 and 140); and the many overt, textual descriptions that candidly undress the exotic body.[14] In other cases, however, the text or image might require some measure of intuition on the part of the viewer or reader—yet not overly much. When Olfert Dapper pronounces that Maronite priests in Syria do not wear any "underwear"—the original Dutch version uses the words for both undershirt and underpants—or that female priests in Soulang (Jiali, Taiwan) strip off their clothing and "rag[e] in a phanatick distraction," this encourages readers to peek, along with the author, underneath their subjects' exotic vestments.[15] And when de Bruijn describes the "drawers" of Turkish men and women, which have "no slit either before or behind," the reader, once again, can glimpse vicariously at both the exotic undergarments and the exotic body virtually visible beneath.[16] In this way, exotic sources implicate the European consumer of geography, once again, in the act of seeing or witnessing exotica and, more particularly, in a form of erotic voyeurism.

This voyeurism surely would have been by design. Sources of geography, in numerous instances, present the exotic body with an almost wanton disregard for what might be considered "European" standards of decency. They offer uninhibited views of the non-European body—images or accounts that might have been considered unduly titillating or even perverse in other contexts—and they describe or depict bodies in ways that may not have been possible if directed toward anything but exotic subjects. The results could be provocative in both senses of the word. After Jacob van Meurs published Arnoldus Montanus's description of Japan, a volume replete with tales of whoring, infidelity, sodomy, bestiality, and casual abortion—all of this taking place in the Asian tropics—Montanus came under attack (as discussed in the previous chapter) from Cornelis Hazart, a Jesuit author in Antwerp. While the kernel of the two men's dispute lay in a cross-confessional controversy over Jesuit-performed "miracles" (Montanus doubted them, Hazart emphatically did not), the broader criticism encompassed the superfluous sexual content of Montanus's volume and the explicitness of his ethnographic descriptions. The indignant Hazart (who himself penned a study of global Christianity and Catholic martyrdom in Japan) found the text well beyond the norms of decorous literature, and the images were to him gratuitously salacious. He found them offensive, and he counterattacked in print.[17] When Kaempfer wrote about Japan, he too included vignettes on the licentiousness of the local women, yet he reserved

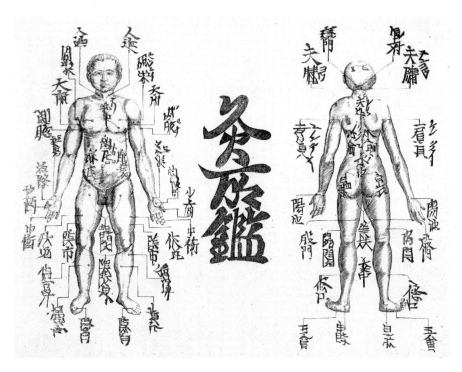

FIGURE 81. Moxibustion (engraving), in Engelbert Kaempfer, *Amoenitatum exoticarum politico-physico-medicarum fasciculi V* (Lemgo, 1712). Princeton University Library.

his most tantalizing fare for the *Amoenitatum exoticarum*—"Exotic Pleasures"—a volume that ranged across the vast Orient and its dissipated habits. Descriptions of acupuncture and moxibustion (a healing process that entails burning with moxa or mugwort) appeared, as it happens, in both of Kaempfer's books: these procedures, typical of traditional Chinese (and, by the early modern period, Japanese) medicine, occasioned several arresting illustrations of uncovered exotic flesh, a female figure used for acupuncture and a male for moxibustion.[18] Yet the "Exotic Pleasures" also reveals to its European audience tumors of the scrotum in Malabar (were there no occurrences of this malady in Kaempfer's native Germany?); the bodily effects and "superb benefits" of various Persian opiates; and the workings of a remarkable drug-cum-spell used in Makassar (South Sulawesi) that could induce or suppress male erections (no illustration is provided).[19] In these and other instances, the reader or viewer is invited to see—or better, to gawk at—the wondrous physical state of the non-European and to take pleasure in the extraordinariness of the exotic body.

Kaempfer's "exotic pleasures" also conveyed commercial benefits: several of the objects he described—valuable plants, rare collectibles, precious mineral products—had obvious market value. More broadly, there was a discernible commercial flavor to many of the descriptions and sightings of the exotic body, a suggestion of profit in corporality. Discussions of exotic bodies, that is, and of the sexual practices to which they may have been subject often came attached to, or were suggestively situated with, intimations of market transactions. These transactions could be blunt: geography texts are rife with reports of prostitution in the non-European world, male no less than female, and there are numerous discussions, as well, of the global trade in slaves (a traffic that could also ensnare European bodies). Yet connections could also be insinuated in more understated terms, in an allusive metaphor or simile, or perhaps a careful juxtaposition that conflated exotic corporality with the world of commercial exchange. Olfert Dapper's rendition of "India," the rubric under which he and Jacob van Meurs delivered their full-service geography of Persia, Central Asia, and South Asia, might be distinguished for two signal qualities. The region gets high marks for its "costly Traffick, and its abundance of high-valu'd Commodities, which . . . exceeds Europe also, and may well stand in competition with the new-found World America." And it stands out for the richness of its sexual perversions. "The Persians," the reader discovers, "exceed most Countreys in Wantonness and venerial Exercises: for besides their great number of Wives, they are very much inclin'd to variety of Women, and in all their Cities, except *Ardebil* [Ardabil, identified as a holy city], are kept publick Brothel-houses, under the Protection of the Magistrates." The peoples of these regions, moreover, "are extremely addicted to the horrid Sin of Sodomy," and, along with other Muslim nations, they like to cross-dress. In this case, the connection is thematic: van Meurs's India volume switches back and forth between envious descriptions of the rich commodities trade and lurid descriptions of the rich sexual trade. In Aphra Behn's evocative portrait of the young African warrior whom she fetishizes in *Oroonoko*, a morality tale of the transatlantic slave trade, the physicality of the novel's hero is at once central to the plot—Oroonoko wages epic combat on the African battlefield, then singlehandedly leads the slaves of Suriname in a failed uprising—and intricately bound up with overseas commerce. In exquisitely sketched prose, Behn likens the exotic body of Oroonoko to those costly import wares that "were Japan'd," or lacquered: delicately darkened and made smooth. In this case, a striking simile links the bodies of Africans (exported to America) to the commerce of Asian decorative arts (exported to Europe). Both earned plaudits and profits.[20]

Behn's lavish attention to the flesh and physical presence of Oroonoko and his fellow Africans—she observes for her readers the gleam of "the Trunk of their Bodies," a prose painting that compares well to Valkenburg's canvas—offers one of the rare instances of a female author gazing intently at the non-European male physique, the exception that points to the more general rule of a masculine perspective to the exotic body. This applies, above all, when the exotic body is sexualized: whether the subject of this sexual gaze is male or female, the viewpoint tends to be male. And the viewpoint tends to testify to predatory, "lustful" behavior, whether it be in the form of adultery, child (male) prostitution, concubinage (usually presented as involuntary), or rape. Adultery per se did not need to be predatory, of course, yet the variants narrated in volumes of exotic geography commonly were.

The most horrific such episode—a tale brimming with lurid descriptions of the exotic body and with appalling details of salaciousness, licentiousness, voyeurism, violence, and more—was the vivid account in Struys's *Reysen* (1676) of the flaying by a Central Asian "gentleman" of his putatively unfaithful wife. The story (broached in the opening of this chapter) takes place in Shamakhy, in the eastern Caucasus (present-day Azerbaijan), although the dramatis personae had more vague and perhaps all-purpose affiliations. The principal "body" in question belonged to a so-called Polish woman, described also as a "slave" and a "wife"—one of thirteen, thus part of an Oriental seraglio—who is tormented by her "husband," the latter classified generically as a "Persian" and thus implicitly as a Muslim. The woman's crime is never fully clarified: she is suspected of an unspecified misdeed, while a later reference to "chastity" may allude to a sexual impropriety. Yet her punishment is described in painfully precise detail: the victim is stripped naked, crucified on wooden stakes, and flayed alive. All of this was perpetrated by the husband himself and witnessed by the narrator ("I stood myself . . . and heard her cry out most bitterly"). It marks a crescendo of sorts to an altogether shocking volume of exotic violence.[21]

The Shamakhy affair pinpoints the brutal, gory, almost unimaginable treatment of the exotic body (the wife's designation as Slavic in no way diminishing her exotic status to western Europeans).[22] It also intimates how the gothic violence meted out in the exotic world—"the horrible spectacle" endured by the wretched woman—pertains to, and in certain ways derives from, the sexual excesses of non-European men. The central episodes of the incident have a whiff of both sex *and* violence, and they blend motifs of both Christian and classical flavors: the suffering of Christ at the hands of nonbelievers (the woman is crucified); the ghastly death of the apostle Saint Bartholomew (who was flayed, reputedly, in Azerbaijan or Armenia); the flaying of the corrupt judge Sisamnes by the Persian ruler Cambyses II; and, of course, the ancient Greek myth of Marsyas.[23] Yet the Shamakhy story also suggests, in its lurid detail, how much more intense the abuse of a non-European body could be—how utterly demeaned, degraded, and debased it was fast becoming to a European audience.

The story begins vaguely with an accusation of a "quarrel" and some other unspecified "misbehaviour." This leads the accused woman, distraught and desperate, to throw herself at the mercy of a European diplomat stationed in Shamakhy, who harbors her until the local authorities dictate that she be returned to her husband. At this point, her physical ordeal begins (quoting from the contemporary English translation): "The Man having as was said permission to punish her at his own Discretion had already provided a Wooden Cross, upon which, with the help of his Servants, he bound her fast, being mother naked, and with his own hands flea'd her whilst yet living." Crucified and viciously flayed, her troubles were not yet over, and the narrator now reverts to a plotline of gruesome excess, incredulous even of his own account: "Yet none thought that his cruelty was of so high a nature ["more than beastly," in the Dutch original] till we saw the Carcase, thrown out into the street where it lay an hour or two, and afterwards by his [the husband's] order was dragged into the Fields, to be devoured of the Eagles, and other Birds of prey." And still, there was more: "But he not satisfied herewith took the skin and nailed it upon the Wall for a Monument and Warning for his other Wives, which were 12 in number, who never saw it but trembled, as indeed I my self did, so often as I went by the House."[24] The exotic body had thus been stripped "mother naked"; skinned like a prized animal ("flea'd," in the English translation, combines both "flayed" and "fleeced"); cast out indecorously to the wild beasts; and finally nailed to the wall to serve as an object lesson—the flesh of the woman had been literally objectified—and a notice to others of the cruelties to which the body may be subject in the non-European world.

How were European readers to make sense of such a dreadful story? In part, through the fold-out picture used to illustrate it, which invokes several well devel-

FIGURE 82. Jacob van Meurs (atelier), Flaying of a Polish woman (engraving), in Jan Jansz Struys, *Drie aanmerkelijke en seer rampspoedige reysen* (Amsterdam, 1676). Special Collections, University of Amsterdam (O 63-41).

oped themes and techniques of exotic geography. At the core of the engraving—which is reputedly "drawn by the author himself, after life," yet unsigned and unlikely to be the genuine work of Jan Struys, by training a sailmaker—lies a female body: full-figured, fully nude, and fully splayed out and exposed for all to see. The woman lies on a wooden cross to which a servant diligently straps her limp left arm; her torso and legs are already tightly fastened with rope. At her side, in the composition's foreground, lie a woman's robe and a suggestive pair of silk slippers, the latter being of the sort commonly found in Dutch genre painting, particularly those exhibiting so-called wanton women.[25] Another servant, at the other end of the cross, holds down her right ankle, as a "Persian" gentlemen—his status is signified by a fine jacket and feathered turban—works his knife intently over the skin of the woman's right shin. If the action taken by these men is shocking and alien to the European viewer, the setting is not: a bourgeois interior that suggests a domestic sitting room, with a pair of windows shaded by partly drawn curtains, a high mantle held aloft by classical columns, and a slender cupboard off to the side. Both the cupboard and the mantle bear impressive garnitures: in each case, three pieces of ceramics—imported porcelain?—comprising pairs of elegantly shaped bowls, long-necked vases, and decorative plates. Off to the side in another room, which is entered through a modest but graceful landing of stairs and a theatrically pulled-back curtain, the "Persian" man gestures toward the final product of his labors, the ghoulish hide of the woman nailed to a wall (a hammer leans on a railing). This room also holds ceramics: a three-shelf case hanging on the wall, illuminated by sunlight that pours in from two arched windows of a sort not uncommon in well-appointed Dutch interiors. A group of women—these, presumably, constitute the living remainder of the seraglio—look demurely toward their gesturing husband or cast their eyes downward; a dog in the bottom left corner of the composition scampers down the steps and out of the picture frame, his head hanging sympathetically low.

The sexual content of the image is plain and made more so by the gratuitous nudity fully on display. The presence of the other women of the seraglio as well as a proverb quoted in the text—to the effect that the husband's suspicion obtained from his own insatiable lust, a disposition typical for a region where men are "generally prone to Venery" and thus never sexually satisfied—hint at the origins of the tragedy in the wife's suspected infidelity. What began in a shroud of secrecy, however, ends in a public and readily viewable display of a stripped exotic body. The reader—or rather, viewer—plays the part of voyeur. The domestic interiors of the composition and the casual presence of decorative arts, however, link two modes of exotic consumption, the sexual and material. They also add a bizarre note of normalcy to a scene that would otherwise seem remorselessly, relentlessly shocking. *Seeing* the body, in all events, and the titillation induced by this sight, is central to the affair. This is a point slyly made in a coda to the Shamakhy vignette. After concluding the story of the flayed woman and briefly explaining the customs of the seraglio, which strictly precluded women from being witnessed by a man other than their husband (or a eunuch) lest their virtue be compromised, the narrator relates another incident that "happened once" when his patron requested that he fetch a precious saddle for his horse. This required the narrator to walk through several rooms of the house, in one of which, as he confesses, "I found my Patroness standing naked in the bath." The narrator fears that his "peeping" (as he calls it) would cost him dearly, but he is assured by the lady herself that he need not worry: "*Ho! ho! don't run away* [she cried], *go thro' and fulfill your Lords Commands*. This she said with a smiling Countenance, which cured me of the Palsie [paralysis], that the sight of her had already struck me into."[26] The "sight" of the exposed woman, in other words, brings both pleasure and potential pain. And "sight," once again, serves as a central device for exotic geography—in this case, a means to convey the exotic body—whether the seeing takes place on the part of the narrator or his reader-viewer.[27]

Exotic Perversions: Pleasure, Pain, Paradox (and the Market)

A male perspective in exotic geography in no way precluded attention to the male body. This meant "seeing" exotic men, both clothed and not. On the frontispiece of Louis Hennepin's *Nouvelle decouverte d'un tres grand pays situé dans l'Amerique* (1697), a book that follows the journey of Hennepin and Sieur (Robert) de La Salle through the western waterways of New France, chiefly in the region of the Great Lakes and upper Mississippi, stands a robust male figure meant to represent a native North American (figure 83).[28] With broad shoulders and short-cropped hair, the Indian poses *contrapposto* and holds an oversized calumet, or ceremonial pipe. He is seen from the rear, and he torques his body gracefully to display the whole of his backside along with his delicate profile. And despite the potential chill of these northerly climes—the decorative palm trees notwithstanding, the landscape is intended to illustrate New France in the region of Lake Michigan or perhaps the upper Illinois River—he stands utterly naked. His powerful, statuesque body, all but flawless in its musculature, would have been familiar to students of classical or even Mannerist sculpture (think Farnese Hercules). Be that as it may, the audience for this relatively inexpensive print, delivered in a highly popular volume—printed in duodecimo and translated from the French into Dutch, German, Spanish, and English—was far broader and perhaps less erudite, and it would have seen this image more straightforwardly and crudely for what it was: a gratuitously nude male body, depicted from the rear, holding a large and indubitably phallic object. The illustration was no less alluringly homoerotic than the bare-breasted woman in Kaempfer's acupuncture plate may have been heteroerotic—two terms

FIGURE 83. Caspar Luyken, frontispiece (engraving) to Louis Hennepin, *Nouvelle decouverte d'un tres grand pays situé dans l'Amerique* (Utrecht, 1697). Courtesy of the John Carter Brown Library at Brown University.

that may not fit the vocabularies or the categories of early modern sexual desire, yet that speak all the same to the erotically charged bodies, male no less than female, that featured in exotic geography.

Exotic geography did not merely allow its audience to glimpse the exposed male body. It also catalogued the poses, practices, and "perversions" of exotic men, characterizing even the most basic male-to-male sexual relations as "wanton" deviations from a presumed European norm of monogamous heterosexuality.[29] In many ways, the "perverse," or inverted, sexuality imagined and described in many of these sources correlated roughly to Europe's sense of geography: when they took place outside of Europe, sexual practices fell outside of the norm. They were perilously, albeit provocatively and intriguingly, exotic. This applied above all to homosexual practices, which functioned as an important "parameter of 'civilization,'" as Rudi Bleys terms this in his pioneering study of European homosexuality. Homosexual relations were presented and configured as critical signs of cultural difference and social deviation.[30] Such a notion of exotic sexual alterity was not entirely new. "Within the narratives of discovery and conquest," writes Bleys in regard to the early samples of post-1492 literature, "same-sex behavior was employed as a *signifier* of the cultural difference of the people of both *India Orientalis* and *India Occidentalis*, and Africa too was submitted to a similar, if perhaps less visible, symbolizing discourse."[31] This becomes especially apparent to readers of the initial Spanish accounts of the conquistadors' advances in America. Same-sex behavior served as a signifier of indigenous American inferiority and thus as an excuse for the harsh and punitive conquest of the Indians that ensued. What had changed by the middle and later decades of the seventeenth century, however, was the extent and richness of this signification and the colonial "neutrality" of the perspective. Exotic sexuality and illustrations of exotic homosexual "perversion" flourished everywhere in the literature (and prints) of circa 1670–1730. They could be located and "witnessed" across the globe—in virtually all settings and theaters of European contact, whether or not these matched a specific imperial geography of conquest (as was the case for Castilian literature on America).

"Sodomy" provided European authors with the most comprehensive rubric for male-to-male sexual relations, a catchall category for various acts and actors linked to homosexuality. Sodomy was "very common among the Turks," as de Bruijn and numerous others reminded their readers, and it was pervasive in places like Persia, India, and Siam, where the men were "lazy and slow," according to Joost Schouten. This comment is echoed by Wouter Schouten (no relation to Joost), who also singled out the languid and indolent men of Siam for their "unchaste" habits. Joost Schouten, who traveled extensively around Asia in the mid-seventeenth century, may have been a better-than-average witness to the homosexual practices he records, since he apparently engaged in more than a few of them himself. For his crimes—for sodomy was a capital offense in his native Holland—he was tried, convicted, and ultimately executed, his sentence denouncing "how abominable this filthy and vile *sodomitical* sin is in the eyes of God and man, so that for this reason the Lord God has destroyed Lands and Cities with fire from Heaven, as an example and warning to the whole world," Siam apparently included.[32] Arnoldus Montanus dedicated a section of his book on Japan to the practice of sodomy in the Far East, an account that accords with a prior description of male sexual customs in Japan recorded by François Caron. A longtime VOC employee who gained fluency in Japanese dialects, Caron singled out the Edo ruling class—"much given to Sodomy"—and the Japanese Buddhist priests for their regretful proclivities to sodomy.[33] Montanus also offered details of homosexual habits in his book on the New World, which included well-known—that is, oft-repeated—descriptions of American *berdaches*, or transvested ("two-spirited") males.[34] And, likewise, Olfert Dapper described the practices of Central African "Chibados" ("quimbandas" in Spanish and Portuguese sources): men who dressed like women and assumed, along with their status as healers and spiritual figures, a "nonmasculine," passive role in male-to-male relations.[35]

In descriptions of American *berdaches*, African *chibados*, and ubiquitous Asian sodomites, the exotic male body becomes not only a site of "perverted" sexual practices; it also becomes feminized and distorted from its presumed natural form. Descriptions of the non-European male body accentuate these inversions: lack of masculine facial or body hair (famously among the American Indians, yet also in descriptions of the Chinese, Japanese, and sub-Saharan Africans); feminine dress, grooming, and "mien"; and a predisposition to sexual deviance, generally of the homosexual variety. In this context, the most "unnatural" exotic body belonged to the hermaphrodite, who made an appearance most frequently in descriptions of American Indian societies. Louis Hennepin reported that "there are numerous hermaphrodites" among the native inhabitants of the New World, a disproportionate number of whom embodied, from his perspective, a feminine role ("usually . . . women"). It is not altogether obvious what Hennepin meant by "hermaphrodite," a word of classical vintage that could imply someone of genuinely mixed (male/female) or ambiguous (homo/hetero) sexual characteristics, or someone who did not fully embody his or her gendered role—an effeminate male or a virile woman, for example. But it is apparent, in all cases, that the narrator of Hennepin's account considers hermaphrodites "unnatural" creatures, who possess critically flawed bodies and "shamelessly commit the sin against nature"—namely, sodomy. "They have boys whom they dress like girls, because they use them for this abominable sin," Hennepin remarks. "These boys only do women's work and abstain from hunting as well as warfare. They are very superstitious." Hennepin's final comments allude to *cultural* transgressions: a lack of proper religion (superstition and "sin") and an inability to pursue male-gendered roles, such as hunting and warfare.

Yet his observations otherwise underscore a perceived *somatic* shortcoming of the exotic (in this case Native American) body: an improperly gendered body and the many inversions and abuses to which it apparently could be subjected.[36]

The exotic male body, as perceived by the European (typically male) observer, exhibited several such inversions and underwent numerous abuses, which collectively tend to highlight, on the one hand, exotic sexuality and, on the other hand, the anxieties provoked by that sexuality. The non-European body was *unseemingly* sexualized. The Khoikhoi ("Hottentots") of southwestern Africa possess exceptionally large penises (their "manhood"), the reader learns, yet they also lack one testicle, typically the right, which permits them to run faster. (The Khoikhoi women appeared in European sources invariably with elongated breasts, which allegedly permitted them to nourish their young children while they were strapped to their backs.)[37] In Persia, it was reported, holy men known as "Benjanen" sit cross-legged by the roadside: "they never pair their Nails; some have locks of Hair hanging down their Backs of 4 or 5 Feet long, others never Shave their Heads or Beards, which makes them appear more like Devils than Men" (figure 84). More to the point, they endure uncommon attention to their bodies, particularly their "privy members," over which local women fawn in a "scandalous" way:

> They always appear Naked, having only a piece of Cloth wrapt about the middle. The *Indian* Women resort to them in great Numbers out of Devotion, to touch the extremities of their Fingers, or to Kiss their Privy Members in a most humble Posture; which they admit of, without shewing the least sign of sensibility thereat, for if they should do otherwise, they would be look'd upon as unfit for that Holy Seat.[38]

Muslim "Kalenders," or Qalandars—Sufi mystics described in Dapper's volume on Ottoman Syria—also went naked and had recourse to a purpose-made accessory meant to maintain their holiness: an iron ring "which was placed over the skin of their male member" with the intent of ensuring their chastity. The Qalandars endured several further bodily embellishments and mutilations: "carvings" of the flesh (compare Oroonoko's "cut" and "carved" body), swords through their abdomens, spikes piercing their biceps, and so on (figure 85).[39] A form of the penis ring, or ampallang (male genital piercing), also appears in accounts of Pattani (in southern Thailand), where the men were "addicted to Venery"—specifically with women, the text makes clear—yet were also prone to jealousy and sodomy. As a consequence, "they have an Ancient custom since enacted into a Law, that to check that enormous Vice of Sodomy, the men are obliged to wear constantly two or three small Bells made of Gold, Silver or Lead, betwixt the prepuce and the glans, or the head of the Yard."[40]

Goegys of Benjaenfe Heijligen.

FIGURE 84. Willem vander Gouwen, "Goegys of Benjaense Heijligen," in Johan Nieuhof, *Gedenkwaerdige zee en lantreize door de voornaemste landschappen van West en Oostindien* (Amsterdam, 1682). Special Collections, University of Amsterdam (KF 61-4601).

This perversely picturesque image—bells on the genitals of Siamese sodomites—illustrates some of the wildly contradictory qualities of exotic bodies, or at least of the European depictions of them. For while the men of Pattani were "addicted to Venery"—enthusiasts of those sexual pleasures associated with Venus, as the etymology of the word implies, or devoted to the delights of "vrouwvolk," as

CHAPTER THREE

the Dutch edition unstintingly clarifies—they were also expert sodomites with an insatiable appetite for men. Furthermore, whether men or women drove Siamese male desire, the bells that the men were legally compelled to wear would appear to have been utterly ineffective, a device more likely designed to heighten European interest than to explain non-European sexuality. In fact, the men persist in their pursuits, as the very next passage further reports. "Adultery is very frequent among them," the reader discovers, "by reason of the extraordinary Lasciviousness of the Women"—this, after detailing the lust of the men—"who are very desirous, and

BALHAOVA

FIGURE 85. Jacob van Meurs (atelier), "Balhaova [Qalander]" (engraving), in Olfert Dapper, *Naukeurige beschryving van gantsch Syrie, en Palestyn of Heilige Lant* (Amsterdam, 1677). Special Collections, University of Amsterdam (OM 63-114).

love to wallow in Pleasures."[41] As with the Persian holy men, whose sanctified bearing and modest demeanor nonetheless entice female sexual desire—the women's avid interest in the ascetics' private parts—the Pattani men wear accessories that inhibit their sexual abilities even as they exceed all expectations in their hetero- and homosexual prowess. The sexual ability of exotic males is both celebrated and neutralized in these sources, and this might suggest not only European male voyeurism but also European male anxiety.

None of this should imply that there was a lack of material in these sources to incite European *female* anxiety. Exotic geography catalogues countless more examples of sexual curiosities—of peculiarly "lewd" practices, of social and sexual "perversions," of the all-around maltreatment of the non-European body—and these place women in a no less, and very often more, precarious position than men. The Persian holy men's provocation, sitting all but naked by the side of the road, leads also to the Persian women's humiliation: "it is scandalous," comments the narrator parenthetically of the female devotees' attention to the men's genitalia.[42] In detailing the religious practices of Japan, Montanus pauses to cite Herodotus—one of several such Herodotean interludes in these volumes—on the coupling of women and goats in the ancient Egyptian temple of Mendes (Tell El-Ruba). This segues to a discussion of Japan's famous Temple of Apes and the innuendo that female bestiality (and its obvious degradations) blends naturally with sacred practices across the exotic world.[43] In another Herodotean sleight of hand, this one in the *Reysen* of Jan Struys, a discussion of the alleged practice of incest among the Chermis (or Mari), who lived along the Volga and Kama rivers in Russia, leads to an observation of a similar practice among the Singhalese in Sri Lanka, whose men purportedly deflowered their daughters on the eve of the latters' marriages. In both cases, exotic social-cum-sexual practices demean exotic women—by implication, in several sites spread around the world. And while vignettes of this ilk certainly may have delivered a titillating charge to their male audience, they just as certainly would have generated unease among their female readers.[44]

Scenes and stories that incorporate exotic bodies could elicit a range of reactions, more generally, from mild titillation to more serious anxiety about the rude handling and outright abuse of the non-European body, male no less than female. And while many of these narratives and images highlight the potential bodily pleasure experienced in the non-European world—for men, in the ubiquitous brothels, infamous seraglios, and pervasive sodomy; for women, in the more flirtatious, less inhibited world of extra-European sexuality—they also indicate the potential for bodily pain and anguish. A delicate narrative thread or a shrewd ethnographic image might connect these themes: a penis ring could seriously impair the pleasure of a lustful Siamese man, while a whiff of adultery in Persia could lead to the appalling corporal punishment of an accused woman. In certain cases, a single event or figure might demonstrate both pleasure and pain, incipient sexuality and impending violence, blended into a complex whole. Women, all things considered, typically got the worst of it.

A fine illustration of this subtle combination of themes occurs in a truly colossal source—a canvas measuring nearly three by two meters—which also had considerable influence in the visual arts: Albert Eckhout's stunning *African Woman and Child* (see plate 9). This remarkable image stands out for several reasons. It was among the relatively few life-sized portraits of an exotic subject, painted by one of the rare European-trained artists to work on-site in the colonial world. And while painted images of sub-Saharan Africans do occur in the European tradition—depictions of the magi not uncommonly include a dark-skinned visitor from Africa, for example, and innovative painters like Peter Paul Rubens and Rembrandt (and before them Albrecht Dürer and Jan Mostaert) sometimes experimented by incorporating or even spotlighting African subjects in their work[45]—rarely did a composition make an African woman's body so pronouncedly and centrally its subject, and rarely did a composition embrace the breadth of ethnographic detail and exotic furnishings included in Eckhout's massive canvas. Commissioned originally by Count (later Prince) Johan Maurits of Nassau-Siegen, the governor of Dutch Brazil in the mid-seventeenth century, the painting is veritably unique in the history of early modern European art, and it served in subsequent decades as an iconographic source for a far broader production of graphic and material arts that borrowed from the its motifs: prints, ceramics, textiles, furniture, and so on.[46]

On a most basic level, the composition is plainly arresting. A statuesque, well-proportioned, finely muscled, and lightly clothed woman faces the viewer straight on, with one hand holding a basket aloft and the other resting on a young boy's head. A vast, clouded sky behind the woman, an assortment of tropical flora scattered mostly to her right, and a calm, low-horizon seascape with a smattering of ships in the background fill out the considerable canvas. The central female figure is meticulously accessorized. A double string of white pearls gleams against her smooth dark skin, and another double rope of red-coral beads, falling slightly lower on her chest, highlights her full, round breasts. The boy, who is entirely naked except for his own modest jewelry (earrings and a necklace) and who is somewhat lighter in flesh tone than his mother (one presumes), points an ear of corn toward the woman's upper thighs. This gesture and a woven basket that practically overflows with a cornucopia of ripe tropical fruit suggest the fecundity and palpable sexuality of the female figure. She wears a light cotton skirt cinched at the waist and held in place by a stylish red sash, out of which pokes a white clay pipe—an erotic symbol in the context of Dutch Baroque painting, where pipes hinted simultaneously at the habits of wanton women and the critical anatomy of their male suitors.[47] Eckhout's woman, in all events, cuts a striking figure. She is beautiful and alluring and presents a visual version of the fictional character "Imoinda," whom Aphra Behn would memorialize in her novel of just a few years later as "a Beauty . . . [a] beautiful *Black Venus*."[48]

Like Imoinda, Eckhout's protagonist would appear to hail from Africa, yet the setting, artifacts, and flora that surround her spell out a somewhat more complicated itinerary, with more broadly Atlantic traces. Along with the red-coral beads, most of the ethnographic objects she bears do have origins in Africa, specifically the West African coast near the equator and those regions associated with European commerce: the so-called Gold and Slave Coasts and the area to the south, near the mouth of the Congo River. The woman's superbly woven basket is meant to be Bakongo, or Congolese, and her exquisite hat, adorned with colorful peacock feathers, likewise derives from producers and traders (who may have imported the feathers) active in the vicinity of the Congo River's Atlantic estuary. The clay pipe may be of African or European manufacture, yet it was unmistakably associated with an indigenous American natural product, by this time common enough in West Africa: *nicotiana tabacum*. Other *naturalia* point, as well, to both sides of the Atlantic, its tropical African and American coasts. A wax palm (*copernicia alba*), native to Brazil and other sultry South American environments, frames the left side of the composition, while a papaya tree (*carica papaya*), likewise indigenous to tropical America, stands at a distance in the painting's background. And while the cherubic boy clutches a quintessentially American ear of corn in his right hand, on his left index finger perches a red-headed (or red-faced) lovebird (*agapornis pullarius*), a species native to Africa. The bird, as it happens, provides further allusions to the woman's sexuality: by its association with the mating and grooming habits of the species ("love" birds); by its closer proximity (than the corn) to the woman's groin; and by way of the Dutch word *vogel* (bird), which, in the context of Dutch Golden Age visual traditions, puns on the verb *vogelen*, a contemporary slang term that means "to fornicate."[49]

The female subject of Eckhout's "African" painting, in short, presents an alluring mingling of exotica. Yet she also embodies an intricate mixture of messages and intersection of themes that speak to the distinctive presentation of the exotic body to an early modern European audience. For while she beckons the viewer with her frank and unobtrusive sexuality, her body itself has greater cultural significance in the context of the seventeenth-century Atlantic world, and her story offers more than might first meet the eye. In the painting's background and in its backstory lie several clues. First, the background: Behind the woman and to the right of the boy's torso float four seagoing vessels, barely visible on the horizon. And in the lower right of the composition stand several indigenous Brazilians—likely Tupinambá, identifiable from their loose cotton costumes—who busy themselves gathering a net on the beach and tending to other fishing paraphernalia; one of their group

FIGURE 86. Detail of Albert Eckhout, *African Woman and Child* (1641), oil on canvas.
© National Museum of Denmark, Ethnographic Collection.

stands atop a lookout ladder, gazing out toward the distant ships. The scene is comparatively slender, a marginal comment on an otherwise vast and crowded canvas.
Yet the reference it makes to the world of commerce and economic activity is pivotal. Ships convey goods across the Atlantic—from Africa to America to Europe—
and among the most central of the products trafficked in this period, even more
costly than the exotic artifacts modeled by the statuesque woman portrayed, were
exotic bodies: chattel slaves, which were exported from Western Africa and supplied abundantly in this period to fuel the plantation economy of Brazil.[50]

Now, the backstory: While it is notoriously difficult to peek into processes of
painterly production, in the case of Eckhout's canvas we do possess figure studies
that offer invaluable perspective on the *African Woman* and her construction. One
of the most important of these is not by Eckhout (ca. 1610-1666) himself but by
Zacharias Wagenaer (1614-1668), a longtime employee of the Dutch West India
Company (WIC) and a well-traveled, journal-keeping, amateur draftsman who
would later serve the Dutch East India Company (VOC), as well, in Africa and
Asia. German by birth, Wagenaer came to Amsterdam as a young man and worked
for Willem Blaeu, the renowned mapmaker. He later enlisted with the WIC and
happened to be in Brazil at the time Eckhout worked on his "African Woman"
composition (circa 1641). His WIC training and tenure in Blaeu's atelier provided
Wagenaer with basic drafting skills, and this enabled him to produce per manuscript drawing—along with several other sketches of the local scene and occupants
of Dutch Brazil—several annotated copies of Eckhout's portraits. A version of the
African woman, labeled in the manuscript "Molher Negra" (from the Portuguese

FIGURE 87. Zacharias Wagenaer after Albert Eckhout, "Molher Negra" (ca. 1641); watercolor on paper (in the *Thierbuch*). Kupferstich-Kabinett, Staatliche Kunstsammlungen Dresden.

mulher negra: black woman), faithfully reproduces the female figure with her basket, jewelry, outfit, and boy, yet without much of the adjacent *naturalia* or any of the deeper landscape or background scenery. The woman's carefully sketched body does include, however, a vital detail not present in the painting: a branding mark, visible just below the woman's left clavicle, featuring a crowned capital "M." As Wagenaer explains in the notes that accompany the image: "These blacks are brought to Brazil from Africa" and sold as slaves, mostly to Portuguese sugar-plantation owners (who treated them, Wagenaer adds, rather brutally). This particular *mulher negra*—and, by extrapolation, the individual model for Eckhout's African woman—belonged *not* to a Portuguese owner, however, but to the WIC-appointed governor of the Dutch colony, Johan *Maurits*, to whom the branding refers. For the Dutch had appropriated the Portuguese habit of treating African bodies as valuable chattel, as Wagenaer also comments: "Our people, like the Por-

CHAPTER THREE

tuguese, recently decided it would be a good idea to put certain signs or marks on men, women, and children."[51]

The mark on the black woman's body adds critical context to her portrait. Or rather, it adds a different, if perhaps complementary, perspective to a painting that might otherwise be taken to represent *merely* an alluring, exotic, African woman, bearing the rich artifacts and surrounded by the fertile nature of the tropical Atlantic world. The branding both clarifies and complicates the subject's status and the painting's broader message. While the bejeweled "African" woman in the painting is plainly not meant to represent a slave—no one of that humble status would have been so richly attired—the origins of her image in a bona fide slave's body hints at the mostly degrading standing of the preponderance of African migrants who ended up, overwhelmingly by force, in the European-American colonial orbit. The branding, moreover, renders the other devices of Eckhout's canvas thematically thicker. The woman's obvious sexuality now has a less-than-fully-obvious purpose, while her fecundity has a distinct value: the production of healthy offspring, preferably male, who might toil as future slaves. (The mortality rate of Brazilian slaves was notoriously high, while the fertility rate of female slaves in the tropics was grimly low.) The pipe, associated in Dutch genre painting with lusty behavior, also featured in images of American slaves, who smoked tobacco as a respite from the drudgery of the field (where they might also labor to produce crops of tobacco).[52] The painting is packed, in effect, with signs of colonial production and overseas commerce, from the costly African artifacts and sumptuous jewels coveted by wealthy European collectors, to the exotic natural products gleaned and cultivated in the tropics, to the ships looming on the horizon, which conveyed all of this—including the bodies of African slaves—across the Atlantic. Most of all, the European-issued brand on Wagenaer's sketched figure, juxtaposed with the glistening flesh of Eckhout's painted African "Venus," indicates how the exotic body could encompass two important sets of qualities, which simultaneously contradicted and coalesced: desire and degradation, enchantment and humiliation, physical allure and bodily abuse, exotic sexuality and exotic violence.

Exotic Violence (and Sex)

The exotic body transformed almost effortlessly from a site of pleasure to a site of pain, from a source of European titillation to a locus of non-European anguish. In a passage and print that appeared in Olfert Dapper's widely circulated geography of China, an exotic body undergoes titillation, literally (from the Latin *titillare*, to tickle), yet the tickling promptly devolves into unambiguous torment. The engraved version of the scene offers equal doses of shock and spectacle. A naked woman is shown stretched across the picture frame, bound to and suspended from a bamboo pole, with her body fully exposed to the viewer's gaze. Her back arches slightly, as her waist-length hair, lashed to her bare ankles, serves to bend her legs painfully toward her buttocks and thereby to leverage her body. And although she is trussed horizontally, stomach facing downward, her right breast is readily visible to all onlookers. Two sturdy men clasp the pole at either end, while a third male figure maneuvers a grotesquely large feather, allowing its delicate tip to graze the soles of the woman's feet. This elaborate tickling operation takes place in a distinctly mundane setting: a Chinese domestic interior decorated with slender vases of flowers (the vases likely made of porcelain), several covered storage drums, and a fringed silk rug draped from an open window. Three figures standing outside the window engage in ostensibly convivial conversation, while a fourth glances casually into the room, taking in the scene of torment that is well under way. He and the volume's readers alike

FIGURE 88. Jacob van Meurs (atelier), Titillation (engraving), in Olfert Dapper, *Gedenckwaerdig bedryf der Nederlandsche Oost-Indische Maetschappye, op de kuste en in het keizerrijk van Taising of Sina* (Amsterdam, 1670). Special Collections, University of Amsterdam (OM 63-124).

CHAPTER THREE

witness, that is, an exotic female body, fully displayed, in a state of palpable suffering. In this case, however, the sexualized female figure must endure what can only be regarded as perverse abuse: unambiguous and unstinting torment.[53]

Such extravagant, to our eyes stunning, abuse—physical cruelty purposefully inflicted on an unprotected human body, or, more bluntly, torture—is replicated in several other exotic scenes, not least in the printed geographies of Olfert Dapper, which were published and illustrated principally by Jacob van Meurs and his atelier. In another illustrated vignette from Dapper's China book, the victim is now male, yet he is shown in much the same manner, in an agonizing and sexually compromised position (see plate 10). Stripped from the waist down, a Chinese gentleman—his status is confirmed by the mandarin costume cast off to the side— braces to receive a blow from his tormentor, the latter vigorously wielding a bamboo cudgel that will momentarily strike the victim's bare buttocks. The locus of torture, once again, is a domestic interior, an oddly cheerful space decorated with many of the trappings of an imagined elite, or at least comfortable, Chinese life: a framed landscape painting, which the victim is forced to face; a set of ceramic jars and bowls (lubricants, perhaps, yet possibly and more simply service for tea); a heavy drapery against the rear wall, pulled back to show an open window and background foliage. Just outside this centrally staged window—a compositional technique that suggests the same illustrator as the "titillation" print—stand three men, one of whom leans into the room, arm akimbo, taking in the act of caning with studied nonchalance. Such casual detachment notwithstanding, the scene playing out in front of these hypothetical spectators—and, more vitally, for the volume's European audience—is one of unvarnished torture: workmanlike figures toil to torment, mangle, and cruelly abuse the bodies of their victims. They exploit the exotic body in violent, dramatic, and spectacular fashion, and their maltreatment is pointedly observed: by the Chinese figures engraved into the picture frame, as well as the European spectators and consumers of exotic geography.

If the non-European body could be sexualized in sources of European geography, it could also—and often simultaneously—be subjected to pitiless violence. The abuse of the exotic body was pervasive in this period. Across the globe, as depicted in visual and textual materials alike, the exotic body was made to suffer intense, grisly, graphic, and ostentatious violence. Its abuse was presented, moreover, as a "spectacle" intended for the consumption of an implicitly European observer. Bodies were hacked to pieces, forcibly disemboweled, savagely cannibalized, aborted in fetal form, and habitually tortured in Persia, India, Bengal, Siam, Malacca, China, Japan, and innumerable other "tropical" locales—and all of this occurs in the single narrative of Wouter Schouten, whose *Oost-Indische voyagie* conveys the author merely to the East Indies. Body parts were gouged, pierced, sliced, flayed, seared, crushed, blistered, mauled, and gorged upon by wild beasts—once again, just in the

FIGURE 89. Jacob van Meurs (atelier), Hindu procession (engraving), in Wouter Schouten, *Oost-Indische voyagie* (Amsterdam, 1676). Special Collections, University of Amsterdam (OG 77-17).

account of Schouten, once again over the course of only a single Asian journey.[54] Bodily abuse, in addition, was garishly displayed. Indeed, the most salacious examples of somatic violence merit vivid illustration from Schouten's Amsterdam publisher—as when the author describes his acute unease at the sight of the "awful" bodily contortions performed by "pious" Hindus, which Schouten reports to his reader per text and which he is also depicted "witnessing" per engraving (in one instance, while hoisting a flute of beer) during his sojourn in Bengal.[55]

In sources of geography produced in the milieu of Schouten's popular volume, exotic bodies undergo flamboyant, extravagant, and, in several regards, innovative forms of violence.[56] For years, it had been de rigueur for European narrators to report the occurrence of sati (ritual immolation) in South Asia, cannibalism in South and Central America, and "Moorish" cruelties across the Mediterranean, whether these heinous deeds had actually been observed or not. Yet now, in materials dating from the later seventeenth and the early eighteenth centuries, it became routine also to revel in the gory details of *seppuku* in Japan; widespread cannibalism across Asia (as well, of course, as in the Americas); scarification in West Africa; and sadistic torture, dictated by emerging "Oriental despots," in the empires of China, Russia, and Ottoman Turkey. In many of these reports, furthermore, a visual component made the accounting of exotic violence all the more lurid and lucid. This entailed inevitable claims by narrators of "eye-witnessing"—a statement of *seeing* the violence they describe—and, fairly commonly too, the graphic illustration of corporal abuse. Images of exotic violence might also include a well-placed European spectator, who was meant to stand in for the volume's author and, effectively, for its reader. Pictures were designed, in an important sense, to double the process of witnessing: the reader sees the putative author seeing the exotic body suffer. Somatic pain multiplied in the exotic world.[57]

The violence visited upon exotic bodies could be truly baroque. Descriptions invariably catalogued bodily mutilations of the crudest sort; they also underscored the systematic nature of somatic violence. Exotic bodies were not just haphazardly inflicted with pain, but subjected to regimes of justice and forms of governance that routinely and methodically dole out horrific physical punishment. In the Dutch printing of Jean de Thévenot's *Travels*—a much revised version of the original French edition, amplified in Amsterdam ateliers by copious plates from the engraver Jan Luyken—the reader gets a vivid and pervasive perspective on exotic violence. The frontispiece starts things off with an illustration of a freshly severed head (figure 90, bottom right) presented to an allegorical figure of the Levant, suggesting, in crisp visual shorthand, the cruel regard taken in the Eastern world toward subject populations. The reader then learns, within the body of the volume, of "the typical punishments of Egypt," including impalement. This is shown in an explicit composition (signed by Luyken: figure 91) that depicts the three stages of this torture: hammering a sharp-tipped stake through the victim's groin and buttocks (it emerges through the lower neck), waiting alongside the reamed figure as he succumbs to the pain and profuse loss of blood (Thévenot mentions one man who lasted three days, passing his time by smoking a pipe), and, finally, abandoning the victim—still suspended on the stake—to expire. In another Luyken illustration, likewise meant (in the context of

FIGURE 90. Jan Luyken (?), frontispiece (etching) to Jean de Thévenot, *Gedenkwaardige en zeer naauwkeurige reizen van den Heere de Thevenot* (Amsterdam, 1681–1682). Special Collections, University of Amsterdam (O 63 5229).

the narrative) to demonstrate the awesome power of Eastern potentates, a richly dressed Persian shah commands the son of "an elderly Lord" to lop off his father's ears and nose. At the victim's feet lie two vividly depicted, freshly severed ears, soon to be joined by the Lord's nose, through which the son obediently works his knife (figure 92).[58] Similarly, on the frontispiece of Johan Nieuhof's China volume the "Great Cham" lords over an assortment of miserable subjects, who writhe in the foreground in obvious pain: some shackled in iron chains, one yoked in a wooden cangue (see plate 19). Further reports await the reader within the text: of maimed limbs, shrunken feet, castrated infants, and other diversely mutilated bodies. And in Petrine Russia (as

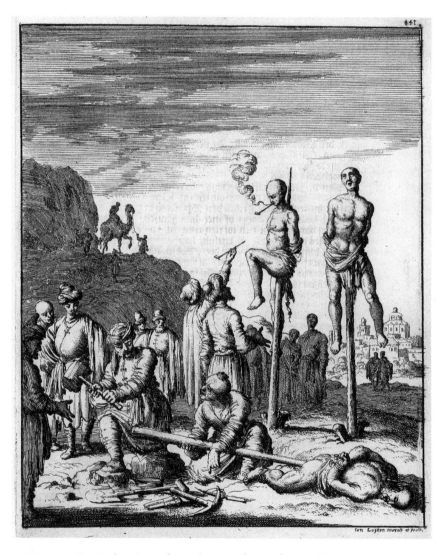

FIGURE 91. Jan Luyken, Typical punishments of Egypt (etching), in Jean de Thévenot, *Gedenkwaardige en zeer naauwkeurige reizen* (Amsterdam, 1681–1682). Special Collections, University of Amsterdam (O 63 5229).

FIGURE 92. Jan Luyken, A lord punished (etching), in Jean de Thévenot, *Gedenkwaardige en zeer naauwkeurige reizen* (Amsterdam, 1681–1682). Special Collections, University of Amsterdam (O 63-5229).

we discover from Cornelis de Bruijn), the tsar is "an absolute Monarch" whose punishments embrace the burning, beheading, and burying alive of his "enslaved" subjects, not to mention the whipping, lashing, branding, and further torture of those judged guilty of lesser, non-capital crimes. Even in the relatively peripheral sultanate of Aceh (or Achin), the "Absoluteness of their Kings" translated into the repugnant control of their subjects' bodies: "In former Ages the Kings used to surrender the miscreant"—this regarding "the least Trespass" of the sultan's command—"to the Man-eaters [of the land], who after they had chop'd of their Hands, Arms and Leggs, threw Pepper upon the Trunk of the body and devoured it."[59]

Thus exotic castigation. And while European regimes clearly—and commonly—abused their own subjects' bodies, the non-European rulers described in sources of exotic geography far outdo their European counterparts, time and again, in their inventively violent forms of punishment. In a world of sadistic one-upmanship, the most gruesome tales may pertain to Persia, at least the version of Persia narrated and illustrated in the van Meurs–published account of Olfert Dapper. Here the fullness of royal hegemony over the subject corporality, and the sheer cruelty perpetrated against it, render the exotic body a site of utterly shocking violence. Dapper's narrative marries two themes, princely power and somatic pain, which come together in the exotic body. "The Government of this Countrey," Dapper writes of the Safavid dynasts, "is by absolute Monarchy, for the King being the Chief, hath all things in his own power, to do whatsoe're he pleases, being able to make or break Laws without any contradiction, nay, to take away any ones Estate or Life, though he be the greatest Lord in the Countrey." Criminals are punished "with extream severity," typically by mutilation—of noses, eyes, hands, feet—although they might also be flayed alive, disemboweled, or strung up by their feet. Dapper's descriptive mode seems to linger on and almost to savor the excruciating pain:

> They make two Holes in the Malefactors Legs behind the Ancle, between the Bone and the great Tendon, through which they put a Rope, whereby they hang them on a Tree so high, that their Heads do just touch the Ground; in which manner, if the Malefactor be condemn'd to die, they let him hang two or three days, till after an intolerable Number of pains he gives up the Ghost; or if he die not in that manner, then they shorten his time by ripping open his Belly. Others for smaller Offences [sic] are hang'd up an hour or two with their Head downwards. He that Ravisheth a Woman, and is convicted by her Swearing three times, or commits Sodomy, hath his Genitals cut off.[60]

For Dapper, torture and its descriptors only intensify. A usurer in Persia ("worse than a *Jew*") might have his teeth knocked out with a hammer; criminals under Shah Abbas (r. 1587–1629) could be sandwiched between wooden boards and sawed in half; and the victim of one particularly sadistic "king" (Abbas or perhaps Shah Sefi, his grandson) was compelled to eat the flesh that had been carved out of his own arm. In China according to Dapper (this in another volume), death came in one stunning instance not by a mere thousand but by *ten* thousand cuts.[61]

These affronts to the body, once again, gain the attention of illustrators. Dapper's China volume, designed and produced in van Meurs's atelier, contained three remarkable engravings of the Great Khan's regime of torture: the tickled female and the thrashed male figures (both discussed above: see figure 88 and plate 10),

Pag. 204.

Cruautéz in-oüies des sauvages Iroquois.

FIGURE 93. Jan van Vianen, "Cruautéz in-oüies des Sauvages Iroquois" (engraving), in
Louis Hennepin, *Nouveau voyage d'un pais plus grand que l'Europe* (Utrecht, 1698)
(shelf mark 866.c.6). © The British Library Board. All Rights Reserved.

and the depiction of another half-naked male victim, who lies grimacing, face in
the dirt, as he receives a blow from a stoic, cudgel-wielding executioner (see figure
173). Another engraved image, this time of the "Cruelty of the Savage Iroquois"
and printed in a volume designed by the Utrecht publisher Antoine Schouten, reveals the grisly regard of North American natives for their enemies' bodies: a collage of scalping, slicing, carving, bleeding, burning, and crucifying various non-
European bodies, the remnants of which are left to scavenging dogs.[62] Perhaps the
most vivid—which is to say, most graphic and brutal—depictions of exotic bodies
and the violence they could endure appeared in a series of images by Romeyn de

Hooghe (1645–1708), who ranks (along with Jan Luyken) among the leading graphic artists of the late seventeenth century. De Hooghe's illustrations for *Les Indes Orientales et Occidentales et autres lieux* (circa 1700)—a sequence of oblong etchings, minimally captioned, intended as a kind of visual summa of religious, political, and social practices of the non-European world—serve as a veritable catalogue of the exotic body: at work, at prayer, and, almost obsessively, at points of pain and torment. Bodies toil in mines and prostrate obscenely at royal courts; they writhe ecstatically in smoke and idol-filled temples; and they yield to the sharp knives and long nails of religious ascetics.[63] Above all, they submit to all manner of vicious "justice." In a print of miscellaneous "Asian Punishments," variously garbed officials—"Asians"—deploy large wooden pestles to stamp a collection of human heads in a barrel; in "Persian Tribunal," servants of the shah gouge out the

FIGURE 94. Romeyn de Hooghe, "Tribunal des Persans" (etching), in *Les Indes Orientales et Occidentales* (Leiden, ca. 1700). Koninklijke Bibliotheek, The Hague.

FIGURE 95. Romeyn de Hooghe, "Supplices des Asiatiques / Alle Asiatische Straffen" (etching), in *Les Indes Orientales et Occidentales* (Leiden, ca. 1700). Koninklijke Bibliotheek, The Hague.

eyes and flay the bodies of their distressed victims; and across scattered prints covering much of the non-European world, bodies are routinely impaled by stakes, pierced by hooks, suspended from buildings, dragged by horses, and staked onto crosses—crucified, in Christian terms—in every imaginable way.[64]

In what might count as the climax to this orgy of pain, one etching shows bodies that are made to suffer from the ingenious torments of "Turkish" slavery and incarceration. The baroque profusion of corporal misery represented in this remarkable print allows de Hooghe to register both the obscene methods of subjugation and the exotic body in its fullest range of somatic torment. A male figure (left foreground) with trussed ankles and bound wrists is shown in a dramatically foreshortened perspective, his mouth shaped in a silent howl to express the visible pain he endures as he is dragged off by a galloping horse. Another nude figure (center middleground), this time female, lies with one arm crooked above her head, the other arm limply stretched out, and a single knee halfway extended—the pose is almost Michelangelesque—as her lifeless body nourishes two dogs and a raven. Yet

FIGURE 96. Romeyn de Hooghe, "Esclavage et Prison chès les Turcs / Turkse Slaverny en Gevanknis" (etching), in *Les Indes Orientales et Occidentales* (Leiden, ca. 1700). Koninklijke Bibliotheek, The Hague.

another hapless victim is suspended from a tower, high above the mayhem, his torso and groin savagely pierced by a monstrous, six-hook contraption; his arms and legs contort in a fashion that simultaneously highlight his anguish and display his well-muscled body. Slightly lower in the composition, halfway toward the raven-pecked woman, a figure "lies" horizontally, staked by a high wooden pale, his stabbed chest arched upward toward the sky and his arms and legs crisscrossed in spectacular pain. There is a perversely violent beauty, de Hooghe's print seem to insinuate, to the brutal abuse of the non-European body.[65]

De Hooghe's aesthetic of exotic violence—and the descriptions of somatic cruelty visited upon the non-European body that were otherwise pervasive in the prints and texts of his day—had indubitably broad appeal. Several of de Hooghe's plates had previously appeared in publications by Simon de Vries, a composer of omnibus anthologies of "wonders"; and their success in these earlier volumes encouraged Pieter van der Aa, among the leading printers in the Netherlands, to acquire the plates for *Les Indes Orientales et Occidentales*. Van der Aa circulated the images widely: his vivid picture book generally required no translation, since the plates were only minimally captioned (in both French and Dutch), and *Les Indes*—undated on the title page—may have appeared in at least two editions, printed in the late seventeenth and early eighteenth centuries, respectively.[66] The prolific van der Aa also used the etchings for several other of his publications, a phenomenal record of print that reached its zenith in the sixty-six-tome pictorial tour de force *La galerie agreable du monde*. And the de Hooghe images were also appropriated (and pirated) by other printers for other picture-rich books—including, for example, Schouten's *Oost-Indische voyagie*.[67] In all of these cases—and in the numerous others where the exotic body featured so centrally and circulated so widely in print and text—the non-European world served as a locus of vivid and visible, sensational and spectacular violence: it was a much displayed and much viewed "spectacle." The exotic body in this period—again, from circa 1670 to 1730—is subjected by European authors, etchers, and printers to horrific abuse and cruel torment. It functions as an encyclopedic register for torture and pain, and it is routinely anatomized, in gory detail, for the European consumer of exotic geography. Why was this so?

Violence was hardly new to the European consumer or spectator. In both its exotic forms and its myriad homegrown varieties, violence regularly descended upon early modern Europe, in textual and visual media no less than in actual, tangible, physically devastating manifestations. The power of despotic princes had long piqued European interest—Egyptian pharaohs, Persian kings, and Greek tyrants all got their due in historical accounts—as did all manner of foreign customs perceived to entail "marvelous" bloodshed or "wondrous" carnage. Sati, to cite one of the most legendary examples, had intrigued European readers already for decades. Jan Huygen van Linschoten, a Dutch merchant-traveler of the late sixteenth century, furnished what may have been the iconic image of this rite: a putatively eyewitness account, described and illustrated in van Linschoten's much cited *Itinerario* of 1596 and regularly copied for decades to come.[68] Van Linschoten also reported on and provided graphic depictions of the power of the Chinese emperor and the control he exercised over his subjects' bodies (even if van Linschoten could not possibly have viewed such power himself), and these illustrations likewise circulated widely. Just a few years later, Theodor de Bry produced several engravings of Chinese techniques of torture—one shows a variation of caning, doled out by double executioners; another depicts hapless victims squashed and stretched in pain (figure 98); while a third, plainly adopted from van Linschoten, illustrates the harshly regimented nature of Chinese society—and de Bry's style of picture-heavy publication, with its emphasis on curious customs and exotic mores, may have served as a guiding influence on bookmakers working the better part of a century later.[69] Still more violent—and pervasive—were representations of Ottoman "cruelties," which proliferated after 1453 and more intensively in the 1520s. In the first

N. ursloird

Bramenes cum mortuus est, secundum eorum legem crematur. uxor
autem ejus, præ amore, ese vivam in ignem cum illo conjicit.

De Bramene doot wesende wort nae haer wet verbrant, en zyn
vrouwe wt liefde haers mans, verbrant haer levendich met hem.

Ioannes a Doetchum fecit

FIGURE 97. Johannes van Doetecum, "Bramenes cum mortuus est, secundum eorum legem crematur" (engraving), in Jan Huygen van Linschoten, *Itinerario, voyage ofte schipvaert van Ian Huygen van Linschoten naer Oost ofte Portugaels Indien* (Amsterdam, 1596). Koninklijke Bibliotheek, The Hague.

instance, this related to the obvious anxieties provoked by the fall of Constantinople and the shifting geopolitical balance of power in southeast Europe (and perhaps also the migration to western Europe of Greek humanists bearing an anti-Ottoman animus); while in the second instance, highly polemical depictions of bloodthirsty "Turks"—Ottoman soldiers shown with violently slaughtered Christian peasants and horribly skewered Christian babies—pertained to the imperial and religious struggles going on in the heart of Europe. Both the wars of religion sparked by the Reformation and the Habsburg imperial crises of the 1520s encouraged propagandists—especially German woodcut artists—to locate a common enemy in the Ottoman Turk, a useful diversion for the emperor Charles V from the nuisance of Protestant upstarts and Castilian *comuneros*.[70]

In fact, Europe had been positively awash in violence, real and descriptive, for the two centuries or so preceding the late seventeenth-century surge in production

FIGURE 98. Johannes van Doetecum, Manner of Chinese punishment (engraving), in Theodor de Bry, *Collectiones peregrinationum in Indiam Occidentalem et Indiam Orientalem* (Frankfurt am Main, 1598). Special Collections, University of Amsterdam (OF 63-745).

of "exotic" violence. These earlier images and texts, however, which date from the early sixteenth century and continue through the mid-seventeenth century, relate mostly to the exceedingly rancorous and distinctly internecine conflicts that wracked the Continent. Chief among these, of course, were the struggles over religion and faith, which collectively constituted what might be seen as a European civil war and which contributed to several of the preeminent national conflicts of the early modern period: the Dutch Revolt; the French Wars of Religion; and, above all, the ongoing military clashes in the German-speaking lands that commenced following the Augsburg Confession, carried on in the Schmalkaldic War, and culminated in the horrific brutalities of the Thirty Years' War. Broadsheets produced in the wake of the Protestant Reformation positively reveled in graphic and often gratuitously violent imagery. Visceral scenes of Hell, pornographic renditions of nuns,

scatological portraits of religious leaders: woodcuts and engravings from this polemical milieu often present masterpieces of visual propaganda, efforts to which
both sides of the conflict readily contributed. These largely German-made images, in
turn, served as models for the rival combatants of the French Wars of Religion, and
they also influenced the prolific polemicists of the Low Countries, Catholic no less
than Calvinist, who further refined the art of savaging the enemy with depictions of
the enemies' imagined savagery. Much of this production involved, as well, representations of violence, in visual no less than textual form; and the *non*-exotic body—of
the Dutch rebel, the French Calvinist, the German Lutheran, and their respective
antagonists—regularly appeared in hacked, hewed, hanged, pierced, stripped,
raped, burned, and disemboweled form. Europeans were everywhere in Europe tortured to points of extreme pain. Richard Verstegen's *Theatrum crudelitatum haereticorum nostri temporis* (1587) offers a catalogue of cruelties no less ferocious than
anything done a century later in products of exotic geography—or, for that matter,
than in any of the plentiful French Huguenot prints (and paintings) depicting the
Saint Bartholomew's Day Massacre (1572); the Dutch tracts recording Spanish/
Catholic cruelties in the Netherlands (which date from 1568 and which Verstegen

FIGURE 99. Adriaen Hubertus (?), "Horribles cruautez des Huguenots en France" (engraving), in Richard Verstegen, *Theatre des cruautez des hereticques de nostre temps* (Antwerp, 1588). Special Collections, University of Amsterdam (O 62-1655).

FIGURE 100. "Antwerpen" (engraving), in *Tweede deel van den Spiegel der Spaensche tyrannye gheschiet in Nederlandt* (Amsterdam, 1620). Special Collections, University of Amsterdam (O 61-5588 [2]).

consciously copied); or the etchings done by Jacques Callot showing the appalling "miseries," as his print series terms it, of the Thirty Years' War (1633).[71]

Much of this production centered on the printing presses of northwest Europe, with the Netherlands playing a particularly pivotal role from the mid- to late sixteenth century. First Antwerp and later Amsterdam ateliers adopted German Lutheran and French Huguenot images, which were soon superseded by homegrown inventions of graphic violence that, in turn, were themselves widely copied. This process intensified over the course of the Dutch Revolt (1567–1609), which segued into the Eighty Years' War (1568–1648), which spilled over into the Europe-wide Thirty Years' War (1618–1648). There was, as well, an "exotic" component to Dutch propaganda: the profusion of images depicting Habsburg "tyranny" in America, which culminated in the phenomenal printing of Bartolomé de las Casas's *Brevísima relación de la destrucción de las Indias*, a tract rendered by the Dutch as the

CHAPTER THREE

"Mirror of Spanish Tyranny in the West Indies" and often printed with a compendium volume, the "Mirror of Spanish Tyranny in the Netherlands." A popular version of this book bore engravings, and these portray the savagely tortured bodies of Native Americans, shown in all manners of pain; it appeared originally at the turn of the seventeenth century and for several decades following. Yet this form of propaganda died down by the middle decades of the seventeenth century and certainly after the signing of the Peace of Westphalia in 1648, which brought Europe's major religious wars (and the Dutch conflict with Spain) effectively to a close. There was another outburst of violence around 1672–1674—the Third Anglo-Dutch War and the invasion of the Netherlands by the armies of Louis XIV—when a young Romeyn de Hooghe was enlisted to etch several gruesome scenes of French "atrocities" in a work known as the "Mirror of French Tyranny" (circa 1674): bodies, once again, were graphically impaled, cleaved, chopped, burned, and shockingly violated.[72] Yet this proved to be only a brief interlude in what became a period of relative peace for both the Netherlands and its corner of northwest Europe (even while Louis XIV's martial ways persisted).

All of these images, it should be emphasized, delineated intra-European pain and bloodshed; the bodies mutilated belonged overwhelmingly to indigenous (as it were) European subjects. Even the work of Las Casas—as assiduously recalibrated and printed by ateliers in the Netherlands—centered on European rivalries and efforts of Dutch polemicists to blacken the reputation of their Habsburg rivals. American Indians stood in for Dutch rebels, and the joint depiction of the two groups in mutually reflecting "mirrors"—each "nation" presented with nearly identical, mostly nondescript, and all but interchangeable bodies—makes this conflation clear.[73] More to the point, the Dutch appropriation of Native American bodies for their revolt against Habsburg Spain vividly demonstrates the strategic formulation of geography for the impassioned, intraconfessional antagonisms of the day, in this case recasting Calvinists and Catholics in the guise of Indians and conquistadors. Reformed though they may have been, the Dutch rebels knew well enough to invoke traditional images of Christian suffering for their cause—as did Lutherans, Huguenots, and Catholics before them, and indeed Las Casas in his original tract.[74] More generally, the depictions of mutilated European bodies in these earlier sources derive overwhelmingly from the religious hostilities of the day: the fratricidal, intracontinental, cross-confessional bloodshed of the sixteenth and first half of the seventeenth centuries. Yet as the religious and imperial enmities of this era dissipated, European violence did as well, at least in its descriptive forms: it shifted to the non-European world. Depictions of violence, in other words, were displaced to the exotic world—mostly to non-European bodies, and all but exclusively to non-European perpetrators of dreadful "cruelties" and "tyrannies." The new visual and textual production of violence reflected the new cross-confessional (if not quite postconfessional) attitudes of those whom geography texts increasingly referred to as "Europeans." The architects of these sources—the authors, engravers, and printers of exotic geography—were less inclined to cast aspersions on *European* perpetrators of violence (who certainly continued to flourish) than on exotic entities, above all the imperious, despotic, and often "Oriental" potentates of the exotic world. By the late seventeenth century, in short, there was a shift in interest in violence and an alteration of its mimetic purpose.

The Renovation of Violence and the Exotic Body

The new exotic violence flourished in Dutch ateliers, where it developed its most influential form. The contrast of these new forms of descriptive bodily pain, moreover, with both the older and contemporary (non-Dutch) varieties could be stark. Compare, once again, the nearly contemporary accounts of Japan from the Jesuit Cornelius Hazart, who narrated the saga of Catholic missionaries to Japan in the context of his broader global history of Christian faith, and from Arnoldus Montanus, the titular author of a characteristically capacious and amply illustrated volume of geography-cum-history that rolled off the presses of the van Meurs atelier in 1669. As a rule, the Jesuits reported avidly and fairly regularly on their far-flung travels, especially to Asia and even more so to the Far East, where Francis Xavier arrived in the mid-sixteenth century, reaching Japan in 1549 and establishing one of the earliest European beachheads in the region. Yet their reports tended not to be published and, even when they were, tended not to carry the same impressive level of illustration as comparable Dutch-made volumes.[75] Jesuit accounts, in addition, were presented in starkly confessional terms: they reported the successes and sufferings of Catholic missionaries overseas, and they offered their narratives as testimony of the Roman Catholic Church's tribulations in these challenging times. They advocated for the Jesuit cause. Hazart, a pugnacious polemicist for the Catholic squad in the scrum of the Reformation, certainly stayed true to form in his *Kerckelycke historie van de gheheele wereldt* (Ecclesiastical history of the whole world, 1667–1671). He directed his report "especially" to the martyrdoms and "other brave deeds" of his brethren in faith, and his volume's illustrations (executed by the Antwerp printer Michiel Cnobbaert) highlight the "sacred" and "pious" agonies of European Catholics (chiefly Jesuits, yet also mendicant friars), who undertook godly labors in distant lands. Hazart penned a narrative *apologia* of the Jesuit project in Japan; he celebrated the glorious gains and lamentable setbacks of the Roman Church in its expanded theater of operations.[76]

Montanus, by contrast, historicized the Japanese martyrdoms, generalized the Christian suffering, and globalized the exotic "tortures" that he so keenly delineated. In fact, his dark tales of "persecutions" of "[those] of the Christian religion"—note the broadly defined subject of *Christian* persecutions rather than *Catholic* martyrdoms—are remarkable simply for what they are not: an opening for a Dutch-Calvinist author to criticize his Jesuit antagonists for their missionary missteps and to revel in Protestant *Schadenfreude* over Catholic misfortunes abroad. To Montanus, conversely, the saga of Christian faith in Japan afforded an opportunity to narrate "wonders"—"horrible cruelties" and "inhuman tortures" suffered in an exotic setting—and the attraction of the persecution vignettes rested more in the gothic pain endured by its victims than in the sacred narrative they embodied. Rather than underscore the unfortunate fate of the Jesuit missionaries—men sent from Rome, Antwerp, Madrid, and other capitals of the Counter-Reformation—Montanus describes, in macabre detail, the stunning violence committed against "wives and children," and the marvelous "martyrdoms" of so many common "Christians." For while the author does on occasion invoke the category of "Roman Christians" and even identifies certain Jesuits by name, he speaks more often of generic "Christians" or victims of "faith," categories long familiar to European readers of all stripes from the cross-confessional tradition of Christian martyrology.[77]

Mostly, though, Montanus records the exotic violence devised by the inventive tormentors of early modern Japan. The pain is sensational and invariably somatic. "Their bodies," Montanus writes in his description of the "horrible cruelties" and "endless tortures" meted out to, in this case, a group of Japanese-born Christians, "[were] wash'd with scalding Water, stigmatiz'd with red hot Irons, beaten with sharp Canes or Reeds, at Noon-day set naked in the Sun, at Night in the Cold, and also in Tubs full of Serpents. . . . These kind of Afflictions some endur'd thirty, forty, nay sixty days, before they would Apostatize."[78] Montanus also describes the fate of those "miserable wretches at Singok," who suffered the scalding waters of a sulfurous pool that "eats through Skin and Flesh, to the Bones."[79] And he goes into grisly detail narrating a notorious form of upside-down hanging, whereby the victim would be suspended

> by their Legs on a Gallows, with their Heads down in a Well, over which a Gibbet was plac'd, and at the end thereof, a Block was made fast, through which a Rope was drawn, and they ty'd to the Legs of the sufferer, who being thus ty'd, was let down with his Head into the Well, so low, that his Feet appear'd just on the top thereof; In the Heads of those that hung [*sic*], several Wounds were cut crosswise, to the end [that] the bloud might by degrees drop out, and not overwhelm their hearts; some liv'd five, six, any more days, before they gave up the ghost.[80]

An illustration of this baroquely sadistic mode of punishment, along with several others depicted in similarly voyeuristic detail, crowd a van Meurs–atelier engrav-

FIGURE 101. Jacob van Meurs (atelier), "'t Ziedende water van Singock" (engraving), in Arnoldus Montanus, *Gedenkwaerdige gesantschappen der Oost-Indische Maetschappy in 't Vereenigde Nederland, aen de Kaisaren van Japan* (Amsterdam, 1669). Special Collections, University of Amsterdam (OM 63-363).

ing, which is intended broadly to catalogue the horrific experience of Japanese torture (as did the nearly contemporaneous etching of Ottoman torture by de Hooghe). Ultimately, though, the van Meurs–Montanus depiction of Japanese persecution presents a more markedly clinical than confessional approach to pain: it is strikingly *post*confessional, even apolitical (within its European context), in its attention to technique rather than victim. Whereas Hazart focused on sacred narratives of Catholic martyrdom, Montanus produced a desacralized portrait of exotic violence, in which the abused bodies of the victims, rather than the Church's missionary history, took center stage.[81]

In other revisions of Jesuit accounts—for van Meurs and Montanus had to rely on bona fide reports, typically from Jesuit authors, to compile their works of geography—similar redeployments take place, whereby a more plainly interested narrative of martyrdom or imperial punishment becomes reformulated and converted in a Dutch-made account to demonstrate postconfessional violence. The resulting "exotic" rendition not only stripped the violence of its original and often religious (in the case of Jesuit narratives) meaning, but also had the effect of transforming horrible torture into lurid spectacle. Jesuit accounts of China offer another case in point. The many reports filed by Jesuit voyagers to the Far East in the late sixteenth and seventeenth centuries normally passed into the central offices of the order unpublished. They contributed to the Society's knowledge of global religion (and politics) and to their strategy for expansion—yet not necessarily to the common European pool of geographic knowledge. Even when letters were printed in a streamlined form, they were not ordinarily made into consumer-oriented volumes of geography. What publications there were, moreover, bore fewer engravings than Dutch-made products, and these images only infrequently illustrated scenes of torture and the like.[82] When Jesuit texts do turn to the topic of corporal violence, they emphasize the in-the-line-of-duty suffering of their members or, in cases of Chinese judicial punishment, the rank and standing of the victim—a distinction of great importance to the Jesuit project of evangelization, which entailed gaining access to Chinese elites. (And the most successful Jesuit missionary to China in the seventeenth century, Johann Adam Schall von Bell—a persistent thorn in the side of Dutch commercial endeavors—did achieve the rank of mandarin.) Dutch narratives, by contrast, even when reliant on Jesuit sources, pay closer attention to the *techniques* of torture, which are meant to highlight the mores of the Chinese. The subject's status was less relevant than his (and sometimes her) sensational pain.

The van Meurs–Dapper account of China offers, once again, an instructive comparative example. Dapper's descriptions of Chinese corporal punishment and "torture"—he uses that term bluntly—pay less attention to those on the receiving end of the rod than the rod itself: "Canes are seven Foot long, below a handful thick, but broad and smooth on the top, that they may hold them the better."[83] Dapper also details how and how often these canes reach their victims' bare flesh and the considerable pain (or even death) that ensues. Caning features, as well, in two van Meurs–atelier engravings, both of which derive from original sketches by the Spanish Jesuit Adriano de las Cortes, whose manuscript, typically, never circulated in print (see plate 10 and figures 173 and 174). Yet while de las Cortes offers a simplified drawing that stresses the mandarin status of the victim—the all-important tunic with rank badge and the hat with *wushamao* (the oval-shaped side flaps) jointly occupy the center of the composition—van Meurs provides enough added detail that these vestments of rank recede into the background. In one print, which shows a tormented figure bound (vertically) against a wall, a hat lies on an unobtrusive bench hidden in shadows; while in the other print, which features a tortured victim sprawled (horizontally) in an open courtyard, the hat is barely discernible just below the executioner's rod. Far more prominent in both compositions are the dynamic executioners, who wield their thick cudgels with obvious bravura, and the numerous spectators—an addition derived entirely from van Meurs's imagination—who occupy two well-placed windows: front and center in one engraving, which includes an onlooker leaning over the window frame and into the scene of torture; and, in the other engraving, on the upper floor of a set-back structure, from which two figures peer out onto the action below. In both cases, these "framed" witnesses observe the processes of punishment and thereby render acts of torture into open theater: exotic violence becomes public spectacle.

Such cases—and there are many more—might be considered *revised* violence: prior traditions of representing violence are adapted or reformulated for alternative, yet recognizably cognate, purposes. These images may fall under similar rubrics (corporal punishment, for example, or religious martyrdom), yet they are relocated to exceptional locales—old (European) wine in new (exotic) bottles. In other instances, however, revisions are more strenuous and projections of violence by the printer or engraver or narrator are more emphatic and appalling. Narratives or depictions of violence, in these cases, even if inherited and refashioned from older and established forms, may develop into something altogether different and more distressing than the originals—so much so that they indicate a wholly new type of descriptive violence. This is the case with what may be the most disturbing motif in sources of exotic geography: images of exotic rape.

Descriptions of rape, exotic or otherwise, were scarcely fresh fare in European art and literature. Rape featured centrally in several of the foundational myths of Europeans: the rape of Europa, the rape of the Sabine women, the rape of Lucretia (the first two of which entailed something closer to involuntary abduction than outright sexual violation).[84] And these ancient myths and motifs experienced a revival of sorts among Renaissance artists and authors—famously in canvases by Titian, Nicolas Poussin, and Rembrandt, also in poetry and drama by Poliziano, Shakespeare, and John Heywood. Rape had also earned a place in classical geography, particularly in the histories of Herodotus, who, in a much-cited passage, contrasted European and Asian regard for women's honor and their forcible abduction: "We of Asia regarded the rape of our women not at all," he quotes the Persians broadly declaiming, "but the Greeks, all for the sake of a Lacedaemonian woman [Helen of Sparta, later of Troy], mustered a great host, came to Asia, and destroyed the power of Priam."[85] Rape reared its dreadful head, as well, in early modern depictions of war, in both visual and textual sources, and this goes especially—once again, as with other representations of violence—for images related to Europe's ongoing struggles over religion. It served as a much-invoked theme in the annals of the French Wars of Religion and, perhaps even more so, in the chronicles and prints describing the Dutch Revolt. Particularly in the first half of the seventeenth century, anti-Habsburg materials produced in the Netherlands made rape a central aspect of their polemical attacks. Rape resonates in Dutch sources almost rhythmically according to the pulse of the war. Vignettes of sexual violence—perpetrated by "tyrannical" Spanish troops upon "innocent" Dutch women and girls—appear in the wake of the Dutch Revolt and then fill the pages of rebel pamphlets and prints in the period leading up to and following the Twelve Year Truce (1609–1621), when such stories served the dual purpose of vilifying the enemy and unifying the new, as yet fragmented, Dutch Republic. Rape also featured, literally and metaphorically, in several works of literature penned in the lead-up to the war's final resolution (1648), when "patriotic scripture," once again, was pressed into action—for example, in P. C. Hooft's *Geeraerdt van Velzen* (1619) and Joost van de Vondel's *Gijsbrecht van Amstel* (1637), the latter roughly retelling Roman foundational stories in the context of Holland. Images of rape resurfaced in the early 1670s, too, when the double threat of English naval attacks and French military invasions, once more, prompted rhetorical counterfire. This occasioned Romeyn de Hooghe's highly explicit etchings of French atrocities, which illustrate, vividly and frontally, crude episodes of sexual violation.[86]

Rape, in other words, was highly visible in certain forms of European art and literature, much of it pertaining to intra-European conflict. This shifts subtly, however, in the final decades of the seventeenth century, a strategic reorientation made vivid in what may count as the dramatic culmination of these images of rape, as well as the motif's all-but-last gasp in the polemical context of northern European and specifically Dutch politics, a work of theater that situated rape, as it happens, in the exotic world: John Dryden's *Amboyna*. Written and produced for the London stage in 1673, *Amboyna* was an explosive and pointedly topical play. It dramatized controversial events from 1623—it revived, in this sense, half-century-old propaganda—in the context of ongoing Anglo-Dutch competition over colonial trade, particularly in the Maluku Islands. On the tropical island of Ambon—or at least Dryden's dramatic rendition of it—the Dutch had tortured and executed their English rivals under false charges of treason, with the aim of gaining the upper hand in the spice trade. These putative crimes and punishments had originally sparked intense controversy—fifty years prior, a fierce debate had taken place, also in print—yet in the throes of the Third Anglo-Dutch war, Dryden's play assumes an unequivocally British perspective. It impugns England's commercial rival, and it revels in the ungodly violence committed against "innocent" Englishmen by the "cruel" Dutch (a sharp shift of identity for the traditionally underdog

Republic). Plot devices are meant to follow historical incidents—competition over the spice trade and colonial governance—yet the play quickly devolves into baroque melodrama, which Dryden serves up with heaping measures of hot, steaming violence. English victims suffer exquisite torment from the Dutch, most spectacularly from a procedure whereby water is poured on and around the victim's head to induce the sensation of suffocating—waterboarding in the vocabulary of modern torture. All of this takes place, moreover, following a climactic incident of rape: by a spiteful Dutch character against a woman of the island, who had recently been wed to the incoming English factor. Although "exotic" in its staging, the rape is European in its execution; it is perpetrated by a European (the covetous son of the Dutch governor, Harman Junior) against a Europeanized "native" (Ysabinda), who stands in for and brings out the gallantry of an English gentleman (Gabriel Towerson). The drama depicts *intra-European* violence, if partly by proxy and in an exotic setting. Indeed, the brutal massacre that ensues—carried out, once again, by the Dutch—claims mostly European lives (English and Portuguese), with the native Ambonese serving mostly as theatrical props.[87]

Nevertheless, Dryden's depiction of Dutch-perpetrated rape (and otherwise of vicious intra-European violence) appeared on the London stage simultaneously with several other images of rape that were unambiguously exotic. Many of these were channeled by the London impresario and Royal Geographer John Ogilby, delivered to his audiences via the translations that began to appear under Ogilby's name of the several volumes of geography published by Jacob van Meurs. And in these cases—in descriptions of sexual violence in Japan and America by Montanus, in Persia and China by Dapper, and so on—victims and perpetrators were entirely and explicitly exotic. Dapper himself had translated Herodotus just a few years earlier (1665) and was certainly conversant with the stereotypes of Asian sexuality, and Montanus had included depictions of rape (and of female bestiality) already in his Japan book of 1669. Van Meurs and Johannes van Someren would soon publish (and graphically illustrate) scenes of Georgian, Russian, and Persian rape in their editions of Struys's *Reysen* (1676), and rape would loom ominously in numerous other volumes of geography produced and widely translated in these years. In almost all of these cases, rape occurred *outside* of Europe, and its victims and perpetrators had an exotic provenance—or worse. For there also emerges from this literature a new and far more disquieting form of sexual violation, with racialist implications: the sexual violation of exotic women by lascivious simians, or what Montanus somewhat loosely characterized (in his *Japan*) as "ape" rape. This was a whole new order of exotic violence.

The "lecherous" attacks by simians of various breeds against women of various lands mark a novel motif in the representation of the exotic body. It blends a crude mode of "wild" violence and a bizarre insinuation of sexual interbreeding to create a wholly repugnant formulation, which would endure for years to come and greatly influence the European colonial imagination.[88] To locate a precise source for the motif may be less vital than to identify a decisive moment of proliferation, which lies in the intense decade of geographic production that took off with the publication of Nieuhof's China book. In that volume, readers learn of the "bestial lust" of certain monkeys who prey upon the mountain-dwelling women of China:

> In the Province of *Suchu* lyes a Mountain called *Toyung*, upon which are Monkies or Baboons, which for bigness and shape are very like a man. These Creatures are more than ordinarily addicted to Venery, so that they often attempt to surprise Women on purpose to satisfie their bestial lust, and have their wills on them. The *Indians* call them *Wild Men*, and the *Indian* Women are in such fear of them, that they dare not come near those Woods where they frequent.[89]

A remarkably similar passage appeared a few years later in Dapper's volume on China, where a slightly modified emphasis clarifies that the women are (in the Restoration translation of Ogilby) "ravished": "In the Country *Cungkingfu* in the Province of *Suchuen*, on the Mountain *Tayung*, are Baboons, which in bigness and shape are very like a Man, and so furiously lustful after Women, that oftentimes surprising them in the Way, they Ravish them."[90] And in Montanus's digressive account of Japan (published within months of Dapper's China book), the scene has shifted to Borneo, where "courtship" comes into play and the suggestion of reciprocal participation by those exotic women in question: "The Baboons in the Island *Borneo* dare encounter with Armed men, and will set upon Women; and if by their kindness and courtship they cannot vitiate, they will force them."[91] The motif finally reaches Africa a few years later—also by way of the van Meurs atelier, which might be the chief engine of its dispersal—in the *Reysen* of Jan Struys. On the island of Madagascar, the author observes: "There are besides these [simians] another kind of white Apes [*sic*], that go almost right over end, and are so lecherous that even the Women in that place, cannot be secure for [i.e., from] them, which they ravish if they find an opportunity, one holding her, till another has perform'd his Task."[92] Once again, the non-European body must endure vulgar and violent abuse, yet the none-too-subtle nuances of this particular accounting—conspicuously "white" apes, who operate vaguely anthropomorphically—impart a distinctly racialist innuendo to the developing narrative of the exotic world.[93]

These proliferating reports of the sexual violation of exotic women by unruly simians—incidents of "ape rape," both loosely implied and explicitly described, first in textual accounts and later in engraved images (figure 103)—make two separate, though hardly exclusive, points. One relates to the awful brutality, sexual vio-

FIGURE 102. Jacob van Meurs (atelier), Courting apes (engraving), in Arnoldus Montanus, *Gedenkwaerdige gesantschappen der Oost-Indische Maetschappy in 't Vereenigde Nederland, aen de Kaisaren van Japan* (Amsterdam, 1669). Special Collections, University of Amsterdam (OM 63-363).

lation, and sheer pain that the exotic body must endure in sources of the later seventeenth century and beyond: violence is ever more "exotic." The second pertains to the non-European body itself, which, as configured in these many vignettes of violence, has seemingly bifurcated from the European body. The exotic body not only acts and looks different; it also feels sensations and experiences pain differently. It is physically and somatically distinct; it is, implicitly, a "race" apart.

Race, of course, has a history. Yet it is precisely at this moment in that ongoing history when one of the most critical touchstones in the discourse of race appeared in print: François Bernier's *Nouvelle division de la Terre, par les différentes Espèces ou Races d'hommes qui l'habitent* (1684).[94] A veteran traveler to the courts of the Levant and South Asia—and, just as crucially, to the salons of northern Europe—Bernier (1625–1688) counts among the first authors to use in print the term "race" in its modern sense and to classify humans based primarily on bodily difference. Although he personally journeyed only as far as Bengal—he never quite saw all of

FIGURE 103. Johann-Eberhard Ihle after John Chapman, "The Orang-Outang Carrying off a Negro Girl" (1795), hand-colored engraving. Wellcome Library, London.

the "species" that he categorized—he posited the existence of "four or five Species or Races of men so notably differing from each other that this may serve as the just foundation of a new division of the world."[95] Bernier gave the "physico-biological notion of race foundationalist status" by conceiving human distinction "exclusively based on *physical* criteria": based on the body.[96] His efforts reflect a well-established impulse among early modern savants to sort things—a taxonomic instinct expressed particularly in natural history and, to a lesser degree, in geography. Yet Bernier also innovated. His approach differed from the typical "bricolage" (as Stephen Greenblatt terms it) of sixteenth- and earlier seventeenth-century ethnography, and the categories he proposed were more insistently somatic and physically observable than the culturally attuned rubrics invoked in the past.[97] They coincided with comments and currents of contemporary geography. Thus, where Ogilby (in his translation of Nieuhof on predatory monkeys) might conflate ethnic Chinese with generic "Indians"—and affiliate the entire lot with the medieval species known as "wild men"—Nieuhof could refer to the "brown" races of the world (identified in India), and Kaempfer could invoke the "black" nations of Asia: "The Kingdom of *Siam* is the most powerful, and its Court the most magnificent among all the black Nations of Asia."[98] They all, in short, observed bodies per color and racial type.

They all, moreover, perceived in bodily hues and somatic differences something akin to cultural distinctions and racial divisions: different colors bespoke different cultures and, more broadly, different bodily qualities. Color was a surface, or topical, indicator—it was sometimes observed disinterestedly, although more often not. While the English translator of Jean-Frédéric Bernard's *Ceremonies et coutumes religieuses des tous les peuples du monde* (1723–1743)—that much-heralded "objective," "authentic," and "enlightened" tableau of global religion—initially pronounced, somewhat subversively, the bodies of all men to be equal (even while their "Intellects and Dispositions, their religious and civil Institutions," could come in copious varieties), he later highlighted precisely the racialist differences among mankind, defined in terms of corporal complexion: "The *Negroe* Idolaters are involved in an Obscurity much darker than their own Complexion."[99] The darkness of the body, in this particular discussion of sub-Saharan Africa, indicated the dimness of the soul and its incapacity for godliness. And just as a capacity for godliness might vary among the spectrum of global bodies (and souls), so too might other capacities—for pain, for example. The non-European body, in this conception of it, was dissimilarly constituted from the European body and unevenly capable, albeit in multifaceted ways. The darkness of Aphra Behn's heroic prince-turned-slave Oroonoko—he of "perfect ebony, or polished jet" skin—is not only pivotal to the protagonist's noble character; it is also central to his otherworldly capacity for bodily torment: in the first instance, in the ritual scarification of his black body, an aesthetic marking of his princely status; in the second instance, in his capacity to endure horrific somatic pain, notably the physical torture that comes at the end of the novel.[100]

Outside of Europe, bodies functioned and performed differently, and more often than not, they endured pain. Pain was veritably pervasive. Even in the most basic forms of geography, physical anguish could be ubiquitous in the exotic world—as (to take a relatively mild example) in the decorative cartouches of maps,

PLATE 1. *Interior of a Shop Dealing in Asian Goods* (Holland, 1680–1700); gouache on paper, mounted onto a wooden panel (originally a fan); 26.3 × 43.6 cm. © Victoria and Albert Museum, London.

PLATE 2. Cornelis de Bruijn, "Pyramides" (engraving, printed in color and further colored by hand), in *Voyage au Levant* (Delft, 1700). Special Collections, University of Amsterdam (OF 06-275).

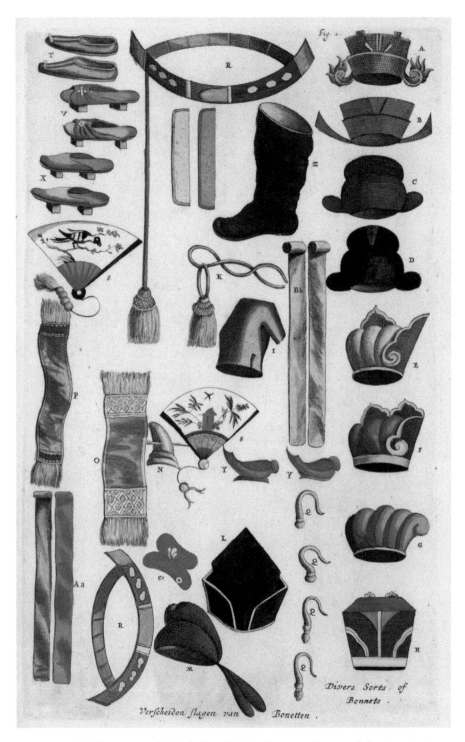

PLATE 3. Jacob van Meurs (atelier), "Verscheiden slagen van Bonetten" (hand-colored engraving), in Olfert Dapper, *Gedenkwaerdig bedryf der Nederlandsche Oost-Indische Maetschappye, op de kuste en in het keizerrijk van Taising of Sina* (Amsterdam, 1670). Special Collections, University of Amsterdam (OM 63-124).

114. Raven Bek.

115. Formosa.

116. Douwing Royal.

117. Brocade.

118. Mauritius Oud Wyf.

X.

PLATE 4. After Samuel Fallours (?), "Raven Bek, Formosa, Douwing Royal, Brocade, Mauritius Oud Wyf" (hand-colored engraving), in Louis Renard, *Poissons, ecrevisses et crabes* (Amsterdam, 1718). Special Collections, University of Amsterdam (OF 80-41).

PLATE 5. "Bala" (engraving), in Hendrik Reede tot Drakenstein, *Hortus Indicus Malabaricus* (Amsterdam, 1678–1679). Special Collections, University of Amsterdam (483 A 1-12).

PLATE 6. "Tab. LXII [Pythons, ibis, shama]" (hand-colored engraving), in Albertus Seba, *Locupletissimi rerum naturalium thesauri accurata descriptio* (Amsterdam, 1734–1735). Special Collections, University of Amsterdam (OL 63-1941).

PLATE 7. "Het Amboinsche Cruijdeboek," frontispiece to Georgius Everhardus Rumphius, *Het tweede boek van het Amboinsche Cruijdeboek* (1690 manuscript); pen and wash; 43 × 28.5 cm. Leiden University Library (ms. BPL 1924: 2, fol. 1r).

PLATE 8. Dirk Valkenburg, *"Slave Play" on a Sugar Plantation in Surinam* (1706–1708); oil on canvas; 58 × 46.5 cm. National Gallery of Denmark, Copenhagen © SMK Photo.

PLATE 9. Albert Eckhout, *African Woman and Child* (1641); oil on canvas; 282 × 189 cm. © The National Museum of Denmark, Ethnographic Collection.

PLATE 10. Jacob van Meurs (atelier), Caning in interior (hand-colored engraving), in Olfert Dapper, *Gedenckwaerdig bedryf der Nederlandsche Oost-Indische Maetschappye* (Amsterdam, 1670). Special Collections, University of Amsterdam (OM 63-124).

PLATE 11. Nicolaes Visscher, *Novissima et Accuratissima Totius Americae Descriptio*; hand-colored engraving. Special Collections, University of Amsterdam (33.22.40).

PLATE 12. Jan van Kessel, *Africque* (central panel showing "Temple des Idoles") (1664–1666); oil on copper; 48.5 × 67.5 cm. Alte Pinakothek, Bayerische Staatsgemäldesammlungen. © Blauel/Gnamm, Artothek.

PLATE 13. Jan van Kessel, *Americque* (central panel showing "Paraiba en Brasil") (1664–1666); oil on copper; 48.6 × 67.9 cm. bpk, Berlin. Alte Pinakothek, Bayerische Staatsgemäldesammlungen/Art Resource, NY.

PLATE 14. Jan van Kessel, *Asie* (central panel showing "Jerusalem") (1664–1666); oil on copper; 48.5 × 67.5 cm. Alte Pinakothek, Bayerische Staatsgemäldesammlungen. © Blauel/Gnamm, Artothek.

PLATE 15. Jan van Kessel, *Europe* (central panel showing "Rome") (1664–1666); oil on copper; 48.4 × 67.1 cm. bpk, Berlin. Alte Pinakothek, Bayerische Staatsgemäldesammlungen/Art Resource, NY.

PLATE 16. Willem Kalf, *Still Life with a Chinese Bowl, a Nautilus Cup, and Other Objects* (1662); oil on canvas; 79.4 × 67.3 cm. Museo Thyssen-Bornemisza, Madrid, Scala/Art Resource, NY.

PLATE 17. *Turbo marmoratus* (East Indian turbo shell) decorated with fauna (ca. 1650–1699); carved, engraved, and painted. Amsterdam Museum.

PLATE 18. Johann Friedrich Eberlein (with Peter Reinicke) after Johann Joachim Kändler (Meissen Manufactory), Table centerpiece (*Allegorical Figure of America*) (ca. 1750); hard-paste porcelain painted with enamel colors and gilt; 27 cm (height) × 30 cm (length) × 17 cm (width). Wadsworth Atheneum Museum of Art / Art Resource, NY.

PLATE 19. Jacob van Meurs, frontispiece (hand-colored engraving) to Johan Nieuhof, *Het gezantschap der Neêrlandtsche Oost-Indische Compagnie* (Amsterdam, 1665). Special Collections, University of Amsterdam (OM 63-116).

PLATE 20. Beauvais Tapestry Manufactory after designs by Guy-Louis Vernansal, *The Emperor on a Journey* (ca. 1690–1705); tapestry of wool and silk; 254 × 415 cm. Getty Research Institute, Los Angeles (83.DD.339).

Above left PLATE 21. Drug pot (ca. 1700); Japanese porcelain overdecorated in Delft; 22.8 cm (height) × 18.5 cm (diameter of mouth rim). Collection Groninger Museum. Photo: Marten de Leeuw.

Above right PLATE 22. Drug pot (ca. 1700); Japanese porcelain overdecorated in Delft; 18.5 cm (height) × 16.3 cm (diameter of mouth rim). Collection Groninger Museum. Photo: Marten de Leeuw.

Below PLATE 23. Tea saucer and bowl, Meissen Manufactory (ca. 1725); decorated by Lauche; hard-paste porcelain painted with enamel and gold. © The Trustees of the British Museum.

PLATE 24. Wall panel with scenes of corporal punishment (ca. 1700) (detail); silk backed with linen, gilded silver thread, and metallic thread; 328 cm (height per panel) × 96 cm (width per panel). Courtesy of Bayerische Verwaltung der staatlichen Schlösser, Gärten und Seen.

FIGURE 104. Johannes van Keulen, *Nieuwe Pascaert van Oost Indien* (ca. 1680–1689) (detail); engraving. Special Collections, University of Amsterdam (OL 63-1579).

which not infrequently display vignettes of torture to allegorize exotic spaces. In Johannes van Keulen's *Nieuwe Pascaert van Oost Indien*, a maritime chart that delineated the entire sweep of the Indian Ocean and its adjacent lands, the upper cartouche shows a scene of gruesome violence: the bloody decapitation of a prisoner, as witnessed by a turban-wearing, parasol-shaded overseer. Tableaux of corporal violence function here as visual shorthand, a pictorial device to demonstrate the social and political qualities that define the East. Another van Keulen product, this time depicting the eastern Mediterranean, illustrates a mostly nude male figure on one knee, entreating an Ottoman pasha for his life (figure 105). Between this Oriental potentate and his desperate supplicants—a queue of victims that includes a woman, two children, and two stripped-down male bodies—lie the tools of torture (whip, rod, shackle) that implicitly will be applied to the exotic body.[101] Such intimations of violence are wholly absent from cartouches that belong to maps of European lands, which typically express social organization and political hierarchy in the form of heraldry, weaponry, and royal emblems. The exotic world is depicted otherwise. It stages a cast of characters who endure otherworldly violence; it offers bodies that are practically primed for pain.[102]

In these several variations and representations, in the myriad texts and images that describe exotic violence, the non-European body suffers a type of physical ordeal that has been mostly expunged from Western Europe. This denoted a fundamental shift in the geography of violence—as occurred, simultaneously, to Europe's geog-

FIGURE 105. Johannes van Keulen, *Paskaerte vande archipel en de eylanden daer omtrent gelegen* (detail); engraving. Special Collections, University of Amsterdam (OL 63-1576).

raphy of "perversion"—whereby somatic abuse, in its descriptive form, had been transferred elsewhere, banished from the boundaries of Europe. Violence had been exoticized (not to mention eroticized). This reflected also a critical shift in the epistemology of pain, which now served different ends and possessed correlatively different meanings for Europeans. By the late seventeenth century, pain and suffering had been largely *desacralized*, a realignment that corresponded to the declining religious warfare among European factions.[103] In Europe's postconfessional world—not in actual fact, perhaps, as religious antagonisms certainly persisted, but in state-posited theory, as sovereign powers legislated cross-confessional settlements—it made little sense to advertise and valorize intra-European violence. This shift in purpose, in turn, effected a shift in the space of violence. Pain and torture moved outside of Europe, accordingly, and were displaced to the non-European body— thus, exotic violence. Violence and physical torment, furthermore, not only afflicted the non-European world; they were also understood to flourish there, as if

CHAPTER THREE

somehow innately suited to the exotic body. The cruel treatment of the non-European body and its numerous experiences of somatic suffering served to delineate exotic "species" and to set apart European bodies—increasingly free of such torturous pain—from non-European ones.[104] In a sense, a "sacramental" understanding of bodily pain yielded to a "racialist" one: the body suffered less and less for religious reasons and more and more for racial ones.[105]

This shift took place rhetorically and incrementally. It is true that, in some accounts of European travel and in certain descriptions of the exotic world, pain was still inflicted upon European bodies and suffering continued to carry a thinly veiled religious message. In Jan Struys's gruesome tales of Central Asia, violence not only maimed European bodies—Struys's much mangled figure, vividly portrayed on the frontispiece in assorted Christ-like poses; the "Polish" woman's horribly abused corpse, flayed and crucified like Saint Bartholomew—but also conveyed a message of Christian suffering and martyrdom.[106] Struys's popular book provided readers with a narrative of Christian endurance and spiritual redemption; it conformed to a long tradition in European literature, which was not so easily discarded. More broadly, however, brutalities visited progressively more non-European bodies than European ones and, by the late seventeenth century, in ever more extravagant ways. Or, rather, they did so in ways remarkably similar to the ingenious techniques of punishment and horrific corporal violence depicted in the polemics of the Reformation and the internecine religious wars of the prior century—which were now, however, increasingly rare. For while the specter of violence was no longer welcome in Europe, it was readily witnessed abroad; and while "confessional" violence made less and less sense in a European context, "colonial" violence, visited upon racially marked non-European bodies, became, by contrast, more and more useful. As Talal Asad has observed, the "inhuman" treatment and "torture" of non-Europeans—the latter considered to be victims of "Oriental despotism" and cruel "tyranny"—usefully justified European interventions in the colonial world.[107] Violence, in other words, found new bodies and new uses abroad.

A final point about the emergent motif of exotic violence: whether suffered by Europeans (as in Struys) or by non-Europeans (as in scores of other texts, prints, maps, and so on), the dreadful violence that violated bodies in the expanding exotic world was consistently presented to the European reader and viewer of these materials as "spectacle." Violence was something both to marvel at and to *observe*. And no matter who ended up suffering the abuse, the violence was invariably meted out by non-European tormentors, who, as described in sources of geography, staged full-out theaters of cruelty. The scenes of brutality so vividly engraved in the Struys volume—reflected in special "mirrors" and advertised on macabre human hides—call attention to the role of viewing the bodily abuses described within; the reader is not merely an incidental voyeur but an active, lingering witness. The engravings of torture that accompany Nieuhof's and Dapper's descriptions of China make excruciatingly visible the pain suffered by the victims of imperial justice. Van Meurs's atelier emphasized the act of *seeing* torture by enhancing their engraved scenes with witnesses and casual bystanders; by including balconies and windows to accommodate these viewers; and by transforming physical torment, more generally, into public spectacle. The effect is to make exotic torture— particularly in the case of imperial China, which began to supplant Ottoman Turkey in these sources and these years as the capital of corporal punishment—appear public as well as pervasive. These editorial enhancements and enrichments, as it were, reveal not so much actual regimes of Chinese punishment—recent scholarship has, if anything, downplayed the relative cruelty of Qing judicial practices and exposed how greatly misconstrued they appear in Western sources—as they show how firmly the image of Eastern torture and bodily defacement had become lodged in the Western mind. Van Meurs's engravings and the larger picture they formulate of the exotic body under duress illustrate a key chapter in the history of "Oriental torments and the Western imagination" (as several historians of China have recently phrased this).[108] They begin to codify a conception of the exotic body that would influence European consumers and colonial planners for years to come.

The non-European body and its spectacular torment play an essential role in defining the exotic world. Chinese torture—to take one of the more dramatic expressions of the exotic body's ordeal—may not in actual fact have been the public, didactic, decadent, sadistic, or theatrical tableau of cruelty it was made out to be. Nor did the non-European body otherwise experience anything like the baroque theater of violence (or rampant sexual excess) reported in sources of exotic geography. But scenes of Chinese torture, both in their timing and their circulation, had a profound impact on their European consumers. First, these images turned out to be immensely influential in the graphic and other visual arts. The van Meurs–manufactured vignettes, in particular, were recycled in books, prints, maps, and the material arts (more on this in the coming chapter), and they served to consolidate the association of the East (in this case) with somatic torture. Its validity notwithstanding, the motif of "Chinese torture" became through these sources "a fictive déjà vu."[109] Second, the rise of Chinese judicial and civic torment coincided with the decline of European torture—at least in its representational forms—and this allowed China to supplant the West in this regard as the principal terrain of wanton "cruelty." Cruelty, to the early modern mind, also implied "tyranny," and a political-philosophical form of these images circulated further in the prose of Montesquieu and the numerous other "enlightened" critics who denounced the scourge of "Oriental despotism" over the coming decades.[110] By the turn of the nineteenth century, George Henry Mason would dedicate an entire (and heavily illustrated) volume to the subject of Chinese torture, *The Punishments of China*

(1801), a source that propelled the motif of Asiatic "cruelty" through the concluding century of imperial China.[111] Third, it was the body, ultimately, that served as the site of these "tyrannies," the physical manifestation of these exquisitely described acts and images, the palette on which European writers and engravers demarcated their divergence from the exotic world. Corporal violence made concrete the distinction between European bodies and their exotic counterparts. The body revealed, in highly dramatic fashion, the exotic world as a locus of cruelty and despotism; it showed the capacity of exotic subjects to endure otherworldly torment and pain; and, not unrelated, it made vivid and tangible the injustice of these somatic abuses. Finally, it is worth pointing out the obvious: the spectator of these dramas of cruelty and the witness to these vicious abuses of the non-European body—and the witness to its "perverse" sexual practices—was the European consumer of exotic geography in the period circa 1700.

For *Englishmen* require Certainty, and are apt to despise any Art where they meet with such endless Difference, without being able to discover where the Truth lies. In short, if this Method was duly pursued, I am persuaded Geography would soon recover the credit it has lost among us, and be delivered from the Danger of relapsing into Error, by putting a Stop to those spurious Compositions which are daily obtruded on the Public by ignorant or mercenary Hands; because in such Case, nobody would buy Maps for Use which wanted Vouchers [assurances] or did not agree with them.

—JEAN-BAPTISTE DU HALDE, *Description geographique, historique, chronologique, politique, et physique de l'empire de la Chine et de la Tartarie chinoise* (circa 1738)

With *Indian* and *Chinese* subjects greater Liberties may be taken, because Luxuriance of Fancy recommends their Productions more than Propriety, for in them is often seen a Butterfly supporting an Elephant, or Things equally absurd; yet from their gay Colouring and airy Disposition [they] seldom fail to please.

—*The ladies amusement; or, Whole art of japanning made easy* (circa 1760)

CHAPTER FOUR

EXOTIC PLEASURES

Geography, Material Arts, and the "Agreeable" World

Exotic Space and Exotic Things, or Consuming
the Early Modern World

It is a curious fact that, over the course of the early modern period, exotic place names came to stand for exotic goods. That is—to put this more precisely and technically—geographic nomenclature associated with several of the lately encountered foreign spaces of the early modern world became appropriated by Europeans as a linguistic means to identify a range of material objects, particularly the sorts of consumable luxury items lately flooding the fashionable courts and better households of Europe. This did not apply to all exotic lands or to most exotic goods. Yet over the course of the early modern period and most intensively from the second half of the seventeenth century and into the early decades of the eighteenth—once again, from circa 1670 to 1730, more or less—a significant number of foreign regions engaged with by Europeans metamorphosed into words that belonged to the milieu of consuming and collecting material arts, especially those material arts that correlated to the world of luxury consumption. These words were originally affiliated quite firmly with the regions and polities that occupied Europe's diplomatic, commercial, and, not least, geographic imagination in this period. In each case, however, they subsequently developed, typically by the early decades of the eighteenth century, into words—non–proper nouns as well as verbs—that designated a range of material goods broadly sought after by connoisseurs and collectors across Europe. Places, in short, became things—consumable things and luxury items—as exotic geography segued into collecting and the material arts.

To wit: *China*—an empire that had partially opened up to European traders over the course of the sixteenth century, yet had been much admired long before for its production and export of various luxury articles coveted by European princes and merchants—came to be associated by the mid-sixteenth century with the porcelain imported from the Ming empire; and *china ware*, a term used already in Johan Nieuhof's printed geography of 1665 and later shortened to *china*, soon became a generic term for the ceramic plates, bowls, tea services, and so on imported (by the later seventeenth century) from the Qing empire.[1] *Japan* was also invoked as a geographic place name by the sixteenth century—like China, it was one of several terms originally used to reference a region only rarely visited by Europeans. Yet it also came to mean, by the final decades of the seventeenth century—by which time the region was more securely embedded in the European imagination—a varnish of exceptional hardness used in the practice of lacquering. As a verb, it designated the art of lacquering: the technique of producing an increasingly popular material art or furniture. (It also could mean the lacquered object itself.) It was used as such by John Stalker and Robert Parker in their widely consulted *Treatise of japaning and varnishing* (1688), and it was likewise invoked, several decades later, by Jean-Baptiste Pillement, the well-traveled painter and draftsman who designed the "exotic" engravings of *The ladies amusement; or, Whole art of japanning made easy* (circa 1760).[2]

These are well-known cases, yet numerous others can also be cited. The term *Ottoman* was employed by early modern Europeans almost interchangeably with *Turk* as a noun or adjective to describe a person or political-cum-cultural quality of the Levant, generally speaking; while *ottoman* as "a low upholstered seat without a back or arms" comes from the French *ottomane*, used in print by the first third of the eighteenth century. *India*, long associated with South Asia and indeed a vast expanse of Asian terrain east of the Indus River, came to designate by the early eighteenth century a type of silk cloth favored by well-to-do European women (with time, it was used for various other Indian cloths, as well). And, peering only slightly ahead in terms of chronology, *Java* came to stand by the late eighteenth century, just as *Mocha* had been used slightly earlier in this sense (from at least the 1760s), for a good cup of coffee.[3] In none of these instances does the non–proper noun or verb become a synecdoche per se; geographic and material meanings remain technically distinct. Rather, these doubly vested words serve to indicate the blurring process of early modern geography, whereby geographic space, particularly the space of the exotic world, becomes a commodity, as it were, most typically a luxury item.[4] This linguistic phenomenon also demonstrates a broader conceptual approach to the world and to worldly things. It illustrates how the early modern European culture of collecting and consuming had merged with the aesthetic of exotic geography—how exotic places came to be correlated with consumable things.[5]

This correlation of exotic space with exotic thing points, as well, to the broader affiliation of geography circa 1700 and the contemporary material arts: of the links between two-dimensional, generally printed sources that engaged with the world—books, prints, maps, and the like—and the many three-dimensional objects that similarly flourished in this period, also engaged with the world, and fit broadly under the less-than-satisfactory rubric of "decorative" arts: ceramics, both imported (typically from China and Japan) and European-made (above all from Delft); textiles, including tapestries, silks, and a range of woven fabrics that adorned early modern domestic interiors; natural objects, which might be variously embellished and thus technically hybrid (natural-artificial) products, such as decorated marine shells, coconut shells, ostrich eggs, ivory tusks, rhinoceros horns, and so on; carved woods, both of exotic provenance and from European species; and much more. Sources of early modern geography possessed a quality of "objectness," or materiality, that allowed them to be readily rendered into consumable forms of material arts, and the material arts of this period, likewise, borrowed in all sorts of ways from forms (in this case) of print geography. Two-dimensional sources gesture in this way toward three-dimensional ones, and the reverse pertains as well.[6] This overlap not only encompassed a shared nomenclature, which allowed place names on early modern maps to double as rich vocabulary for early modern material arts. It also meant shared motifs and a common trove of iconographic material; shared design strategies and overlapping modes of production; shared atelier practices and mutual habits of borrowing and replication; and productive exchanges among media, which encouraged a shared aesthetic of exoticism to develop and circulate broadly among disparate early modern sources. Frontispieces of Dutch-made volumes of geography—to cite but one quick example of these exchanges—not only depicted all manner of consumable exotic objects; they also supplied motifs that decorated those very goods when designed in early modern European workshops (as many of the "exotic" material arts often were).

Common habits of cultural production and savvy workshop practices—tricks of the exoticism trade, so to speak—reflect a significant overlap between, on the one hand, ways of thinking about, describing, and depicting exotic space (geography) and, on the other hand, the many so-called decorative or material arts that developed so distinctively in this period (ceramics, lacquer, textiles, and so on). Exotic geography and the material arts—not all genres and forms, but certainly many among those that flourished from the final decades of the seventeenth century—shared strategies of production, aesthetics of presentation, and even what might be seen as epistemological foundations of invention: ways of *understanding* and thus *making* the respective objects of their production. The two "fields" made common reference to one another, and there were, as well, numerous instances of cross-fertilization—hence the double-directional gesturing. This meant, furthermore, that critiques of exotic geography and of the "decorative" arts—in both cases, reactions became increasingly negative and even disdainful by the early to middle decades of the eighteenth century, the great "Age of Classification"—also focused on a shared range of qualities, which could be dismissed as "spurious" (by the English editor of Du Halde's scholarly geography of China) and without "propriety" (by the premier eighteenth-century manual on the art of lacquering).[7] Exotic geography and the material arts alike fell under the dubious category of mere "fancy," as both Du Halde (in another derisive comment made in the *Description*) and the author of *The ladies amusement* agreed. Works of this ilk were inattentive to the "truth" and without a firm sense of "certainty," overly inclined to take "liberties" and apt to traffic in "endless difference," prone to "error" and to "absurd" conflations of forms, and designed by "mercenary hands" and peddling, at best, trifling "amusements." Mostly, the products of exotic geography and the decorative arts could be faulted for their facile recourse to "charming descriptions," as Du Halde disparagingly terms it in his critique of prior brands of—by inference—Dutch-made geography, and for their less-than-serious instinct "to please," as the author of *The ladies amusement* blithely proclaims. At a certain level, sources of geography and material arts afforded their respective audiences variations of exotic "pleasure," and for this they were roundly ridiculed: as basely commercial ("mercenary"), trivially feminine ("ladies"), and generally "spurious" objects of consumption.[8]

This chapter investigates the correlations between exotic geography and the material arts that developed in tandem over a pivotal period falling roughly from the final third of the seventeenth century through the first third of the eighteenth. In his classic account of European artistic engagements with the exotic world in the wake of Cook's Pacific voyages, Bernard Smith drew attention to the affiliation of an "aesthetic of the exotic" and the decorative arts, an association that Smith, an art historian, dates expressly to the second half of the seventeenth century. "Baroque exotica," Smith proposes in his landmark *Imagining the Pacific*, where he dedicates a lengthy opening chapter to this highly influential "aesthetic mode," "flourished most congenially in the decorative arts." To this Smith adds a coda: "of the Catholic south."[9] That Smith vaguely dismisses the role of the Dutch in the production of this new and powerful form of exoticism speaks more to his approach to his subject strictly from the perspective of canonical visual arts—painting and watercolors, above all—than to the rich and richly suggestive sources of print geography. His narrowly visual approach—undoubtedly sensible for certain topics—obscures the contributions of Dutch ateliers, producers of exotic geography par excellence, and the methods and motifs they developed for representing exotic things, at this precise moment, in books, prints, maps, and also the visual and material arts. Interrogating the "aesthetic of the exotic" from the perspective of geography not only adds valuable source materials that help to elucidate its origins and developing form in this period; it also suggests a more nuanced and rigorous way to understand the "decorative" materials that Smith, as well, seems to slight in his analysis. The goals of juxtaposing early modern geography and material arts are thus several: first, to illustrate the striking overlap of these two modes of production and their fertile exchanges in the period circa 1700; next, to demonstrate how productive these relations could be both for the discipline of geography and for the practice of material arts—the former could function more "decoratively" and the latter more "narratively" than is often imagined—and, finally, to explore the mutual investment of both modes in exotic "pleasure," a leitmotif and aesthetic disposition that played a critical role in shaping how early modern Europeans perceived the world.

Exotics on the Map: Geographic Icons, Material Objects, and European Values

To locate the "decorative" proclivities of early modern geography and the "geographic" disposition of contemporary material arts, one need look no further than a map—a map produced in the Netherlands, that is, preferably dedicated to the exotic world—and more particularly to its cartouche. Cartographic materials are, in many ways, the quintessential geographic sources—for what delineates space more expressly than a map?—yet they turn out to be, as well, a brimming font of motifs for early modern decorative arts, which borrowed liberally from embellished maps; and they also provide a form of visual celebration of those material objects from the exotic world that Europeans so keenly craved. Maps, more generally, had gained considerable popularity over the early modern period as consumable objects in their own right. Cartographic data, vital to the operation of commercial ventures, imperial projects, and evangelical missions alike, acquired an added cachet in the wake of Renaissance Europe's voyages abroad: maps were avidly collected and prominently displayed, both in the elite courts and relatively modest homes of early modern Europe. From the second half of the fifteenth century, moreover, maps shifted starkly in their appearance, reshaped not only by the latest reports of overseas explorers, but also by the fundamental shift from schematic, so-called T-O maps, which fulfilled a primarily sacred and ideological function, to the Ptolemaic map, a mathematical format that, while no less ideological than the medieval genre it replaced, presented geographic data on uniform grids and in a simply reproduced format: the square, printed sheet map. This new mode of cartographical presentation became the predominant form that shaped the European image of the early modern world, and Dutch-made maps, by the mid-seventeenth century, became the commercial version of this form that dominated the European market.[10]

And *market* offers an appropriate matrix on which to fix the flourishing cartographic business of this period. Maps were commodities, bought and sold on the
open market. Notions of secret or classified cartographic data, while perhaps relevant to the Iberian model of production—where the monarchy played a central
role in controlling the flow of information and print culture was less vibrant than
in northern Europe—do not easily apply to the Dutch cartographic enterprise.
Printed maps, in truth, bore limited relevance to bona fide navigation, and while
they certainly imparted fresh data about distant lands (and distant waters: maritime maps sold briskly in this period), they served mostly as commercial commodities. Well designed, vividly embellished, not infrequently hand-colored, and
sometimes even gilded by an illuminator, maps might be seen as "decorative" arts
in their own rights, alluring objects of impressively broad consumption. Maps, correspondingly, adorned numerous spaces of early modern Europe. As luxury objects, they hung in princely courts and the residences of wealthy merchants; as inexpensive, single-sheet wares, they might be tacked onto the walls of a vast swath of
"middling" homes, affordable even to the lower stratum of the urban classes. Maps
also came in the form of mosaics, laid out as ornamental floors; in the medium of
ceramics, often as tiles that formed grand tableaux; and in the fabric of tapestry,
which, like the ceramic tableaux, could move among and decorate multiple interior areas. In all cases, maps commonly *decorated*: both domestic spaces and, needless to say, copious products of print geography.[11]

Of all of the decorated spaces on the early modern map, the cartouche typically
offered the most ornate piece of the affair. It functioned, as well, as the most critical
element of the cartographic enterprise: if a map might be said to be the quintessential form of geography, the cartouche was the quintessence of the map. It lay, moreover, at the heart of the map's decorative scheme. Like the frontispiece of a book,
the cartouche epitomized the contents of a map, reformulating in a condensed and
often allegorical form the space depicted on the larger cartographic image. Just as
the printed frontispiece "framed" the narrative of an early modern book, the decorative cartouche "staged" the space of an early modern map. This was achieved visually, typically in an engraved vignette that was designed (in some cases, by the
leading graphic artists of the day) to distill a geographic space: to offer a visual en-
capsulation of a region, its inhabitants and qualities; to provide a pictorial perspective or thematic portrait of a distant locale. Distilled does not mean undecorated,
however, and designs for cartouches became, if anything, more elaborate, baroque,
and substantial over the course of the seventeenth century. The cartouche, correlatively, gained prominence and space on the early modern map, and this granted it
still more authority as the interpretive key to the cartographic whole.[12]

This had "decorative" consequences, as well. As the early modern cartouche
gained in substance and prominence, its design acquired more visual value and re-

quired more attention. Producers took note. Designs for the cartouche of a decorative map could simultaneously derive *from* other media—from a prominent frontispiece, for example, or a narrative illustration in a volume of print geography—and contribute motifs *to* other media, especially to the material arts. In this way, the cartouche could serve as an important hinge between print media and the material arts: a well-conceived design might "swing" (as it were) from source to source, medium to medium, transferring a visual device or allegorical motif to a wider audience and to a revised context. The mapmaker's atelier, much like the bookmaker's, necessarily engaged in the canny borrowing, recycling, and replication of designs, thereby instigating a process by which exotic imagery could be transferred, adapted, and repurposed from one medium to another—from "learned" geography, not infrequently, to "decorative" arts. As they gained prominence, in other words, motifs of exotic geography gained fluidity—and the ability to traverse multiple media. The engraved frontispiece to Philip Baldaeus's *Naauwkeurige beschryvinge van Malabar en Choromandel* (1672), a broadly circulated volume devoted to the religious and social mores of southern India and Sri Lanka, furnished the design for Hendrick Doncker's equally prevalent map of South Asia (circa 1680): the geographic regions invoked in this case mostly overlap, even while the purposes of the designs have shifted (figures 106 and 107).[13] These motifs moved—to other maps, to sundry atlases, and, ultimately, to the material arts—since they possessed easily pliable, broadly interchangeable, and evidently compelling iconographies. The original frontispiece design, likely the invention of the printers Johannes Janssonius van Waesberge and Johannes van Someren, assembles a series of iconic images of Asia—a large-tusked elephant, a resplendent Oriental potentate, a seminude mahout—that could be smartly reconstituted in other media and for other ends. Along with its allegorical figures (the elephant, in particular, had long associations with Asia), the frontispiece also presents a sumptuous feast of material objects, which spill into the foreground of the print: pearls, gems, ivory, ceramics, and fabrics of various fashion and stripe. This cornucopia of consumable goods is common to the genre and a hallmark of Dutch-made frontispieces in particular.[14] But this design also fit into the genre of cartography, it turns out, and into several other exotic contexts. And its mode of presentation points to the close kinships and easy affiliations between the graphic realms of books and maps—in the form of the frontispiece print and the device of the decorative cartouche—and the material arts, which the engraved sources readily advertise.

Several of these strategies and devices can be instructively observed in what ranks among the most influential and fluid cartouche designs of the early modern period, which embellished one of the most broadly disseminated maps of Europe's exotic world: Nicolaes Visscher's *Novissima et Accuratissima Totius Americae Descriptio* (circa 1658) (see plate 11). Visscher's map was enormously successful. From

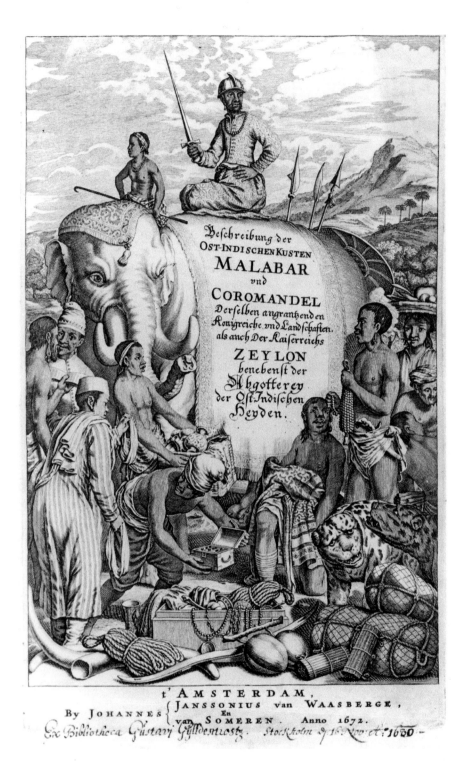

FIGURE 106. Frontispiece (engraving) to Philip Baldaeus, *Wahrhaftige ausführliche Beschreibung der berühmten Ost-Indischen Kusten Malabar und Coromandel* (Amsterdam, 1672). Getty Research Institute, Los Angeles (84-B22317).

FIGURE 107. Homann Erben, *Peninsula Indiæ citra Gangem hoc est Orae celeberrimae Malabar & Coromandel cum adjacente insula non minus celebratissima Ceylon* (detail); engraving. Special Collections, University of Amsterdam (33-13-22).

its debut in the mid-seventeenth century, it appeared in scores of further editions, unsanctioned reproductions, and creative revisions, which carried the map's designs and visual messages deep into the eighteenth century.[15] Its iconic cartouche, invented by the esteemed landscape painter (and prolific graphic artist) Nicolaes Berchem, shaped an enormous range of images across several media, becoming effectively a standard—if not *the* standard—allegorical depiction of America. (This pertains chiefly to the lower of the map's pair of vignettes [figure 108], yet the upper cartouche, also designed by Berchem, inspired frequent imitation as well.) To put this in context: what Jacob van Meurs's famous frontispiece to Johan Nieuhof's book did for the representation of China and the birth of chinoiserie, Berchem's cartouche did for America and what Hugh Honour once dubbed "américainerie."[16] It played this role and achieved this status for its superb staging of the central figure of "America," which Berchem at once allegorized and distilled into its essential qual-

FIGURE 108. After Nicolaes Berchem, Allegory of America (engraved [lower] cartouche), detail of Nicolaes Visscher, *Novissima et Accuratissima Totius Americae Descriptio*. Special Collections, University of Amsterdam (33.22.40).

ities. It was all there: the alluring figure of "America" herself, decked out in a dainty feathered skirt and colorful feathered headdress; the pearls, faintly visible around her neck, demonstrating the region's endemic richness; the classic bow and arrow, just to her right, alluding to her habit of hunting ("America" also bears a stylized club); the mounds of freshly mined gold (or perhaps silver) piling up at her feet, alongside stacks of ingots, which indicate the substantial mineral wealth of the continent; a pair of queerly coiled snakes, which reveal the exotic *naturalia* of the New World; a central parasol, which shades "America's" head from the tropical sun.

Visscher's map and Berchem's cartouche had an immediate and substantial impact. First, the map: Soon after its original issue and frequent reprints by Visscher and his heirs, Dutch cartographers—the likes of Frederick de Wit and Justus Danckerts, among others—published revised editions of the map, sometimes with privileges, although also without. English, French, and German printers followed suit, brazenly copying the map and its design, in whole or in part, for their own atlases and geographies (generally without privileges). John Ogilby, the onetime Scottish dance-master who had obtained the inflated rank of "His Majesty's Cosmographer and Geographic Printer" (to take a fairly egregious example), relied on Visscher for his standard-issue map of America—albeit with a London imprint and revised dedication to an English baron—which Ogilby published on its own and in his van Meurs–derived volume on America (1671). This English-stamped rendition launched a slew of London-made Americas, which circulated in British salons and studies for decades to come.[17]

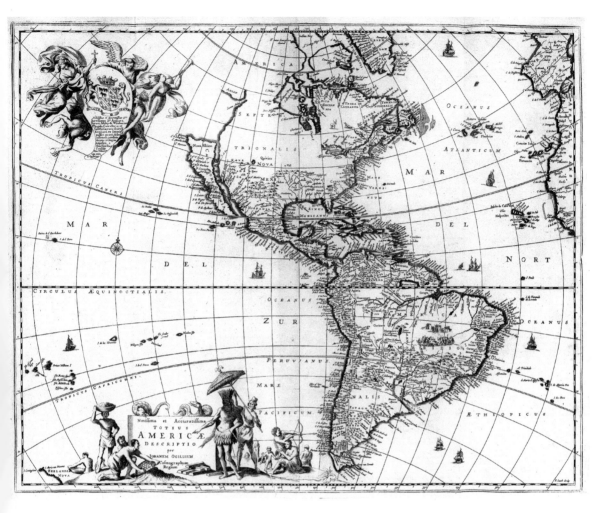

FIGURE 109. F. Lamb after Nicolaes Visscher (with revised cartouche), *Novissima et Accuratissima Totius Americae Descriptio per Johanem Ogiluium* (1671); engraving. Courtesy of the John Carter Brown Library at Brown University.

Next, the cartouche: The allegory caught on in several forms, most simply as the go-to decorative cartouche for maps of America—when a printer copied a map, he often retained its embellishments—yet also in revised and reformulated adaptations, which distilled and refined the core elements of Berchem's design. In these forms, the map's imagery dispersed widely. The designer of the "Carte de la Nouvelle France" (1683), done at the behest of Louis Hennepin following his explorations of North America's interiors, incorporated a variant of Visscher's upper cartouche, which offered an allegory of religion among the New World's "heathen"(compare figures 123 and 110).[18] Further afield is the frontispiece to one of the earliest Russian *Americana*, a translation commissioned by Peter the Great of Johann Hübner's *Kurtze Fragen aus den neuen und alten Geographie*. The "Description of America" in that

FIGURE 110. Nicholas Guerard, "Carte de la Nouvelle France et de la Louisiane Nouvellement decouverte" (engraving), in Louis Hennepin, *Description de la Louisiane, nouvellement decouverte au Sud'Oüest de la Nouvelle France* (Paris, 1683). Courtesy of the
John Carter Brown Library at Brown University.

geography (1719) opens with a crudely engraved rendering of Berchem's allegory of
"America," complete with feathered skirt, necklace of pearls, shade of parasol, ingots
of gold, slithering snakes, and, for this parochial adaptation, background beavers
(the fur of which would have played an important role in the Russian economy).[19]
Closer to home—but furthest-reaching in terms of impact—was a modification of
the allegory drafted by Berchem himself: a design invented for a frontispiece in
Joan Blaeu's monumental *Atlas major* (1662; figure 112). In this variant, the artist
enhanced the allegory somewhat by bringing the upper and lower cartouches together in a single composition and enlarging the figure of "America," who now
bears her own bow and arrows and gains an accompanying alligator (an animal
associated with the continent since Cesare Ripa's 1603 edition of the *Iconologia*).[20]
This immensely influential depiction, in turn, begot several more cycles of imitation, replication, variation, and so on. These effectively corroborated and codified
the essence of "America" in visual terms: her essential attributes, her allegorical
meaning, and her—and the continent's, by extension—exotic qualities.

This intense replication and circulation notwithstanding, "America" proved to
be a less fixed image and less stable allegory than might be expected. For despite

FIGURE III. "Ameriki opisanie [Description of America]" (engraved frontispiece), in Johann Hübner, *Zemnovodnago kruga kratkoe opisanie. Iz staryia i novyia gegrafii po voprosam i otvietam chrez IAgana Gibnera sobranoe* [A short description of the terra-queous globe (. . .)] (Moscow, 1719). Courtesy of the John Carter Brown Library at Brown University.

these obvious and resolute iconographic inventions, which had been deliberately devised by Berchem to *fix* the continent's qualities and to affiliate a series of visual cues with the New World, his "America" demonstrated remarkable fluidity. Its origin in the medium of cartography and intrinsic association with the terrain of America aside, the design moved readily across space and media. It transferred not

FIGURE 112. Joan Blaeu after Nicolaes Berchem, "America" (engraved frontispiece), in *Geographia maior; sive, Cosmographia Blaviana* (Amsterdam, 1662–1665). Courtesy of Dartmouth College Library.

FIGURE 113. Hendrick Doncker, *Pas-caert van Guinea* (detail); engraving. Special Collections, University of Amsterdam (33-21-08).

only to other maps and other graphic genres—to the Blaeu frontispiece and the Russian-adopted engraving, for example—but also to other geographic regions and other media of representation, and these shifts could substantially change the meaning of the design. Not long after Berchem's "America" appeared in print, a nearly identical engraving—the same heaps of gold, curling snakes, and feather-clad figure standing under the shade of an identical parasol (all engraved in reverse)—turned up on a map of West Africa (1665), the allegory and her attributes meant, in this case, to designate the region of Guinea along with the Ivory and Gold Coasts. The mapmaker—Hendrick Doncker, active in Amsterdam in the second half of the seventeenth century—has taken the "exotic" qualities of the original allegory and simply reassigned them to another tropical milieu.[21]

The parasol in particular, as a distinctively exotic accessory, drifted across space and media, sometimes shading a feathered, quasi-American figure, although other times not. The shrewd Jacob van Meurs promptly picked up the design and redeployed it in several of his vastly dispersed publications. A parasol shades the "king" of Florida in an engraving for the van Meurs–Montanus volume *America*—in this case, the regal figure wears a feathered headdress much like Berchem's "America" (figure 114)—and a parasol with a virtually matching tilt keeps the hot Japanese sun off a samurai ("chevalier") who inhabits the van Meurs–Montanus geography of

FIGURE 114. Jacob van Meurs (atelier), Habit of a Floridian king (engraving), in Arnoldus Montanus, *De nieuwe en onbekende weereld* (Amsterdam, 1671). Courtesy of the John Carter Brown Library at Brown University.

Japan. In Qing China, as observed in the van Meurs–Dapper description of that empire, a parasol provides shelter from the elements for high- and modest-born women alike; and a parasol crowns Shah Jahan as depicted in a van Meurs–atelier engraving for the Dapper volume on the Mughal empire. Even the "Grand Tartar Cham," as presented on the much-imitated frontispiece to Nieuhof's China book—an image that quickly became iconic in its own right—sits under a prominent parasol, which shades the Chinese imperial throne (see plate 19). In this case, the round shape of the umbrella's canopy corresponds formally to the vast globe grasped by the Cham, the two objects jointly serving to center the van Meurs–designed print.[22]

The exotic parasol, along with much of the rest of the "American" allegorical ensemble, passed in this way to other genres and media. And even in instances where it retained a good deal of its original form and arrangement, the newly cre-

SCHAH IEHAAN

FIGURE 115. Jacob van Meurs (atelier), "Schah Iehaan [Shah Jahan]" (engraving), in Olfert Dapper, *Asia: of Naukeurige beschryving van het rijk des Grooten Mogols, en een groote gedeelte van Indien* (Amsterdam, 1672). Special Collections, University of Amsterdam (OM 63-115).

ated images could still incorporate other spaces and alternative purposes. Toward the close of the seventeenth century, by which time the parasol had already circulated in scores of maps and tomes of geography, a new rendering of the feathered and shaded "America" appeared on a mezzotint printed in London. This latest version (engraved by John Smith after a design by William Vincent) depicted "The

The Indian Queen

J. Smith ex.   W. Vincent fe.

FIGURE 116. John Smith after William Vincent, *The Indian Queen* [Anne Bracegirdle as Semernia] (ca. 1700); mezzotint. Houghton Library (B TCS 45), Harvard University.

Indian Queen," as the caption plainly proclaims, on what served effectively as an early modern playbill.[23] The print portrayed the well-known English actress Anne Bracegirdle as she would have appeared in her leading role in *The Widow Ranter*, a tragicomedy composed by the dramatist Aphra Behn and first performed in 1689. The caption's clarity is both provocative and misleading. For the heroine of the play was the character Semernia, a fictional native of Virginia—thus an "Indian" princess—and a protagonist in Behn's fictive narration of Bacon's Rebellion of 1676; she is not to be confused with the eponymous heroine of John Dryden's earlier and well-known play *The Indian Queen*.[24] But the allusion to America is clear, as are the recognizable borrowings from Berchem's cartouche. A female figure sports a garishly feathered crown and elaborate gown—propriety dictated something more substantial than a flimsy skirt, yet out from the lower hemline of the dress peek decorative feathers that recall "America's" native costume—and poses beneath the shade of a parasol. The latter is borne by one of two cherubic lackeys who likewise wear feathers—both headgear and skirts—and, in case the point is not wholly obvious, Semernia clasps in her left hand a bouquet of still more feathers. This Indian queen bears rich strings of pearls around her neck and arm; thick pearls also adorn her feathered headdress and confirm her princely status and wealth. But the fair-skinned and delicate-boned "queen" does not otherwise seem especially "Indian," nor does the landscape behind her appear especially exotic. She looks, if anything, English, and her thickly hatched attendants might as well be Africans. Yet the by now recognizable assemblage of parasol, pearls, and feathers identifies Bracegirdle as plainly exotic and putatively American. More to the point, the intricate and dense conflation of forms—borrowed from Berchem and no doubt other allegorical, possibly cartographical, and in all cases "geographical" vignettes, and incorporating simultaneously European, African, and American elements—combine to fashion an "Indian Queen": an exotic figure with an identifiably "American" lineage.

The subtly restyled Berchem-Bracegirdle "America" enjoyed its own popularity—the print went through several states and republications—and followed its own iterations and itineraries.[25] Once again, too, shifts in form and settings reveal the flexible presentation and loose understanding of exotic space and geographic meaning. Feathers and pearls garnish an "American" figure cut into Silesian glass sometime in the early eighteenth century—in this case, an Asian elephant serves as the allegory's attendant beast (figure 117). And feathers, pearls, and heaps of (mostly mineral) treasure decorate a gathering of "Americas" designed by Lodewijck van Schoor and woven into tapestry by a Brussels factory around 1700—in this case, the alligator has returned to his rightful place by America's side, and traditional bows and arrows abound (figure 118).[26] In a slightly later composition painted by the Augsburg artist Johann Wolfgang Baumgartner, a pearl-clad America herself holds a parasol over a duskier male companion who, similarly festooned with pearls, grips a large "American" bow (arrows lie in the background) (figure 119). And while a snarling alligator can be seen hissing off to the side, the centrally obtruding elephant tusks (and the brown skin tone of the male figure) suggest a more complex blend of Africa and America—and point, perhaps, to the earlier cartographic cocktail mixed by Hendrik Doncker (see figure 113). Then there is the trade card printed for John Cotterell, a "China-Man & Glass-Seller" of mid-eighteenth-century imperial London (figure 120). Produced as an advertisement for his busy shop, Cotterell's handbill features a logo that all but replicates the Bracegirdle mezzotint: two

FIGURE 117. Standing cup with figures of the Continents (Silesia, ca. 1700); honeycomb-cut and engraved glass; 21 cm (height) × 12.7 cm (diameter). Cooper-Hewitt, National Design Museum, Smithsonian Institute/Art Resource, NY.

dark-hued lackeys (joined in this case by a third figure) hold aloft a parasol and train for a well-dressed woman who wears pearls and bears a posy of feathers. And logically so: Cotterell sold his wares "At the *Indian Queen* & Canister," an exotic enough shop-name to encompass the mélange of global consumable goods he had on offer. "China and Lacquer'd"—that is, japanned—"wares" from Cotterell's shop joined "Various sorts of fine Teas, Coffee, Chocolate"—beverages of pronouncedly Asian and American provenance—along with "Snuff" (tobacco, presumably from America yet possibly from Asia), "Indian Fans and Pictures" (likely South Asian), "et cetera." Cotterell's Indian Queen roamed widely.[27]

More generally, many of these images and objects, even while featuring plainly "American" iconography and motifs—or Asian or African, for that matter—exhibit a familiar sort of capaciousness when it comes to representing geographic space. There is a quality of looseness to the design of these materials, a mix-and-match approach to the exotic world and its formulation. Provenances are casually blended, and subjects, even when ostensibly affixed to place or region, could swiftly

FIGURE 118. Lodewijck van Schoor and Pieter Spierincx, *Allegory of America* (ca. 1700); tapestry of undyed wool warp with dyed wool and silk weft; 341.3 × 496.6 cm. Courtesy of the National Gallery of Art, Washington, DC.

decamp to other exotic locales. The peregrinations of the "American" parasol exemplify this process. The parasol, certainly, had a well-established Asian lineage that long predated Berchem and his Baroque cartouche. It functioned for centuries as an icon of the Orient, associated in pre-1492 iconography with the majesty of ancient Assyrian, Egyptian, and Persian rulers—an early carved relief (now in the British Museum) shows the Assyrian king Ashurnasirpal II under the shade of a parasol—and it turns up slightly later in Greek and Roman sources, as well (it fades from view in the European Middle Ages).[28] The effect of Berchem's American cartouche was both to revive the parasol imagery and to attach this plainly "exotic" accessory—along with the feathers, pearls, and other increasingly standard accoutrements of his allegory—to the New World. By appropriating the parasol for his design, however, Berchem also departicularized it. He inserted it into the source pool of exotic geography, and this effectively rendered it an icon of exoticism writ large. Its replication in scores of maps and prints granted the parasol mobility, and this allowed an originally Oriental symbol to become a marker of an American al-

FIGURE 119. Johann Wolfgang Baumgartner, *America* (ca. 1750); oil on canvas; 25 × 38 cm. Städtischen Kunstsammlungen Augsburg, Deutsche Barockgalerie.

FIGURE 120. *John Cotterell China-Man & Glass-selle*r (London, ca. 1750); engraved trade card. Bodelian Library (object number 6 [181751]), University of Oxford.

legory. It allowed a generically "exotic" icon to move across myriad sources and spaces of geography, until the Orient met up, once again, with the Occident in John Cotterell's shop: a "China Man" at the "Indian Queen."

The modus operandi of exotic geography, furthermore, allowed the entire ensemble devised by Berchem—his original design for "America"—to traverse allegorical and imperial space: to sail across the Atlantic, as it were, from the Americas to tropical Africa. In Hendrick Doncker's efficient appropriation of Berchem's cartouche, "America" deftly becomes "Africa"; parasols, pearls, and feathers nimbly bridge the Atlantic, reconstituting themselves in and for another exotic locale. The Berchem allegory thus moves from the new "golden land," as America had come to be known by its European "discoverers," to an older landscape of gold and ivory coasts, as the Doncker map pronounces in a cartouche that invokes the traditional nomenclature for western equatorial Africa, affiliated by Europeans for years with luxury goods (and, more recently, with slaves, yet this would have been covered by another map).[29] Once again, it should be noted, exotic space has come to stand for material things—*Gold* Coast and *Ivory* Coast—and, more particularly, for the consumable goods and luxury items that served the expanding European market for exotic imports. In the case of West Africa, in fact, space is named *after* thing. For while Doncker's map does designate the larger region "Guinea," it labels the subregions along the Gulf of Guinea with non–proper nouns long associated with European luxury consumption (as do scores of other early modern maps and geographies). The West African coast *was* gold.

Looseness, capaciousness, and spatial discursiveness may not amount to "decorativeness," yet there is an outward quality of frivolousness to the deployment of exotic motifs like so many ornaments to be moved around a decorative map. And this suggests a kinship between the digressiveness of geography and cartography, on the one hand, and the playfulness often associated with the material arts of this period—chinoiserie, for example—on the other hand. The *américainerie* instigated by the Berchem cartouche offers one of several instances where exotic geography produces what might be thought of as exotic icons: discreet images or motifs, visual tropes or vignettes, that come to stand for exotic space in a generalized or generic sense. They obtain this status through replication.[30] For even while a context may exist for an original motif or vignette—a parasol does imply hot sun and, in its ancient Near Eastern setting, royal grandeur (the parasol is nearly always held by a lackey)—this context falls away as the motif moves to other spaces and sources with other settings and meanings. Once a marker of Asian majesty, the parasol devised for Berchem's cartouche shades an American Indian who—in a breathtaking irony—must toil to extract mineral wealth out of the murky mines of the New World. (This extraction is alluded to by the figures descending to the left in the

Berchem cartouche and illustrated more vividly, in the background right, in the Berchem-designed frontispiece for Blaeu's atlas: see figures 108 and 112.) The parasol's earlier meaning is wholly inverted in Berchem's American design, even as that previous sense is partially restored by Jacob van Meurs's frontispiece for Nieuhof's China volume, where an imperial Cham sits grandly under a parasol (there is, however, little sense of sun). In both settings, however, the parasol has an identical and unambiguous meaning: it signifies exoticism.

This process recurs in scores of other cartouches, designed for numerous other maps, using various other indicators of exoticism. Palm trees, among the most ubiquitous markers of the non-European world, flourish in the landscape of northerly "New England" in Johannes van Keulen's decorative vignette for a sea chart that covers the coasts of and frigid waters off northeast America and Maritime Canada. A seminude Indian stands under the shade of a palm tree on the left side of van Keulen's cartouche; while on the right side, a scene of European-American barter, in the vicinity of the aptly named Winter Bay (in present-day Maine), takes place beneath the fronds of a putatively indigenous New England palm.[31] Both palm and parasol protect Europeans and Indians from the tropical sun beating down in the "Northern Part of Virginia," as depicted on a cartouche adorning a map of the North Atlantic and its New England and Canadian coastlines.[32] "Virginia" in this

FIGURE 121. Johannes van Keulen, *Pas-kaart vande zee kusten inde boght van Niew* [sic] *Engeland tusschen de Staaten Hoek en C. de Sable* (detail); engraving. Special Collections, University of Amsterdam (V 9 X 8).

CHAPTER FOUR

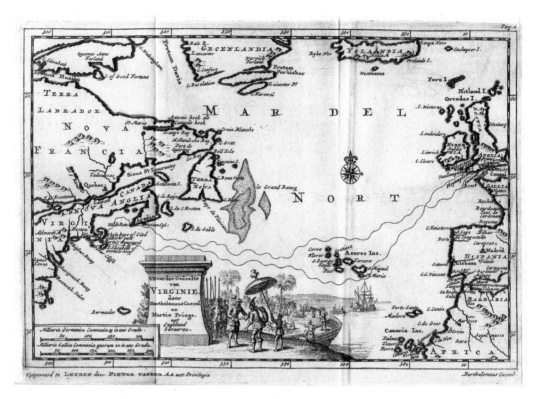

FIGURE 122. Bartholomew Gosnold, *'t Noorder Gedeelte van Virginie* (engraving). Special Collections, University of Amsterdam (O 63-290).

context designates England's aspirations for "New England," and the map's image illustrates Bartholomew Gosnold's virgin encounter with the Penobscot Indians in present-day Maine—a more wintery than tropical climate, even in the most sunny accounts of English colonists. More generally—and more globally—palm trees find a place in countless maps of the exotic world, where, even as they are uprooted from their tropical context, they thrive all the same in northerly and southerly climates. They also recur as background in geography illustrations produced in this period: for example, in the many landscapes incorporated into Nieuhof's China book, in which the printer-engraver van Meurs inserted palms, since the traveler-draftsman Nieuhof did not think to include them in the sketches he made of a northward journey to non-tropical Beijing.[33] And palms are pervasive, of course, in the material arts. In almost all of these cases, palm trees function not so much as a bona fide representation of landscape as they do an embellishment of an object or print or map; they add an ornamental, or "decorative," element that marks the scene as "exotic." Like the parasol that shades the American Indian and the Chinese Cham alike, the ever-present palm tree becomes indigenous to spaces and climates across the globe—at least the forms that decorate exotic geography.

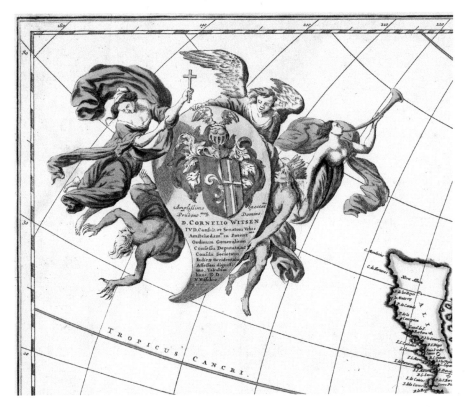

FIGURE 123. After Nicolaes Berchem, Allegory of Faith (engraved [upper] cartouche), detail of Nicolaes Visscher, *Novissima et Accuratissima Totius Americae Descriptio*. Special Collections, University of Amsterdam (33-22-40).

Did the palm or the parasol have any further meaning? Are exotic icons merely decorative, or do they speak to broader conceptions and configurations of the non-European world? In the case of Berchem's influential cartouches—the top as well as bottom components—these devices most certainly did have meaning and conveyed narratives that pertained pointedly to America and its message. That these devices and narratives proved so nimble and mobile, moreover, is an essential part of that meaning and of the European understanding of the exotic world. The often misconstrued upper cartouche of Nicolaes Visscher's *Novissima et Accuratissima Totius Americae Descriptio* is, in fact, a key to the map and provides critical context to the vignette below.[34] In the upper-left quadrant of the sheet, a cluster of allegorical figures surrounds and supports a free-floating, shield-like device, which bears a patron's coat of arms and the map's dedication (to Cornelius Witsen on the original state, yet this varied with each printing). The predominant figure, a woman hovering in the very upper-left corner of the printed sheet, represents Christian Faith: relatively plainly dressed, she points with one hand to a cross that she holds in her other hand and positions centrally above the cluster of figures and the crest. She also glances below to a broad-shouldered, sharp-taloned figure who tumbles out of the sky, as it were: an allegory of diabolism, ejected by the Christian Church. An angel opposite and above gazes, mouth agape, at this falling devil and the wondrous turn of events; while another heavenly figure, just to the angel's side, announces per clarion the plunge of diabolism and spread of the gospel. Finally, an Indian—who is situated closest to the American landmass and wears the same feathered headdress as the "America" figure occupying the cartouche below, in this way linking the two vignettes (figure 108)—gazes in wide-eyed astonishment at the allegory of Faith above, whose good works have apparently converted him. The cartouche describes, in short, the Church's labors in the New World: their success in casting out false faiths and diabolisms and in evangelizing among the American natives.

The upper and lower cartouches are linked formally and iconographically, and together they communicate a larger message pertaining to America and its indigenes, to Europe and the exotic world. The parasol, in a very basic way, acts as a formal device: it points from the lower to the upper cartouche and thus trains the viewer's eye from the larger title cartouche to the dedication cartouche above, forging a narrative connection. (The upper Indian, were he to fall from his heavenly perch, would land directly on the lower Indian's parasol spike.) The parasol also broadcasts America's tropical environs—a deep shadow falls behind the central allegorical figure and those attending her, indicating a torrid tropical sun (the parasol nearly abuts the engraved words "Tropicus Capricorni")—and it underscores the region's climatic distinction from Europe, the latter understood as the temperate and northerly zones of that continent, which would have been the target audience for the map. The parasol places "America" in another spiritual-solar environment, both literally (the tropical sun that it shields) and figuratively (the cast-out devil that it points to). The other conspicuously tropical feature of the print, the two coiling snakes who nestle prominently on the central block that bears the map's title, also allude to the presence of the devil among the heathen of America; they evoke the original "fall" of mankind from prelapsarian grace to earthly sin— the original sin that necessitated labor. Berchem clarifies this theological nuance in a preparatory drawing for the cartouche (now in Windsor Castle), where, rather than to the map's title, the central allegorical figure points to a scene, sketched on to a slab-like tableau, of "heathen" kneeling in prayer around a temple of idols (figure 124). If the upper cartouche shows the ejection of diabolism from America, in other words, then the lower alludes to its presence.

And it alludes to America's copious gold. The connection? This harks back to a proverbial wisdom that circulated in late medieval and early modern Europe about the inverse relation of "god" and "gold": wherever the latter flowed abundantly, it was proposed, the former was typically scarce (and the reverse). Such a

FIGURE 124. Nicolaes Berchem, *Allegory of America* (design for a cartouche) (ca. 1650); pen and brown ink with brown and gray wash over black chalk; 14.6 × 27.4 cm. Royal Collection Trust © Her Majesty Queen Elizabeth II 2014.

conception of America and her endemic riches-cum-heathenism justified much of the Habsburg's early colonial action in the New World—the conquest and simultaneous conversion of the Indians. Yet it also carried an implicit moral message, which gained traction among critics of the Habsburg *Conquista*, especially in northern Europe. A late sixteenth-century poem, which captioned the Dutch and German editions of an engraved allegory of America, commented poignantly on this contradictory relationship between the European god and American gold (words that punned even more in the original: *god* and *goud* in Dutch):

> Europe has discovered me and introduced me to God
> Gold, that otherwise leads to nobility, has enslaved me
> With riches I have become impoverished in my own land
> Since my natural endowments have been taken to other regions.

Here the marvelous mineral wealth of America fosters her own decline; she goes from benighted idolatry to miserable slavery. The allegory (engraved by Adriaen Collaert after a design by Maarten de Vos) expresses sympathy for the doubly abused Indians.[35]

Several decades later, by which time Visscher and Berchem would have been hard at work on their map (the mid-seventeenth century), the correlation of godliness and gold had been further refined: less to comment on the shortcomings of Habsburg Spain and its colonial agents in America than to make sense of the abundant assets of America and of those other extra-European lands similarly rich in material wealth and poor in Christian inhabitants. The association spoke less polemically—anti-Habsburg sentiment had by now cooled down—than climatically, so to speak, on the contrasts between temperate and godly Europe and the sinfully rich exotic world. "The riches and goods of this world," wrote the Dutch Calvinist critic Godefridus Udemans, a near contemporary of Nicolaes Berchem, "are generally possessed in the largest quantities by such people who know not God or who serve Him contrary to His will." Udemans made this observation regarding the "Indies" in general, East and West, and in his lengthy meditation on the morality of overseas commerce from which the comment derives—the seven-hundred-page *Geestelyck roer van 't coopmans schip* (Spiritual rudder of the merchant's ship)—he expanded on this point to assail the contradictory, problematic nature of global exchange: that godly Europeans coveted most those material objects that ungodly non-Europeans seemed not only to possess in great quantity but also to grant scant concern. Gold and other precious commodities, paradoxically, mattered least where they flourished most. "Indeed it has been observed of the Americans that they hardly value gold, silver, and pearls, and that they regard feathers much more highly," noted Udemans, in what could have served as a caption to the Berchem cartouche: feathers adorn America's gaudy crown, while gold is dumped unceremoniously at her feet.[36] "A tiny feather from a parrot / Is for them a wondrous present," quipped the great Dutch poet Jacob Cats, again regarding the "innocent" American Indians. As did Udemans, "Father" Cats moralized at length on the covetousness of his fellow Europeans—*their* moral shortcomings.[37] Yet both men's comments reveal something further about the exotic subjects and exotic objects on the other end of Europe's global trade. They expose a widespread belief that Americans and other non-Europeans had a meager or "false" understanding of the commercial value and material worth of those exotic goods they so splendidly possessed. And herein lay a stupendous irony: while exotic *space* may have been affiliated by early modern Europeans with material wealth and luxury objects, exotic *peoples*—and exotic subjects, in the context of colonial America—did not seem to possess the good sense to recognize for themselves the value of the rich consumable goods in their midst.

The contrast of rich goods and impoverished understanding—of exotic things and exotic peoples—rests at the heart of a series of remarkable essays by the critic William Pietz on European expansion and the "problem of the fetish."[38] Pietz's essays offer a wide-ranging, genealogical study of the concept of fetish: its philological as well as material origins, from the ancient marketplace to the European colonial encounter, in this case, in West Africa. To simplify considerably Pietz's careful, subtle, historically rich set of arguments: "Fetish" as word and idea shifts from an originally commercial meaning—the Latin *facticius* appears in the context of Roman market exchange—to a spiritual one in the European Middle Ages, when the Church had to contend with various heresies related to "idolatry"; and these two meanings come together in the sixteenth and seventeenth centuries, when the term is used by Europeans (*feitiços* in Portuguese and the derivative *fetisso* in Dutch documents) to describe dismissively the "false" understanding among West African trading partners of objects and their values. Pietz observes that European merchants trading along the West African coast had a widely conflicted approach to commercial exchange, whereby they disparaged their African counterparts for their failure to understand the true value of an object, especially gold, even as Europeans gained from this "misunderstanding" by proffering for the undervalued object (specie, for example) equally misunderstood "trifles": inexpensive objects highly desired and respected by the Africans, who appeared to worship these material trifles as fetish. "Just as Africans seemed to overestimate the economic value of trifles," Pietz writes, "so they were perceived to attribute religious values to trifling objects." Their lack of economic or material understanding, in other words, found its parallel in their lack of religious or spiritual understanding. "The alleged false religious values of African fetish worshipers," Pietz posits, "were understood to cause the Africans' false economic valuation of material objects." Their lack of god made them misconstrue gold, as Udemans or Berchem might have put it.[39]

Pietz did not discuss nor did he seem to be aware of the Visscher map and the Berchem cartouche, the Udemans text and the Cats poetry, all of which engage with much the same themes: the contradictions of godliness and material wealth, and the European presumption of the non-European's miscomprehension of the two. Nor did Pietz note Doncker's appropriation of Berchem's design and the transfer of the original allegorical figure from America to—of all places—West Africa, where it conveyed an abbreviated form of the original message. This time, however, the allegory would have illustrated the West African indigene's meager understanding of gold and ivory: "the riches and goods of this world," as Udemans termed them. Pietz's essays helpfully underscore a critical cultural difference, more broadly, between early modern Europeans and their "exotic" counterparts, particularly when it came to the commerce in material goods and their (European) sense of exotic geography. "The idea of the fetish," Pietz explains, "originated in a mercantile intercultural space created by the ongoing trade relations between cultures so radically different as to be mutually incomprehensible."[40] He thus highlights the role of exotic consumable objects in delimiting European and non-European cultures: Europeans, even as they dearly coveted them, believed only they understood an object's "true" material value, while non-European peoples, notwithstanding their casual regard of them, failed to grasp the worth of those very goods they so richly possessed. And while this space of encounter belongs to Africa in Pietz's case study, evidence abounds for other cases of unequal trade and "false" valuations in the exotic world, and of the contradictions—for Europeans, at least—between material and immaterial wealth. The very fluidity of this European perspective in many ways confirms Pietz's point. To the early modern European merchant—and traveler, draftsman, cartographer, printer, painter, ceramicist, and the slew of others responsible for designing and producing images and reports of the non-European world—the material contradictions of the exotic world migrate readily across hemispheres. They circulate as effortlessly as the exotic parasol.

The themes of the Berchem cartouche and the Pietz essays point to several related conclusions. Broadly speaking, both sets of sources—and Pietz does invoke several Dutch-made texts from the period circa 1700—productively connect exotic spaces with exotic things, "the riches and goods of this world."[41] They also help to contextualize Europe's growing appetite for these exotic riches and for the material arts that often derived from them, a hunger whetted by a useful, if paradoxical premise: that the peoples of the exotic world possessed only a dim understanding of those highly desirable material objects for which they were such casual custodians. In Berchem's cartouche, the allegorical message relates chiefly to the religious deficiencies of the indigenous Americans, while in Pietz's sources, the matter pertains more directly to commercial value and modes of exchange. It is striking, all the same, how readily these dismissive attitudes toward non-Europeans ricocheted across exotic spaces, from the fetish-worshiping Africans, who attach excessive value to "trifles"; to the idolatrous Americans of Berchem's drawings, who indifferently regard God and gold alike; to the Guineans of Doncker's derivative cartouche, who inhabit "gold" and "ivory" coasts whose worth they cannot adequately recognize. In Doncker's map of West Africa, space is entirely reduced to thing: the land gains its name and identity wholly from the rich, consumable goods of the exotic world. There is an obvious irony or contradiction to these exotic misapprehensions, which both Berchem and the authors of Pietz's sources intuitively seem to realize: that an African merchant bartering precious gold might dearly covet a mere "trifle," or that an American Indian—forced to labor in gloomy mines to furnish wealth for European masters—might stand under the shade of a regal parasol. And this leads to a further point: that images of parasols, of "trifles," and of the rich material goods obtained on African and American shores—objects commonly described in geography texts and depicted on embellished maps—ultimately become interchangeable to Europeans, markers of exotic space and examples of "decorative" things whose meaning, likewise, could shift across space and context.[42]

Imperfect (and Perfect) Chaos

Around the time that Jacob van Meurs launched the first volume of what would turn out to be arguably the most successful series of geography books printed in early modern Europe, the Flemish artist Jan van Kessel began to unveil a sequence of geographically inspired panel paintings, which depicted the world as a set of "continents" (as they had begun to be called). Van Kessel's *Continents* (1664–1666) consists of four separate compositions, each discreetly labeled in an exquisite contemporary calligraphy painted directly on their frames: "Europe," "Asie," "Africque," and "Americque." Each continent comprises a larger, framed central panel, which is bordered, in turn, by several smaller individual panels (sixteen per work), these miniature paintings similarly framed and labeled with geographic nomenclature—typically more localized place names meant to fall within the specific conti-

FIGURE 125. Jan van Kessel, *Europe* (1664–1666); oil on copper with wood; central panel 48.4 × 67.1 cm, outside panels 14.5 × 21 cm. bpk, Berlin. Alte Pinakothek, Bayerische Staatsgemäldesammlungen/Art Resource, NY.

nent. And while van Kessel's compositions share with Berchem's cartouches the habit of allegory—each of the larger panels features a principal female figure who is surrounded by scattered objects and costumed inhabitants intended to invoke the qualities of her quadrant of the globe—they are otherwise difficult to classify: as an intricate complex of panel paintings, as pictorial (and indeed textual) geographies, as allegorical-cartographical tableaux, or even as a form of "decorative" art. In fact, the van Kessel series might best be described as a hybrid ensemble, meticulously painted and framed objects—oil paintings on copper panels, encased in wooden frames and inscribed with fastidious calligraphy—that fit somewhere among several categories of visual, textual, graphic, and even plastic arts. The panels offer, in all regards, superb examples of exotic geography.[43]

While collectively sui generis, the van Kessel *Continents* do follow an internally coherent strategy of presentation, more or less, which holds the ensemble together.

FIGURE 126. Jan van Kessel, *Asie* (1664–1666); oil on copper with wood; central panel 48.5 × 67.5 cm, outside panels 14.5 × 21 cm. Alte Pinakothek, Bayerische Staatsgemälde-sammlungen. © Blauel/Gnamm, Artothek.

Each central panel has its own inscribed frame, which gestures toward a more particular geographic or cultural milieu—"Rome" and "Jerusalem," for example, stand in for Europe and Asia, respectively—and the surrounding panels all depict an assortment of flora and fauna in the foreground (presumably indigenous species, yet actually often not), with cityscapes or harbor views shown in the background. The middle panels themselves also conform to consistent compositional patterns (see plates 12–15). Each features a female allegorical figure—seated, although not necessarily in the compositional center—who is joined by a male attendant (also not quite central, except in the case of *Europe*) and two or three cherub-sized boys.[44] The allegorical figures and their entourages inhabit imposing, indoor-outdoor structures of mostly classical design—the paintings have typically been labeled "curiosity cabinets," yet the grand architecture presents anything but cabinet-like proportions—while in the background, under passages of bright, Tiepolo skies, other secondary figures mill about in "native" costumes. All of these figures, however,

FIGURE 127. Jan van Kessel, *Africque* (1664–1666); oil on copper with wood; central panel 48.5 × 67.5 cm, outside panels 14.5 × 21 cm. Alte Pinakothek, Bayerische Staatsgemäldesammlungen. © Blauel/Gnamm, Artothek.

serve almost as accessories, and the buildings as elaborate stage sets, for the true essence of the paintings: the abundance of material stuff that spills onto the floors, hangs on the walls, perches on pedestals, fills every niche, and provides the viewer with a magnificent panoply of objects meant collectively to exemplify and illustrate the qualities of each particular continent. These include miscellaneous artifacts related to religious and military practices (standard organizing categories of geography texts and allegorical imagery of this sort); stunning displays of *naturalia*, incorporating all manner of insect, plant, fish, shell, bird, and the occasional beast (all of which reflects van Kessel's professional specialty as an illustrator and painter of nature); and, perhaps most distinctively, sumptuous displays of material arts, embracing global ceramics and textiles, richly decorated gold and silver vessels, glassware and carved wood, statuary of various size and form, decorated chests and boxes brimming with valuables, exotic shells, and other miscellaneous collectibles. This bounty spreads out before each of the graceful Continents and fills the

FIGURE 128. Jan van Kessel, *Americque* (1664–1666); oil on copper with wood; central panel 48.6 × 67.9 cm, outside panels 14.5 × 21 cm. bpk, Berlin. Alte Pinakothek, Bayerische Staatsgemäldesammlungen/Art Resource, NY.

cavities of nearly every available space. The panels offer, in short, a brilliant display of "the riches and goods of the world."

To achieve this dazzling effect, Jan van Kessel (1626–1679) drew on a wide range of forms and techniques. Trained as a painter of still lifes with further expertise in minutely observed depictions of flowers, insects, shells, and other *naturalia*—these objects were greatly prized by Baroque collectors, as were the meticulously rendered paintings of them—van Kessel came from the illustrious Brueghel clan of Antwerp. He was a grandson of Jan Brueghel the Elder (thus a great-grandson of Pieter Brueghel the Elder), also known as "Velvet" or "Flower" Brueghel for his exquisitely executed floral compositions and their miraculous sheen; and he was a nephew of Jan Brueghel II, a painter of allegories and animals (Jan the Elder also painted allegories, famously in collaboration with Rubens). His extended family also linked him to Antwerp's prolific printing houses—likewise, intergenerational firms—and van Kessel had access throughout his career to a vast and wide-ranging trove of engraved materials and printed books. He also had access to, and drew inspiration from, the tradition of visual culture in Flanders and the many visual artists who moved in and out of Antwerp—a strikingly cohesive yet also cosmopolitan group of painters, engravers, miniaturists, naturalists, and cartographers, which included Joris Hoefnagel, who specialized in astonishingly detailed botanical drawings (also including insects); Roelandt Savery, who gained renown for his packed paintings of exotic animals, most of these closely observed (and, like Hoefnagel, a long-term guest at the court of Rudolph II in Prague); and, not least, Abraham Ortelius, the leading geographer of the era and printer extraordinaire of all things cartographic. Finally, van Kessel may have worked from nature—"ad vivum"—and may have possessed his own collection of specimens: a reasonable assumption, at least for the insects and flowers, yet not at all a certainty based on his apparent methods of composition.[45]

All of these influences—together with van Kessel's own considerable skills as a painter, his vivid application of color, his exacting delineation of figures, and his inventive sense of design—produced the tour de force that was the *Continents*. Yet even while van Kessel's series is sui generis, it does correlate in certain ways to other forms of representation and particularly to forms of geography that were being developed at this time—for example, in van Meurs's atelier. In their strategies of composition, in the way they habitually and productively cite other sources—borrow, adopt, and blend a mixture of visual motifs and vignettes designed originally for other compositions—and in their manner of assembling and staging a magpie collection of far-flung objects, the *Continents* partake of several techniques of exotic geography and, of course, other visual and literary forms that also served the makers of geography. The very shape of the individual *Continents*—a central framed image, surrounded by sixteen smaller panels that reference and elaborate on the larger

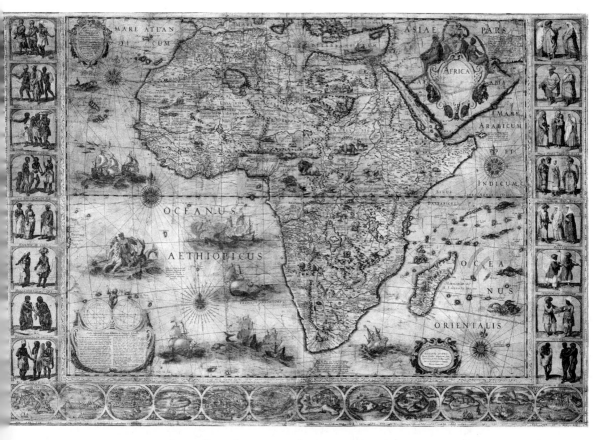

FIGURE 129. After Willem Blaeu, *Nova Africae Geographica* (Blaeu-Verbist, 1644; 1st ed. 1608); hand-colored engraving (wall map). Royal Museum for Central Africa, Tervuren.

whole—replicates a well-established formula of early modern cartography: the decorative map, often in the form of a wall map, with a centrally depicted space framed by peripheral scenes of peoples, cities, and other regional fare. This form was not exclusive to the mapping of the extra-European world, yet it became increasingly popular after the publication by Willem Blaeu of his celebrated maps of the continents (first published in 1608 and thereafter in several versions printed well into the second half of the century). Each of the continents—Blaeu counts the same four as van Kessel—is flanked by sixteen side panels that illustrate exotic peoples, typically in their local habit; each is bordered below, as well, by another twelve panels depicting principal cities and harbors.[46] The tradition of a "major" image or text commented upon by several "minor" images or texts enjoyed, moreover, a long history in European graphic and literary genres; medieval books commonly layered their texts in this way. Van Kessel's *Continents* in this structural, almost hermeneutic sense resembled not only a map but also a book: books in their printed form, to be sure, with their many supportive strata of paratexts, yet also books in their earlier form of illuminated manuscripts, which built up their decorated pages in this elaborately artful fashion.[47]

The paintings certainly resembled books of *geography*, more specifically, in the way they compiled central and peripheral detail to construct broader themes and arguments. Van Kessel's *Continents* further approximated volumes of geography, particularly those forms of exotic geography pioneered by van Meurs and others, in the way they assembled those arguments: by borrowing, quoting, and citing other visual sources, and by mining material that often had little genuine relation to the allegories at hand. Like the cannily constructed composite volumes of Jacob van Meurs or the massively accumulated "galleries" of Pieter van der Aa, the *Continents* came together by clever accretion. Van Kessel took an eclectic and opportunistic approach to the *Continents*. He took what he could, and he took as efficiently and expeditiously as he could. In fact, van Kessel borrowed liberally from those very volumes of exotic geography made in the Netherlands, often snatching prints and designs that had barely left the printer's workshop. In the allegory of Asia, a picture within the central panel—a painting within the painting, as it were, hung on the wall directly behind and above Asia herself—features several figures and elements taken indiscriminately from Johan Nieuhof's book on China (1665), which had been published at most a year earlier.[48] They derive from three distinct engravings in van Meurs's publication, including one of the famous "Porcelain Pagoda." Van Kessel, however, rearranges these elements to fit into a single composition and thereby achieves a more intensive, if decontextualized, effect (see plate 14 and compare figures 157, 158). An adjacent painting-within-painting also borrows from various van Meurs prints, as do some of the statuary in the Asia panel. In the latter case, van Kessel adopts graphic work from van Meurs to replicate the form of sculpture, albeit in the medium of painting—a dizzying feat of visual quotation.[49] Van Kessel also borrows an engraved scene of Indian sati from the *Itinerario* of Jan Huygen van Linschoten, in this case for his allegory of America—"Indians" of all types populate that promiscuous panel (see plate 13 [lower right] and compare figure 97). And he models two of the statues in the open-air arches behind "America" (left and right of the central door) on prints by Georg Marcgraf (based on designs by Albert Eckhout), which had been published in the first edition of Piso's *Historia naturalis Brasiliae* (1648). The latter volume represents the summa of natural history work done in Dutch Brazil under the auspices of Johan Maurits of Nassau-Siegen, and van Kessel counts among the earliest adopters of the Mauritian oeuvre and of the Nieuhof China illustrations—a corpus of images that, in both cases, would go on to have a remarkably influential afterlife in the decorative arts.[50]

More generally and more voraciously, van Kessel relied on a vast number of earlier painted and printed sources for his depictions of exotic as well as European

FIGURE 130. Jan Brueghel the Elder, *The Temptation in the Garden of Eden* (ca. 1600); oil on oak panel; 53 × 84 cm. © Victoria and Albert Museum, London.

FIGURE 131. Jan van Kessel, "Londres" (peripheral panel from *Europe*) (1664–1666); oil on copper; 14.5 × 21 cm. Alte Pinakothek, Bayerische Staatsgemäldesammlungen.

Harpyæ prima icon.

FIGURE 132. "Harpyae prima icon" (woodblock print), in Ulisse Aldrovandi, *Monstrorum historia cum Paralipomenis historiae omnium animalium* (Bologna, 1642). Biblioteca Universitaria di Bologna.

species. An artist highly regarded for his scrupulous natural history painting, both in his own day and in art history's later judgment, van Kessel in practice methodically copied numerous animals from the works of others: a cost-effective and shrewd production strategy to create the immense inventory of *naturalia* that he crammed into his *Continents*.[51] "London" horses come from an earlier *Garden of Eden* (circa 1600) painted by van Kessel's grandfather, Jan Brueghel the Elder (see figures 130 and 131), as does a purple gallinule in the panel painting of "Stockholm"—the species, in reality, is indigenous to the Americas—and a penguin who wobbles about in "Baía de Todos os Santos" (Brazil).[52] A harpy that resides in an interior painting within the central panel of *Africa* and a queer cock from the "Mexico" side panel of *America* originate in Ulisse Aldrovandi's *Monstrorum historia* (1642) and *Ornithologia* (1599), respectively (see plate 12 [upper left] and compare figure 132); a porcupinefish and "admirable" breed of whale begin their lives as woodcuts in Carolus Clusius's *Exoticorum libri decem* (1605) before they swim ashore in van Kessel's vignette of "Tunis" (see figures 133 and 134); and a Clusius-derived armadillo—American thus—ambles across a beach in Aden. Going back even further in terms of vintage are the Bactrian camel that inhabits the port of

FIGURE 133. "Cete admirabilis forma [beaked whale?]" (woodblock print), in Carolus Clusius, *Exoticorum libri decem* (Leiden, 1605). NCB Naturalis Holland.

FIGURE 134. Jan van Kessel, "Tunis" (peripheral panel from *Africque*) (1664–1666); oil on copper; 14.5 × 21 cm. Alte Pinakothek, Bayerische Staatsgemäldesammlungen.

"Ormuz" (the Persian Gulf) and the giraffe posing by an indeterminate American harbor (the beast is properly of Africa), both of which derive from illustrations in the *Historiae animalium* published by the great Renaissance zoologist Conrad Gesner in the mid-sixteenth century—over a hundred years before the "exactly painted" variants of these species land on van Kessel's panels (figures 135 and 136). All of these visual extractions and many more reflect van Kessel's canny approach

FIGURE 135. Lucas Schram (?), "De Camelo [Bactrian camel]" (woodblock print), in Conrad Gesner, *Historiae animalium* (Zurich, 1551–1558). Zentralbibliothek, Zürich.

FIGURE 136. Jan van Kessel, "Ormuz" (peripheral panel from *Asie*) (1664–1666); oil on copper; 14.5 × 21 cm. Alte Pinakothek, Bayerische Staatsgemäldesammlungen.

to compiling paintings, his greater regard for the synthetic (and aesthetic) whole than for "scientific" detail, his casual disregard for regional niceties, his catholic collection of creatures and curiosities—in short, his deployment of techniques of manufacture that would hardly have been alien to Holland's impresarios of print geography.[53]

One more way van Kessel's *Continents* bear comparison to other forms of exotic geography: the manner in which the paintings present the material arts and riches of the world. Each of the four central panels extensively illustrates—or, more accurately, painstakingly inventories and all but obsessively stages—the consumable objects and material arts that were at once associated with and becoming vital media of the non-European world. The paintings positively brim over with exotic *things*. In the center of *Africa*, between the principal allegorical figure and her male companion, lies a trove of Ming blue-and-white porcelain, surrounded by branches of red coral and assorted exotic shells; silver and gold *tazze* of elaborate design; a hybrid drinking vessel, incorporating a coconut shell and crafted sea monsters; finely fluted glassware (invented, according to Pliny, by the Phoenicians, thus in the Levant); intricately shaped pipes of various material (and rolls of tobacco); and other miscellaneous exotica (see plate 12). Treasures on a table to the right of "Africa" include a superb mounted nautilus shell, a stout ceramic and silver jug, strings of pearls—all of which rests on a brightly patterned (Persian?) carpet. Meanwhile, "America" sits amid more pearls, corals, and shells, which spill out of an intricately embossed barrel made of gold, while colorful batches of feathers and breeds of parrot flitter throughout the panel (see plate 13). "America" also lays claim to a set of gamelan gongs at her feet—one of her "boys" is busy at play—while face masks, ingeniously contrived from exotic shells, decorate the walls around her, and a suit of Japanese armor (of the sort collected by Europeans) rests incongruously in the corner. As for "Asia," her floor space may be the most cluttered of the non-European continents (see plate 14). A heavy, possibly Anatolian rug drapes partly over a chair and partly over framed insects in the lower-right corner, while an ornate shield made of ebony and inlaid mother-of-pearl is propped up in the lower left corner. In between these exotic bookends, the attentive eye takes in a range of rich textiles (a silk sheath of arrows lies on a lovely brocaded table covering); intricately ornamented samples of metalware (a large ewer of gold and silver, a golden baton topped with a crescent, a silver censer tugged upon by the two cherubic "boys"); sundry statuary, ceramics, gemstones, pearls, medallions, fans, and more. Even the continent *Europe* boasts some manner of exotica: a cluster of tropical shells occupies the heart of the composition, filling the space between "Europe" and her male escort (see plate 15).[54]

This profusion of foreign (and invariably European) stuff and the bountiful material arts that characterize the *Continents* correlate to the "objectness" otherwise prevalent in sources of exotic geography. Jan van Kessel's painted compositions point in this way to related strategies of presentation in cartography—the overflowing cartouches that decorate maps of the non-European world; the cleverly "framed" designs on the margins of global wall maps—and in other sources of print geography. The layout and the material contents spread across the central panels of the *Continents* correspond, perhaps even more closely, to the frontispiece of an Amsterdam-made volume of geography: the teeming treasures of the Baldaeus *Malabar* cover image (which also moved to cartography; see figures 106 and 107), the style of frontispiece created for almost any book on Asia (an exotic space particularly susceptible to this treatment; see figure 6), or simply one of the many van Meurs–designed opening engravings that revel in the riches of the world (see figure 60). Objects in these prints pile up in similarly splendid heaps of consumable luxury and in comparably chaotic disarray. Material goods and material arts advertise the exotic world with an analogous disregard for putative place of origin or for the regional context of an object or practice—porcelain in Africa, sati in America, armadillos in Aden. Van Kessel's paintings and contemporary sources of print geography alike present the non-European world on similarly decentered, decontextualized grounds: a global stage for exhibiting an abundance of widely gathered, materially alluring, exotic objects.

Depictions of a world saturated with exotic objects and images that celebrate the splendor and variety of global consumable goods were not the least bit foreign to early modern Dutch visual culture. The genre of Dutch still-life painting, especially in its most exuberant, mid- to later seventeenth-century form, also accumulated in a single picture frame the far-flung riches of the material world. The splendidly appointed tables laid out by Willem Kalf and Abraham van Beyeren heave with imported porcelain, mounted nautilus shells, decorated silver and glass vessels, and—rather than van Kessel's armies of insects—glorious fare assembled from across the globe (see plate 16). These so-called *pronk* (sumptuous) still lifes gathered and fabricated, often with brilliant luminosity, what Roland Barthes once derisively described as the superficial "sheen" of worldly things. Barthes's essay on "Le monde-objet" ("The world as object") took on precisely the *objectness* of early modern Dutch culture, its ostensible dedication to material accumulation, and its "empire of things," in which Barthes perceived "an early form of commodity fetish" (a characterization that neatly intersects with William Pietz's interrogation of material culture and fetish in early modern West Africa).[55] In his own broad-ranging analysis of the Dutch Republic's "embarrassment of riches," Simon Schama revisits Barthes's essay, the genre of *pronk* still life, and Dutch visual culture of this period. Schama, however, discerns in these paintings' "flamboyant" gathering of global bounty and in their profusion of glimmering things—the exotic stuff of Dutch still lifes—a pervasive anxiety about material wealth: a moral unease with "the riches and goods of this world," as *predikant* Udemans understood them.[56] With a greater focus on the consumable contents (literally) of still lifes—food, drink, tobacco—Julie Hochstrasser also draws attention to the gathering of worldly goods that takes place in Dutch painting. Hochstrasser catalogues the colonial origins of the paintings' products to make a case for their correlation to Dutch commercial culture—in a sense, returning to Barthes's original materialist preoccupations and, in all events, emphasizing once again the objectness and exotic reach expressed in these sources.[57]

Still-life painting—along with the lesser-studied genre of curiosity-cabinet painting, as developed, for example, by Jan van der Heyden (see figure 4)—no doubt piled up objects from around the world, sometimes with boisterous abandon, in order to illustrate the impressive "empire of things" lately amassed by global commerce. Yet these compositions do not call attention to their combinations in quite the same way that van Kessel's *Continents* do. While the tables of exotic goods in a Kalf still life may mingle the same breadth of objects that spill on to the floors of a van Kessel continent, the Kalf painting manages these mixtures more subtly and artfully than the van Kessel composition. Whereas a typical *pronk* still-life painting inconspicuously draws together the riches of the globe—the point is precisely the cumulative accumulation of far-flung luxury—van Kessel's designs feature a more discordant hodgepodge.[58] Or, to come at this from a more constructive angle, van Kessel creates in his compositional mixtures more cacophony and chaos; he veritably amplifies the global jumble and stresses the spatial conflations. He does this, moreover, in a form that might otherwise be expected to orchestrate global difference and articulate global distinction: a set of discreet continents, presented as individual allegories. Whatever else they are, the allegorical *Continents* would seem to proclaim their purpose in their titles and form: they claim to illustrate and delineate the four distinct "parts" of the world. That they ultimately do not, however, speaks both to their larger thematic purpose and to the developing aesthetic of exoticism.

Van Kessel's *Allegories of the Four Continents*—to give them a full and proper title—operate on two levels: they *distinguish* among the geographic regions of the world, while they also *conflate* the geographic regions of the world. The paintings draw distinctions on the basis of three essential criteria: the religions, natural histories, and material goods that flourish in the separate spaces of the globe. Religion ranks at the top of the list. The world's rival systems of faith and competing devotional practices were, in truth, standard tropes of social comparison, and van Kessel's most easily identified organizational scheme rests on this older tradition. "Asia," who sits beside an open-faced Koran, which occupies its own stately chair—a seat of honor—is associated with Islam as well as Buddhism, the latter embodied by a large bronze statue of a Buddha perched on a pedestal. Off in the distance is Istanbul's Hagia Sophia, and a Chinese pagoda can be glimpsed on a wall painting.[59] For "Africa," the central-frame inscription announces the region's allegiance to "Le Temple des Idoles" (The Temple of the Idols): a sketchy scene of idolatry looms in a rear cave, entered through a monumental arch. The newest continent, "America," would appear to lack all form of religion—so European commentators often opined—although strategic references to sati, cannibalism, and other rites of violence hint at a darker form of heathenism.[60] As for "Europe," van Kessel scatters throughout the panel symbols of Christianity in its most optimistic, pre-schismatic form: a pope's tiara, a cardinal's hat, the pontifical keys to heaven, a propped-up Latin Bible, and so on.[61] Yet this sense of a unified European faith is slyly subverted by allusions not so much to Protestantism as to the invasive sins of the day: playing cards, a backgammon board (both related to gambling), a wine jug (drinking), a tennis racquet (gaming), a debtor's bill, and the like. These devices also appear in contemporary emblem literature, where they insinuated, as did a popular Roemer Visscher emblem that incorporated much of the same imagery, the crisis of Christianity: "Pessima placent pluribus" (most people prefer the worst things).[62]

The *naturalia* and material artifacts that van Kessel blends into the *Continents* also point to global distinctions, while at the same time studiously undermining these. "Europe" admires a cornucopia of fruits and flowers, including a ripe pomegranate—a species native to Persia—while her male companion gestures toward painted and framed flowers and insects, both of indigenous and exotic origins. "Asia" similarly surrounds herself with insects of varied provenance, framed and otherwise—this device carries through all four continents, playing to van Kessel's strong suit as a painter of delicate *naturalia*—and she casts her glance toward a painting of exotic birds. A toucan and macaw—South American breeds, easily recognizable—peer down on her from a peripheral panel depicting Osaka. Along with her wealth of Chinese porcelain, "Africa" also possesses an abundance of tobacco. *Nicotiana* came overwhelmingly from the Americas in these years, although African labor played a critical part in its production. A dark-skinned male figure and a young boy sit off to the side and puff away through one of the many clay pipes—typically Dutch made—strewn across the composition.[63] "America" may be the richest of the continents in terms of animal life—birds, fish, insects, mammals, and even a marsupial loiter about—and in terms of sheer treasure: gold and silver specie along with other precious booty spill out of a golden drum, a suggestion of America's surplus of mineral wealth. In the context of this allegory's absence of any obvious religious paraphernalia, this composition may also allude to the proverbial wisdom on the inverse rapport of God and gold—and thus may relate to the contemporary cartouche designed by Nicolaes Berchem for the oft-reprinted Nicolaes Visscher map of America.

What seems perfectly clear, in all cases, is the tendency in *America*, as in van Kessel's other continents, to muddle matters by mixing and matching the regions of the world—especially the exotic world. These blended concoctions are as rife as they are obvious. If *Africa* features Ming porcelain laid out front and center, *America* boasts Javanese gamelan gongs, similarly situated in the foreground, and a distinctly Japanese suit of armor that anchors the middle section of the composition (the corner where the two walls of statuary join). An ersatz "Brahmin" figure fills a

Canarim

Lascaryn

Balhadeira

Agricola Indus Canaryn dictus
Een Indiaens lant ofte bouwman
genaemt Canaryn.

Indorum liberi pro eorum consuetudine pudendis
tantum rariori tela contecti.
Indiaensche kinderen als slants manier is, leen die scha:
melheyt met een dun linnen doeckskens lickt bedecade.

Miles Indus quem lascarin
nominant
Een Indiaens soldaet lascarin
geheeten.

Inda meretrix, saltando et canendo
victum queritans.
Een Indiaensche lichte vrouwe met dans:
sen en singen haer cost winnende.
58 en 59

Ioann: a Doet: fec.

FIGURE 137. Johannes van Doetecum, "Balhadeira" (engraving), in Jan Huygen van
Linschoten, *Itinerario, voyage ofte schipvaert van Ian Huygen van Linschoten naer Oost
ofte Portugaels Indien* (Amsterdam, 1596). Koninklijke Bibliotheek, The Hague.

central niche of this "American" room—the statue stands adjacent to the wall-
painting of sati—while the woman skipping through the rear door derives from an
engraving of an *East* Indian "Balhadeira" (dancer).[64] Meanwhile, between the Indian dancer and the Japanese armor waddles an iconic American armadillo (a sly
visual pun: the Spanish name means small "armored" one); yet below and center
stands an *African* crowned crane, whose curving neck guides the viewer's eye to a
perched macaw and toucan—two birds typically affiliated with tropical America.[65]
The peripheral panels of the *Continents*, both in their gathering of global fauna and
their invocation of global place names—the geographic nomenclature painted directly onto the frames—only compound this sense of conflation. Giraffes crop up
in Asia and South America; llamas and capuchin monkeys leave their indigenous
American home for coastal Africa; and a wayward opossum, another obvious New

World native, visits in Calicut—the other Indies. These mélanges, once again, appear to be by design, since the allocation of space in the larger compositions, as demonstrated by the dispersal of city and harbor views, would seem to be similarly blended. Angola and Morocco relocate to the continent of Asia, Ceylon (Sri Lanka) and Elmina (Ghana) surface in the Americas, and Athens and the pyramids can be visited in Asia: there are numerous such brazen admixtures. The single and conspicuously unblended continent is Europe, and this also seems by intent. The *non*-European world designed by van Kessel hosts a jumble of species, spaces, and objects, thrown together with a loose conception of geographic place, a blithe sense of regional disorder, and a design plan of obvious incongruity. The *Continents*, in short, convey an aesthetic of exoticism: of purposeful conflation and orchestrated chaos.

If van Kessel's panel paintings partake in an aesthetic of exoticism, they do so in a larger context that crosses (and sometimes merges) several genres and media. For the *Continents'* depictions of the exotic world not only conflate; they also digress and zigzag in much the way printed geography books of this period likewise shift haphazardly from space to space and from narrative to narrative. They gleefully reconstitute the non-European world, as well, in much the same way contemporary visual and "decorative" arts mingle motifs and replicate exotic icons with manifest disregard for original context. The *Continents* and these other forms reflect a broader exotic style: a tendency, among a wide range of sources produced circa 1700, to mix and match geographic spaces; to treat exotic things and non-European peoples as fluid and interchangeable (an American Indian adorning a West African map); to present far-flung material objects or exotic imagery by subtle and often witty analogy (a suit of Japanese armor pointing to an American armadillo); to tolerate within non-European settings, indeed even to cultivate, an aesthetic of disorder. Texts of the type produced by Jacob van Meurs and his publishing cohort successfully traded in this style: a discussion of earthquakes in Japan could provoke a seismic history of Mexico (as occurs in Arnoldus Montanus's *Japan*), while a narrative of South Asian religion could blend Calvinist authorship with Jesuit texts (as exemplified by Philip Baldaeus's *Malabar*). Designers of geographic images, both of the painted and graphic variety, casually appropriated and thereby decontextualized what soon became standard markers of exoticism: palm trees flourishing on maps of New England or opossums wandering through views of Calicut. And makers of objects that engage with exotic things, in terms of both their material and their motifs, inclined similarly toward incongruity, often with an apparently playful intent: an East Indian turbo shell embellished with a West Indian armadillo or a Meissen teapot—one of countless ceramic objects that could be cited—that brings together ostensibly Chinese figures and feathered American Indians (under a ubiquitous palm tree, no less) (see plate 17 and figure 138).[66]

FIGURE 138. Teapot, Meissen Manufactory (ca. 1735); hard-paste porcelain painted with enamel colors and gilt; 11.3 cm (height). © Metropolitan Museum of Art. Image source: Art Resource, NY.

These conflations or digressions, as it were, occur regularly and seem to come effortlessly not only in forms that blur the different parts of the globe—as in van Kessel's hodgepodge of continents—but also in ways that blend the very forms that were enlisted to represent those global parts. A remarkable passage in Aphra Behn's *Oroonoko* (discussed in another context in chapter 3) illustrates this habit of description. The titular hero of the novel—an African-born prince captured and transported in chains to tropical America—clearly fascinated Behn, who devotes several passages of enthusiastic description to Oroonoko's physical appearance. These prose sketches paint a keenly tactile picture of Oroonoko's bodily form—his very physical being—which, inter alia, invoke a full inventory of material arts. The prince's scarified flesh, the reader learns, is "delicately Cut and Rac'd all over the fore-part of the Trunk": the analogy here is to engraving ("cut") and the work of the print shop, as well as to forms of chasing or embossing—"rac'ed," or raised, flesh points to the art of inscribing or incising in a form of relief. The prince's body "looks as if it were Japan'd": Behn now highlights the darkness and slick smoothness of Oroonoko's skin, the worked-over body compared to a piece of Japanese lacquered wood. In the very next clause, however, the author reverts to the nubbly texture of lacework: "the Works [of scarification] being raised like high Poynt round the Edges of the Flowers."

And the hero (in this passage referred to by his given slave name "Caesar") also resembles a form of notched statuary: "Some [princes of Africa] are only Carv'd with a little Flower, or Bird, at the sides of the Temples, as was *Caesar*; and those who are so Carv'd over the body, resemble our Ancient *Picts*, that are figur'd in the Chronicles, but these Carvings are more delicate." The geography of Behn's description thus encompasses the four parts of the globe. An African prince, transported and rechristened in America, physically resembles the Asian art of japanning and the European techniques of lacework, engraving, and chasing. The end result, furthermore, brings to mind "our Ancient Picts," the quasi-mythical ancestors of the British, whose likeness was famously reproduced in engravings printed by Theodor de Bry to illustrate Thomas Harriot's *Briefe and true report of Virginia*—a description thus of the Carolina Algonquians.[67]

Behn's sensibility, van Kessel's sense of design, Dutch ateliers' fashion of geography: all were of a piece, and all reflected an "aesthetic of the exotic," as Bernard Smith termed this in another context. They blended and digressed, and they departicularized and decontextualized, as they devised a "disorderly" and jumbled model of the exotic world. Producers across several media formulated what Georg Rumphius, in his own attempt to assemble the plants of the tropical world in word and image, categorized as an "imperfect chaos"—"onvolmaakte *Chaos*" in the Dutch version or "indigestum supererat Chaos" in the Latin, which stresses the sense of muddled disorder—by which Rumphius meant an expressly unruly presentation of global things.[68]

While they did not invent "exoticism" as such, these authors, printers, painters, naturalists, mapmakers, designers, and cultural commentators did devise a distinctive mode of presentation. And they did invent a suitably exotic idiom to express this aesthetic: *sharawadgi*, a word coined right around this moment by the well-traveled English diplomat Sir William Temple (1628–1699), who sought, in an essay of 1685, to come to terms with the appearance and apparent "irregularity" of the exotic world. Temple, whose travels never actually took him beyond the borders of Europe yet who did spend substantial time in the global entrepôt that was Holland, invokes this rare phrasing in ruminations on the diversity of gardens. Toward the end of his essay "Upon the Gardens of Epicurus; or, of Gardening in the Year 1685," Temple muses on the differences between "regular"—by which he meant orderly and symmetrical—and "irregular" gardens, and this prompts him to posit a distinction between formal European and Chinese-style gardens, the latter devised by "a People, whose way of thinking, seems to lie as wide of ours in *Europe*, as their Country does." What is particularly striking in Temple's description of what he takes to be the Chinese horticultural style is the way his evocation of that aesthetic mirrors the brand of exoticism otherwise prevalent across several contemporary cultural products. "Among us," writes the English statesman, the Beauty of Building and Planting is placed chiefly in certain Proportions, Symmetries, or Uniformities; our Walks and our Trees are ranged so, as to answer one another, and at exact Distances. . . . But their greatest reach of Imagination, is employed in contriving Figures, where the Beauty shall be great, and strike the Eye, but *without any order or disposition of parts*, that shall be commonly or easily observ'd.[69]

Temple bestows on this aesthetic a vernacular name, meant to be Chinese—*sharawadgi*—and he notes its pervasiveness in other exotic arts: "And whoever observes the Work upon the best Indian Gowns, or the painting upon their best Skreens or Purcellans, will find their Beauty is all of this kind, (that is) *without order*." The phenomenon, in other words, crosses material forms and geographic lines: Japanese screens, Indian silks, Chinese porcelains. And this aesthetic can be superbly observed, it turns out, not in China or in England—Temple discourages his readers from even attempting this tricky horticultural feat—but in the gardens of the Dutch Governor of the Cape Colony, in Africa, where Temple learns (secondhand, inevitably) that "so as in this one Inclosure [of the colony's garden] are to be found the several Gardens of *Europe*, *Asia*, *Africk*, and *America*."[70] A Dutch-designed garden, cultivated in a southern African outpost, gathering and commingling the four parts of the world: if not *sharawadgi*, nor even "imperfect chaos," this was indubitably an "aesthetic of the exotic."[71]

On Replication and the Exotic World

Temple's theories were not quite Bernard Smith's theories—Smith's aesthetic of exoticism—although there are several instructive and productive overlaps worth noting. In a lengthy and oft-cited essay on early modern Europe's "visual mode" of engagement with the non-European world, Smith identified an "aesthetic category" of exoticism and located its development specifically in the second-half-of-the-seventeenth-century moment that coincides with the multidisciplinary works of van Kessel, van Meurs, Behn, and Temple. Samples of "Baroque exotica" thrived above all in the decorative arts, Smith contended. "One of its most favored subjects was the Continents," he added, "[which] provided a sumptuous opportunity to commingle and conflate the animals, plants, artifacts, and indigenes of the non-European world within highly colorful, decorative schemes."[72] "Decorative," as an aesthetic, material, and sometimes functional category, is pivotal to Smith's argument—it comes up several times in his essay—and even while he does not mention them, Smith might as well have been referencing the richly "commingled" and "conflated" *Continents* of Jan van Kessel and other geography sources of that ilk.

Yet he also makes a critical distinction, which suggests another approach to these jumbled products. For Smith, the "decorative" exotica of this period lack "narrative" content: these forms carefully "describe" and "replicate" the exotic world, yet "there is no coherent 'story'"; nor is there any coherent order.[73] Decorative objects do not *narrate* so much as they *represent*; they offer the visual pleasure of discreet (and curious) things, yet they provide no account of these things or of their relation to one another. Smith explains this design strategy with reference to what he describes as the "spatial problematic" of material (by which he means non-fine) arts: "the covering of a variety of shaped surfaces" prevents "decorative" objects from maintaining a coherent compositional center. Exotic designs, if fully capable of replicating exotic motifs "realistically"—palm trees that looked like bona fide palm trees—had "illogical space" and an unrealistic sense of spatial correlations, and this made them incapable of formulating progressive, historical narratives. They accumulated things without a sense of order; they "presented [exotica] in a confused jumble" and with a scrambled sense of "realism"; they delivered decontextualized bric-a-brac and (in a slightly adjusted context) digressive geographies. Smith's aesthetic of exoticism resembled, in short, an "imperfect chaos."[74]

Smith's theoretical contribution (one of the few assessments of early modern exoticism in the scholarly literature) prompts several questions pertaining to the form and function of exotic things: to the narrative scope both of "decorative" objects that incorporate exotic motifs and of exotic geography in its multiple printed genres, the two forms alike trafficking in decontextualized content; to the meaning of exotic motifs as they appear in shifting media and contexts—a palm tree engraved on a map, described in a book, painted on porcelain, and so on—and to the fundamental "coherence" or "logic" of various "commingled" and "conflated" exotica, whatever their ultimate form. Form, in fact, rests at the heart of these inquiries, whether a matter of the spatial arrangement of exotic vignettes or the misplaced "realism" of their configuration. By the former—"spatial problematics"—Smith has in mind the absence of linear perspective or flat forms in certain-shaped material arts: round pieces of ceramic, multifaceted furnishings, and the like. Yet this plainly overlooks the easy possibility of perspective in tapestries (the Gobelins Manufactory produced one of the most enduring forms of exotic imagery in its series on *Les Anciennes Indes*, which Smith briefly invokes); in engraved copper plates (the prints designed by Romeyn de Hooghe for *Les Indes Orientales et Occidentales* offer "a baroque profusion of [exotic] images," as one of de Hooghe's modern editors has remarked, yet does so on the flattest of media); or even on the surfaces of smoothly lacquered furniture.[75] It presumes, moreover, the presence of single-point perspective and the invocation of narrative in most genres of paintings—although this is hardly the case. In the second case—the tendency to insert "realistic" or mimetically convincing forms in an exotic pastiche: finely delineated

Ming porcelain, for example, painted into an allegory of Africa—Smith brushes up against, yet does not address head on, questions of context. What does it mean to appropriate images from disparate, often unrelated sources, and then to reinsert them into "exotic" designs? How does the "logic" of an exotic image and its ideological content shift as it changes settings, genres, and media? And why is it that exotic motifs seem to lend themselves so easily to processes of media transfer and workshop replication?

These questions, in turn, suggest one further, valuable correspondence between the field of geography and the decorative arts: their shared habit of replication. The design and manufacture of decorated material arts and the construction and presentation of print geography—the astonishing output of those impresarios of print discussed in chapter 1—entailed remarkably similar processes of invention and production. The modus operandi of these respective ateliers, that is, involved parallel practices of borrowing, appropriating, reformulating, or simply duplicating materials. This occurred across genres, forms, and media; it shaped the production of maps, prints, and a vast range of books (encompassing texts and images); it guided the design of ceramics, textiles, decorated furniture, and more. And it occurred conspicuously with exotic motifs. This tactic of manufacture inverts a common understanding of early modern exotica and their value as "curious," exceptional things. Wondrous objects collected and exchanged among aficionados, as Paula Findlen has argued in her rich study of early modern natural history and the origins of museums, gained value for their implicit quality of "incomparability": they were perceived to be outstanding and presented to the viewer as unique.[76] Yet in the business of exotic geography and in the design of "decorative" arts with exotic motifs, production values point to the opposite approach: to a limited and regularly repeated repertoire of images and icons; to the recourse in print ateliers to a form of stereotype (a term derived from the economy of print, albeit in a later period); and to the basic, if evidently effective, practice of replication.

The most simple form of replication, fairly rife in the context of early modern print, was clear-cut and unapologetic copying. A commonly used cost-saving procedure, the practice of direct duplication was employed by printers and draftsmen to squeeze the most out of a copper plate or to extract maximum benefit from a well-conceived design (possibly copied onto a new plate): hence the concept of "stereotype."[77] In certain cases, a printer might use a print or design successfully across several publications made within his own workshop. Jacob van Meurs did this with various Brazilian sketches by Frans Post and Albert Eckhout, which served for a generic book on America (by Montanus) and a separate volume on the East and West Indies (by Nieuhof) that incorporated substantial Braziliana. The Post and Eckhout illustrations had originally been intended for and partly incorporated into a book on Dutch Brazil published by Joan Blaeu, and they were used

FIGURE 139. Tapuya (Tarairiú) couple (woodblock print), in Willem Piso et al., *Historia naturalis Brasiliae* (Leiden and Amsterdam, 1648). Peter H. Raven Library, Missouri Botanical Garden. Image courtesy of the Biodiversity Heritage Library.

again in a wholly separate volume on natural history produced by the renowned Elsevier firm.[78] The images circulated in this way among different printers, and this businesslike process of borrowing points to another convention of replication. High-quality designs could migrate across several ateliers, the legality of these movements (and appropriations) varying from the legitimate sale of plates to an allied printer to unambiguous pirating. The convoluted history of a series of engravings that illustrate "The Ten Avatars of Vishnu" demonstrates the value—and longevity—of a well-executed set of designs. Based on original Indian images obtained by the Dutch artist Philips Angel during his service in Malabar (likely via a Jesuit intermediary), a series of full-folio plates depicting the Hindu god's ten incarnations appeared in 1672 in a volume attributed to Philip Baldaeus (figure 141). That same year a similar series of avatars from a rival printer—van Meurs in this case taking on the Amsterdam publishing tandem of Janssonius van Waesberge and van Someren, who produced the Baldaeus book—also hit the market. Both groups of engravings circulated widely, also in translation.[79] (Another, slightly cruder set of avatars appeared in Athanasius Kircher's *China illustrata*; these were published in 1667 by *both* Janssonius van Waesberge and van Meurs, who clearly kept tabs on one another's activities.)[80] Both sets of images, furthermore, experienced an iconographic re-

FIGURE 140. Tapuya (Tarairiú) couple (engraving), in Johan Nieuhof, *Gedenkwaerdige zee en lantreize door de voornaemste landschappen van West en Oostindien* (Amsterdam, 1682). Special Collections, University of Amsterdam (KF 61-4601).

naissance, as it were, around 1730—more than half a century later—when they were adopted for rival, this time grander, publication projects. The Baldaeus avatars were appropriated by the engraver Bernard Picart for his *Ceremonies et coutumes religieuses des tous les peuples du monde* published in the 1720s and 1730s (and in further editions, printed well into the 1740s; figure 142), which was right around the time Pieter van der Aa included a version of the van Meurs avatars in his *Galerie agreable du monde* (circa 1729).[81] Both of these publications—each lavishly produced and broadly circulated to Europe-wide acclaim—extended the life of the plates and influence of the images deep into the eighteenth century, allowing them to become the clichéd versions—the standard exotic stereotypes—of Vishnu's avatars.

This process, it bears emphasizing, was hardly unique to works of geography; printers across many fields sought to enhance their profits by whatever means possible, including direct copying. But even such basic patterns of replication, for similar sorts of books or within the same genre, look somewhat different when set in the context of geography, a discipline predicated precisely on making distinctions. The effects of such replications for *exotic* materials, moreover, and in genres such as cartography stand out all the more for their subversion of their expressed purpose: to *differentiate* among, not duplicate, spaces and things. Nicolaes Berchem's car-

FIGURE 141. Coenraet Decker (?) after Philips Angel, First Avatar of the God Vishnu (engraving and etching), in Philip Baldaeus, *Naauwkeurige beschryvinge van Malabar en Choromandel* (Amsterdam, 1672). Special Collections, University of Amsterdam (KF 61-5258).

touche design for Nicolaes Visscher's map of the Americas offers a stunning example: the essence of America, as presented in an allegorical image of the continent, comes to stand in the duplicated cartouche of Hendrick Doncker for Africa. A genre (cartography) and a form (allegory) that are meant to define space and distill qualities do the exact opposite: *a* stands not for *a* but for *a* or *b*. In the case of Jan van Kessel's numerous borrowings for the *Continents*, especially in his detailed design of the *naturalia* in the central compositions and peripheral landscapes of his paintings, the habit of copying reflects, it is true, a long tradition in flower and in-

Premiere incarnation.

FIGURE 142. Bernard Picart after Philips Angel, *Premiere incarnation* (engraving and etching), in J. F. Bernard, *Ceremonies et coutumes religieuses des tous les peuples du monde* (Amsterdam, 1723–1743). The Getty Research Institute (BL75.C4 1723), Los Angeles.

sect illustration and in the printing of natural history books. But the results stand out in sharper relief when the *Continents* are seen in combination with one another: flora, fauna, and native objects from one part of the globe appear incongruously in another, and this subverts the viewers' sense of distinct regional "continents." The results suggest what Sachiko Kusukawa has described as a loss of "argumentative function." In her analysis of the presence of pictures in early modern printed volumes of natural history (using as case studies the relentlessly plagiarized engravings taken from works of the botanist Leonhart Fuchs and the anatomist Andreas Vesalius), Kusukawa considers the effects of purposeful, printerly replication: a sacrifice of context, almost by definition, that leads to a further loss of "the original, descriptive, and argumentative function for which the images had been designed." The replicated images may still serve some function—they do not become "merely" decorative—yet they cease to retain their originally intended meaning.[82]

This mode of modification through duplication is all the more evident when images move not only within a genre—map to map, print to print, book to book—but also across genres and between media. The frontispiece to Philip Baldaeus's book on the regions of Malabar and Coromandel, including a lengthy section on Hinduism in Sri Lanka, served as the launching point for a cartouche to a map of India (see figures 106 and 107). An image originally devised to entice readers to explore the social and religious mores of South India—for this was the chief focus of Baldaeus's 1672 geography—the design later functioned in a series of maritime maps as the navigators' gateway to the Indian subcontinent. It endured as such well into the middle decades of the eighteenth century, a three-quarter-century run as the prevailing image of religion-cum-commerce in India.[83] In the case of the Berchem cartouche, which was sketched for the engraver of the Visscher map sometime around 1650, the allegory's steady replication in other and often competing maps and in other affiliated forms of geography (the influential frontispiece in Blaeu's *Atlas major*, for example) made it part of the standard repertoire of American imagery for decades to come. This enabled it to move readily from cartographic to generic prints and from there to the plastic arts. A variation of "America" by the south German artist Gottfried Bernhard Goetz for a stand-alone print (published in Augsburg circa 1750) transformed Berchem's standing, vertical design into a sitting, horizontal figure, with the allegorical America now astride an alligator (a beast that featured in the Berchem-Blaeu frontispiece). This more squat version rendered the design more adaptable to a sculptural form of table decoration fashionable at that time. The Goetz arrangement likely inspired the Meissen modeler Johann Joachim Kändler, who translated print into porcelain to produce a highly popular *Allegorical Figure of the Continent of America*, designed to be used as part of a dinner service (see plate 18).[84]

In traversing genres and media, exotic images and motifs would naturally have forfeited some of their argumentative function, as Kusukawa suggests, yet they often retained part of their original sense and augmented that, as well. The mediated version would have alluded to earlier forms while also adding new layers of context and material meaning. There might exist, moreover, a productive tension

FIGURE 143. Balthasar Sigmund Setlezkÿ after Gottfried Bernhard Goetz, *America* (Augsburg, ca. 1750); hand-colored engraving; 46.7 × 71.3 cm. Courtesy of the John Carter Brown Library at Brown University.

between context and material, the old motif and the new medium. Such occurred in an all-inclusive set of exotic scenes that were etched originally by Romeyn de Hooghe over a sequence of sixty plates, and which ultimately moved through an impressive range of genres and materials. Even after their several iterations, how-ever, these images preserved a critical element of their "exotic" message, whatever their form, which may have been additionally enhanced by these mediations. Orig-inally designed around 1680 to illustrate a wide-ranging, so-called popular text by Simon de Vries—a sprawling tour of the "wondrous things in the East and West Indies" (one of several such omnibus titles churned out by the indefatigable de Vries, a prolific *veelschrijver*)—de Hooghe's etched vignettes collectively seek to display the *entire* range of exotic peoples, places, customs, and objects that inhab-ited the early modern European world.[85] They offered a particularly "blended"

FIGURE 144. Romeyn de Hooghe, "Lakwerken" (etching), in Simon de Vries, *Curieuse aenmerckingen der bysonderste Oost en West-Indische verwonderens-waerdige dingen* (Utrecht, 1682). Special Collections, University of Amsterdam (OG 63-1453).

variation on this theme. "De Hooghe's etchings," writes the print specialist Ilja Veldman, somewhat censoriously, "are overcrowded and include elements from very different cultures in a single composition without any attempt at classification": par for the course, in other words, for this form of exotic geography.[86] The images moved from de Vries's book into a more visually enhanced product when they were printed in an oblong format, two illustrations per sheet, in Pieter van der Aa's *Les Indes Orientales et Occidentales et autres lieux* (circa 1700). This volume contained virtually no narrative text—it was a picture book, pure and simple. And by adding trompe l'oeil "frames" and "hinges" to the original etchings—the latter design rendered the prints ersatz diptychs—van der Aa further emphasized the

FIGURE 145. Pieter van der Aa after Romeyn de Hooghe, "Thee, Cha, en Palmiten" and "Lakwerken" (etching), in *Les Indes Orientales et Occidentales et autres lieux* (Leiden, ca. 1700). Special Collections, University of Amsterdam (OL 76).

process of *seeing* the exotic world as so many sundry vignettes. This visual formula is highlighted anew when the images find their way into the grand, magisterial, wholly pictorial, and indubitably elite form of *La galerie agreable du monde* (circa 1729), where they contribute to van der Aa's summa of global geography.[87] At this very moment, however, the images migrate from the world of print to furniture: to a likewise grand, in this case gilt and green collector's cabinet, also manufactured around 1730. The Dutch-made cabinet is lacquered or "japanned"; this provides a material allusion to its role as a storage place for exotica. By further decorating the cabinet doors with images taken from de Hooghe's prints, including—hardly by accident, one imagines—a scene of lacquer production (on the right front panel: compare figures 144 and 146), the makers doubly advertise the exotic message of the ensemble. The "overcrowded" chaos of the whole, in this case, generates a co-herent message: of exotic design to house exotic things.[88]

To create consistent order from this chaos, producers could turn to another device for duplication: pattern books, purposefully assembled to transform images culled from print geography into workable models for material arts. These books

FIGURE 146. Collector's cabinet on stand (Holland, ca. 1700–1730); oak japanned with paint and gilt; 166 cm (height) × 115 cm (width) × 42 cm (depth). Courtesy of the Bridgeman Art Library.

not only ensured the multimedia proliferation of exotic images; they also codified the links between print geography and objects of "decorative" arts. Stalker and Parker's *Treatise of japaning and varnishing* (1688) may have promised "above [a] hundred *distinct* patterns for JAPAN-work, in imitation of the INDIANS," yet many of these images came directly from van Meurs's atelier, adopted from prints relatively hot off the press. Pillement's updated version of these images in *The ladies amusement; or, Whole art of japanning made easy* (circa 1760) may have moved away from original forms of geography—a full century stood between Pillement's pastiches and any primary source—but the intermediary pattern books of Johann Christoph Weigel and Pieter Schenk, each with close links to the world of geography, retained these affiliations.[89] Ateliers also compiled in-house pattern books for the use of their own draftsmen, the best known of these emanating from one of the richest fonts of exotic imagery: the sketchbooks drawn by the porcelain painter Johann Gregorius Höroldt and his colleagues at the celebrated Meissen workshop, which supplied motifs for tens of thousands of pieces of porcelain.[90] In all of these cases, easily accessed anthologies assured ongoing affiliations between, and systematic appropriations by, ateliers of material arts and printers of exotic geography. Ease of use also meant ease of replication, however, and the greater likelihood of separation: from context, from original meaning, from any semblance of congruence. These habits of production would have necessarily induced the sort of dizzying disorder that characterizes Jan van Kessel's *Continents*; the lack of "Certainty" and "endless Difference" that offended Enlightened geographers such as Jean-Baptiste Du Halde; the absence of a "coherent 'story'" and discernible "narrative" that agitated the critic Bernard Smith.

All that said, it is worth noting that these habits of production were not only acceptable; they were reasonably common and evidently successful. Serial replications and chronic appropriations occurred in numerous sources of exotic geography, since systematic "chaos" plainly sold, and not merely illustrated books and decorative maps but also painted ceramics and gilded cabinets. The duplicated images resulted not only in stereotypes of the exotic world—an image of Vishnu that could circulate across several prints and publications over a sprawling period of time—but they also spread beyond printed sources to a wider range of media, including (and especially) the material arts. To what effect? Rather than a loss of coherence or "argumentative function," an absence of "certainty" or discernible "narrative," an "overcrowded" jumble "without any attempt at classification," these sources indicate a viable strategy of production. They reflect a sensible and profitable approach on the part of their makers to present an exotic world that was intentionally decontextualized and scrambled by design—and readily recognized as such. The sheer volume of materials that exhibit this "aesthetic of the exotic" suggests that, to the producer and consumer at least, there did exist in these sources a discernible narrative "logic" and a form of legibility, which may have derived in part from this very process of replication.

The zenith of this process of replication, at least in the orbit of print, took shape in one of the most prolific workshops of early modern Europe, directed by one of the most successful publishers of the period, who died a rich man: Pieter van der Aa (1659–1733).[91] Among the most industrious and certainly innovative figures in the history of print geography (if also among the least well known), van der Aa veritably operated on the principle of replication. He acquired, fairly habitually,

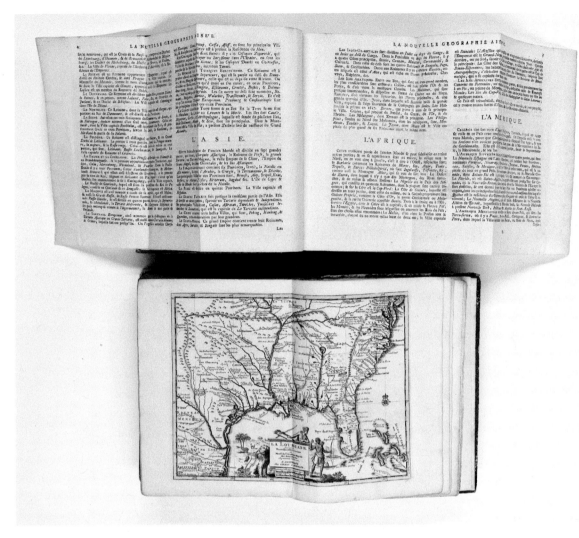

FIGURE 147. "La Louisiane" (engraving of map with accompanying text), in Pieter van der Aa, *Nouvel atlas, très-exact et fort commode pour toutes sortes de personnes, contenant les principales cartes géographiques* (Amsterdam, ca. 1730; 1st ed. 1714). Special Collections, University of Amsterdam (OG 63-6454).

previously published texts, prints, and maps; and he reproduced, reconstituted, or just plain copied these for his ever-expanding list of publications. His repeated success with this model of replication drove his business, which, over a remarkable six-decade span, took on more and more ambitious projects, culminating in the colossal collection of previously printed materials *La galerie agreable du monde*. Throughout all of this printerly production, it was not the originality of sources that generated van der Aa's interests or sales, but the novelty of their presentation—old stuff in newly designed formats. His *Nouvel atlas* (1714), for example, was anything but: its maps plainly and admittedly (by the publisher, on the title page) derived from earlier sources, in this case French cartographers.[92] Yet the maps were "new" and "improved," as van der Aa boasted on the title page, and in truth there was novelty: the volume was printed in the less common form of oblong folio, with certain pages folded in to create a quarto-size book, albeit with larger-sized maps. As with *Les Indes Orientales et Occidentales* and his adaptation of the de Hooghe etchings, van der Aa reconfigured older materials in an inventive format (in both cases, oblong), which lent the new product a fresh and distinctive appearance. Even more impressive was van der Aa's *Naaukeurige versameling*, a twenty-eight-volume anthology of previously published travel literature, reworked and reformatted for coherence and appearance, and further embellished with plates, maps, indices, and the like. Again, size mattered: the series appeared in a relatively handy octavo, which could fit in one's pocket and thus allowed the books to be taken (conceivably) on a journey. And, once again, material form trumped subject matter—as was the case with so many of van der Aa's products. The reprinted contents of the *Naaukeurige versameling*, as the title page cleverly phrases it, were "never before been seen *in this manner*"—even if they were undoubtedly seen before in other manners and in prior publications.[93]

Replication was built into the van der Aa production process. The publisher acquired maps and plates that could be readily reused for other publications, he designed cartouches and captions that could be easily reformulated for and translated into other languages (for use in other publications), and he printed over-whelmingly visual fare that could be re-engraved or rearranged in other forms and sequences (for use, again, in other publications). The form of *La galerie agreable du monde* distilled, in many ways, a central argument of Dutch exotic geography—the primacy of the visual and the value of replication. It also prompts a central question of exotic production in this period: to what purpose did producers of geographic materials and van der Aa, more particularly, reprint and reformulate so relentlessly the exotic world (which was the principal focus of his publications)? Van der Aa's aggressive sales pitch in his scattered prefatory comments points to a basic concern for profits: old prints sold well. Yet these comments also hint at a specific strategy deployed, at least in part, to attract the paying customer: the promise of "pleasure" or "delight," which came in the form of easily recognized, blandly "amusing," and indistinctly "decorative" pictures.[94] This sentiment is perfectly expressed in the title to the publisher's most ambitious project of replication, *La galerie agreable du monde*. A truly phenomenal feat of early modern (or, for that matter, modern) publishing—an exceptionally "grand number" of pictures, suffusing sixty-six tomes, printed in some thirty volumes—this agreeable gallery makes three germane points already on its title page: on the purposefully amusing or "pleasing" (*agréable*) quality of van der Aa's brand of print geography; on the superlative grandeur of his

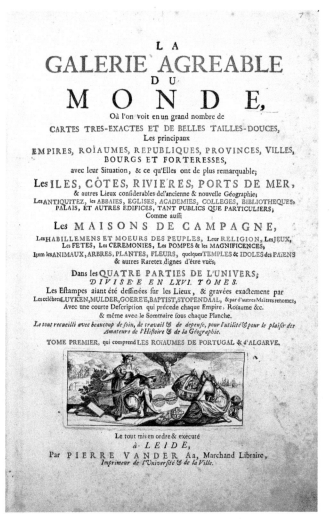

LA
GALERIE AGREABLE
DU
MONDE,

Où l'on voit en un grand nombre de
CARTES TRES-EXACTES ET DE BELLES TAILLES-DOUCES,
Les principaux
EMPIRES, ROÏAUMES, REPUBLIQUES, PROVINCES, VILLES,
BOURGS ET FORTERESSES,
avec leur Situation, & ce qu'Elles ont de plus remarquable;
Les ILES, CÔTES, RIVIERES, PORTS DE MER,
& autres Lieux confiderables de l'ancienne & nouvelle Géographie;
Les ANTIQUITEZ, les ABBAIES, EGLISES, ACADEMIES, COLLEGES, BIBLIOTHEQUES,
PALAIS, ET AUTRES EDIFICES, TANT PUBLICS QUE PARTICULIERS;
Comme auffi
Les MAISONS DE CAMPAGNE,
Les HABILLEMENS ET MOEURS DES PEUPLES, Leur RELIGION, Les JEUX,
Les FETES, Les CEREMONIES, Les POMPES & les MAGNIFICENCES;
Item les ANIMAUX, ARBRES, PLANTES, FLEURS, quelques TEMPLES & IDOLES des PAÏENS
& autres Raretez dignes d'être vuës;
Dans les QUATRE PARTIES DE L'UNIVERS;
DIVISE'E EN LXVI. TOMES.
Les Estampes aiant été deffinées fur les Lieux, & gravées exactement par
Les celébres LUYKEN, MULDER, GOERE'E, BAPTIST, STOPENDAAL, & par d'autres Maîtres renomez,
Avec une courte Defcription qui précede chaque Empire, Roïaume &c.
& même avec le Sommaire fous chaque Planche.
Le tout recueilli avec beaucoup de foin, de travail & de depenfe, pour l'utilité & pour le plaifir des Amateurs de l'Hiftoire & de la Géographie.

TOME PREMIER, qui comprend LES ROÏAUMES DE PORTUGAL & d'ALGARVE.

Le tout mis en ordre & executé
à LEIDE,
Par PIERRE VANDER Aa, Marchand Libraire,
Imprimeur de l'Univerfité & de la Ville.

FIGURE 148. Title page to Pieter van der Aa, *La galerie agreable du monde* (Leiden, ca. 1729); letterpress with engraving. Collection Antiquariaat Forum BV, 't Goy-Houten, The Netherlands.

ultimate project of duplication—literally, thousands of reprinted prints—and the obvious triumph of his publication strategy; and, not least, on the *objectness* of these duplications and, by extension, of the type of illustrated geography so successfully produced by van der Aa, which subtly affiliates exotic prints with material arts (a "gallery").

The *Galerie agreable* certainly replicates with gleeful abandon: hundreds of images taken from van der Aa's massive stock, accumulated over a lengthy career in print geography; hundreds more simply borrowed from competing publications; and all of these systematically reformatted and often re-engraved to produce a profusely magnificent volume. Many of the *Galerie*'s illustrations go back decades—some date from the sixteenth century—although a large number come from the surge of exotic geography that begins with the books of Jacob van Meurs. By dint of their replication in the majestic *Galerie*, however, these images circulated anew and became codified as canonic representations of the exotic world. Johan Nieuhof's depictions of Chinese "mendicants" and "idols" (in both cases, designed by van Meurs); Olfert Dapper's renditions of Asian justice and Chinese "torture" (as it is frankly labeled in one van der Aa print, based, once again, on a van Meurs original); Albert Eckhout's portraits of the indigenous peoples of Brazil (revised from images in Arnoldus Montanus's book on America): all gained a new life and major boost from their republication in the *Galerie*. They also gained fresh form, and this meant, in many cases, more impressive and imposing form, as van der Aa had many of his print stock reissued in larger formats and imposing double folio. He also engraved into some of his plates decorative "frames": trompe l'oeil borders that mimicked the appearance of bona fide picture frames and thereby added depth and

FIGURE 149. After Jacob van Meurs (atelier), "Autre maniere de donner les Bastonnades chez les Chinois" (engraving), in Pieter van der Aa, *La galerie agreable du monde* (Leiden, ca. 1729). Collection Antiquariaat Forum BV, 't Goy-Houten, The Netherlands.

enhanced the visual impact of these gallery-worthy images. This framing device also drew attention to the *objectness* of the prints. It lent to the flat form of graphic reproduction a three-dimensional aspect—van der Aa added frames to many of his maps and city views, as well—and this reinforced the conceit of the volume: a leisurely stroll through an agreeable "gallery" of the exotic world. Finally, van der Aa included numerous prints that display material objects per se: prints depicting a sequence of fashionable "bonnets," which are given a catalogue-style presentation (adopted from a Dapper-volume illustration); engravings of rare coins and medallions, likewise laid out like merchandise available for purchase; and actual decorative objects, which seem innocuously to fill out certain engravings, such as the porcelain vessels resting atop a mantel in "*La torture chez les Chinois*" or the delicately shaped ointment jars on a background table in "*Bastonnades chez les Chinois*" (an engraving that illustrates corporal punishment by cudgel or "baston," also known as the bastinado). In all these ways and over several thousand prints, van der Aa's *Galerie agreable* at once exemplifies and celebrates exotic geography.[95]

Transmediation and Decorative Torture

It is through these replications and production processes, these images and imagined objects, that van der Aa's virtual gallery makes a broad case, as well, for the affiliation of geography—describing the world, in this case in pictorial form—and the material arts. The repetitively printed images of the *Galerie agreable*, adroitly "framed" or otherwise "agreeably" enhanced, gesture toward the recurring images that adorn assorted "decorative" arts. And the *contents* of these replicated images further underscore, inadvertently or not, the fluid passage of exotic motifs from one medium to another: from print to print, naturally, yet also from prints to those material arts that often bear the same replicated scenes as illustrated in the graphic arts (as does the gilded lacquer cabinet of circa 1730, painted with the de Hooghe–etched exotic scenes). This movement of images, motifs, and vignettes from genre to genre and medium to medium approximates what the art historian Craig Clunas refers to as "iconic circuits." Clunas enlists this term (borrowed from the Renaissance historian Carlo Ginzburg) to describe an iconographic congruence among different visual sources of mixed media: "an economy of representations in which images of a certain kind circulated [among] different media in which pictures were involved."[96] "Iconic circuits" helps Clunas explain the movement of replicated images in the context of the dynamic visual culture of late Ming China, and the term might also be used to describe the migration of motifs across the many forms of early modern European geography and on to the material arts. It can also help elucidate the affiliations of these respective spheres of production—geography and material arts—both of which thrived on replication. It does not fully explain, however, processes of what might be called *transmediation*: the transfer and translation of images across media, and the way shifts in media—mediations, as it were—affect form and meaning. *Iconic circuits* entail pictorial movements to different forms and focus on the changes or the stability of a particular icon or image. *Transmediations* also follow the movement of images, yet pay attention, as well, to the media of origin and arrival, and to how the mediated route can shape meanings. To pursue transmediations across sources of exotic geography and material arts is to explore how replications function and how media matter.

Charting the circuits and mediations of exotic imagery confirms the steady march of motifs across genres and media. It further demonstrates the thick relations of print geography and the material arts, which shared numerous visual byways and sometimes, notwithstanding these dizzying circuits and mediations, similar "narrative" paths. Consider the course of an image that arguably launched this rich moment of early modern exoticism: the celebrated frontispiece design to Johan Nieuhof's recurrently published book on China (see plate 19). An engraved full-plate folio and the opening illustration of the volume—and thus of van Meurs's substantial output of exotic geography—the frontispiece centers on a regally dressed figure who sits, one arm akimbo, upon a baroquely carved throne. The figure's second arm rests on a bulky globe that features the just-discernible outlines of China and its imperial domains; the globe's round form mirrors that of a tilted parasol, which is held aloft by a lackey and crowns both the central sitter and his throne. This is the Great Khan, who positively radiates imperial hegemony. Surrounding the mighty Chinese emperor stands a fierce cadre of men bearing arms and banners, while at his feet writhes a cluster of supplicants in various forms of restraint: chains, manacles, the cangue. These obsequious prisoners sprawled at the base of the engraving (just above the printer's cartouche) allude to the Khan's full control over his subjects' bodies, and the frontispiece image, more generally, sends a message (echoed in the text) of Chinese imperial puissance. It speaks, more broadly, to the contemporary European awe of the Great Khan's majesty and to the admiration—especially among certain elite observers—of his absolute political and juridical control.[97]

While the origins of this image are not at all clear, its considerable afterlife is eminently traceable. There exists no original Nieuhof draft for this imaginative imperial scene, which is implicitly attributed to the volume's author. While the manuscript from Nieuhof's China voyage does contain an illustrated title page, this bears no resemblance to the engraved frontispiece of the printed book. The latter derives, rather, from van Meurs's workshop and not unlikely from the sketchpad of the printer himself, who trained as an engraver. It extracts the figure for the Great Khan from an on-site drawing made by Nieuhof of "an old viceroy," who wears the

FIGURE 150. Johan Nieuhof (?), Viceroy, in Nieuhof, "Iournaal" (1658); pen and wash. Société de Géographie (coll. Muller 14-IV-1984), Bibliothèque Nationale, Paris.

same brocaded gown, beaded chain, fur-lined hat, and jaunty feathers as the engraved emperor. And it gussies up this relatively austere, stand-alone sketch with layers of regal extravagance: the armed guards, humbled prisoners, and stately trappings of power.[98] The combination proved compelling. For while the portrait of the Great Khan on his own is relatively rare, the imperial entourage appears as such in multiple prints and the decorative arts. It served, unrevised, as the frontispiece to the French (1665), German (1666), and Latin (1668) editions of Nieuhof's book—all products of the van Meurs atelier—while a copy of the design, mildly modified by the Bohemian etcher Wenceslaus Hollar, fronted an English edition of the volume printed by John Ogilby in 1669. Other, unrelated geographies of China adopted the basic layout of the image—enthroned emperor, flanking attendants, wretched supplicants.[99] And it is highly ironic that the German publisher of Jean-Baptiste Du Halde's *Description geographique* lifted van Meurs's design largely

Opposite page FIGURE 151. Wenceslaus Hollar after Jacob van Meurs, frontispiece (engraving) to *An embassy from the East-India Company of the United Provinces, to the Grand Tartar Cham Emperour of China* (London, 1669). Courtesy of the University of Wisconsin.

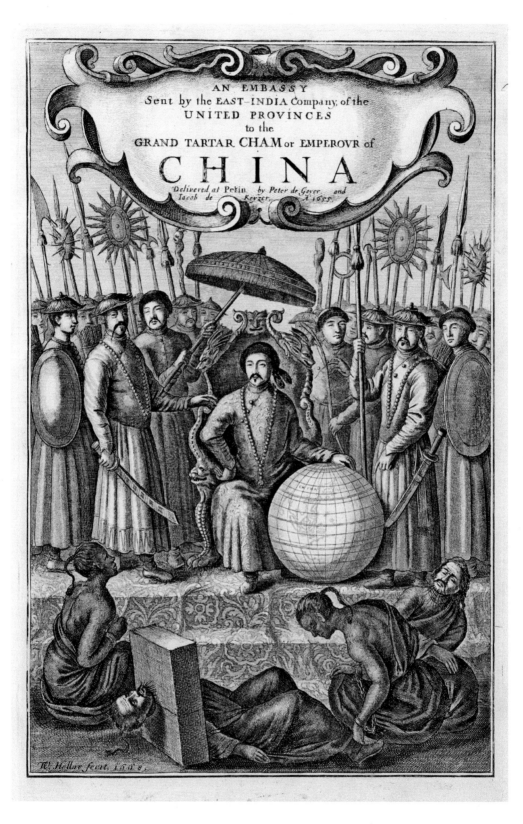

AN EMBASSY
Sent by the EAST-INDIA Company, of the
UNITED PROVINCES
to the
GRAND TARTAR CHAM or EMPEROVR of
CHINA
Delivered at Pekin by Peter de Goyer and
Iacob de Keyzer A.º 1655.

W. Hollar fecit 1668.

FIGURE 152. [J. M.] Bernigeroth, frontispiece (engraving) to Johann Baptista [Jean-Baptiste] Du Halde, *Ausführliche Beschreibung des Chinesischen Reichs und der grossen Tartarey. Erster Theil* (Rostock, 1747). Maastricht University Library.

unchanged, thus pilfering this now iconic image from the very brand of "spurious" geography that Du Halde himself so vehemently rejected: "decorative" pictures illustrating "serious" books.[100] This Du Halde edition appeared in the mid-eighteenth century, and it indicates how fixed this picture had become among Enlightened Europeans: an enduring image of imperial China.

The image of the Khan also moved into the material arts, where it "decorated" a range of goods: ceramics, furniture, tapestry, and so on. The astonishingly productive "Grieksche A Factory" of Delft, the leading European producers of tin-glazed earthenware in the second half of the seventeenth century, manufactured a vase with cover (circa 1675–1680) that featured the emperor and his entourage, transposed virtually unchanged from the engraved print. The disciplined Chinese subjects in this arrangement are painted slightly off to the side of the imperial

FIGURE 153. Grieksche A Factory (attrib.), Vase with cover (ca. 1675–1680); tin-glazed earthenware painted blue; 58 cm (height). Anonymous gift in honor of Eloise W. Martin; Eloise W. Martin Fund, 1998.515a–b, Art Institute of Chicago. Image 00048135-01.

FIGURE 154. Hendrik van Soest (attrib.), Cabinet (ca. 1700); oak veneered with walnut, Brazilian rosewood, and padauk, decorated with inlaid pewter; 66.5 cm (height) ×
37 cm (depth) × 129 cm (length). Grassi Museum für Angewandte Kunst Leipzig.
Photo: Christoph Sandig.

assembly. Yet rather than weakening the message of the Khan's omnipotent power,
this circular, nonlinear arrangement—pace Smith—arguably enhances it: the
viewer observes imperial control and its effects. Emperor, entourage, and globe also
appear under a tilted parasol on a large oak cabinet veneered with walnut, Brazilian
rosewood, and padauk (a tropical wood from Asia or Africa), and decorated with
inlaid pewter (made in the workshop of Hendrik van Soest around 1700). Here the
original composition has changed in subtle ways—the Khan stands, the attendants
recede, and the vignette now includes a richly dressed figure (lower left) who offers
a spread of luxury goods. Yet the side drawers of the cabinet surrounding the central
imperial scene incorporate an array of exotic scenes that also derive from van Meurs
prints and that further illustrate forms of imperial justice and control, particularly
practices of Chinese "torture" (see, for example, figures 161 and 162). The multipli-
cation of somatic punishment in these images intensifies the impression of absolute
imperial power, while the medium itself—exotic woods used to exhibit exotic motifs—only reinforces this message.[101] A series of tapestries designed by Guy-Louis
Vernansal and manufactured in the Beauvais workshops (circa 1690–1705) makes
numerous references to the van Meurs frontispiece, along with other prints from the
Nieuhof volume, in its illustration of "The Story of the Emperor of China" (as the

FIGURE 155. Hendrik van Soest (attrib.), Cabinet (detail of central panel) (ca. 1700); oak veneered with walnut, Brazilian rosewood, and padauk, decorated with inlaid pewter. Grassi Museum für Angewandte Kunst Leipzig. Photo: Christoph Sandig.

tapestries are collectively known).[102] In "The Emperor on a Journey," for example, the Great Khan sits with one arm akimbo under an intricately designed canopy that shades a majestic throne-cum-palanquin (see plate 20). He is borne by attendants and accompanied by mounted escorts who bear arms and royal banners.[103] Although the medium in this instance is neither inherently exotic (like the tropical woods) nor formally so (like the blue-and-white delftware), the message of the magnificent tapestry meshes well with the motifs of the original print: a textile fit for a prince displays the grandeur of the Chinese emperor. While it is not unusual in the European tradition to enlist large-scale tapestry for grandiose themes, the medium's deployment for "The Story of the Emperor of China" well serves this exotic imperial narrative.[104] And, more generally, while the van Meurs frontispiece certainly traveled extensively and circuitously—from print to vase to cabinet to tapestry—its mediations functioned productively, by and large, to augment the original "narrative" of what would come to be known as Oriental despotism.[105]

Numerous more instances of iconic circuits and transmediations establish both the stability and malleability of exotic imagery, which retains as well as yields meaning as it shifts contexts and media. From the van Meurs atelier and particularly the Nieuhof books came several more long-lived icons of exoticism. A pair of designs illustrating "Mendians" or mendicants—assorted roadside ascetics, sketched originally (in a slightly different form) by Nieuhof to show popular religious practices in China—made their way through a typical roster of prints and books: van Meurs–issued editions of Nieuhof, also in translation; van der Aa's picture-rich publications; and other unrelated, omnibus volumes of exotic geography.[106] Yet the mendicants flourished in painting and other material arts, too, both collectively and on their own. A group of them turns up, within a year of their original publication, in Jan van Kessel's *Continents*—they blend into the interior décor of the allegory of "Asia" (circa 1665–1666; see plate 14)—and they soon appear on ceramics, as well. A selection of seemingly misplaced mendicants adorns a tin-glazed punch bowl painted by Samuel van Eenhoorn around 1680 (under the auspices of the "Grieksche A Factory"), while one individual wayfarer—a potbellied figure who raises a boulder menacingly over

FIGURE 156. Johan Nieuhof (?), Roadside ascetics, in Nieuhof, "Iournaal" (1658); pen and wash. Société de Géographie (coll. Muller 14-IV-1984), Bibliothèque Nationale, Paris.

FIGURE 157. Jacob van Meurs (atelier), "Mendians" (engraving), in Johan Nieuhof, *L'Ambassade de la Compagnie Orientale des Provinces Unies vers L'Emperour de la Chine, ou Grand Cam de Tartarie* (Leiden, 1665). Special Collections, University of Amsterdam (OF 86-10).

FIGURE 158. Jacob van Meurs (atelier), "Mendians" (engraving), in Johan Nieuhof, *L'Ambassade de la Compagnie Orientale des Provinces Unies vers L'Emperour de la Chine, ou Grand Cam de Tartarie* (Leiden, 1665). Special Collections, University of Amsterdam (OF 86-10).

EXOTIC PLEASURES

FIGURE 159. Samuel van Eenhoorn (Grieksche A Factory), Punch bowl (ca. 1680); tin-glazed earthenware painted blue and manganese-purple; 25 (diameter) × 11.8 (height) cm. © Fitzwilliam Museum, Cambridge.

FIGURE 160. Plaque with Chinese figures (Holland, ca. 1680–1700); tin-glazed earthenware painted blue; 63 × 92 cm. Rijksmuseum Amsterdam.

CHAPTER FOUR

his head and was understood (according to Nieuhof's manuscript description) to pound stones mercilessly into his chest "until blood spews out"—materializes on a large ceramic plaque, likewise manufactured in Delft (circa 1680–1700). This "religious" figure joins a medley of exotic tricksters and acrobatic stuntmen in a circus-like scene that has ostensibly little to do with asceticism. Palm trees and pagodas place the action in China. (And his companions derive mostly from print geography, too, including engravings from the van Meurs atelier.)[107] This chest-banger later appears with members of the punch-bowl group on the wood and inlaid-pewter cabinet, featured on a drawer just below the central depiction of the Great Khan; while the remainder of the mendicant ensemble reassembles on another cabinet drawer, to the left of the emperor, a design that also incorporates an image of a man plunging a sword into his abdomen—a Sufi Qalandar, it turns out, from a van Meurs volume on Ottoman Syria (see figures 85, 161, and 162). Among this second group of figures, the prostrate "mendicant" who bangs his forehead on a great stone—so violently "that the earth rumbled from it," according to Nieuhof's original description—also shows up on porcelain: a rouleau vase made in Jingdezhen and overpainted in Bohemia by Ignaz Preissler (circa 1720), who added a swooping phoenix.[108] This ornate mendi-

FIGURES 161 AND 162. Hendrik van Soest (attrib.), Cabinet (details of central-drawer panel [above] and left-drawer panel [below]) (ca. 1700); oak veneered with walnut, Brazilian rosewood, and padauk, decorated with inlaid pewter. Grassi Museum für Angewandte Kunst Leipzig. Photo: Christoph Sandig.

FIGURE 163. Ignaz Preissler (?) and others, Vase (ca. 1720); Chinese porcelain (Jingdezhen) overpainted in black and gold (Bohemia); 24.5 cm (height) × 10.6 cm (diameter). © The Trustees of the British Museum.

FIGURE 164. Johann Christoph Weigel, Chinese figures (ca. 1720); engraved print for design book. Museum für Kunst und Gewerbe Hamburg.

FIGURE 165. After Johann Christoph Weigel, Painted wallpaper with Chinese figures (1734–1739), Amalienburg (kitchen), Nymphenburg Palace. Bayerische Verwaltung der Staatlichen Schlösser, Gärten und Seen.

cant and mythical fowl journeyed by way of print—a design engraved by Johann Christoph Weigel around 1720—and thus moved easily to other locales: the painted walls of the hunting lodge Amalienburg (1734–1739), for example, in the Bavarian palace of Nymphenburg, where the wholly transmuted "mendicant" allows his back to prop a preposterously prancing squirrel.[109]

The mendicants' swirling itinerancy impresses on several levels. First, there is the speed by which these figures become adopted and deployed by designers working across several media and over many years: cabinet painting (within a matter of months) and wall painting (seven decades later); delftware and porcelain of diverse forms; opulent inlaid furniture and great ceramic tableaux. Next, there is the manner by which media shaped meaning in both subtle and substantial ways. On the inlaid oak cabinet, the mendicants (and Qalandar) serve to remind the viewer of the Khan's all-encompassing power; they have shifted from self-mutilating ascetics (their original connotation in the van Meurs prints) to subjects of omnipotent imperial control (the overall narrative of the oak cabinet). On the delftware plaque and in its carnival-like pastiche, the boulder-bearing mendicant undergoes a more extreme transformation: from religious actor to circus performer. And on the overpainted vase and the palace wall painting, the sense of performance may be wholly absent: the kowtowing figure, pecked by a phoenix and harassed by a squirrel, has become deracinated décor. In all but these final iterations, however, the "mendicants" do retain a semblance of their original meaning. The notion of bodily pain (which much impressed Johan Nieuhof on his original journey) carries over from the print to the oak cabinet—here the medium of sumptuous furniture works in tandem with the imperial motifs. And the quality of "curious" spectacle—embodied by a roadside ascetic and street-performing artist alike—persists in the ceramic plaque, a medium that would have adorned a well-to-do home and whose curiously large format (really, an outsized tile) may have accentuated its sense of baroque display.

Another set of iconic circuits spins west to America and its exotic milieu, where the indigenes cultivated "marvelous" habits—attention here focused more on the social and natural than on the political and religious (as it did for China)—and where native flora and fauna provoked copious wonder. The drawings of Frans Post and Albert Eckhout, sketched largely in Dutch Brazil under the patronage of Johan Maurits of Nassau-Siegen—landscapes and *vedute* by Post, and natural and ethnographic subjects from Eckhout—served as a crucial catalyst for some of the most productive image-making on the Baroque New World. Post's and Eckhout's drawings came into the hands of Amsterdam and Leiden publishers, for whom they served as models for a steady stream of engravings and woodcuts. These, in turn, illustrated books on Dutch and Portuguese Brazil (published by Blaeu), much-admired natural histories of tropical South America (printed by the Elsevier firm), and several more generally pitched geographies of America. From there the images moved on to other forms of publications—books printed in the van Meurs atelier, maps from Blaeu and his cohort, and nearly all subsequent natural histories with an American aspect. And they also served as models for paintings: both by Post and Eckhout themselves, who produced scores of landscapes (Post), several life-size ethnographic portraits (Eckhout: see plate 9 and compare figure 166), and a series of tropical still lifes (Eckhout); and by other European artists, such as van Kessel, who incorporated the rich "Mauritian oeuvre" (as David Freedberg has called it) into their own exotic paintings.[110] Other material arts, "decorative" and "fine," promptly followed, and the images circulated, accordingly, in ceramics, furniture, textiles, and so on.

Two striking examples demonstrate the range of circuits as well as their divergent, if partly intersecting, patterns of travel. The Brazilian imagery and the Eckhout designs in particular inspired a series of tapestries woven at the Royal Gobelins Manufactory, known collectively as *Les Anciennes Indes*. (Johan Maurits had gifted to Louis XIV an assortment of Brazilian pictures, which served as models for the cartoons.) This superb series depicted Indians and savage animals and hunting scenes; it offered, as did the Beauvais tapestries devoted to China, a royal me-

FIGURE 166. Albert Eckhout, *Woman on Beach* (ca. 1640); oil on paper; 35.5 × 24 cm; Biblioteka Jagiellonska, Krakow.

dium for the noble theme of the hunt. That the hunters were wild "Brazilians" and the animals monstrous alligators, queer tapirs, the odd rhino, and the like only added a whiff of exoticism to this universal theme (see figure 167).[111] In a somewhat different context and a less elevated medium, figures modeled on Eckhout's designs (and van Meurs's prints) turn up on coconut cups carved in the second half of the seventeenth century.[112] Several examples survive, and one of these—mounted in rudimentary silver straps, with an added base and cover (likely later embellishments), and depicting a trio of crudely carved Indians—includes inscriptions that clarify the subject: "A Tapuya [Brazilian] Fisher," "A King of the Tapuya," and "A Tapuya Woman." While the first two of these topics present a traditional theme

FIGURE 167. Manufacture Royale des Gobelins after Albert Eckhout and Frans Post, *Indians Fishing and Hunting* [*Les pêcheurs*, from the series *Les Anciennes tentures des Indes*] (Paris, ca. 1692–1723); tapestry of wool and silk; 356 × 305 cm. Rijksmuseum Amsterdam.

FIGURE 168. After Albert Eckhout, Coconut cup (1653); carved coconut with silver cover and mount; 17.4 cm (height) × 7.4 cm (diameter of cover). Cultural History Collections, University of Bergen (inv. no. B 513).

applied to a less-than-traditional subject—the fisherman-hunter carries weapons and prey, as he might in any variant of this scene, while the king stands one arm akimbo and wears a crown, albeit with little else to cover his masculinity (ditto the fisher)—the third vignette adds a distinctly curious element. Clutching one child by the arm and cradling another close to her right breast (she is similarly depicted naked), the woman wears a satchel strapped to her head which bears plainly discernible human limbs. The hunt has yielded human flesh, and the hunters reside in the kingdom of cannibals (figures 168 and 169 and compare also figures 139 and 140).[113] In the case of this carved coconut shell, a tropical medium conveys a tropical message, as it were. Yet Eckhout's Indian icons have circulated with a telling twist. A less decorous material than royal tapestry—for coconut shells (*cocos nucifera*), if once

FIGURE 169. Zacharias Wagenaer after Albert Eckhout, "Molher Tapuya" (ca. 1641); watercolor on paper (in the *Thierbuch*). Kupferstich-Kabinett, Staatliche Kunstsammlungen Dresden.

elite objects of desire, had come down in price and prestige by the second half of the seventeenth century—delivers a more sensational vision of the exotic world. The medium and message have subtly shifted.[114]

A final set of iconic circuits and transmediations, this time bearing on the theme of exotic violence and torture, illustrates once again the fluid nature of exotic imagery, while it alludes, concurrently, to the rich associations of geography and the material arts. The crude and brutal treatment—certainly to the modern eye—of the human body (a theme broached in the previous chapter) featured in several pictorial sources of exotic geography, from where it moved on to other media and arts. Both the frontispiece to the Nieuhof–van Meurs book on China and one of the two mendicant prints in that volume offer striking depictions of the cangue: the heavy wooden frame worn around the neck of its victim as kind of a portable pillory, used in premodern China as a technique of corporal punishment. (The Chinese device, an awkward and painful contraption that prevented the wearer from eating properly while also attracting humiliation, related in form and function to the European stocks). The image takes on two unrelated connotations in its print debuts—the power of the Khan over his subjects' bodies (the frontispiece) and the habits of "popular" asceticism among exotic "mendicants"— although neither of these can claim a connection to any known original source.

CHAPTER FOUR

Nieuhof's drawing of roadside beggars, like his manuscript's title page, contains no correlative representation of the theme. The cangue image, nonetheless, gained quick and broad popularity. It was reproduced in other Nieuhof volumes and other geographies of China; variants appeared on other frontispieces issued by van Meurs's atelier, dedicated to other geographic spaces; and the original print ultimately received the full van der Aa treatment in *La galerie agreable du monde*: integrated into a double folio trimmed around the edges, which allowed the engraver to add a decorative frame and which enabled the image to reach a fresh and influential audience.[115] The cangued figure also enjoyed—if that is the proper term—wide circulation in the material arts. The Delft-made tin-glazed vase illustrating the Great Khan enthroned reproduced the prisoner in the cangue, who suffers alongside the emperor's other supplicants, while the inlaid oak cabinet also features the stocked subject languishing beneath his omnipotent, imperial sovereign (see figures 153 and 161). In a wholly other context, the cangued figure appears on Samuel van Eenhoorn's ceramic punch bowl with an utterly motley crew: three different "mendicants" (see figure 159); a man wielding a handsaw, attended by a parasol-bearing lackey; two traveling peddlers toting curious baskets (figure 170); and a well-dressed woman receiving a duck.

FIGURE 170. Samuel van Eenhoorn (Grieksche A Factory), Punch bowl (ca. 1680); tin-glazed earthenware painted blue and manganese-purple; 25 (diameter) × 11.8 (height) cm. © Fitzwilliam Museum, Cambridge.

FIGURE 171. Jacob van Meurs (atelier), Chinese tribunal (engraving), in Olfert Dapper, *Gedenckwaerdig bedryf der Nederlandsche Oost-Indische Maetschappye, op de kuste en in het keizerrijk van Taising of Sina* (Amsterdam, 1670). Special Collections, University of Amsterdam (OM 63-124).

Another depiction of the cangue, likewise derived from a print geography of China and likewise issued from the van Meurs workshop—Olfert Dapper's *Atlas Chinensis*, as it was known in its English version—launched another variant of the theme of bodily pain and enforced suffering. Once again, no original manuscript source survives, although drawings by the Spanish Jesuit Adriano de las Cortes, which would be selectively adapted by van Meurs for the Dapper volume, include three sketches of prisoners in some manner of stocks.[116] The printed illustration in question represents one figure bearing a cangue (around the neck, thus) and another in hand-stocks; both offer themselves up for judgment before a seated imperial officer, the cangued man bound, humbled, and kneeling, while his partner in distress stumbles behind him veiled by a blindfold. This striking print design, meant to depict the severe judicial protocol of China, was replicated in other publications per usual—in van der Aa's version, it shared a double folio with another engraving of "Torture by the Chinese" (an image taken directly from de las Cortes). And it migrated before long to the decorative arts: not to the inlaid oak cabinet, as it turns out, which boasted several other vivid vignettes of torment, but to an exceptionally accomplished reproduction (circa 1700) painted on a Japanese drug pot overdecorated in Delft (imported Arita porcelain, which obtained a second application of paint and design in the Netherlands: see plate 21).[117] Drug pots, normally destined for the apothecary for the storage of medicaments and therefore left unembellished (to allow for the later inscription of labels), sometimes found a market niche in their unadorned state. Size and shape made them well suited for other purposes, including as drinking vessels; the pots approximated the form of a large, open-topped ale tankard or perhaps a ceremonial drinking goblet.[118] The quality of the overpainting on the "cangue" pot indicates a discerning consumer and the purposefulness of the adornment: the desire to decorate a foreign-made vessel with scenes of corporal punishment. As with the delftware punch bowl—a utensil similarly enlisted for the consumption of alcohol and also associated with male carousing and camaraderie—a scene of exotic violence has transmuted into an accoutrement for masculine revelry.[119]

Another overdecorated drug pot (circa 1700), more than likely painted by the same hand as the "cangue" pot, features another portrait of violence, in this case a gruesome decapitation (see plate 22).[120] In the central band of the pot, a bound and blindfolded figure cowers on his knees; directly behind him another figure brandishes a broad, sword-sized cleaver, at the ready to strike. Just beside the kneeling victim sprawls a recent casualty of the deadly blade, blood gushing freely from his freshly sliced vertebral arteries, and on his other flank stands a larger figure draped in trousers and a rich crimson robe, who observes the execution from under the shade of a tasseled parasol. The coloration of this second pot (which has slightly smaller dimensions than the first) closely resembles that of the "cangue" cup, as do the decorative borders along the top and bottom of the vessel; the two objects almost certainly derive from the same atelier and not unlikely the same painter. Once again, as well, no manuscript source exists for the execution; nor is there an identifiable engraving on which the pot might be modeled, although the beheading scene does relate to other variants in print geography. A cartouche for a maritime map of the Indian Ocean, for example, designed in the atelier of Johannes van Keulen sometime in the 1680s, presents a well-dressed "Oriental" overseer who stands beneath a parasol and views a similarly ghoulish death sentence by sword (see figure 104).[121]

If there is no direct print source for the second overdecorated drug pot, there are several comparable vignettes of exotic violence on other forms of material art—pastiches of decorative decapitation, so to speak.[122] A side drawer of the inlaid oak cabinet shows a figure flourishing a sword dramatically over the neck of a kneeling captive; to the victim's right stands a fashionably attired observer. This scene speaks directly to the cabinet's central-panel illustration of the Great Khan, contributing cogently to an overall design that emphasizes the authority and hegemony of the

FIGURE 172. Hendrik van Soest (attrib.), Cabinet (detail of left-drawer panel) (ca. 1700); oak veneered with walnut, Brazilian rosewood, and padauk, decorated with inlaid pewter. Grassi Museum für Angewandte Kunst Leipzig. Photo: Christoph Sandig.

Chinese emperor, his life-and-death power over his subjects. A somewhat bulky piece of furniture plausibly geared for the chambers of a gentleman or merchant, the cabinet's invocation of imperial violence and somatic abuse might fit well with the blood-soaked drug pot's representation of an execution: both objects and their designs speak to a world of masculine authority and political violence. Yet this sensibility would not so easily apply to another depiction of decapitation, this time on a Meissen tea-bowl and saucer, manufactured slightly later (circa 1725), which displays a nearly identical scene to the inlaid cabinet: one of the victims on the saucer bears an added cangue, a slightly incongruous touch since it makes a beheading technically more tricky (see plate 23).[123] While taking tea was scarcely an exclusively feminine pastime, it does not easily conjure up an aesthetic of violence. The reverse side of the saucer, more true to type, bears flower sprays and insects painted in matching hues of mauve and brown; the delicate beaker-shaped tea cup, meanwhile, offers scenes of ladies drinking tea in the garden and gliding birds in a pastoral setting. There is no hint of imperial vigor or puissance. Rather, an exotic medium (porcelain, albeit made in Meissen) serves an exotic drink (tea from China or perhaps India), for which a stylized pastiche (of Oriental justice) serves as "decorative" background: exotic décor for exotic refreshment.

One more round of iconic circuits and transmediations, once again showcasing episodes of violence, exhibits the full arc of development of these themes across sources and media, contexts and meanings. Two spectacular scenes of corporal punishment, both printed originally as page illustrations in a Dapper–van Meurs volume, purport to show the Chinese methods of caning that, according to Dapper's text, counted as common practice under the Ming and Qing regimes (see plate 10 and figure 173). In the first image, the victim, stripped from the waist down, with both arms bound to the wall in front of him and both feet posted to the floor, throws his head back in anguish as he prepares to receive a blow on his bare buttocks. His tormentor grips a thick bamboo cudgel and, with one foot raised slightly off the ground, rears back and readies to swing his tool of torture to the exposed flesh. While this first scene takes place in an interior space—three men peer through an open window at the action within—the second illustration shows the condemned figure lying on the bare ground of a grassy courtyard, his buttocks and legs once again exposed to the executioner's brutal blows. Several other men cower in the background, likewise stripped of their clothing, as they await their fate. In the distance loom the trunks of two tall bamboo trees, an allusion to the medium of punishment (the bamboo rod), and a pair of impressive edifices (one of which shelters a pair of spectators), which provide an architectural reminder of the imperial presence.

For the design and setting of these prints there are no known sources on which van Meurs could have relied; yet for the actual, isolated vignettes of violence, van Meurs could turn to the manuscript of Adriano de las Cortes. There the Spanish Jesuit furnishes on-site and fairly clinical observations in the form of drawings and annotations: the placement of the victim, distance of the executioner, form of the

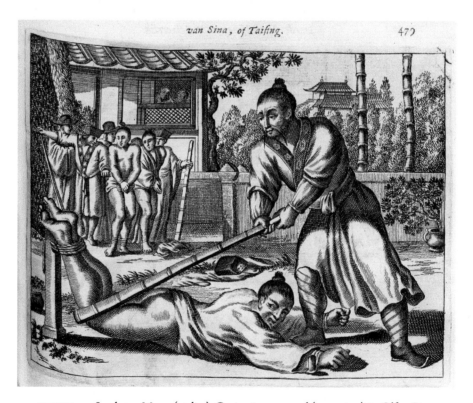

FIGURE 173. Jacob van Meurs (atelier), Caning in courtyard (engraving), in Olfert Dapper, *Gedenckwaerdig bedryf der Nederlandsche Oost-Indische Maetschappye, op de kuste en in het keizerrijk van Taising of Sina* (Amsterdam, 1670). Special Collections, University of Amsterdam (OM 63-124).

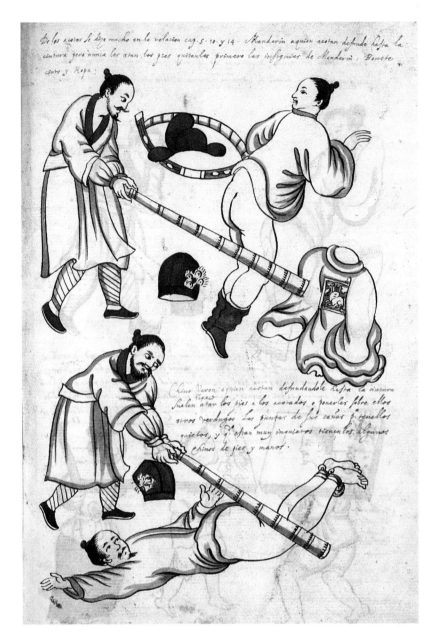

FIGURE 174. Adriano de las Cortes, Chinese corporal punishments, in *Relación del viaje* (ca. 1625); pen drawing (Sloane 1005). © The British Library Board. All Rights Reserved.

implement, location of the impact, and so on. Both in his text and sketches, moreover, de las Cortes highlights the disrobed *costumes* of the victims, which function to emphasize their relatively high social status—the so-called mandarin square, or rank badge, is plainly visible on a discarded tunic in the upper sketch and on two centrally placed hats that appear in both scenes. This, in turn, offers a means of stressing a primary theme of his account: that no one escapes the judicial reach of the emperor, including the high-ranking Mandarins, in particular, whom the Jesuits perceived as possible allies in their efforts to gain access at court.[124] For van Meurs and Dapper, these social matters may also play a role—cloaks and hats feature in both prints, if less prominently than in the original sketches. Yet van Meurs's draftsman, once he has extracted the principal protagonists from the drawings, adds the far more elaborate settings: the tortured victim and his dynamic tormenter, the casual spectators and the shivering prisoners, the interior décor and the imposing architecture. In their published commercial context, the engravings underscore, along with the "absolute" power of the Khan, the *spectacle* of the Chinese judicial process and the drama of imperial discipline.

And once the images had been appropriated, reformulated, and engraved by van Meurs, their most vivid features gained further endorsement in their subsequent iterations. The images circulated widely in other prints and publications, and this process culminated, once again, with their appearance in *La galerie agreable du monde*. There van der Aa both aggrandizes and codifies the pictures as representations of torture and forms of spectacle. He accentuates the images' association with "torture" by placing one of the two caning episodes alongside another set of Chinese scenes, which he unambiguously labels "*La torture chez les Chinois*": the torture of the Chinese. (These illustrations include the horrific image of a woman, stripped and strapped horizontally to a pole, whose upturned feet are crudely tormented—"tickled"—by means of a grotesquely large feather: see figures 175 and 88.) And van der Aa enhances the images' sense of spectacle by recasting them—specifically the courtyard caning scene, now more bluntly labeled "*Les Bastonnades chez les Chinois*": the Chinese bastinado—in lavishly engraved, double-folio prints, one of which he frames with classical columns and architecture that also bear the printer's full signature: "A Leide, *Chez* Pierre Vander Aa, *Marchand Libraire*" (see figure 149). This sumptuously exhibited picture appears, needless to say, in van der Aa's "agreeable gallery," where it and the other representations of frankly identified torture were meant to be visited, viewed, and implicitly enjoyed.[125]

The images of corporal punishment by cudgel—by this point rendered "*torture*" and "*bastonnades*" in the printed texts—also made their way to other media and the material arts, and these further iterations reveal perhaps the most startling effect of their circuits and transmediations: the transformation of exotic violence into "decorative" arts. The critical medium of transmediation, in this case, may have been a pattern book that included an engraved scene of caning. In John Stalker and Robert Parker's commonly cited *Treatise of japaning and varnishing*, a volume meant both to explain and to model the art of lacquering, one of the book's plates features—just beneath two separate designs of a strolling woman under a parasol and a cloaked man heading toward a pagoda—a variation of the open-air caning scene printed by

FIGURE 175. After Jacob van Meurs (atelier), Scenes of Chinese justice and torture ("La torture chez les Chinois") (engraving), in Pieter van der Aa, *La galerie agreable du monde* (Leiden, ca. 1729). Collection Antiquariaat Forum BV, 't Goy-Houten, The Netherlands.

van Meurs.[126] The engraving's descriptive caption proposes that its ensemble of exotic vignettes could be used to embellish "Drawers for Cabbinets to be Placed according to your fancy": to decorate a cabinet that would have been ample enough to accommodate the trio of designs, each of which would have been painted under layers of glossy lacquer ("japanning"). But the caning design had further applications—and broader implications. It was fashioned, as were the volume's other plates, for the arts of "guilding [gilding], burnishing . . . and of painting mezzo-tinto-prints [mezzotints]"; it was suitable for "counterfeiting tortoise-shell, and marble, and for staining or dying wood, ivory, and horn"; and it would have aided in the adornment

FIGURE 176. John Stalker and George Parker, "For Drawers for Cabbinets to be Placed according to your fancy" (engraving, detail), in *A treatise of japaning and varnishing* (Oxford, 1688). Courtesy of Marquand Library of Art and Archaeology, Princeton University. Purchase supported by the Elise and Wesley Wright Jr. '51 Marquand Book Fund.

of ceramics. It belonged, in short, to an all-purpose manual for the decorative arts.[127] Perhaps to make it more adaptable to these several modes and media, the original caning scene was refined and simplified in the Stalker and Parker version. Absent are the background edifices and throng of prisoners; meanwhile, the efficient executioner is replaced by a neatly dressed figure whom the pitiful victim implores, with a single unbound hand, for mercy.[128] While the van Meurs image underscores the power of the Qing judicial regime and of the emperor by extension—present metonymically in the background architecture—the Stalker and Parker design personalizes the exchange, granting more discretion to the caner. In certain ways, it undermines the original message of the emperor's sole authority by vacating him from the scene. It offers a purer distillation of exotic violence.

The second caning scene also underwent several instructive revisions in its transformation from printed book illustration to—in this case—bedroom décor. A wall covering designed around 1700 and ultimately destined for a private bed chamber in the Munich *Residenz* (the Bavarian royal palace) features both scenes of corporal punishment in the form of embroidered silk relief on a black taffeta foundation (see plate 24).[129] The episodes of caning appear on the wall decoration as discreet vignettes, one on top of the other, and they differ in design both from the Dapper–van Meurs illustrations and (in the case of the outdoor scene) the Stalker-Parker model. Like the latter, they are strategically streamlined. The lashing scene originally set indoors now takes place outdoors, and it isolates the cudgel-wielding tormentor and his half-naked victim by ridding the scene of all bystanders and accessories. The tormented figure is bound not to a wall but an exotic tree, and in the background looms another tree, an iconic palm (plus a small, indeterminate hut). The second vignette similarly highlights the thrashed figure and his thrasher, adding only two casual attendants, one of whom watches intently. It retains from the van Meurs print the smaller "Chinese" structure with curving roof gables (on the left), yet not the larger one, and it inserts, rather than background bamboo trees, another prominent palm placed in the heart of the composition. In both vignettes, the robes and hats of the caned men no longer serve to identify or rank them; in both, all the same, the victims have been stripped of most of their clothes, so that they must endure their harrowing ordeal with exposed legs and bare buttocks. These changes in form and setting—a carefully calibrated iconic circuit that lands caning motifs in the bedroom décor of Bavarian royal apartments—naturally affect meaning and function. By isolating the tormentors and their miserable victims, the wall-covering design effectively emphasizes the scenes' inherent violence. By inserting conspicuous palm trees in each of the scenes, the embroidered decoration clarifies the exotic setting of this brutal violence. And by placing all of this on the taffeta wall panels of a private chamber, the designer of the room reconfigures judicial violence as domestic décor. In this way, once again, iconic circuits and transmediations have produced a deracinated form of an exotic design. Corporal punishment, extracted from its global context, has been transformed into decorative pastiche suitable for a bedroom. Exotic pain has transmogrified into domestic pleasure.

Or, perhaps better, exotic pain has transmogrified into *exotic* pleasure, since the form of pleasure imparted by embroidered scenes of torment on silk panels adheres to a well-developed aesthetic of early modern exoticism—as do the strategically placed palm trees in caning vignettes, the parasol-shaded spectators of drug-pot decapitations, the carved cannibals who grace coconut cups, and the many other exotic accessories to what often amounts to decorative torture. While it may be tempting to associate these startling design strategies with a more recognizably modern sensation of delight and desire—bare-buttocked men embellishing risqué bedroom décor, blood-splattered pictures on fanciful drinking cups, and so on—they relate, in truth, to a distinctly earlier form of "exotic pleasures" (as Engelbert Kaempfer called it).[130] In their early modern context, these exotic motifs possessed a quality of "agreeableness" (Pieter van der Aa's term) despite, or even because of, their incongruous settings and seeming inappropriateness. This "aesthetic of the exotic" (Bernard Smith's phrasing) incorporated "misplaced" scenes of violence just as easily as it boasted "misplaced" allegories of continents. This aesthetic not only permitted but wholly embraced the "pleasure" and "delight" that derived from the departicularized objects of the world, from the decontextualized scenes of the world, and from the deracinated palms and parasols, "mendicants" and "torture," that furnished exotic décor. The aesthetics of exoticism adopted, surely by design, a strategy of "imperfect chaos" (as Georg Rumphius branded it).

This early modern aesthetic of exoticism, which bridged genres, media, and global spaces and which encompassed forms of geography and material arts alike, ultimately produced a distinctive and recognizable version of the non-European world. It was a world that inclined toward disorder and digression, conflations and "chaos"; a world inhabited by japanned "Indians" (as modeled by Stalker and Parker) as well as "japan'd" Africans (as fetishized by Aphra Behn); a world adorned with savagely sliced Sufi Qalanders (on inlaid cabinets) and piteously cangued Chinese supplicants (on numerous examples of ceramics and furniture). Violence and torture, when adequately exotic, could both decorate furniture and furnish "delight." This exotic perspective on the world extracted pleasure, too, in worldliness per se, as when expressed by the rich diversity of global objects that could litter paintings, prints, and plaques, even as these exotica were stripped of their original meaning and context: Ming porcelain in allegories of Africa (as in van Kessel's oil panel), verdant palm trees in maps of New England (on van Keulen's engraved cartouche), itinerant mendicants in exotic circus tableaux (on blue-and-white delftware). The non-European world was presented and perceived, furthermore, as a vast and agreeable gallery. It was designed to have broad and even mass appeal—Delft-made ceramics and single-sheet prints of this period reached an extensive range of consumers, even if other luxury items may have appealed to a more elite class of collector—and it was pitched to a loosely prescribed "European" audience.[131] The ateliers that produced the texts, images, and objects that adopted this aesthetic of exoticism shared sources, motifs, and vignettes, which circulated within a vast corpus of consumable goods. By dint of these circulations and mediations, moreover—the routine representation, replication, and reformulation across genres and media of geography and material arts—these texts and images obtained a markedly "European" appearance. A Dutch-designed scene derived from a Spanish-Jesuit drawing could migrate to an English-printed pattern book or adorn a German-decorated bedroom. It is hardly a coincidence that the "exotic pleasures" that feature in Engelbert Kaempfer's hodgepodge volume of that name, just like the "agreeable" contents of Pieter van der Aa's global gallery, are presented on the allegorical frontispieces of those two works to the maiden Europa (in the case of Kaempfer's print, they are delivered literally on a platter: see figures 1 and 2).[132] The pleasures of this exotic world belonged wholly to Europe.

Some Persons, perhaps, may object to the Promiscuous Assemblage of the various Subjects here exhibited, and be ready to wish that they had been allotted in Order and Method. . . . But however desirable such an Attainment might have been to a few *Cognoscenti*, it is very certain that the Majority of the World are not *Methodists*. They love Variety more than Order.

—*A Catalogue of the Portland Museum* (1786)

However, all Persons of true Taste, and a right Turn of Mind, greatly prize the Relations of [World] Travellers, which when *methodically digested*, and drawn up with a *strict Regard to Truth*, are of great Use, especially when they come from the Hands of Men of Penetration and Judgment.

—*Ceremonies and religious customs of the various nations of the known world* (1733–1737)

FROM PROMISCUOUS ASSEMBLAGE TO ORDER AND METHOD

Europe and Its Exotic Worlds

The pleasures of Europe's exotic world flourished around 1700, and its delights endured well into the eighteenth century. The use of the word itself—*exotic*—and its meaning also expanded over this period. Along with its traditional and customary deployment in natural history to designate non-native species, and its technical use in certain other fields of inquiry to describe things foreign or extrinsic to ("outside of") a defined indigenousness, the word *exotic* came to indicate by the mid-eighteenth century things that had not only *foreign* but also *delightful* attributes—things that possessed alien and perhaps curious qualities, yet also things that had wondrous and pleasurable features. This meaning was spelled out directly in the title of Engelbert Kaempfer's *Amoenitatum exoticarum politico-physico-medicarum* (1712): here the "pleasures" of the non-European world blend natural-historical flavors with political and cultural observations to concoct an agreeably "exotic" cocktail. And this is also the sense suggested by the distinguished English lexicographer Samuel Johnson, who commented, just a bit later in the century, on the "exotick . . . entertainment" exhibited in the faddish operas of his day—lovely, lavish affairs, with "Turkish" devices and delightful "Oriental" décors.[1]

The march of exoticism from systematic, semiorderly natural history to "delightful" and cheerfully disheveled bric-a-brac—from a "methodically digested" conception of the world to one that indulges "the Promiscuous Assemblage of the various Subjects" displayed in the Duchess of Portland's museum—proceeded through the terrain of early modern geography. While in the early years of the seventeenth century, in classic accounts such as Carolus Clusius's *Exoticorum libri decem* (Ten books of exotica) published in 1605, *exotic* indicated species that were simply non-native from the naturalist's perspective, by the later seventeenth century it came to mean something broader and less distinctive.[2] It embraced the "imperfect chaos" of Rumphius's ruminations on the Indies, the "pleasures" of Kaempfer's far-flung observations of tropical phenomena, and the "promiscuous assemblage" gathered by Margaret Cavendish Bentinck, the second Duchess of Portland, in her illustrious museum. More generally, an aesthetic of exoticism had developed by the early eighteenth century across volumes of print geography, among the plentifully produced pictures and paintings of global disposition, and in a vast array of material arts. These exotic materials—which commonly relied on shared manuscript sources, visual motifs, and decorative designs, and which borrowed from one another using methods of production that blithely crossed genres and media—traded in a form of representation that strategically incorporated disorder and digression, and expressly highlighted the "pleasure" and "promiscuity" of their global "assemblages." Exotic geography delighted in the world. This is the message articulated explicitly in the products of Pieter van der Aa—not only in *La galerie agreable du monde* but also in his multivolume series "Les délices," which furnished armchair travelers across Europe with the wide-ranging "delights" of the world. And exotic "pleasures" are enlisted to pitch several other global productions of this geographical moment: Kaempfer's *Amoenitatum exoticarum* (1712); a reissue of Olfert Dapper's work under the telling title *Delitiae Orientales* (1712); a catch-all, two-volume compendium of Jacob van Meurs publications (published after the printer's death), *Dapperus exoticus curiosus* (1717–1718), which, if labeled slightly less explicitly, points all the same in the direction of exotic enchantments. Delight sold well.

Exotic delight readily transcended the confines of print geography, too, and this allowed it to further shape other genres and media. Exotic motifs proliferated particularly in the material arts of the late seventeenth and eighteenth centuries, and the notion of "pleasure" in the world emerges in the design and adornment of myriad "decorative" arts. This applies especially for those European-made objects that engaged with forms and materials of exotic extraction (woods, shells, ivories, and so on). Asian-inspired ceramics and lacquered furnishings, decorated textiles and inlaid cabinets, embellished shells and carved minerals, cut glass and metalwork of "curious" form: all could incorporate exotic designs, often borrowing directly from the richly illustrated geography books that circulated so widely in this period. In what meager commentary exists in the special pattern books devised for the ornamentation of these objects, moreover, a comparable emphasis falls on the "pleasing" qualities of exotic design and the conceit of "delight" in a boisterously exotic world. In the aptly titled *Ladies amusement* (ca. 1760), a volume that revised and supplanted Stalker and Parker's *Treatise of japaning* (1688) as the preeminent manual for the embellishment of ceramics and lacquered objects, exotic motifs aim chiefly "to please." They afford their audience "agreeable" images of the world and

"delightful" décor. Inspired largely by ersatz Asiana—chinoiserie in the language of design history—the volume presents "an agreeable amusement" in the form of two hundred copperplate engravings. These exhibit the "great and pleasing variety" of the globe in all of its jumbled profusion.[3] In this regard, the *Ladies amusement* affiliates exotic design with the aesthetic of variety, digressiveness, and "promiscuity" that had long been prevalent in print geography. An "agreeable confusion" guides the presentation of exotic material objects, which incline toward "variety more than order."[4] The delight of this aesthetic of exoticism, whether found in print geography or material design, lay in its digressive and disorienting style: in its "cunning confusion and vast variety and surprising universality," as the bluestocking Elizabeth Montagu observed on visiting the Duchess of Portland's collection (1742); in its "higgledy-piggledy" mode of description and literary presentation, as critics commented on Montesquieu's exotic satire, *The Persian Letters* (1721); in its production of a *sharawadgi* ("beauty . . . without order"), to cite William Temple's appraisal of the "Chinese" gardens invented by Dutch overseas agents in colonial southern Africa (1685).[5] In all these guises, exoticism implied a veritably *perfect* chaos—it was digressive by design.

The ascendancy of exoticism in the eighteenth century did not, however, go unchallenged. As it happens, the "*Cognoscenti*" who "might" have objected to the promiscuity of the Duchess of Portland—to the lack of "Order and Method" in her collection, that is—turned out to be more than just "a few"; and the "Methodists," if not quite a "majority," did hold considerable sway in the eighteenth-century republic of letters.[6] There was, even several years before the Portland collection began to take shape and before exotic motifs became the "amusement" of "ladies," a backlash against exotic geography, with the brunt of the criticism aimed precisely at the genre's lack of "Order and Method." Jean-Baptiste Du Halde, the Jesuit historian who assiduously gathered and organized missionary reports from members of his Order and produced from them (in 1735) a four-volume "Geographical, historical, chronological, political, and physical description" of China—from the very title itself, the volume hewed to a "Methodist" approach—scathingly denounced the brand of exotic geography that had burgeoned over the past years. Du Halde expressed his unambiguous contempt for the "spurious compositions" presently on the market and their lack of "certainty," for geography volumes full of "errors" and the endless replication of "difference"—for their *lack* of order and method and their want of what he calls "exactness"—and, not least, for geography's cunning manufacture "by ignorant or mercenary Hands" rather than the ranks of the learned.[7] One of those "learned" colleagues, the Swiss scholar Johann Gaspar Scheuchzer, prefaced his translation of Engelbert Kaempfer's *History of Japan* (1727) with a similarly censorious critique of contemporary geography, calling out in particular Arnoldus Montanus's *Atlas Japannensis* (the English edition of van

EPILOGUE

Meurs's original). Scheuchzer, who served as in-house librarian for the eminent English colonialist Hans Sloane—the energetic naturalist, tropical physician, "inventor" of milk chocolate, and collector extraordinaire whose massive cabinet of exotic curiosities formed the basis of the British Museum—derided earlier forms of (in this case) print geography for their almost decorative approach to global description. These antecedents furnished mere "embellishments" rather than trustworthy accounts. The Montanus–van Meurs volume, Scheuchzer protested, was wholly "without any order" and "full of large digressions"; its rambling text mostly "deviate[d] from the truth." It was, in short, a classic example of exotic geography.[8]

Du Halde's and Scheuchzer's denunciations echoed numerous others from the republic of letters, which likewise made the case that the form of geography that had dominated the market over the past several decades was deeply flawed. Earlier volumes of exotic geography had not been "methodically digested," as the editor of the *Ceremonies and religious customs of the world* (1733–1737) insinuated.[9] They failed to adhere to "a strict Regard to Truth," and they did not issue from "Men of Penetration and Judgment"—from the learned and elite and others who properly "make use of their reason." From this perspective, the species of exotic geography that had evolved in recent years—dating back, more or less, to the van Meurs oeuvre, cited both directly and indirectly in these attacks—imparted too little "order" and too much "pleasure." It amused yet did not enlighten. And if the latter term is not explicitly invoked—the *Ceremonies*' preface speaks only allusively of "reason" and the "rational" reader—it indicates the general inclination of these critiques. "Men of penetration" and "Persons of true Taste and a right Turn of Mind" could no longer abide the embellishments and amusements of exotic geography. They demanded a more "enlightened," or what might anachronistically be called "scientific," approach to the extra-European world. Indeed, no less an authority than Carl Linnaeus weighed in on the "sumptuous" geographies that still circulated in his day (the 1730s, when Linnaeus commenced his own project of describing the exotic natural world), books that overflowed with distracting pictures and extraneous diversions.[10]

Geography thus moved away from an "agreeable" and "promiscuous" vision of the world, which had flourished from the later seventeenth century into the early eighteenth, toward a more "methodically digested" rendition (evident from the 1730s at the latest). It shifted from an ostensibly more ludic posture to a more exacting and didactic one, from the haphazard "delights" and chaotic "pleasures" of Europe's exotic world to Du Halde's Jesuit-sourced "certainties" and Scheuchzer and Sloane's systematically collected "truths." The cause? To a degree, this bifurcation may simply have reflected an ongoing dialectic in the history of travel literature and geography: the oft-stated intent of such sources both to teach and to delight. For most of the genre's history, European travel narratives and descriptions of the world promised their readers what Sir John Mandeville nimbly labeled "lust" and "lore"—pleasurable diversion and moral lesson (or commonly moral lesson *through* pleasurable diversion)—qualities that jointly stamped most "exotic" accounts of the Middle Ages.[11] In the narratives of "discovery" that followed 1492, however, moral lessons typically yielded to more crudely ideological ones—the imperatives of empire, the calls to colonial action, the banners of evangelization of rival European powers—and the "delight" of travel fell largely by the wayside. Yet by the mid-seventeenth century, during a relative lull in Europe's colonial contest, "delight" made a comeback. Adam Olearius, for example, made a point in the preface to his mid-century *Voyages and Travels* (through Muscovy and Persia) to endorse geography's capacity "delightfully [to survey] the strange circulations of humane nature," the "divertissement" and "pleasure" that it afforded, and the genre's many exotic "charms."[12] Comments of this sort mushroomed in Holland-produced sources from the final third of the seventeenth century through the early eighteenth century—a period that coincided, not unrelatedly, with the Dutch Republic's own reduction of imperial ventures. And by the time Pieter van der Aa launched his series of travelers' "delights" and his agreeably global picture gallery, the quality of "lust" in exotic geography and the genre's "promiscuous assemblage" of curious things had reached their zenith. Europeans—as portrayed, for example, on van der Aa's and Kaempfer's allegorical frontispieces—amused themselves by preference with the "pleasures" of exoticism.

The shift in the genre from around the 1730s indicated a new and competing impulse in Europe's conception of the world. On the one hand, an "aesthetic of the exotic" prospered and endured in volumes such as those of Pieter van der Aa, in collections such as those of the Duchess of Portland, and in material arts such as those designed from *The ladies amusement*. These sources and objects presented the exotic world as a locus of "pleasure" and "delight," and they underscored the "agreeable" qualities of exotica, which afforded a manner of "amusement." Yet this amusement and delight bore a distinctive quality. It showcased the dizzying abundance and chaotic bric-a-brac of the world, and it eschewed any coherent sense of global "order." It reveled in a form of "cunning confusion," and it relished what one volume designated, typically, "delightful variety."[13] The consumer of this brand of exotic geography, just as the visitor to Portland's museum, "love[d] Variety more than Order."[14] On the other hand, the competing form of geography that emerged in the early eighteenth century embraced a more "methodical" perspective on the world. It disdained the "large digressions" of earlier offerings of geography, and it aspired, accordingly, to "order and method"—*method* turns up regularly in these texts as a modus operandi. Sources of this provenance stipulated that global things should be "methodically digested": compare the prior mode of exotic geography, which advertised its contents (in this instance, descriptions of tropical *naturalia* from Georg Rumphius) as "*un*digested," a form of "imperfect chaos" (*indigestum supererat Chaos*).[15] Just as important as the method, furthermore, were the "Methodists" who extolled this revised manner of geography: "Men of Penetration and Judgment" and others who valued "a strict regard to truth." The new geography was required to be "strictly agreeable to the truth, and without embellishments"— without, in other words, the ornate illustrations and haphazard digressions typical of earlier variants of the genre.[16]

The incantation of "truth" in these later sources would have been fairly routine for almost all forms of geography (not to mention history and even romance). Yet the invocation of a particular class of consumer—"Men of Penetration and Judgment"—marks another significant departure. The new brand of geography appealed by design to "men" of discernment and good judgment, to "Persons of true Taste, and a right Turn of Mind," as the editor of Jean-Frédéric Bernard and Bernard Picart's *Ceremonies* averred. "True taste" here does not necessarily denote an elite readership (although the audience for Bernard and Picart's seven-volume tour de force would almost certainly have derived from the upper links of Europe's great chain of wealth). It does indicate, nevertheless, a degree of distinction and level of discrimination that set the targeted audience for such global projects apart. Other sources, likewise, carefully pitch to a particular category of consumer. Du Halde flatters his readers (and himself) when he broadcasts the superior attributes of his new geography of China, its keen "exactness," and—invariably—its uncompromised truth. Yet even as he characterizes that truth in terms of its quality of *désintéressement* (disinterest), he contradicts this claim when he catalogues the Jesuit accounts on which such putative neutrality would have been constructed. Outside of those select religious and political circles where Jesuit testimonies might count as unbiased reporting, Du Halde's *Description* offered many European readers a bitter pill to swallow. It presented an updated narrative of Chinese history and geography, yet from a pronouncedly Jesuit perspective. Its easily perceived "religious notions" delivered a dose of "poison," according to one Protestant critic, who promised a countervailing "antidote."[17] Scheuchzer's presentation of Kaempfer's geography of Japan did not convey quite the same biases, yet this Sloane-directed project sprang from the seasoned colonialist's larger endeavor of collecting and assembling the globe—assembling, not at all promiscuously, the foundations of the British Museum and collecting the cultural memorabilia, arguably, of the British Empire. "True taste" in these contexts reflected the perspectives of a French Jesuit and an English empire-builder (Sloane cut his teeth collecting in the West Indies). "Truth," in this latest iteration of geography, obtained from metropolitan centers in London and Paris and from imperially minded men such as Hans Sloane and Jean-Baptiste Du Halde— hardly thus the simple "amusements" and exotic "pleasures" of generic "Europeans."

FIGURE 178. *Charles Vere At the Indian King* (London, 1772); engraved trade card. © The Trustees of the British Museum.

All that said, exotic delights—and exotic geography in its various formulations—did carry on. The new mode of geography that developed in the middle decades of the eighteenth century pursued "order and method," as it aspired to organize and demarcate the spaces of the non-European world. It appealed by design to men of true taste, learned leanings, and enlightened perspectives. Yet it delineated more often than not the spaces of French and British interests. Or rather, it delineated a world that strategically accommodated French and British global interests—typically one or the other, as these interests increasingly competed—at a moment of rising imperial ambitions in the salons of Paris and the merchant offices of London.[18] The older manner of geography, meanwhile, persisted in other forms and venues. A well-entrenched aesthetic of exoticism continued to provide "amusements" for European "ladies" and supply decorative motifs for material arts. There was a certain gendered inflection, that is to say, to this bifurcation, whereby one manner of geography appealed to "men of penetration" and another to ladies drawn to "luxuriance and fancy" (as *The ladies amusement* phrased it).[19] Nonetheless, the "majority" of Europeans were not "methodists" (as the Duchess of Portland's catalogue correctly pointed out), and quite a few were inclined to the consumption of exotica. They genuinely loved "Variety more than Order." They also loved the worldly goods stacked high in the stylish "Chinaman" shops lately materializing in London, such as John Cotterell's "Indian Queen," where customers could purchase a "great variety" of exotic things; or Charles Vere's "Indian King," which stocked "all sorts" of exotica and "a great variety" of Asian, African, and American bric-a-brac.[20] And they flocked to the art dealers and *marchand-merciers* of Paris, such as Edme-François Gersaint, who operated the famous shop "A La Pagode" and whose engraved trading card (designed by François Boucher: figure 179) featured the same manner of exotic variety and global profusion as Jan van Kessel's allegorical *Continents*, as the Duchess of Portland's promiscuous assemblage of exotic miscellany (depicted in an engraving by Edward Francis Burney: figure 177), and as could be found in the several other outlets for consumable exotica.[21] For it was in these years—again, the middle decades of the eighteenth century—that the aesthetic of exoticism spread further to other cultural forms and other media: to theater and opera, fiction and poetry, painting and material arts, and much more. In these forms and in these "mercenary hands" (which so vexed Du Halde and his fellow "methodists"), an aesthetic of exoticism prospered for decades.[22]

A final point: The two forms of geography and their respective visions of the world could, in a critical sense, coexist and even sustain one another. The one conception of the non-European world—of a disorderly, disheveled, cheerfully jumbled space filled with exotic pleasures and global delights—all but asked for the "imperfect chaos" that it envisioned to be sorted out. Meanwhile, the other vision of the world—of an orderly, "methodically digested," clearly demarcated globe, delineated with less untidy "difference" and greater political "certainty"—offered a response to the implicit challenge of exotic geography. Indeed, by rendering the non-European world so emphatically digressive and so brimming with disorderly "delight," exotic geography invited a more rigorous retort. A world rich with exotic pleasures and abounding with consumable goods—goods delivered on a platter to

FIGURE 179. Anne-Claude-Philippe de Tubières-Grimoard de Pestels de Lévis, comte de Caylus, after François Boucher, *A La Pagode* (trade card of Edme Gersaint) (Paris, 1740); etching and engraving; 36 × 21 cm. Waddeson, The Rothschild Collection (The National Trust), acc. no. 3686.1.56.103. Photo: University of Central England Digital Services © The National Trust, Waddeson Manor.

allegorical maidens of Europe—was a world of immense enticement. The monarchs and merchants of Europe, the colonial strategists and imperial schemers of the day, accepted this challenge and seized these enticements. They endeavored, over the eighteenth century and well beyond, to make their own order of this exotic world.

[NOTES]

INTRODUCTION

Epigraphs: Rumphius, *Herbarium Amboinense*, Preface, n.p. (sig. **2v–****r) (signed 1690 and published posthumously): "Ik presentere U E. dan wat nieuws, geen monster uit de wildernissen van Africa gehaalt, maar een vermakelyke, en niet te min nutte Historie, of beschryving van 't jeugd Aard-gewas, dat men in deze uiterste werelts-hoek beschouwen mag, en tot nog toe aan onze Europianen onbekent is" (emphases added).

Defoe, *Plan of the English Commerce*, 192.

Segalen, *Essay on Exoticism*, 13.

1 Aa, *Galerie agreable*. As per his habits of production, van der Aa adopted his frontispiece etching from an earlier print, which had served as the opening image of Carel Allard's *Orbis habitabilis*. The original design was the work of Romeyn de Hooghe, and van der Aa had this image reworked and reframed (a practice he followed for several of the illustrations in his massive "gallery").

2 Aa, *Galerie agreable*, title page, and see also "L'imprimeur au Lecteur" (n.p.). On this remarkable impresario of print—discussed in further detail in chapters 1 and 4—see Hoftijzer, *Van der Aa*; on his masterpiece of printing, see Krogt, *Koeman's Atlantes Neerlandici*, vol. 4.

3 De Hooghe and van der Aa may have collaborated years earlier on *Indes Orientales*, which appeared (undated) sometime in the late seventeenth or early

eighteenth century. De Hooghe died in 1708, so the redesigned print in the *Galerie agreable* would, by necessity, have been the work of van der Aa's atelier, adopting a composition originally formulated by de Hooghe. On the extraordinary career of de Hooghe, see Nierop, *Romeyn de Hooghe*.

4 The tradition of the continents had been revived in the early sixteenth century, instigated by the "discovery" of the Americas—counted as a single continent, namely the fourth—and the iconography of the continents was substantially solidified by the publication of Cesare Ripa's *Iconologia* (1593; with illustrations in 1603). On the development of continental themes more generally, see Lewis and Wigen, *Myth of Continents*. On Europa more particularly, see Wintle, *Image of Europe*, and the classic study of Hay, *Europe*.

5 The globe itself traditionally had several religious associations, especially in late medieval Europe (cf. the iconography of Salvator Mundi): see Cosgrove, "Christian Globe," in *Apollo's Eye*, 54–78.

6 The myth of Europa—of the abduction of a high-born Phoenician woman (Europa) by Zeus in the form of a white bull—dates back to antiquity, and it, too, was revived in the Renaissance, particularly in the visual arts: see Wintle, *Image of Europe*, 102–110.

7 A contrasting message—forcefully polemical and muscularly Habsburg—is conveyed in the Rijksmuseum's *Allegory of the Abdication of Emperor Charles V* (ca. 1630; object no. SK-A-112), painted by

Frans (II) Francken about a century before van der Aa's frontispiece appeared. The Francken image offers a counter-model of allegorical representation and continental homage. Charles receives the bounty of his imperial world from America, Asia, and Europe, as he sits regally enthroned amid signs of his Christian dominions, flags of his imperial possessions (symbolizing his Dutch, Spanish, and Italian territories), and a banner that spells out his powerfully imperial motto: *Plus Ultra* (roughly "ever further").

8 On the articulation of the Self by way of the Other—identity though alterity—there is an enormous literature. Two insightful studies that go back to the foundational moment of Western ethnography are Hartog, *Mirror of Herodotus*, and Hall, *Inventing the Barbarian*. For a provocative exploration of these themes at another pivotal moment in modern imperial geography, see Wey Gómez, *Tropics of Empire*.

9 The phrasing borrows from Cooper and Stoler (discussed below): Cooper and Stoler, *Tensions of Empire*, 3, 13.

10 Shifts in early modern geography have been noted in studies focused chiefly on the Renaissance (that is, earlier) and Enlightenment (later) moments—although only meagerly on the intervening episode ca. 1670–1730 highlighted here. On the earlier transitions, see Rubiés, *Travel and Ethnology*; Rubiés, "Travel Writing"; Brummett, *"Book" of Travels*; and the still useful study of Hodgen, *Early Anthropology*. On the subsequent transitional moment of ca. 1730, see Daston and Park, *Wonders*. Note that post-1648 Europe was by no means at peace—Louis XIV was particularly belligerent—yet there was, by contrast with the previous decades, no sustained, catastrophic, continent-wide conflict that occupied Europe's undivided attention.

11 On the trade of exotic goods, especially in the Netherlands, see McCants, "Exotic Goods." On the role of the Dutch as purveyors and producers of exotica—and on this exotic moment in its broader economic context—see Vries and Woude, *First Modern Economy*, especially 429–448 and 464–481; and Vries, "Luxury."

12 On Amsterdam printing in this period, see the definitive account of Eeghen, *Amsterdamse Boekhandel*, along with Hoftijzer, "Metropolis." On the phenomenon of early modern Dutch printing more generally, see Berkvens-Stevelinck, *Magasin de l'Univers*. And on the outstanding production of maps—especially those dedicated to exotic places—see Zandvliet, *Mapping for Money*.

13 Cook, *Matters of Exchange*, surveys the flourishing commerce in "scientific" exotica, while Davids, "Amsterdam as a Center of Learning," identifies the period from the 1660s to 1730s as a high point in the Netherlands for the life sciences, particularly as they pertain to exotic *naturalia*. See also Bergvelt and Kistemaker, *Wereld binnen handbereik*, and Margócsy, *Commercial Visions*.

14 The definitive study is Aken-Fehmers, *Delfts aardewerk*; see also Dam, *Delffse porceleyne*.

15 On the well-studied case of Post, see Corrêa do Lago and Corrêa do Lago, *Frans Post*. On the many other artists who engaged with the exotic world, see note 51 below.

16 Nieuhof, *L'Ambassade* and *Gezantschap*—published simultaneously in Leiden and Amsterdam, respectively, in 1665 and subsequently in other languages—and Dapper, *Naukeurige beschrijvinge*, likewise published in Amsterdam in multiple editions and languages (both books are discussed in chapter 1).

17 Montanus, *Gedenkwaerdige gesantschappen*. On the volume's convoluted process of creation, see Hesselink, "Memorable Embassies"; Eeghen, "Montanus's Book."

18 Hakluyt has long been singled out for his patriotic approach to geography—he produced his work "[for] the ardent love of my country," as he proudly proclaims (*Principal Navigations*, Dedication to Charles Howard, n.p. [1599–1600 ed.])—and he offers as sharp a contrast as imaginable to the Dutch approach to geography, as noted by the literary critic E. M. Beekman: "This crucial connection between the printed word and the manipulation of a nation's consciousness was recognized in England much earlier than in Holland. Richard Hakluyt . . . published what has been called 'the very papers of empire'" (*Fugitive Dreams*, 26). Beekman misses, however, the strategic purpose of the Dutch approach: precisely to avoid parochial geography and thus to reach a broader audience.

19 Heylyn, *Cosmographie*, Preface ("To the Reader"), n.p. (sig. [A4]r). On Heylyn and his "tub-thumping" patriotism, see Markley, *Far East*, 57–59.

20 Purchas, *Hakluytus posthumus*, and cf. his fiercely antagonistic "Note Touching the Dutch" (n.p.).

21 See Latour, *Science in Action*, which includes his classic account of knowledge production through the mechanism of "centers of calculation" (215–257).

22 The very word "exotic" proliferated beginning in the late seventeenth century—in previous decades, it was deployed almost exclusively in the context of natural history to describe nonnative specimens, as in

Clusius, *Exoticorum libri decem*. And scholarship on the exotic has skewed, accordingly, toward eighteenth-century studies. See Rousseau and Porter, *Exoticism in the Enlightenment*; Knellwolf and Maccubin, *Exoticism and the Culture of Exploration*; Knellwolf, "Exotic Frontier"; and Eaton, "Nostalgia for the Exotic." On the process by which exotic species and European interest in them instigated concerns with *indigenity*, see Cooper, *Inventing the Indigenous*.

23 Court, *Interest van Holland*, cited in Vries and Woude, *First Modern Economy* (675), where the authors also describe the rise and fall of the Dutch Atlantic empire (see especially 396–402 and 464–467). See further Vries, "Dutch Atlantic Economies"; and Emmer and Klooster, "Dutch Atlantic," which dates the Republic's Atlantic decline precisely to the final decades of the seventeenth century. The broader picture is sketched out in Schmidt, "Dutch Atlantic."

24 De Vries and van der Woude speak of a "peak" around 1650 and a decline quickly thereafter: "An era of great prosperity for the VOC came to an end in the 1670s and '80s as forces in both Europe and Asia undermined the viability of the inter-Asian trade ... and reduced the Company's profitability in Europe by forcing down prices." Vries and Woude, *First Modern Economy*, 436. See also Bruijn and Gaastra, "Dutch East India Company's Shipping," which likewise makes a case for the relative decline, from the late seventeenth century, of the Dutch in Asia.

25 Compare Benton, *Search for Sovereignty*, which makes the complementary argument that early modern empires were not necessarily all that territorial.

26 Piso et al., *Historia naturalis Brasiliae* and *Indiae utriusque*. There was also a shift in patronage for the second edition: while the 1648 version was dedicated, unsurprisingly, to Johan Maurits, the 1658 edition bore a dedication to the Elector of Brandenburg, Friedrich Wilhelm. See also Cook, *Matters of Exchange*, on the "ham-fisted editorial interventions" (224), more generally, in the production of Piso's 1658 volume; and Freedberg, "Science, Commerce, and Art," on the contrast between the "entrepreneurial" practices of exotic science of the Dutch and the more courtly model common in Italy.

27 Asad, "Muslims and European Identity." Asad's point had been made earlier, famously—albeit in a more concretely colonial context—by Frantz Fanon: "Europe is literally the creation of the Third World" (*Wretched of the Earth*, 58). It is echoed in much postcolonial scholarship—for example, by Catherine Hall: "Europeans made history and made themselves through becoming colonizers" (*Cultures of Empire*, 13). The theme is also central, if implicitly argued, in the magnum opus of Donald Lach, *Asia in the Making of Europe*.

28 Schouten, *Oost-Indische voyagie*. The volume appeared in some dozen editions, also in French and German translations (produced, per usual, in Amsterdam ateliers).

29 Schouten, *Oost-Indische voyagie*, book 1, 44–47 (quotation on 47). Schouten also comments on the "lamentable" treatment of the Catholics in Japan (26); and compare the similar comments—a Dutch Calvinist narrator showing sympathy for former Catholic rivals—sprinkled throughout Montanus, *Japan*.

30 Pagden, *European Encounters*, especially 17–49; and compare Findlen, *Possessing Nature*, on the concern of Renaissance collectors of exotic *naturalia* to establish the "incomparable" quality of their specimens.

31 Greenblatt, *Marvelous Possessions*. Like Pagden, Greenblatt describes the European desire to "efface the incommensurability" of the New World—to reduce, that is, the profound difference and challenging "singularity" of exotic American phenomena (54).

32 Columbus, *Four Voyages*, 116, 209, and 219; Columbus, *Diario*, 203; and see also Hulme, "Tales of Distinction."

33 Cortés, *Letters from Mexico*, 102–104. See also Hartog, *Mirror of Herodotus*, which comments more extensively on this form of associative description in the context of the ur-ethnography of Herodotus.

34 White [attrib.], *True pictures*; for which see Mancall, *Envisioning America*, 102–103.

35 Loomba, "Periodization"; see also the classic study of Fabian, *Time and the Other*.

36 "Historiae oculus geographia" (Geography [is] the eye of history). The motto appeared on the title-page woodcut of Ortelius, *Parergon* (1592; earlier editions without woodcut from 1579), which served as a supplement to the *Theatrum orbis terrarum*. Ortelius invoked this aphorism following an earlier Renaissance tradition that conceived of geography as an "eye" on the world: cf. Apianus, *Cosmographicus liber*; Chytraeus, *Ratione discendi*.

37 Montanus, *Nieuwe en onbekende weereld*; Montanus, *Japan* (a volume that, in its English form, actually closed with an advertisement for the author's "Atlantick Work": see Montanus, *Atlas Japannensis*, 488).

38 Cooper and Stoler, *Tensions of Empire*, especially vii–ix, 2–4, and 13. See also Said, *Orientalism* and *Culture and Imperialism*; and Segalen, *Essay on*

Exoticism. For a converse approach from another angle, see Barkey, *Empire of Difference*.

The discussion in Cooper et alia of "the production of colonial knowledge" builds on the foundations of an immense body of scholarship generated over the past few decades that seeks to relate colonial knowledge to imperial power—the central thrust of Said's work, which borrows theoretical insights from the work of Michel Foucault. By interrogating early modern processes of producing exotic knowledge—by focusing on modes of mediation that take place between colonial actors and metropolitan producers; between overseas travelers, authors, draftsmen, and collectors, on the one hand, and entrepreneurial makers of exotic books, maps, prints, paintings, material arts, and so on, on the other—this study suggests a reevaluation of this scholarship. Emblematic studies that underscore the knowledge/power relationship as it developed in early modern Europe include Hulme, *Colonial Encounters*; Mignolo, *Darker Side of the Renaissance*; Pratt, *Imperial Eyes*; Fuller, *Voyages in Print*; and Ogborn, *Indian Ink*, all of which focus on writing and literature. More squarely focused on geography and cartography are Harley, *New Nature of Maps*; Winichakul, *Siam Mapped*; Hostetler, *Qing Colonial Enterprise*; and Brückner, *Geographic Revolution*. For natural historical materials, see Schiebinger, *Plants and Empire*; Schiebinger and Swan, *Colonial Botany*; and Miller and Reill, *Visions of Empire*. And studies with an art-historical focus include Tobin, *Picturing Imperial Power*; and Grigsby, *Extremities*.

39 Cooper and Stoler invoke this formulation explicitly and implicitly: see *Tensions of Empire*, 3, 13, and passim.

40 Nor is there mention of Holland, Amsterdam, Leiden—an important center of Oriental Studies from the seventeenth century—and so on (a passing mention of a contemporary Dutch scholar and a dismissive reference aside: Said, *Orientalism*, 24, 210, and passim). Scattered and brief citations of Holland do appear in *Culture and Imperialism*, yet these reference the modern, nineteenth-century chapter of Dutch colonialism rather than the early modern moment of producing proto-colonial geography. The oversight in *Orientalism* seems more critical and germane insofar as Said's earlier, agenda-setting study was meant precisely to present a history of the phenomenon.

41 Defoe, *Plan of the English commerce*, 192.

42 Montesquieu, *Lettres persanes*, for which see *Persian Letters*, 187 (letter 102).

43 Rumphius suggests that readers would enjoy "skimming" his work ("doorbladeren"): *Herbarium Amboinense*, sig. **v. Meanwhile, de Lange offers his global wonders as so many "morsels" to be sampled and tasted by the reader: *Wonderen des werelds*, "Aen de Leser," sig. A2.

44 Lange, *Wonderen des werelds*. See also the preface to Jean de Thévenot's description of the Levant, where the editor explains the volume's strategy of offering quick, scattered accounts of "all that is curious in every place"—rather than sustained, detailed narrative—"and not too much, to cloy the Reader with the repetition": *Travels*, n.p. De Bruijn rationalizes this scatter-shot approach in a chapter titled "Odd Matters," noting that the sheer variety of exotic miscellany and bric-a-brac "would render the Narration Intricate or Defective": *Voyage to the Levant*, 103–104.

45 Montanus, *Atlas Japannensis*, where the word "strange" echoes like a symphonic leitmotif: 119–120, 154–156, 324–325, 394, 412, 488, and passim.

46 Olearius, *Voyages & travels*, "To the Reader" (n.p.); Rochefort, *History of the Caribby-Islands*, 50 (and on both works, whose production and dissemination relied heavily on Dutch book makers, see chapter 1).

47 Bruijn, *Voyage au Levant*. De Bruijn apparently also printed the Dutch edition of 1698 (from which the French was translated) in color, yet no copy remains. The single extant copy of the four-color print French edition is in the Universiteitsbibliotheek Amsterdam. See Gnirrep, *Levant in kleur*.

48 The reference is to Alpers, *Art of Describing*.

49 On the economic effect of these products, see McCants, "Exotic Goods"; on the assemblage of exotic material arts more broadly, see Jackson and Jaffer, *Encounters*.

50 In this way, forms of exotic geography helped to usher in and to set many of the terms for the "enlightened pleasures" of the eighteenth century: see Kavanagh, *Enlightened Pleasures*.

51 The list of painters occupied with exotic motifs is remarkably and surprisingly long—surprisingly, since they go mostly unnoticed in the art-historical scholarship (for an exception, however, see Westermann, *Worldly Art*). Along with Frans Post and Albert Eckhout—on the latter, see Buvelot, *Eckhout*, and Brienen, *Savage Paradise*; on the former, see note 15 above—the roster would include a variety of painters depicting numerous exotic settings across several genres. For landscapes and *vedute* there are works by

Dirk Valkenburg, Andries Beeckman, Ludolf Backhuyzen, Abraham de Verwer, Reinier (Zeeman) Nooms, Gerard van Edema, Hendrik Jacobsz Dubbels, Hendrick van Schuylenburg, Adam Willaerts, Jillis van Schendel, and Gillis and Bonaventura Peeters. There were also artists specializing in *kunstkamer* paintings (e.g., Jan van der Heyden and Jan van Kessel), genre scenes depicting curiosity dealers and their exotic wares (Cornelis de Man), exotic portraiture (Cornelis de Bruijn and Jean Baptiste van Mour), and fantasy scenes set in exotic settings (Willem Schellinks, who painted imaginary pastiches of the Mughal court). And there were many painters who specialized in still lifes with exotica—too numerous to list—and portraits of collectors surrounded by exotica. Several examples of these last two categories are reproduced in Bergvelt and Kistemaker, *Wereld binnen handbereik*, cats. 10–11, 23, 62, 66, 69, 84, 259, 270, 290–295 (this last group comprises works by Otto Marseus van Schrieck, Rachel Ruysch, and Dirk Valkenburg, each of whom concentrated on exotic *naturalia*), and 362. See also Bok, "European Artists," and Terwen-De Loos, *Nederlandse schilders*, both of which amplify this list.

CHAPTER 1. PRINTING THE WORLD

Epigraph: Boswell, *Life of Samuel Johnson*, 247.

1 Nieuhof, *Gezantschap*. The book came out virtually simultaneously in a French edition, also published by van Meurs, also with privileges—*L'Ambassade de la Compagnie Orientale*, printed "Avec Privilege du Roy"—and in Latin, German, and English editions (discussed below).

2 A partial listing can be found in Ulrichs, *Nieuhofs Blick*; see also Landwehr, *VOC*.

3 Nieuhof's final fate is not entirely clear. In 1672, he disappeared on the island of Madagascar after he came ashore in search of water. What scant details of his life that are known can be gleaned from studies of his China book: see Blussé and Falkenburg, *Nieuhofs beelden*; Ulrichs, *Nieuhofs Blick*; and Rietbergen, "Zover de aarde reikt."

4 These events are also reviewed, in the context of the book's patronage, in Peters, "Nepotisme."

5 Linschoten, *Itinerario*, "Prohemio ofte Voorreden totten leser" (n.p.).

6 On the concept of the author-function, see Foucault, "What Is an Author?" and the discussion in Chartier, *Order of Books*, 25–60 ("Figures of the Author").

7 Thévenot, *Relations de divers voyages*, vol. 3 ("Avis," n.p.); see also Blussé and Falkenburg, *Nieuhofs beelden*, 12–13. Melchisédech was the uncle of the well-known traveler Jean de Thévenot, whose descriptions of Asia and particularly the Middle East also appeared in a superb Amsterdam edition (1681–1682), illustrated by the highly regarded etcher Jan Luyken—an edition that, characteristically, supplanted the original, non-illustrated edition printed in Rouen (1665) in terms of translations and reissues.

8 Helgerson, *Forms of Nationhood*, discusses ways new genres could instigate meaning, particularly in literary fields that pertain to geography.

9 The complete van der Aa bibliography is, not surprisingly, gargantuan. See, above all, *Galerie agreable*; *Naaukeurige versameling*; *Grand theatre historique*; *Nouveau theatre du monde*; *Atlas nouveau*; *Nouveau petit atlas*; and *L'atlas soulagé*. Van der Aa's collaborative work includes (among many titles) Munting, *Naauwkeurige beschryving der aardgewassen*, and Rumphius, *Thesaurus imaginum piscium*. See further Hoftijzer, *Van der Aa*, which provides a bibliographic (and biographic) overview.

10 Janssonius van Waesberge (with Elizer Weyerstraten) published both the Latin and French editions of "China illustrata"—*China monumentis* (1667) and *La Chine* (1670)—along with several other Kircher titles.

11 Schouten, *Oost-Indische voyagie*; Struys, *Drie aanmerkelijke en seer rampspoedige reysen*.

12 The bibliography, once again, is formidable. For volumes pertaining to the East, see Landwehr, *VOC*; for volumes focused on the West (chiefly the Americas, yet also the Atlantic world more generally), see Alden and Landis, *European Americana*.

13 See Forrer, *François Halma*.

14 Among ten Hoorn's publications were bestselling works on China and America—for example, Hennepin's *Description de la Louisiane*, which appeared in Dutch as *Beschryving van Louisiana*—and, in another vein, a pioneering publication that veritably launched the pirate literature craze of the late seventeenth and eighteenth centuries: Exquemelin, *Americaensche zee-roovers*.

15 Prices for van der Aa's *Galerie agreable* and Blaeu's *Atlas major* are cited in Koeman, *Atlantes Neerlandici*. Salary figures are analyzed in Vries and Woude, *First Modern Economy*, 611.

16 Scholarship on this literature is thin, yet see Roeper and Wildeman, *Reizen op papier*, which offers

an overview of early modern travel and print, pointing likewise to the generic shifts (formal as well as bibliographic) that took place in the context of Dutch bookmaking.

17 For excellent examples, see the voluminous and haphazardly constructed books of the *veelschrijver* Simon de Vries, including his *Groote historische rariteit-kamer*; *Groot historisch magazijn*; *Groot historisch schouwtooneel*; and *Curieuse aenmerckingen*, the latter weighing in at 3,316 pages. On de Vries's stupendous output (and an excellent case study of a *veelschrijver*), see Baggerman, *Drukkend gewicht*.

18 Freedberg, "Science, Commerce, and Art," which discusses the late seventeenth-century natural history work of Maria Sibylla Merian, Hendrik Reede tot Drakenstein, and Georg Rumphius, among others. On this golden age of Dutch natural history, see, more generally, Jorink, *Reading the Book of Nature*, and Davids, "Amsterdam as a Center of Learning," which singles out the period of the 1660s to 1730s as a "zenith" (306) for natural history and life sciences.

19 Along with the books of Simon de Vries (cited above), this category includes best-selling publications by Georgius Hornius on global polities, Bernard Picart on global religions, Balthasar Bekker on global witchcraft, and Romeyn de Hooghe on global everything (in his van der Aa–published picture book of ca. 1700).

20 Renard, *Poissons, ecrevisses et crabes*; van der Aa, *Galerie agreeable*.

21 Data on Holland's book industry is collected, above all, in Eeghen, *Amsterdamse boekhandel*, whose analysis of practices in Amsterdam are confirmed in several relevant case studies. See, for example, Gnirrep, "Intekenaren" (which also discusses, inter alia, print runs for van Meurs); and Boogaart, "Books on Black Africa." Note that print numbers for European bookmakers more generally (non-Dutch) would have been lower. In their comprehensive study of *Asiana*, Lach and Van Kley suggest print runs of 250 to 1,000 (*Asia*, 3:595).

22 Open-market sales would have raised substantially the total number of books printed, with estimates running as high as three or four thousand: Drijvers, "Cornelis de Bruijn."

23 Hoftijzer, *Van der Aa*, 87 and passim.

24 Eeghen, "Montanus's Book" (for the dowry data, see 264).

25 That granted, it is worth noting the significant role of Dutch publishers of geography, already in the early seventeenth century, in pioneering this broadly European, market-oriented approach to the book business. On this point, see Roeper and Wildeman, *Reizen op papier*, which discusses the innovative careers of Cornelis Claesz ("father of the Dutch travel narrative"; 138) and Barent Langenes, among the leading publishers of travel literature ca. 1600, and which also singles out the innovations introduced by van Meurs ca. 1665.

26 This should not obscure the tremendous publication record of Dutch printers in more modest formats, as well, of which Willem Bontekoe's account of the East Indies, which appeared in a staggering seventy-five editions, and François Caron and Joost Schouten's description of Japan and Siam are particularly fine examples. See Verhoeven and Verkruijsse, *Iovrnael*; and Caron and Schouten, *Rechte beschryvinge*.

27 There is no true bibliography (or biography) for either of these prolific authors. For Dapper, see Wills, "Author, Publisher." And for Montanus (whose volume on Japan has received most of the scholarly attention), see Eeghen, "Montanus's Book," and Hesselink, "Memorable Embassies."

28 Vries and Woude, *First Modern Economy*, 311–314.

29 The control van Meurs exercised over his product was truly remarkable—compare the record, otherwise, of piracy in this period—as were his methods of translation, which generally entailed assistance from foreign scholars residing in the Netherlands. In the case of English editions of Dutch books, which tended to be done in London, the two methods of controlling the product had distinct advantages. Shipping imprinted pages (that is, pages already printed with illustrations), as van Meurs did with Montanus's *Japan*, for example, preserved the printer's ability to bring out later editions, as the market demanded. By contrast, shipping the plates themselves—as de Bruijn did for his Levant book, the plates of which were shipped in 1702 to the London printers Jacob Tonson and Thomas Bennet—signaled the end of the bookmaker's involvement with a particular title. See Eeghen, "Montanus's Book"; and Gnirrep, *Levant in kleur*. On the rampant piracy in this period, especially in the London market, see Johns, *Piracy*.

The utterly extraordinary Greek translation was an edition of Dapper's *Naukeurige beschryving der eilanden, in de Archipel der Middelantsche Zee* (1688). It was translated in 1836—coincident, that is, with the establishment of the modern Greek state—and served, in part, to support the "imagined community" then coalescing in Athens. See Ἀκριβης περιγραφη της Κρητης, μεταφρασθεισα ἀπο την φλαμαντικην εἰς την γαλλικην διαλεκτον (Athens, 1836); on constructions of national identities through the mechanism of print geography, see Anderson, *Imagined Communities*.

30 [Männling], *Dapperus exoticus curiosus*; [Männling], *Dapperi exotici curiosi continuatio*. Note that the "America" in the full title of the 1717 volume references the work of Arnoldus Montanus, which is also included in the digest. The two authors Dapper and Montanus were conflated in other instances, for example, on title pages and in the privileges, indicating yet again the fluid understanding of authorship in these works.

31 Other phenomenal best sellers include Caron, *Rechte beschryvinge*, on Japan, which included a version of Schouten's *Notitie van de situatie* on Siam (Thailand); Schouten's *Oost-Indische voyagie*, a van Someren product dedicated to the eastern reaches of Asia; Rochefort's *Histoire naturelle* on the Caribbean; and Bontekoe, *Iovrnael*, generally describing Asia.

32 See Hoftijzer, "Metropolis"; Hoftijzer, "Dutch Printing and Bookselling."

33 Gnirrep regards the Asia Minor volume as "the most richly illustrated travel description printed in the seventeenth century" ("Intekenaren," 59).

34 Pricing printed volumes was hardly a science and certainly more complex than any simple size- or illustration-to-cost ratio might suggest. In standard folio, *Asia Minor* cost 14 guilders, while *Muscovy* sold for 24 guilders; when printed in "great paper," however, the ratio was 18 to 30 guilders, which is a slightly greater cost differential. In both cases, however, the difference in price exceeded 50 percent, which was the difference in the number of illustrations. By these calculations, *Muscovy*, de Bruijn's second and more lavishly illustrated product, was potentially a bigger money maker. On de Bruijn, his books, and their production, see Drijvers, Hond, and Sancisi-Weerdenburg, "*Ik hadde de nieusgierigheid.*"

35 The vast majority of subscriptions (87 percent), bulk or not, came from nonprofessional buyers. Many subscribers belonged to the author's social network—patrons, supporters, friends, relatives—and many others fall under the broad rubric of collectors (*liefhebbers*). Those remaining who ordered multiple copies presumably did so with the intention of reselling on the secondary market—much the way the book market still works today. See Gnirrep, "Inteke-

naren." Note that some Dutch-language books, even if not translated, might still reach the foreign market. Not only does Valentyn's Dutch-language *Oud en Nieuw Oost-Indiën* contain a subscription list with several foreign names, it also shows up in libraries outside the Netherlands with marks of non-Dutch ownership. Hans Sloane's book plate in one copy of Valentyn's massive publication and Joseph Banks's in another—in both cases, gracing the British Library editions (BL signature marks L.R.265.c.7 and 455.g.3, respectively)—indicate the book's extension into the English market and, more generally, the pervasive British habit of consuming Dutch geography.

36 Uffenbach, *Merkwürdige Reisen*, 3:674–677.

37 This is the broad theme of van Eeghen's magnum opus, *Amsterdamse boekhandel*. See also Kolfin and Veen, *Gedrukt tot Amsterdam*, which considers the phenomenal success in this period also of graphic publications.

38 Economic contexts (and data) are surveyed in Vries and Woude, *First Modern Economy*, 311–318. See also Frijhoff and Spies, *Dutch Culture*, 257–279 ("Books, Printers, Publishers, and Booksellers").

39 Hoftijzer, "Metropolis"; and Eeghen, *Amsterdamse boekhandel*, esp. vol. 5.

40 By and large, bookmaking was a male-dominated industry, and relatively few women were listed as printers on the title page. Those who did were generally widows or daughters of printers, who retained the rights, privileges, and plates of their deceased husbands or fathers, and may have carried on an atelier's work for a number of years—usually until privileges or plates wore out. See Goinga, "Schaduwbeelden"; Vries, "Vrouw en boek"; and Zech, "'Inde Werelt von Drucks.'"

41 Chartier, "Genre Between Literature and History."

42 McKenzie, *Bibliography and the Sociology of Texts*, 13; see also Chartier, "Crossing Borders." Chartier explores this issue, too, in his seminal study of the lives of texts, *Forms and Meanings*, where he asks the basic question: "How are we to understand the ways in which the form that transmits a text to its reader or hearers constrains the production of meaning?" (1).

43 Chartier, *Forms and Meanings*, especially the final essay, "Popular Appropriations: The Readers and Their Books" (83–97).

44 Editorial practices and publishing strategies are discussed in several of Chartier's essays, including "Genre Between Literature and History." See also Verhoeven, "'Brought Together at Great Effort,'"

which highlights the critical role of the publisher in the making/authoring of books; and Vries, "Published . . . and Exploited."

45 Eeghen, *Amsterdamse boekhandel*, 3:247. Note, by contrast, the professional positioning of the London publisher John Ogilby, who takes various degrees of credit for the English version of Nieuhof's China book—yet ultimately leaves his role ambiguous. Ogilby claims the mantle of translator ("Englished . . . by John Ogilby"), which is only possibly the case; of engraver ("several sculptures by John Ogilby"), which is doubtfully the case; of editor ("set forth . . . by John Ogilby"), which is a stretch, at best; and even of author ("printed for the author"). The book was in fact printed by John Macock, reflecting the English custom of dividing the tasks of selling and printing books, so ultimately Ogilby might best be described as the front man, who claimed credit largely because of his status as Royal Geographer.

46 See Eeghen, *Amsterdamse boekhandel*, 4:157–163, where the document cited employs an early modern Dutch term that translates, loosely, as "company."

47 This term appears in the nonpaginated preface to Rochefort, *Histoire naturelle*. See also Wilkie, "Authorship and Purpose," which discusses the possibility of group authorship in works of geography such as Rochefort's (and the active role, otherwise, assumed by the editor-figure).

48 Nieuhof, *Gedenkwaerdige zee en lantreize*, 23. Jan Huygen van Linschoten (1563–1611), whose name graces the title page of perhaps the most important volume of geography of the late sixteenth century, writes similarly of the pressure he felt to publish. "Daily, without letting up," he recalled, "they exhorted me to publish the memories and thoughts of my journey": Linschoten, *Itinerario* (1596), "Prohemio ofte Voorreden totten leser" (n.p.). See also Schmidt, *Innocence Abroad*, 158–164, which discusses this earlier moment of "processed" geography with reference particularly to van Linschoten and his publisher, Cornelis Claesz.

49 See Eeghen, "Montanus's Book," which discusses the battles that took place over travelers' manuscripts; and Nieuhof, *Gezantschap*, which invokes "deze dierbare schatten" in the book's dedication (n.p.).

50 The Nieuhof manuscripts are detailed in Blussé and Falkenburg, *Nieuhofs beelden*; see also Dew, "Reading Travels," which examines the case of the Parisian publisher of voyages Melchisédech Thévenot.

51 Roeper, Walraven, and Buys, *Hamel's World*; Boterbloem, *Fiction and Reality*; Boterbloem, "Met een beschaafder Penne."

52 The geography of China by Olfert Dapper also incorporated Jesuit content, as did the geography of South India by the Dutch *predikant* Philip Baldaeus (an irony, of sorts). On the Chinese materials, see Standaert, "European Images of China"; and on the Baldaeus borrowings, see Stolte, *Angel's Deex-Autaers*.

53 Roeper, Walraven, and Buys, *Hamel's World*, 11, 95–97. See also Roeper and Wildeman, *Reizen op papier*, 47; Landwehr, *VOC* (which offers a bibliography for Saeghman); and, on the elephant in print, Hoetink, *Verhaal*, 142–143.

54 It was in fact not uncommon, and the practice continued as a viable publication strategy well into the eighteenth century. See Darnton, *Business of Enlightenment*; as well as Turnovsky, *Literary Market*.

55 Ogilby scholarship has been slow to catch up with van Meurs: cf. Van Eerde, *Ogilby*, which wholly misses the Amsterdam connection. Blom analyzes the constructed quality of the *America* volume: "Picturing New Netherland."

56 Dedication to Johan de Witt in Dapper, *Gedenkwaerdig bedryf*, n.p. (sig. *3–[*4]). The brief plug for other works of geography attributes to Dapper volumes on Africa (his *Africa* came out that year), America, and Asia. The America book would have been Montanus's *Nieuwe en onbekende weereld*, which was ready for press in 1670; while the Asia book would likely have been a Montanus title, as well (since Dapper had no further publications until 1672, a book on India), the *Gedenkwaerdige gesantschappen [. . .] Japan*, or perhaps the Nieuhof China book (1665). This generous mode of attribution, in all events, suggests that, at least in the context of exotic geography, the author ceded authority to the publisher—van Meurs—who ultimately counts as the maker of all of these volumes.

57 Kolfin and Veen, *Gedrukt tot Amsterdam*.

58 Roeper and Wildeman, *Reizen op papier*, discusses the emergence of the newer, more heavily illustrated forms of the genre, highlighting, too, the role of van Meurs.

59 Several of the plates also appeared in editions of Schouten, *Oost-Indische voyagie*.

60 Clunas, *Pictures and Visuality*, which speaks of "an economy of representations" (46) and also references Ginzburg's discussion of erotic imagery (where Ginzburg makes a distinction among sets of images that circulate in distinct spheres, e.g., private and pub-

lic): "Sixteenth-Century Codes for Erotic Illustration." Clunas's theory of "iconic circuits" is discussed in greater detail in Chapter 4.

61 Dürer's rhinoceros is discussed in Dackerman, "Dürer's Indexical Fantasy"; see also Clarke, *Rhinoceros*. For the Nieuhof variant, see the plate "Reinoceros of Neus-horn," in his *Gezantschap* (see figure 31). Note that the Nieuhof image circulated impressively in the decorative arts—for example in a cabinet of ca. 1695–1700, made in the atelier of Hendrik van Soest for the occasion of the recapture of Namur. See Toussaint and Verbrugge, *Un cabinet*, 10 and 73.

62 Ridley, *Clara's Grand Tour*. Clara was etched in several souvenir prints produced during her 1747 tour and then engraved by Jan Wandelaar for Bernhard Siegfried Albinus, *Tabulae sceleti et musculorum corporis humani* (London, 1749).

63 On Bernard and Picart's production and the derivation of many of their images, see Wyss-Giacosa, *Religionsbilder*; on the afterlife of the work, see Hunt, Jacob, and Mijnhardt, *Book That Changed Europe*. Note that Picart used several sources for his copious engravings, borrowing from van Meurs chiefly for his Asian images: from Nieuhof's *Gezantschap*, Dapper's *Gedenkwaerdig bedryf*, Montanus's *Japan*, etc. Picart used other Dutch sources liberally, as well—van Linschoten's *Itinerario*, de Bry's *Americae*, and so on—which suggests that, while van Meurs was a significant mediator of exotic imagery, he was by no means the only source for Picart or otherwise. On the movement of these images into the decorative arts, see the discussion in chapter 4.

64 Baldaeus, *Naauwkeurige beschryvinge*; Heiden, *Vervarelijke schip-breuk* (with a second, augmented edition, also done in 1675, by van Meurs and van Someren: Heiden, *Vervarelyke schip-breuk*); and Schouten, *Oost-Indische voyagie*. Further bibliographic details for all three publications can be found in Landwehr, *VOC*. Van Someren also collaborated with van Meurs on the travels of Jan Struys, yet in this case pitching to a more modest buyer: Struys, *Drie aanmerkelijke en seer rampspoedige reysen*. The privileges issued for the Struys volume refer to, and make the case for publishing, the three narratives of Schouten, Heyden, and Struys, offering yet more evidence of how bookmakers conceived their publishing projects holistically.

65 These correspond to Dapper, *Naukeurige beschrijvinge der Afrikaensche gewesten* (1668); Montanus, *De nieuwe en onbekende weereld, of, Beschryving van America en 't zuid-land* (1671); and Dapper, *Asia:*

of Naukeurige beschryving van het rijk des Grooten Mogols, en een groote gedeelte van Indiën (1672). Note how, in simplifying the original, more descriptive titles, Ogilby has homogenized the world.

66 See Van Eerde, *Ogilby*. Van Eerde sees the absence of the final (fifth) atlas, which would have been dedicated to Europe, as a case of distracted energies—Ogilby's—yet it would more likely reflect the publication strategy of van Meurs, who never bothered with or focused on European geography and thus never supplied the less capable Ogilby with a ready-made book on Europe to fulfill his publishing promise.

67 The *Atlas Chinensis*, published in two parts, comprised Nieuhof's and Dapper's respective China books, the latter mistakenly credited to Montanus; and the *Atlas Japannensis* presented a version of Montanus's *Japan*. On "local" and "universal" forms of knowledge, see Latour, *Science in Action*, 215–257 ("Centers of Calculation").

68 Genette, *Paratexts*.

69 Lange, *Wonderen*, "Aen de Leser," sig. A2.

70 Duran, *Sefer ha-Tashbets*, cited in Berger, "Invitation to Buy and Read" (translation slightly revised).

71 Kaempfer, *History of Japan*, xliij–xliv. The reference is likely to the works of van Meurs, particularly his lavishly illustrated edition of Montanus's *Japan*.

72 And the frontispiece was much admired. Pepys is exemplary in this regard, in his celebration and collection of frontispieces: Pepys, "My Collection of Frontispieces." See also Remmert, "'Docet parva pictura.'"

73 Churchill and Churchill, *Collection*, 1:iv.

74 The practice of adding prints—common enough in the context of geography publishing—is not to be confused with the practice of assembling an atlas from miscellaneous (loose) prints, which produced the so-called *factice* atlas: see Schmidt, "Atlas Van der Hem." On the coloring of prints, see Goedings, "Kaartkleurders"; and Goedings, "Kunst- en kaartafzetters."

75 On credit, see the classic account of Shapin, *Social History of Truth*; and—considering the matter from the perspective of print—Johns, *Nature of the Book*.

76 Cf. Johan Nieuhof, "Voyage des ambassadeurs de la Compagnie Hollandoise des Indes Orientales, envoyés l'an 1656 en la Chine," in Thévenot, *Relations de divers voyages*, vol. 3; and Nieuhof, *L'Ambassade*. These editions are also discussed in Blussé and Falkenburg, *Nieuhofs beelden*, 16–17 and 89–91.

77 The commerce of cartographic knowledge, in particular—meant to be the most valuable and therefore most closely guarded form of geographic knowledge—is surveyed in Zandvliet, *Mapping for Money*. Royal control of geographic knowledge was perhaps most successful in Portugal and Spain—as exercised by the *Armazém da Guiné* in Lisbon and *Casa de la Contratación* in Seville. Yet the foundation of the Royal Society in London in 1660 (just months after the Restoration of Charles II) and the Académie des Sciences in Paris in 1666 (at the instigation of Colbert and Louis XIV) illustrates the increasing centralization of such projects in England and France. See also Freedberg, "Science, Commerce, and Art," which contrasts the Dutch and Italian cases, characterizing the former as entrepreneurial, commercial, and colonial; and the latter—under the auspices of the Accademia dei Lincei—as aristocratic and "sometimes libertine" (394).

78 Witsen made his considerable library available to Dapper, who was otherwise a wholly Holland-bound writer; he wrote "recommendations" for de Bruijn and housed some of that traveler's exotic artifacts; and he was a regular correspondent with Rumphius and Kaempfer, who were part of Witsen's circle of learned "liefhebbers." On these interactions and exchanges, see Peters, "Witsen and Gijsbert Cuper"; and Peters, *Wijze koopman*.

79 The connections between Dutch commerce and science are underscored in Cook, *Matters of Exchange*. Similar themes are explored in Margócsy, *Commercial Visions*; and Freedberg, "Science, Commerce, and Art."

80 The phrasing is James Anthony Froude's and ranks among the most commonly cited clichés of English nationhood. The original quotation can be found in "England's Forgotten Worthies," 1:446–447, which reprints an essay that appeared first in the *Westminster Review* in 1852. See the discussion of Hakluyt and Englishness in Sacks, "Hakluyt's Navigations in Time."

81 A meticulous overview of the contents can be found in Quinn, *Hakluyt Handbook*; see especially 2:338–460. On Hakluyt and his political contexts, see Mancall, *Hakluyt's Promise*, and Fuller, *Remembering the Early Modern Voyage*, both of which point to the inherent Englishness of Hakluyt's geographic enterprise.

82 On Thevet's project, see Lestringant, *Thevet*.

83 Carrillo Castillo, "World Is Only One."

84 On the imperial agenda of López de Gómara, see Roa-de-la-Carrera, *Histories of Infamy*, which deals with (as the first chapter subheading bluntly phrases it) "Historiography and Empire-Building."

On the imperial agenda of the Habsburg geographers and chroniclers more generally, see Kagan, *Clio and the Crown*.

85 Further examples abound, including manuscript sources, such as Battista Agnese's "Charles V Atlas," with its muscular, imperial iconography on the frontispiece illustration; and published ones, such as Herrera's *Historia general*, composed by the first official historiographer of the Indies (appointed by Philip II). Herrera's work, it is worth noting, was reissued in Amsterdam editions ca. 1622 (in Latin, translated by the Dutch humanist Caspar Barlaeus, and in French); and this version did end up having an afterlife, yet only in the *eighteenth* century and based on these appropriated, reformulated, and refashioned editions of Dutch printers.

The exceptions to this general rule of parochial—and frankly imperial—geography in pre-1650 print would be the collection of Giovanni Battista Ramusio, *Navigationi et viaggi* (1550–1559), and Theodor de Bry's *Collectiones peregrinatiorum in Indiam orientalem et Indiam occidentalem*, which appeared in multiple volumes and editions beginning in 1590 and continuing (also under the direction of his sons) through 1634. Both of these publications, however, offered anthologies of, by and large, previously published, rather than new, travel literature, which makes for a somewhat different print phenomenon (Dutch exotic geography sometimes included anthologies of published materials, yet mostly highlighted original works). Ramusio's and de Bry's collections also concentrated on single-author titles, which they gathered and republished—once again, a subtle yet important distinction from the genre of exotic geography, which tended to favor blended works on regions of the world rather than reports from this or that voyager. In all events, the lavishly illustrated collection of de Bry offers a precedent of sorts, albeit one that appeared in relative isolation when compared to the many publications that flooded the geography market in the final decades of the seventeenth century.

86 The first edition was printed by Janssonius van Waesberge with Elizer Weyerstraten. The second (pirated) edition was printed by van Meurs and prompted a legal confrontation, after which van Meurs agreed to print no further copies (yet in exchange for a tidy sum).

87 The pseudo-traveler Sir John Mandeville also claimed to have seen exotic marvels, of course, and to have experienced personally the global wonders he describes, and he continued to be read as an authority well into the Renaissance—for example, by Sir Walter

Raleigh. His writing's allegorical quality, however, may have distinguished it from the water-and-weather brand of reporting that came to define bona fide travel accounts of the seventeenth century. In certain ways, the quotidian, prosaic, and elemental—daily reports on the weather and water conditions, and of the ship's provisions—defined the factuality of this genre; tedious prose made for truthful prose.

88 For Columbus, see *Select Documents*, especially the agenda-setting opening to his 1493 letter, which brashly broadcasts the admiral's achievement. Vespucci's text is printed in *Letters from a New World*. On the rhetorical construction of Vespucci and his "travels," see Fernández-Armesto, *Amerigo*.

89 See Rennie, *Far-Fetched Facts*, which surveys the history of the fact-fiction phenomenon in travel literature, and Mason, "Ethnographic Portraiture," which considers the conundrum of authorship and authenticity in the case of the flamboyantly fraudulent George Psalmanazar.

90 Cf. Cohen, "Pilgrimages"; Brummett, *"Book" of Travels*; Rubiés, "Travel Writing."

91 This development is also observed by Spary in her study of illustrated natural history books. Spary singles out the richly engraved Dutch volumes of the later seventeenth century—the moment of exotic geography—in which authorship becomes "de-centered" and "denied": Spary, "Scientific Symmetries" (quotations 8–9).

92 Valentyn's is a subtle, craftily composed work. On the one hand, it is prefaced with a note meant to establish its author's credentials based on his lengthy experience overseas, his familiarity with Asian languages (and hence geography), and his orderly prose style (hardly a fair assessment, it turns out). In this regard, the author is certainly present. Yet on the other hand, for the remainder of this massive, five-volume opus—a "continent of a work," by Henry Yule's estimation—the author largely disappears. And with good reason: much of the text is derivative—"purloined" from Rumphius and others—and the volume suffers from its catch-all flavor, more omnibus "description" than a person-specific narrative. E. M. Beekman, in his fairly stinging critique, takes Valentyn to task for his "unacknowledged borrowing" and "incondite work." The text, Beekman writes with a barely concealed sneer, shows "utter disregard for narrative or geographic consequence," an observation that, if largely accurate, misses the context of Dutch geography publications, in which such narrative strategies were par for the course. See Beekman, *Fugitive Dreams*, 55–80.

93 Schouten's *Oost-Indische voyagie* (1676) went through numerous editions (eleven at least), in Dutch, German, and French; see Landwehr, *VOC*, 144–147. Valentyn's *Oud en Nieuw Oost-Indiën* (1724–1726) was prohibitively vast to merit republication, yet the book apparently did circulate on the international market (see note 35).

94 "The Translator to the Reader," in Bernard and Picart, *Ceremonies and religious customs*, 4:i–ix (quotations ii and viii). The eight-volume French original dates to 1723–1743, while the six-volume Dutch translation appeared in 1727–1728.

95 Thévenot, "Avis," in *Relations de divers voyages*, vol. 3. Truth, travel literature, and curiosity in their early modern registers are explored in Evans and Marr, *Curiosity and Wonder*.

96 On the book's remarkable construction, see Hesselink, "Memorable Embassies."

97 Jacob van Meurs, Dedication, in Montanus, *Japan* (n.p., emphasis added).

98 Cf. Shapiro, *Culture of Fact*.

99 Stagl and Pinney, "Travel Writing to Ethnography" (emphasis for first quotation in the original).

100 Not only did the VOC ask its employees to record data of the ship's progress and its merchants' profits, it also required that journals derived from VOC voyages be published through the Company. They sought to retain control, that is, over knowledge retrieved from VOC-sponsored missions. This turned out not to be fully feasible or possible—far too many manuscripts circulated in the Republic—yet it indicates all the same an awareness of the value of geography. Note that the VOC also requested sketches of overseas sites, structures, and even landscapes. See Zandvliet, *Groote waereld*, 85–86, which reproduces the text of these directives, and Roeper and Wildeman, *Reizen op papier*, 46, which discusses the handling of these journals by Dutch printers.

101 This is a point made, regarding the Dutch case, by Zandvliet, *Mapping for Money*. The Iberian case can be illustrated by the simple fact of publications: Van Linschoten's *Itinerario* spread the news of Portugal's overseas empire (based on Portuguese sources), while López de Gómara's *La istoria de las Indias* (1552), describing Spanish America, was widely published despite the censorship of Charles V (as were also the renowned letters of Hérnan Cortés).

102 See Rubiés, "Instructions for Travellers"; and also Pagden, *European Encounters*, which analyzes the traveler's "discourse of privileged vision" in a broader discussion of "the autoptic imagination" (51–88, quo-

tation on 67, where Pagden cites the seminal work of Clifford Geertz on this issue).

103 On Dapper, see Jones, "Decompiling Dapper"; and cf. Cortes, *Voyage en Chine*, which contains much of the material (especially visual) that was incorporated into Dapper's China book. On Montanus, see Hesselink, "Memorable Embassies."

104 Hesselink, "Memorable Embassies," where the digressiveness of the volume is also noted: "Although . . . there is an original journal (or at least snippets of one) hidden in the first 283 pages, it is almost smothered out of existence by the author's ruminations on the geography and ethnography of the world at this time" (101).

105 On Baldaeus's remarkable plagiarisms—a Calvinist *predikant* borrowing from Jesuit authors to forge a narrative on exotic religions—see Stolte, *Angel's Deex-Autaers*, 84–92; Bergvelt and Kistemaker, *Wereld binnen handbereik*, 186–187; and Lach and Van Kley, *Asia*, 3:494–495.

106 Roeper and Wildeman note how the VOC instructed authors to address a prescribed set of subjects, including "the presence of hostile (Portuguese or other European) powers." It seems significant that, in the printed version of these authors' journals, this form of enemy report was dropped out: *Reizen op papier*, 48.

107 Hazart, *Kerckelycke historie*, whose full title reads: "Kerckelycke historie van de gheheele wereldt, namelyck van de voorgaende ende teghenwoordighe eevwe, inde welcke verhaelt worden de ghelegentheden der landen, manieren, ceremonien, ende religien der inwoonderen, *maer namelycke de verbreydinghe des H. gheloofs, martelaren, ende andere cloecke Roomsche Catholycke daeden*, inde vier ghewesten des wereldts, met over de veertigh copere platen verçiert. Beschreven door den Eerw. P. Cornelius Hazart, priester der Societeyt Iesu. Het eerste deel. vervattende de rycken en landen van Japonien. China. Brasilien. Mogor. Florida. Bisnagar. Canada. Peru. Paraquarien. Mexico. Maragnan" (emphasis added). Hazart also penned the anti-Montanus pamphlet *Sots-caproen*.

108 Eeghen, "Montanus's Book," details how privileges were obtained for publication in the Holy Roman Empire. Note also that the pirated Dutch edition of Nieuhof's China book, published in 1666 under the name of "Michel Cnobbert"—Hazart's Antwerp collaborator—is effectively a changed text; the publisher has excised all passages that are inadequately sympathetic to the Jesuits. See Blussé and Falkenburg, *Nieuhofs beelden*, 16; and Meersbergen,

"Uitgeversstrategie," which argues that the "Cnobbert" edition was actually done by van Meurs (making it a pseudo-pirated edition).

109 Du Halde, *Description geographique.*

110 Du Halde, *Description of the Empire*, 2:ii. The author of this note was likely the translator, Emanuel Bowen.

111 The reference is to McLuhan, *Understanding Media.*

112 Boswell, *Life of Samuel Johnson*, 247 (quotation mildly modified): "Why yes, (said he) as one reads such a book; that is to say, consult it."

CHAPTER 2. SEEING THE WORLD

Epigraphs: Johnson, *Vanity of Human Wishes*, ll. 1–2.

Bruijn, *Reizen over Moskovie*, 210: "Nu zal ik dit lichaem, om zo to spreken, openen om u een gezicht van het binnenste te geven." This passage extends the metaphor of sight at length, also in its various translations (citing here the English edition): "The spectator first sees . . ." (*Travels into Muscovy*, 2:11).

1 Cf. Mitchell, "Pictorial Turn," in *Picture Theory*, 11–35 (originally published in *Artforum* 30 [March 1992]: 89–94). See also Curtis, "'As If,'" together with the other contributions to *Culture, Theory and Critique* 50 (2009) (special issue: "The Pictorial Turn"), and Curtis, *Pictorial Turn*. For an insightful and strikingly novel approach, which focuses on sight and *early* modernity, see Clark, *Vanities of the Eye*.

2 See the discussion of seeing/revelation and its association with "discovery"—*descubrimiento*—and of "the autoptic imagination" in Pagden, *European Encounters*, 5–7 and 51–87. The *Oxford English Dictionary* (*OED*) entry for *discover* is extensive, yet see the first non-obsolete entry (no. 3a): "To disclose or expose to view (anything covered up, hidden, or previously unseen), to reveal, show."

3 Johnson's poem (see epigraph) was invoked and riffed upon regularly in the eighteenth and nineteenth centuries—for example, by Oliver Goldsmith, who cleverly paraphrases and triplicates (tongue, no doubt, in cheek) Johnson's act of observation: "Let observation with observant view, Observe mankind from China to Peru." On the metaphor of seeing in Johnson, see Donaldson, "Samuel Johnson and the Art of Observation."

4 Thévenot, *Travels* (quotation on 1, emphasis added and punctuation modified). The original French edition of this work came out in three volumes published in 1663, 1674, and 1684. A more visu-

ally resplendent Dutch version appeared in 1681, with plates by the well-known engraver Jan Luyken, and this edition formed the basis of several more in Dutch, French, and German.

5 On which see the seminal work of Law, "Long Distance Control" and "Social Explanation of Technical Change." Also germane is Latour's discussion of "action at a distance" in *Science in Action*, 215–257 (on "Centers of Calculation"); Rennie, *Far-Fetched Facts*; and Bourguet, Licoppe, and Sibum, *Instruments*.

6 Ortelius, *Parergon*. Compare similar comments by Joan Blaeu in his introductory remarks to the *Atlas major*, nearly a century later (1663): "Geography is the eye and the light of history . . . maps enable us to contemplate at home and right before our eyes things that are far away" (cited in Alpers, "Mapping Impulse").

7 This conception of geography's relation to history—its visualization of history—was something of a humanist commonplace by this time, and Ortelius invoked his aphorism following an earlier Renaissance tradition. Compare Apianus, *Cosmographicus liber*, where a distinction is made between the "face" (cosmography) and "eye" (chorography) of history; and, closer to Ortelius's day, comparable comments in Chytraeus, *Ratione discendi*, sig. 2f.

8 Kaempfer, *Amoenitatum exoticarum*, n.p. ("quam ut Icones illis adderem, aeri prius incidendas, sine quarum lumine & adminiculo exotica difficilime intelliguntur"), and see the English translation (which I have modified slightly) in Kaempfer, *Exotic Pleasures*, xix.

9 Churchill and Churchill, *Collection*.1:iv (emphasis added).

10 "Introduction by the Translator," Kaempfer, *History of Japan*, sig. xliij–xliv.

11 "Avis," Thévenot, *Relations de divers voyages*, n.p. (also cited in Blussé and Falkenburg, *Nieuhofs beelden*, 13).

12 These volumes—along with Peter Heylyn's *Cosmographie* of 1652—are discussed in the Introduction and the previous chapter. For a full bibliography, see Alden and Landis, *European Americana*. On de Bry—who offered a good preview of what would come—see Groesen, *Representations*.

13 See Remmert, "'Docet parva pictura'": "As a result of [the Jesuit] concern with the visual, an intensive culture of frontispieces and engraved title pages began to flourish in the 1620s" (241). See also Remmert, *Picturing the Scientific Revolution*, and, on the Jesuit "style" and its intensive use of visual devices, Bailey, "'Le style jésuite.'"

14 Ortelius, *Theatrum orbis terrarum*, whose frontispiece is a recognizable proscenium. Cf. also—in the context of exotic geography—the Amsterdam-produced and plainly theatrical frontispiece to Kircher, *China monumentis*, discussed in Reed and Demattè, *China on Paper*, 150.

15 Bruijn, *Reizen van Cornelis de Bruyn*.

16 Instructions to VOC officials posted overseas, and particularly to those leading embassies, make clear the desire for descriptions and *pictures* (including maps) of the "cities, towns, palaces, rivers, forts, and other important buildings that [they] may pass by." See, for example, the directives to the 1655–1657 embassy to China (from which this quotation comes), which calls expressly for a "skilled draftsman": "Bataviaes Uitgaand Briefboek," 1655, Instruction f. 366–398 (cited in Blussé and Falkenburg, *Nieuhofs beelden*, 13–14).

17 To offer but one of the scores of examples: Nicolaes Witsen engaged, for a 1696 expedition to the west coast of Australia, a draftsman named Victor Victorsz. to ensure "that whatever strange or rare things they meet with may be accurately depicted." See Venbrux, "'Wild and barbaric manners'" (quotation on 167). On Witsen's extensive activities as a collector and patron of *materia exotica*, see Peters, *Wijze koopman*; on Johan Maurits as a collector-patron, see Boogaart et al., *Johan Maurits*. More generally, see Waals, "Exotische rariteiten."

18 On which see Bergvelt and Kistemaker, *Wereld binnen handbereik*, especially Noordegraaf and Wijsenbeek-Olthuis, "Wereld ontsloten"; Veen, "Met grote moeite"; and Waals, "Exotische rariteiten." The great collector Laurens van der Hem was also known to offer writers and printers access to his collection: see Schmidt, "Atlas Van der Hem."

19 On the practice of natural history in the Netherlands, see Jorink, *Reading the Book of Nature*.

20 On the reconfiguration of pictures, particularly for exotic ethnography, see Mason, "Ethnographic Portraiture"; and, more generally, Mason, *Lives of Images*. Van der Aa's practices are studied in Hoftijzer, *Van der Aa*.

21 Ogilby required van Meurs's support to produce Montanus's *Japan* (to cite but one example) as follows. Once the Dutch and German editions of the book were completed, van Meurs sold the plates for the smaller illustrations (those which shared the page with text) to Ogilby; meanwhile, the larger (full-page) illustrations were prepared and printed in van Meurs's atelier in Amsterdam, and the sheets—which

required no further text—were then shipped, as well, to Ogilby's London shop.

22 Eeghen, "Montanus's Book," 250.

23 There were something in the order of 82 sketches and 149 printed engravings, yet the former number is less certain than the latter, as it is based on the unsigned manuscript. See the survey of the images and their production in Blussé and Falkenburg, *Nieuhofs beelden*, 61–91.

24 Blussé and Falkenburg, *Nieuhofs beelden*, folio 27 (following page 32) and pages 69–71.

25 We do not know the name of these artists, yet we do have record of the engravers working on this volume, including Abraham Coenradus, Cristoffel Bruijn, Melchert Cornelis, and Adriaen Haelwech; see Ulrichs, *Nieuhofs Blick*, 28.

26 Dürer's ur-exotic beast was in fact still prevalent and beloved in this period, appearing in a range of prints, books, and material arts, and across a spectrum of exotic geography: the exceedingly "popular" account of Nieuhof no less than the learned tome of the physician Willem Piso, which covered the natural history of the Indies (originally and more thoroughly focused on Brazil, but later also including material on the East). See the oddly placed rhino at the very center of the frontispiece to Piso et al., *Indiae utriusque*.

27 Along with the images reproduced here (figures 32-33), compare Blussé and Falkenburg, *Nieuhofs beelden*, folios 37 (following page 32) and 167 (following page 48); and Sun, *Wandlungen*, 228 (fig. 113) and 252 (fig. 160), respectively. Falkenburg proposes that Ming porcelain may have been used as a source for some of these decorative adornments, which would indicate a fascinating process of borrowing: European printmakers adopting Ming design for putatively eyewitness accounts of China, thereby producing images (van Meurs's prints) that would later serve as some of the chief sources for European decorative arts (as will be described in chapter 4).

28 "Qui en a veu une, les a vees toutes" (quoted in Blussé and Falkenburg, *Nieuhofs beelden*, 89).

29 Dapper's book includes a narrative of Balthasar Bort's expedition along the Fujian coast in 1663–1664; as with the report on the Beijing embassy, the account came from members of the expedition, yet not necessarily its high-ranking leaders. On these Dutch voyages, see Wills, *Pepper, Guns, and Parleys*, and *Embassies and Illusions*.

30 Some of the images, however, are plainly based on drawings by Pieter van Doornik; see Ulrichs, *Nieuhofs Blick*, 108–115. Note that the volume's text is

likewise derivative. Dapper would have used a combination of VOC-generated journals and non-Dutch materials, especially the work of Martino Martini, which he openly registers in his literature list.

31 See the partial bibliography in Landwehr, *VOC*, 326–330, which lists nine editions in the years 1670–1676 alone.

32 Other exceptions—not always listed on the title page, yet evident on signed illustrations or by their easily identifiable styles—include Jan Luyken, who did work (for example) for the Dutch-made editions of Spon and Wheler (*Voyage*) and Thévenot (*Reizen*) and for Pieter van der Aa; and the tireless Romeyn de Hooghe, who etched several frontispieces for Simon de Vries and also did work for van der Aa.

33 Dapper, *Naukeurige beschrijvinge* [Africa], title page ("na 't leven getekent, en in kooper gesneden"); Montanus, *Nieuwe en onbekende weereld* [America], title page ("verciert met af-beeldsels na 't leven in America gemaekt").

34 This is the conclusion also of Jones, who otherwise deconstructs the whole of Dapper's volume: "Decompiling Dapper."

35 Baldaeus, *True and exact description*, title page; and cf. *Naauwkeurige beschryvinge*, title page ("na het leven, in Indiën afgeteekent, en kurieus in kooper gesneden"). On the convoluted production of the Baldaeus volume, see Schmidt, "Accumulating the World"; on the Angel images in particular, see Stolte, *Angel's Deex-Autaers*. Also useful is Lach and Van Kley, *Asia*, 3:874–876 and 911–912.

36 Struys, *Drie aanmerkelijke en seer rampspoedige reysen* ("Met verscheydene curieuse koopere platen, door den auteur selfs na het leven geteekent, verçiert"; title page); and cf. *Perillous and most unhappy voyages* ("illustrated with divers curious plates, first designed and taken from the life by the author himself"; title page). See further Boterbloem, *Fiction and Reality*, who speculates that Johannes Kip (who later moved to England) and Coenraet Decker were largely responsible for the images.

37 The privileges appear in the opening pages of Struys, *Drie aanmerkelijke en seer rampspoedige reysen*; Schouten, *Oost-Indische voyagie;* and Heiden, *Vervarelyke schip-breuk*.

38 Shapin, "Invisible Technician"; and Shapin, *Social History of Truth*, 355–408.

39 The document and dispute are discussed in Eeghen, "Montanus's Book."

40 Roeper, Walraven, and Buys, *Hamel's World*, reviews the various published forms of the journal

and provides a modern edition; see also Landwehr, *VOC*, 218–221. Note that the most popular seventeenth-century edition, which came from the atelier of the well-regarded publisher of travel literature Gillis Joosten Saeghman, relied wholly on stock images.

41 Hennepin, *New discovery* (London, 1698, based on Utrecht, 1697: *Nouvelle decouverte*) (cited in Dickenson, *Drawn from Life*, 107).

42 "Avis au Lecteur," in Hennepin, *Nouvelle decouverte* (Leiden: Pieter van der Aa, 1704), n.p. (cited in Dickenson, *Drawn from Life*, 106 [emphasis added]).

43 Aa, *Gedenkwaardige West-Indise voyagien*.

44 Montanus, *Gedenkwaerdige gesantschappen*; Schouten, *Oost-Indische voyagie*.

45 Fabian, *Time and the Other*.

46 Du Halde, *Description of the Empire of China*, 1:iv.

47 Braun and Hogenberg, *Civitates orbis terrarum*.

48 Romeyn de Hooghe, *Indes Orientales*.

49 Hung, *Double Screen*, especially 183 and 246–259. See also Mitchell, *Picture Theory*, 35–82: "the principal use of the metapicture is, obviously, to explain what pictures are—to stage, as it were, the 'self-knowledge' of pictures" (57).

50 Vries, *Curieuse aenmerckingen*. Each volume had a separate frontispiece, each etched by de Hooghe (who also did several of the volume's illustrations).

51 Hooghe, *Indes Orientales*, plate 23.

52 Nieuhof, *Embassy*, 244.

53 Nieuhof, *Gedenkwaerdige zee en lantreize*, 198–199 (plate 30/1: "Clove Tree").

54 Ogilby [Dapper], *Atlas Chinensis*, 680–681 (rhubarb) and 691–692 (pineapple). Note that, in both cases, van Meurs may have borrowed from Michael Boym's *Flora Sinensis*: for the rhubarb, in format, and for the pineapple, in format as well as form, the van Meurs's illustration closely resembling the Boym model.

55 Witsen, *Noord en Oost Tartarye*: "Goude cieraeden, opgedolven uit aloude Tartersche [*sic*] graven in Siberien" (illustration following 748 in 1705 ed.); and cf. *Peter the Great*, 192–203, which illustrates a remarkably similar set of objects from the collection of Tsar Peter (now in the State Hermitage Museum). There was, of course, a taxonomic aspect to these presentations, as well, yet the two approaches to exotica—commercial and scientific—were not mutually exclusive, as a taxonomic approach to natural history could also have a commercial component. On this point, see Cook, *Matters of Exchange*, and Margócsy, *Commercial Visions*.

56 Kaempfer, *History of Japan*, plate 9, which collects, along with two examples of the kirin, several other mythical beasts.

57 Bruijn, *Reizen van Cornelis de Bruyn*; Willughby and Ray, *Ornithologia*. Note that the English edition of de Bruijn's book, *Voyage to the Levant*, appeared in 1702, following the French edition of 1700 (*Voyage au Levant*) and the Dutch original of 1698.

58 The modern term and concept of "science" has long earned quotation marks when invoked for early modern practices. See Shapin's concise review of the matter in *Scientific Revolution*.

59 On de Bruijn, his books, and his pictures, see the biographical sketch in Hond, "Cornelis de Bruijn."

60 Bruijn, *Reizen over Moskovie*, 209, where the author promises "to show that which can be shown," thus multiplying his emphasis on his visual-pictorial performance. See also Sancisi-Weerdenburg, "'Yver, aendacht en naerstigheit.'"

61 *Reizen van Cornelis de Bruyn*. On the book's publication (and popularity), see Drijvers, "Cornelis de Bruijn"; and Gnirrep, "Intekenaren."

62 Hannema, "'Groot gelt gespilt.'" It is also worth noting the enduring influence of many of de Bruijn's images. The "Filander," for example, would inspire George Stubbs's famous rendering of a kangaroo, which went on display in London in 1773 and came to exemplify not just this exotic species but also the broader project of reproducing exotic *naturalia* in the age of Cook (see figure 50).

63 The episode is narrated in Raven, *John Ray*. Note that the word *exotic* is used here in its technical sense, as it would have been understood for much of the seventeenth century: as a way to designate nonnative species (thus, from Ray and Willughby's perspective, all non-English flora and fauna).

64 Willughby and Ray, *Ornithologia*.

65 Willughby and Ray, *Historia piscium*, with a separate title page: Francisci Willoughby, *Icthyographia . . .* Sumptibus Societatis Regalis Londinensis, 1685. On the volume's production, see Kusukawa, "'Historia Piscium'"; for Ray's ideas about pictures, see Ray, *Further Correspondence*, 99 (emphasis in the original). Note that Pepys appears to have paid for sixty, yet put his name down for as many as eighty copies, which puts the limited sales of the book into still sharper relief.

66 See Kusukawa, "'Historia Piscium,'" which describes the fish book as a "flop"; cf. Bruijn, *Reizen over Moskovie*.

67 Freedberg, "Science, Commerce, and Art."

68 It is worth noting that both Merian and Rumphius did face challenges in bringing their books to publication: the former was a woman—a significant hurdle in the business of early modern bookmaking—and the latter's manuscript was mishandled several times en route to the publisher. Yet the system in place—printers and engravers, draftsmen and translators—made their ultimate success in print a far more feasible proposition than would have been the case anywhere in Europe outside of the Netherlands.

69 Spary, "Scientific Symmetries," invokes specifically the Dutch-made volumes of Levinus Vincent as examples of authorship "de-centered" and "denied" (8–9).

70 On generic patterns of earlier volumes of natural history, see Ogilvie, *Science of Describing* (which, unfortunately, does not analyze books of the later seventeenth century).

71 Beverley, *History*; and, on the "anthropology of religion," see Gaudio, "Space of Idolatry."

72 Wyss-Giacosa, *Religionsbilder*; and cf. Hunt, Jacob, and Mijnhardt, *Book That Changed Europe*.

73 Beverley, *History*, 1:252 (see also 1:200 on "figures," added to "suppl[y] the Defect of Words"). Gaudio, "Space of Idolatry," discusses the confessional context of Beverley's *apologia*.

74 "The Translator to the Reader," in Bernard and Picart, *Ceremonies and religious customs*, 4:viii.

75 Remmert, "'Docet parva pictura'"; Bailey, "'Le style jésuite.'" Note, however, the relative absence of pictures in works of Jesuit geography: Guy, *"Ad Majorem Societatis Gloriam.'"*

76 See, for example, Benjamin, "Work of Art"; yet compare the important counterargument, taking into account both the traditional chronology and geography of modernity, in Clunas, *Pictures and Visuality*.

77 Jay, *Downcast Eyes*; see also Schwartz, *Spectacular Realities*.

78 Daston and Park, *Wonders*, 329–331 and passim.

79 Hond, "'Vermaarden Cornelis de Bruyn.'" On the collection of van der Hem, see Groot, *Seventeenth-Century Collector*.

80 Tobin, *Picturing Imperial Power*, 277 (in a discussion of Martin Jay and Bruno Latour).

81 Leonhart Fuchs, preface to *De historia stirpium comentarii insignes* (Paris, 1543), x–xi (emphasis added); quoted in Ackerman, "Early Renaissance 'Naturalism,'" 17. See also Kusukawa, "Fuchs" (Fuchs cited on 411 in a mildly different translation); and, more generally, Swan, "Uses of Realism."

It is worth noting how long this notion of pictures persisted. Compare the strikingly similar comments (to Fuchs's) made two centuries later by the great English naturalist Mark Catesby: "The Illuminating [of] Natural History is so particularly Essential to the perfect understanding of it, that I may aver a clearer Idea may be conceiv'd from the Figures of Animals and Plants in their proper Colours, than from the most exact Description without them: Wherefore I have been less prolix in the Discription, judging it unnecessary to tire the Reader with describing every Feather, yet I hope sufficient to distinguish them without Confussion" (Catesby, *Natural History*, 1:xi–xii).

82 Renard, *Poissons, ecrevisses et crabes*, title page and "Avertissement" (sig. A2r).

83 "Temoignages et Certificats," in Renard, *Poissons, ecrevisses et crabes* (sig. A2r). Note, however, the irony (one of of many for this volume) of Valentyn's testimony: the latter was himself accused of plagiarism, as detailed in Beekman, *Fugitive Dreams*, 55–95.

84 Shapin and Schaffer, *Leviathan and the Air-Pump*; see also Shapin's earlier essay, "Pump and Circumstance."

85 Smith, "Science in Motion"; and see note 58 above.

86 Findlen, *Possessing Nature*, 201 and 208.

87 Important examples of performance might include the display of exotic objects and peoples, and the geographic décor—cartographic paintings, tapestries, murals, mosaics—exhibited in princely settings. On the latter, see Kagan and Schmidt, "Maps and the Early Modern State."

88 The reference is to Bruijn, *Reizen over Moskovie*, 210; and see the argument connecting *autopsia* to Herodotus—the father of exotic geography—and to the practice of history in Spiegel, "Task of the Historian."

89 Vesalius, *De humani corporis fabrica*. *Autopsia*, pictures, and printed books come together brilliantly, of course, in Rembrandt's *Anatomy Lesson of Doctor Nicolaes Tulp* (1632; Mauritshuis, The Hague), where a grand dissection takes place—pictorially—also in the presence of a book (lower right corner), which is thought to be an edition of *De humani corporis fabrica*.

90 Kusukawa, "Uses of Pictures" (quotation on 77); see, more broadly, Kusukawa, *Picturing the Book of Nature*.

91 Kusukawa, "Fuchs," 411 (emphasis added).

92 Francis Bacon, *Great instauration* (preface), cited in Alpers, *Art of Describing*, 100.

93 Comenius, *Orbis sensualium pictus*.

94 Evelyn, *Sculptura*, 122; and see the discussion of Comenius and the visual (also citing Evelyn) in Alpers, *Art of Describing*, 91–99.

95 Thus Praetorius on de Bruijn's pictures, which "merit the attention and suffrages of learned men, and lovers of antiquity, *more than any other relation which I have yet seen*"—here pictures trump relations—and Salmon describing his decision to add "enige kopere platen, om den Lezer te beter bevatting te geven, *van 't geen de woorden alleen niet zoo klaar voor 't verstand brengen.*" See "Remarks of Cornelius Le Bruyn, on the Plates of the Antient Palace of Persepolis Published by Sir John Chardin and Mr. Kempfer," in *Travels into Muscovy*, 2:215; and Salmon, *Hedendaegsche historie*, sig. *3v.

96 This ecumenical approach, in van der Aa and several other sources, may account for the phenomenal mobility of Dutch visual materials, which could sometimes function as pan-national products. Gary Schwartz makes a related point when he critiques the idea of a Dutch "national" art: Dutch painters, he argues, helped to create "national" images in Poland, Denmark, and elsewhere in Europe; and the "Dutch" style borrowed extensively from (and lent habitually to) others. In this sense, the skill of marketing images extended beyond the field of geography and the style of exoticism. See Schwartz, "International Identity." On the geography of Dutch art, see further Kaufmann, *Toward a Geography of Art*; Kaufmann, "Independent Dutch Art?"

97 Dickenson, *Drawn from Life*; Kusukawa, *Picturing the Book of Nature*.

98 Renard, *Poissons, ecrevisses et crabes* (for which see the excellent facsimile edition, with commentary, *Fishes, Crayfishes and Crabs*); and see also Pietsch, "Renard's Fanciful Fishes" (quotations on 60 and 63).

99 Reede tot Drakenstein, *Hortus Indicus Malabaricus*. The work has a staggering 794 plates in most editions.

100 In fact, on the title page of the Latin edition, van Reede claims a role in preparing the images ("Adornatus [which can mean to prepare or make ready, yet also to adorn or embellish] per Henricum van Rheede . . ."); while in the Dutch translation of 1689, he accepts credit only for "gathering"—that is, compiling, organizing—the images ("By een vergaderd door den Ed. Heer Henric van Rheede van Draakestein . . .").

101 Along with the prefatory material to the *Hortus Indicus Malabaricus*, see Heniger, *Van Reede tot Drakenstein*.

102 That said, the reputation of the *Thesaurus* was indubitably based on its illustrations' alleged fidelity to nature. This is the forthright pitch of its prospectus, which promises that "Each of the . . . curiosities [described in the prospectus] and many others, too numerous to mention here, have been drawn from nature by the author and engraved on copper plates. The prints are so realistic that the famous Professor Herman Boerhaave of Leyden University has publicly declared that this work was unequalled." See Landwehr, *Dutch Books with Coloured Plates*, 69.

103 Seba, *Locupletissimi rerum naturalium thesauri*, 1: tabula 102 (hydra). See, further, the many and various monstrous dragons (chiefly in vol. 1); the marvelous, two-headed African deer (1: tabula 45), likely based on a sketch sent to Seba; and the malformed goat of Curaçao with (by contrast) one head and two bodies (1: tabula 46).

104 Pietsch, "Samuel Fallours" (and note that Valentyn also included an image of the mermaid in his *Oud en Nieuw Oost-Indiën*). On Linnaeus's interest in Seba's collection—visited on at least two occasions in 1735—see Verkruijsse and Kwa, *Aap, vis, boek*.

105 Compare the coiled and embellished serpents pictured in the body of the book with the illustrated frontispiece, which shows Seba holding a preserved snake stuffed in a jar with, as backdrop, a wall lined with jarred specimens. It is also worth contrasting the images in the first two volumes, the production of which was overseen by Seba—these are the books comprising the stylized snakes and nature narratives—with the second round of publications (volumes 3 and 4), which appeared posthumously more than two decades later (1758–1765) and affect a wholly different style: more restrained, less embellished, without the "living" arrangements of the earlier plates, and largely influenced by the "scientific" style of Linnaean natural history.

106 Although not even Merian's famous tropical insects-cum-plants were fully drawn from life: see Reitsma, *Maria Sibylla Merian*, which details the processes of construction that took place both in South America, where Merian was assisted by indigenous assistants gathering specimens in the field, and in Amsterdam, where she worked from sometimes "muddled" notes and from dried—thus hardly "on site"—specimens (182, 186, and passim).

107 See Ulrichs, *Nieuhofs Blick*, figs. 60 ("Cinnamonium") and 61 ("Caneel Boom"); and cf. Sun, *Wandlungen*, which shows a full range of Boym's and Nieuhof's (figs. 43–58 and 186–203) relevant engrav-

ings. Note that Nieuhof's manuscript contains only one expressly drawn depiction of a plant (cotton) and one of an animal ("vogel Louwa" or Chinese cormorant); these are reproduced in Blussé and Falkenburg, *Nieuhofs beelden*, folio 139 (following page 46) and folio 124 (following page 44), respectively.

108 There are multiple ironies to this adaptation in the Nieuhof volume, among them the very conspicuous presence in the original Saenredam print of an on-site artist sketching ad vivem—a pivotal detail left out by van Meurs in his exotic reengraving.

109 This is the central insight, as well, of Clark, *Vanities of the Eye*.

110 Rumphius, *Ambonese Curiosity Cabinet*, lxviii.

111 Rumphius, *Amboinsche rariteitkamer*; Rumphius, *Herbarium Amboinense*; and see also Rumphius, *Ambonese Curiosity Cabinet*, lxvi, for the author's own promise (in a letter to the VOC directors) to draw from life.

112 Rumphius, *Ambonese Curiosity Cabinet*, lxviii; Rumphius, *Thesaurus imaginum piscium testaceorum*, title page ("in locis reperta").

113 The frontispiece, intricately drawn and colored, is implicitly attributed to the blind Rumphius—a bibliographic paradox, as it were. Note that in the printed editions of the *Amboinsche rariteitkamer* and the *Herbarium Amboinense*, both of which appeared posthumously and by which time Rumphius's reputation as a naturalist was well established, the author portrait shows Rumphius at his desk rather than in the field, a scholar grasping at his specimens with no apparent physical sight, if irrefutably endowed with inner wisdom.

114 For an example in the *Amboinsche rariteitkamer*, see the image of crabs borrowed from the Delft collector Hendrik D'Acquet and reproduced in Bergvelt and Kistemaker, *Wereld binnen handbereik*, 132 (cat. 263); and cf. *Wereld binnen handbereik*, 125 (cat. 260), which demonstrates how D'Acquet's own collection of "ad vivem" drawings were themselves commonly copied. Likewise, Seba copied numerous specimens that, if purportedly drawn from life and based on items in his own collection, derived from the cabinets of others, who sent him illustrations (and later complained that their rarities had been claimed by him): see Müsch, "Seba's Collection," 11.

115 Kolb, *Naaukeurige en uitvoerige beschryving*; and cf. Kolb, *Caput Bonae Spei hodiernum*. The Dutch edition, per usual, had "more maps and illustrations than the original, executed in ways that were more technically sophisticated than the original." It

also formed the basis of most subsequent editions, including the French (1741, 1742, 1743) and the second German edition (1745). See Good, "Construction of an Authoritative Text" (quotation on 90).

116 See the three-volume expanded edition of the text, Senebier, *Essai sur l'art d'observer*, 1:117; cf. also 1:122, where Senebier calls Huber's work a "masterpiece of logic and observations." On Huber and observation, see Singy, "Huber's Eyes" (whose French translations I have followed).

117 Schouten, *Oost-Indische voyagie*, title page ("door den Schrijver in Indien self geteeckent"); and see, for example, the account of the "magicians" of India/Bengal, described by the author as "verschrickelijcke te *sien*" (book 3, 115; emphasis added).

118 Schouten, *Oost-Indische voyagie*, book 2, 225: "door loofwaerdige oogh- en oor-getuygen," implying the act of witnessing or offering testimony. This admission comes in an otherwise revelatory passage, where the author confesses to offering a less than thorough account—he absolves himself, in other words, of detailed, credible, on-site reporting—with the understanding that such a description would be tiresome, and the reader would surely prefer lighter and brisker fare.

119 See, for example, the copy in the Robert E. Gross Collection of Rare Books in Business and Economics, housed in the Rosenfeld Library of University of California, Los Angeles (DS 411.1 S3760).

120 Montanus, *Gedenkwaerdige gesantschappen*, which appeared in English as the *Atlas Japannensis* (the title by which it came to be known among nineteenth- and twentieth-century collectors); and cf. Kaempfer, *History of Japan*. There were also editions of Montanus's *Japan* in German and French, the most recent of which had appeared in Amsterdam in 1722.

121 "Introduction by the Translator," in Kaempfer, *History of Japan*, sig. xliij–xliv (emphasis added). Scheuchzer, who served as Sloane's librarian, wrote emphatically from the perspective of the learned: he was officially named a Fellow of the Royal Society a year after the publication of *History of Japan*.

122 Eeghen, "Montanus's Book," 257; see also the title-page claim: "Verceirt met een groot getal afbeeldsels in Japan geteikent." Note that elsewhere in the volume van Meurs makes the paradoxical case for Montanus's objectivity based on his distance: that he had *not* been to Japan (*Gedenkwaerdige gesantschappen*, Dedication [n.p.]). The assumption, all the same, was that illustrations derived from on-site sketching, be these from the author's hand or otherwise.

123 Geerts, *Catalogue des livres japonais*, also cited in Eeghen, "Montanus's Book," 257.

124 Hazart, *Sots-caproen*, on which see Eeghen, "Montanus's Book": "Why then are these reproduced as they are? And if they do go about naked, why bother to give us a picture of the fact? Wasn't it enough to state it verbally?" (255–256).

125 Bosman, *Nauwkeurige beschryving*, and see the preface to the English edition, *New and accurate description*, sig. A2r–v. On the complex construction of Bosman's book, see Dantzig, "Bosman's 'New and Accurate Description.'"

There are several other instances of this backlash against Dutch geography and particularly its use of pictures. Linnaeus, for example, who was in the Netherlands in the 1730s, took issue with the "sumptuous" books of exotic natural history produced by the Dutch: see Heller, "Linnaeus on Sumptuous Books." And from deeper in the eighteenth century, when such swipes became more or less commonplace, there is the case of Johan Splinter Stavorinus—like Bosman, of Dutch background and the author of an African account—who piles on Dutch bookmakers for their habit of stuffing their volumes with pictures, often recycled and unrelated to the subject at hand: Stavorinus, *Reize van Zeeland*; and see the brief discussion in Beekman, *Fugitive Dreams*, 18.

126 Kaempfer, "Author's Preface," in *History of Japan* (n.p.), where the author claims that "though perhaps less elegant and perfect, [the representations] are yet strictly agreeable to the truth, and without embellishments." See also Bodart-Bailey, *Kaempfer's Japan*, which describes the transformation of the manuscript en route to publication.

127 Biographical details are culled from Drijvers, Hond, and Sancisi-Weerdenburg, *'Ik hadde de nieusgierigheid'*; and Hond, "Cornelis de Bruijn."

128 Bruijn, *Voyage to the Levant*, 1.

129 De Bruijn continued on to Bandar Abbas and from there voyaged to Batavia by way of Cochin and Sri Lanka. This second journey lasted seven years, from 1701 to 1708.

130 Publication history is reviewed in Hannema, "'Groot gelt gespilt,'" which also discusses the prompt and positive reviews of de Bruijn's books in the *Bibliotheca librorum novorum*, *De boekzaal van Europe*, and the *Journal des sçavans*.

131 Cox, *Reference Guide*, 1:218.

132 On these working methods, see Drijvers, "Cornelis de Bruijn," 95, which also cites the description of Zacharias Conrad von Uffenbach, a well-known bibliophile who visited de Bruijn in Amsterdam and admired the watercolors and detailed pictures executed (so Uffenbach avers) in loco.

133 Bruijn, *Travels into Muscovy*, plate 100 (described on 1:226). See also "Backer-Kara" (pl. 93, 1:224), which offers an excellent example of de Bruijn's shadowing, in this case of birds shown in the form of dead game, as might be depicted in a typical Frans Snyder still life; and "Fruits Singuliers" (pl. 198, 2:91), which, along with the "Citrouïlles" engraving, bears a remarkable resemblance to the style of still-life painting done by Albert Eckhout.

134 Bruijn, *Travels into Muscovy*, plates 7–8; see also the lovely, dynamic group portrait of a Tartar family (plate 100), with two animated boys tugging on their mother's hands, one also pulling on the fur lapels of his father's coat.

135 Bruijn, "The Author's Preface" in *Travels into Muscovy*, (n.p.).

136 Bruijn, *Voyage to the Levant*, 114–115.

137 Bruijn, "The Author's Preface," in *Travels into Muscovy* (n.p.).

138 Bogaert, *Historische reizen*, esp. "Voorreden aan den lezer" (n.p.); and see also Hannema, "'Groot gelt gespilt,'" 27–29. Note that Bogaert was referencing the interventions of Praetorius, a German scholar and friend of de Bruijn, who did contribute to the volume (as will be discussed).

139 On Cuper, see Chen, "Digging for Antiquities"; on his debate with de Bruijn, see Drijvers, "Cornelis de Bruijn."

140 Chardin, *Voyages*; on which see also Ferrier, *Journey to Persia*.

141 Bruijn, *Aanmerkingen* (see 3 on chatter in the "Boekzaal").

142 Sancisi-Weerdenburg, "Through Travellers' Eyes."

143 Cornelis de Bruijn, "Remarks of Cornelius Le Bruyn, on the Plates of the Antient Palace of Persepolis Published by Sir John Chardin and Mr. Kempfer," in *Travels into Muscovy [. . .] together with remarks on the travels of Sir John Chardin, and Mr. Kempfer, and a letter written to the author on that subject*, 2:198–223 (quotations on 199).

144 Bruijn, *Reizen over Moskovie*, 210.

145 Drijvers, "Cornelis de Bruijn," 92 (citing Uffenbach's description of "Herrn Prätorius").

146 See Drijvers, Hond, and Sancisi-Weerdenburg, *'Ik hadde de nieusgierigheid,'* 179–180 ("Appendix II," also listing further editions).

147 *Persepolis illustrata*. Vickers, "Views of Persepolis," discusses the poor state of alternative illustra-

tions. Note also that pictures (and plates) from the *Levant* volume likewise gained quick popularity, with evidence of a sale already in 1702 to an English bookseller, suggesting the strong demand more generally for de Bruijn's illustrations.

148 Hannema, "'Groot gelt gespilt,'" 38–40, which cites several other, similarly positive reviews. The reference is to Kaempfer's *Amoenitatum exoticarum*, a publication that also contained pictures of Persepolis.

149 This is a central argument of Daston and Park, *Wonders*, which discusses the *content* and scholarly approach of eighteenth-century "science" (see especially chapter 9, "The Enlightenment and the Anti-Marvelous," 329–363). Yet the shift I am underscoring pertains also to the *form* of science—namely, the textual and pictorial manner in which learning (geography and natural history, in this instance) was delivered (a point taken up in the Epilogue).

150 Emerson, "Sir John Chardin"; see also Ferrier, *Journey to Persia*.

CHAPTER 3. EXOTIC BODIES

Epigraph: Behn, *Oroonoko*, 40.

1 Gibbon, *Decline and Fall*, book 1, chapter 6: "The grave senators confessed with a sigh that, after having long experienced the stern tyranny of their own countrymen, Rome was at length humbled beneath the effeminate luxury of Oriental despotism" (ed. J. B. Bury, 7 vols. [London: Methuen, 1897], 1:144). Compare the classic study of Wittfogel, *Oriental Despotism*.

2 Verhoeven and Verkruijsse, *Iovrnael*.

3 Struys, *Drie aanmerkelijke en seer rampspoedige reysen*; see also Boterbloem, *Fiction and Reality*.

4 Nierop, *Treason*, which reproduces an appalling image of the torture of Jan Jeroenszoon, a Catholic lawyer who hailed from Hoorn, not far from Wormerland (plate 13 and cf. plate 5).

5 This control took its most abhorrent form in the practice of early modern slavery, for which there is an extensive historiography: see, for example, Blackburn, *New World Slavery*; Emmer, *Dutch Slave Trade*; Welie, "Patterns of Slave Trading." While it will inevitably touch upon slavery—a practice and institution of increasing importance in these years—this chapter's primary focus is on sources of geography (rather than more direct accounts of slavery) as they have been broadly invoked otherwise in this study.

6 Said, *Orientalism*, especially 186–190.

7 Bruijn, *Voyage to the Levant*, 102 and 123–124.

8 Kaempfer, *History of Japan*, 439, where the author explicitly challenges the account of François Caron (*Rechte beschryvinge*), who claimed to have encountered relatively few brothels in Japan.

9 Bruijn, *Voyage to the Levant*, 101–102, and 136.

10 Nieuhof, *Gedenkwaerdige zee en lantreize*, 2:36; and cf. Nieuhof, *Voyages and travels*, 2:202. This anecdotal observation may have had its origins in Amerigo Vespucci's well-known "Lettera," which contain a similarly misogynistic report on Arawak female sexuality and—relatedly—male impotency. See Vespucci, *Letters*, esp. the letter to Lorenzo di Pierfrancesco de' Medici (45–56).

11 Bruijn, *Voyage to the Levant*, 96; Schouten, *Oost-Indische voyage*, book 3, 23, 45, 83; book 2, 103 ("De Reys-lust waerlijck is een krachtige passie van de ziel"). See also the opening pages of the volume, where the author comments similarly on his "lust" to travel (book 1, 1–2).

12 Bruijn, *Voyage to the Levant*, 39–40, and see plates 34, 35, and 37.

13 Allard, *Orbis habitabilis*, plates 38, 43, 46, 57, 59, and 60. These so-called costume plates were printed as well in Aa, *Galerie agreable*.

14 For Kaempfer, see *History of Japan*, plate 43; for Eckhout, see Buvelot, *Eckhout*, which reproduces the paintings and several of the derivative images—for example, in print geography (45) and tapestry (39). Valkenburg's painting is currently labeled by the Statens Museum for Kunst, Copenhagen (where it hangs), *"Slave Play" on a Sugar Plantation in Surinam* (the quotation marks perhaps underscoring the museum's own ambivalence).

15 Dapper, *Naukeurige beschryving van gantsch Syrie*, 49–56 (comment on "hembden [en] onderbroeken" on 54); Ogilby [Dapper], *Atlas Chinensis*, 16–17.

16 Bruijn, *Voyage to the Levant*, 92 and cf. 94.

17 Hazart, *Sots-caproen*.

18 Kaempfer, *Amoenitatum exoticarum*, with plates facing 582 (acupuncture) and 600 (moxibustion); and cf. Kaempfer, *History of Japan*, "Appendix" (separate pagination) and plates 43 and 44.

19 Kaempfer, *Amoenitatum exoticarum*; and cf. the partial English translation, *Exotic Pleasures* (quotation on 186 of this edition). See, as well, the fascinating study of Bowers and Carrubba, "Drug Abuse."

20 Dapper, *Asia*, for which see Ogilby [Dapper], *Asia*, n.p. (sig. Av) and 49. Behn, *Oroonoko*, 40; see also Chi-ming Yang, "Asia Out of Place."

21 Struys, *Drie aanmerkelijke en seer rampspoedige reysen*, 286–287; quotations from English edition: *Perillous*, 270–271.

22 Wolff, *Inventing Eastern Europe*.

23 The Struys narrative brings together several strands of early modern notions of the Near East. Along with the widely popular story of the flaying of Saint Bartholomew (claimed by both Armenian and Azerbaijan traditions), the story of "The Flaying of Sisamnes" (and "The Arrest of Sisamnes") was known through the well-regarded paintings of Gerard David done in 1498 for the town hall of Bruges, and this may have circulated images of this narrative among northern European audiences. Herodotus also tells the story of Sisamnes, and this would have been available to readers in a Dapper-translated edition printed in 1665.

24 Struys, *Perillous*, 270–271; and cf. Struys, *Drie aanmerkelijke en seer rampspoedige reysen*, 286–287.

25 Franits, *Paragons of Virtue*; Franits, *Dutch Seventeenth-Century Genre Painting*.

26 Struys, *Perillous*, 272.

27 The sight of the abused Polish wife—the terrifically graphic engraving of the Shamakhy affair—may have been too much even for some viewers. In the Huntington Library copy of the second English edition (1684), the engraving is missing: either torn out by a prudish, indignant owner, or perhaps discreetly removed, to be used for some other, possibly private purpose. The former seems more probable, however, as this edition also has contemporary manuscript markings that include a strong line through the title of this particular engraving ("A woman flea'd alive") where it is listed in the "Directions for the Bookbinder." This suggests that the plate was expressly taken out and censored by the owner ("J. H. Middleton," who signs, in the same hand, on the title page). See *The voiages and travels of John Struys through Italy, Greece, Muscovy, Tartary, Media, Persia, East-India, Japan, and other countries in Europe, Africa and Asia: containing remarks and observations upon the manners, religion, polities, customs and laws of the inhabitants* (London: Abel Swalle and Samuel Crowch, 1684) [HEH shelf mark 71373].

28 Hennepin, *Nouvelle decouverte* (1697). The work came out in several further editions in French, Dutch, German, Spanish, and English, mostly based on the Utrecht original. Note that the Indian pictured on the frontispiece was meant roughly to stand for a member of the Inoka or Illinois Confederation.

29 "Perversion" is used, of course, in a qualified sense: see Bleys, *Geography of Perversion*. The literature on early modern homosexuality has flourished in recent years; along with Bleys, see Betteridge, *Sodomy*; and Borris and Rousseau, *Sciences of Homosexuality*.

30 Bleys identifies a "descriptive pattern . . . that connected [a] discourse on sexuality to representations of cultural and ethnic difference": *Geography of Perversion*, 18.

31 Bleys, *Geography of Perversion*, 35 (emphasis in the original). See also Bernand and Gruzinski, "Redécouverte," especially 13–15.

32 Schouten, *Notitie*, quoted from the modern edition, Caron and Schouten, *True Description*, 107; and Schouten, *Oost-Indische voyagie*, book 3, 45. On the execution, see Caron and Schouten, *True Description*, 142 (mildly modified), which cites the original pamphlet reporting the affair: *Extract, ofte cort verhael van 't schip Nieu Delft* (1648).

33 Montanus, *Atlas Japannensis*, 316; Caron, *Rechte beschryvinge*, for which see Caron and Schouten, *True Description*, 23–24 (on the shogun) and 43 (on the priests: "Their Priests, as well as many of the Gentry, are much given to Sodomy, that unnatural passion, being esteemed no sin, nor shameful thing amongst them").

34 Montanus, *Nieuwe en onbekende weereld*. On *berdaches*, see Trexler, "Making the American Berdache"; and, more broadly, Trexler, *Sex and Conquest*.

35 Dapper, *Naukeurige beschrijvinge*, 617. See also Sweet, "Mutual Misunderstandings." Bleys also mentions the transvested harem of Queen Anna Xinga, who kept a group of young male concubines dressed as women, thus allowing her, dressed as a man, to assert her royal authority while maintaining her (male) seraglio: *Geography of Perversion*, 33.

36 Hennepin, *Nouvelle decouverte*, 219–220; and see Bleys, *Geography of Perversion*, 42, whose translation I have followed.

37 Morgan, " 'Some Could Suckle' "; and cf. the frontispiece of Dapper, *Naukeurige beschrijvinge*, which offers a fairly typical depiction of the female African body (see figure 19). Observations of Khoikhoi genitalia come from Nieuhof, *Gedenkwaerdige zee en lantreize*, 2:10–12. The English translation conveys the full eroticism of this passage: "The Men have very well made Legs, but slender Calfs, and are so nimble as to be able to outrun a strong Bull, and stop him in his full career. . . . The Mens Privities or Yards are very large, but have only one stone; for so soon as

a Male Child is born, the Mother cuts out the right stone to make it [i.e., the boy] the more fit for running, and afterwards gives it some Sea water and Tobacco." Nieuhof, *Voyages and travels*, 2:188.

38 Nieuhof, *Voyages and travels*, 2:230.

39 Dapper, *Naukeurige beschryving van gantsch Syrie*, 260.

40 Nieuhof, *Voyages and travels*, 2:218; and cf. the Dutch original, which clarifies the location of these bells ("klootjes") "tusschende voorhuiten 't hooft van de roede" (*Gedenkwaerdige zee en lantreize*, 2:63). Note that piercing the male penis or prepuce (foreskin) is also done to enhance sexual pleasure, an idea that would not appear to be within the realm of the possible to the European authors of these accounts.

41 Nieuhof, *Voyages and travels*, 2:219.

42 Nieuhof, *Gedenkwaerdige zee en lantreize*, 2:82.

43 Montanus, *Atlas Japannensis*, 154–156: "Herodotus relates also, That the *Mendesier* Women make themselves common with Goats, that so they might obliege [*sic*] them, and be big, and bear Children, by their Sacred Seed" (154). On the pages that follow, Montanus discusses the "shameful Worshipping of Apes" in Japan. Dapper, as noted, did a translation of Herodotus around this time (1665), which would have meant easy access to this text for Montanus.

44 Struys, *Drie aanmerkelijke en seer rampspoedige reysen*, 176; and see the discussion in Boterbloem, *Fiction and Reality*, 85, which cites Adam Olearius as a possible source for this story and also describes an account of the same variety from yet another, in this case VOC-generated, source of exotic geography.

45 See Bindman and Gates, *Image of the Black*; Earle and Lowe, *Black Africans*; and Kolfin and Schreuder, *Black Is Beautiful*, which discusses images by Rubens and others (pp. 76, 77, 175 [Rubens]; 82, 242, 251 [Rembrandt]; 90 [Dürer]; and 255 [Mostaert]).

46 On the painting and its various contexts, see Buvelot, *Eckhout*, 76–78; Kolfin and Schreuder, *Black Is Beautiful*, 234–235, 237; and Brienen, *Visions of Savage Paradise*, 144–154. Variants of *African Woman* were engraved into printed works by Caspar Barleaus (*Rerum in Brasilia et alibi gestarum*, 1647), Willem Piso (*Historia naturalis Brasiliae*, 1648), Montanus (*Nieuwe en onbekende weereld*, 1671), and Nieuhof (*Gedenkwaerdige zee en lantreize*, 1682); woven into several tapestries made by the Gobelins Manufactory (and others); and painted onto canvases, ceramics, and more. Many of these forms are traced in Whitehead and Boeseman, *Portrait of Dutch Seventeenth-Century Brazil*.

47 Gaskell, "Tobacco."

48 Behn, *Oroonoko*, 14. On the perceived sexuality (and fertility) of images like the *African Woman*—Venus, after all, was the goddess of love—see Nederveen Pieterse, *White on Black*; and Brienen, *Visions of Savage Paradise*. Note that a possible pendant painting, Eckhout's *African Man*, features a large and strikingly phallic date palm.

49 Whitehead and Boeseman, *Portrait of Dutch Seventeenth-Century Brazil*, 74–75; Buvelot, *Eckhout*, 78; Brienen, *Visions of Savage Paradise*, 147–149, 256–257.

50 At the time the Dutch commenced their colonization of Brazil around 1630, about 40,000 slaves were already in the province of Pernambuco alone (the administrative center of the Dutch colony), and it is estimated that another 26,000 slaves would be imported under their colonial auspices. See Postma, *Atlantic Slave Trade* (especially table on 21).

51 Wagenaer is quoted from the *"Thierbuch,"* 174–175, a volume that focuses on its author's watercolors, his "most precious legacy" (as deemed by Whitehead and Boeseman, *Portrait of Dutch Seventeenth-Century Brazil*, 48). See also Pfaff, *Wagener*, which provides biographical details. Note that there were other colonial drawings in circulation at this time, and it is possible that Wagenaer's images are copies of Eckhout's own preliminary studies; copies of earlier copies from another hand; or—as is generally argued—original work, done at the time and in the context of Eckhout's painting (and there are also debates regarding the time and place of the paintings: see Mason and Egmond, "Albert E(e)ckhout"). In all events, the drawings would have recorded the incontrovertible reality of the model's status as a branded slave.

52 See, for example, the classic image of a slave family in Suriname, featuring a pipe-smoking woman spinning cotton in the field, originally printed (after William Blake) in John Gabriel Stedman's *Narrative of a Five Years Expedition against the Revolted Negroes of Surinam* (and discussed in Kolfin and Schreuder, *Black Is Beautiful*, 222, 238–239).

53 Dapper, *Gedenkwaerdig bedryf*, 480. The words "torture" and "torment" in this section are invoked somewhat loosely—while the former relates mostly (and often technically) to judicial proceedings, a process enlisted as a means of persuasion or to extract a confession of guilt, the latter is commonly used to describe great suffering or anguish (sometimes physical yet not necessarily). Sources of early modern geography tend to be less than precise in their

nomenclature, yet they do sometimes state forthrightly (as is the case, it turns out, with several of the images discussed below) that an event or illustration represents "torture." A useful discussion of these distinctions and usages, especially as they pertain to Western conceptions of "Asiatic [or Chinese] torture" (as it would come to be known), can be found in Brook, Bourgon, and Blue, *Death by a Thousand Cuts*, 9, 43, 46; and see the classic discussion in Foucault, *Discipline and Punish*, 34.

54 Schouten, *Oost-Indische voyagie*, passim.

55 Schouten, *Oost-Indische voyagie*, book 3, 114 (with illustration between 114 and 115).

56 Schouten's *Oost-Indische voyagie* appeared in Dutch, German, and French; in multiple editions and reprints; in anthologized and excerpted versions; and so on. It was printed by the dynamic publishing duo of van Meurs and van Someren at the height of their productivity and in the very year (1676) they printed the equally graphic travels of Struys. By these measures, Schouten's book can surely be categorized as "popular," and its print milieu soon broadened to encompass several other global descriptions and sources of geography.

57 Compare the discussion in Hung, *Double Screen*, 246–259, which describes a similar process of picturing, framing, and multiplying imagery (also of the body) in the context of "meta-pictures."

58 Thévenot, *Reizen*. Note that the original edition in French (*Relation d'un voyage fait au Levant*, 1664) was a wholly different animal: without the baroque frontispiece (the 1681-1682 Bouman edition had three, one for each volume), the plentiful plates (several of these signed by Luyken), and the other apparatuses of Dutch-made geography.

59 Nieuhof, *Gezantschap*, frontispiece and passim; Bruijn, *Travels into Muscovy*, 43; and (on Aceh) Nieuhof, *Gedenkwaerdige zee en lantreize*, 2:74–76, for which see Nieuhof, *Voyages and travels*, 2:227 (note, however, that in the Dutch original, they both salt *and* pepper the body).

60 Dapper, *Asia*, for which see Ogilby [Dapper], *Asia*, 74–75.

61 Ogilby [Dapper], *Asia*, 75 (where further tortures are delineated with zest: "malefactors," particularly women, could be cast from the towers of mosques; highway robbers were half buried—"the upper part of their Bodies inclos'd with great Posts"—and thereby starved to death; and so on); and Ogilby [Dapper], *Atlas Chinensis*, 430.

62 "Cruautéz in-oüies des Sauvages Iroquois," in Hennepin, *Nouveau voyage* (illustration facing page 204).

63 Hooghe, *Indes Orientales*, in which see, more particularly, figs. 2 (mines), 19 (courts), 8 (temples; cf. also the grisly sacrifices in "Mexican" temples in 32), and 31 (ascetics, an image that borrows, nota bene, from a van Meurs engraving published several years earlier in Nieuhof's China book).

64 Hooghe, *Les Indes*, figs. 7 (punishments), 25 (tribunal), and passim.

65 Hooghe, *Les Indes*, fig. 22. On the author, his phenomenal range, and his mode of production, see Nierop, *Romeyn de Hooghe*.

66 The bibliographic entry in Nierop, *Romeyn de Hooghe*, 275, is indeterminate ("17XX.02") and based, in all events, on a collation of older secondary literature. Individual copies of *Les Indes* can differ slightly in the order and number of the illustrations, which leads to various dating: ca. 1685 by the Getty (shelf mark 92-B13189), ca. 1710 by the Royal Library at The Hague (131 C 52), ca. 1700 by the Newberry [Ayer 135 .H72 1700], and so on. The etchings certainly circulated by 1682, when they appeared in Vries, *Curieuse aenmerckingen*.

67 Schouten, *Oost-Indische voyagie*. The edition/ copy in question belongs to the Gross Collection of the Rosenfeld Library, University of California, Los Angeles (shelf mark DS 411.1 S3760). Since Schouten's volume is dated 1676, this would mean either that de Hooghe had completed (some of?) the etchings by then or—more likely—that a later printer or bookmaker decided to include these illustrations in a later version of the book. On van der Aa's appropriation of earlier graphic material—a regular practice for him—see Hoftijzer, *Van der Aa*, and the discussion in chapter 4.

68 Linschoten, *Itinerario*, 58/59 (untitled plate marked "58 en 59"). The image was regularly revived and revised in print, well into the eighteenth century, and it also shaped numerous representations of sati in painting and the materials arts (for example, in Jan van Kessel's *Americque* [1666], a composition taken up in chapter 4).

69 Bry, *Collectiones*; the Chinese material appears in volume 8 (*Pars Octava*), printed in 1607. De Bry's China illustrations are meant to embellish (among other texts) Juan Gonzáles de Mendoza, *Historia de las cosas más notables, ritos y costumbres, del gran reyno de la China* (Rome, 1585), which describes various "cruel torments," including the technique of squeezing and crushing the fingers and feet of the victim. On de Bry's visual style of publication, see Groesen, *Representations*. The original van Linschoten images of China—derived, most likely, from Dirck Gerritszoon Pomp, also known

as Dirck China, who served in Goa, later journeyed to Japan and China, and finally settled in Enkhuizen, where he apparently knew and befriended van Linschoten (Jan Huygen himself never reached China)—are discussed in Boogaart, *Verheven en Verdorven Azië*.

70 Meserve, *Empires of Islam*; Bisaha, *Creating East and West*.

71 Verstegen, *Theatrum*, which also circulated in French: *Theatre des cruautez des hereticques de nostre temps* (Antwerp: Adrien Hubert, 1588). For a fine example of painted (Protestant) propaganda—with a surfeit of abused bodies—see François Dubois, *Le massacre de la Saint-Barthélemy* (ca. 1572–1584; Musée Cantonal des Beaux-Arts, Lausanne); for Dutch (rebel) propaganda, see the illustrated *Tweede deel van de Spieghel der Spaensche tyrannye gheschiet in Nederlandt* (Amsterdam: Jan Evertsz. Cloppenburg, 1620). Jacques Callot's eighteen etchings of the Thirty Years' War were printed as *Les misères et les malheurs de la guerre* (1633).

72 Hooghe, *Schouburgh der Nederlandse veranderingen*; and see the cacophony of bodies in the print "Spiegel [Mirror] der France tirannye gepleecht op de Hollantsche dorpen." Compare also the horrific image of bodily abuse, produced in the same period as de Hooghe's etching and attributed to Jan de Baen, *The Corpses of the Brothers De Witt, on the Groene Zoodje at the Lange Vijverberg in The Hague, 20 August 1672* (ca. 1672–1675; oil on canvas; Rijksmuseum, Amsterdam).

73 Schmidt, *Innocence Abroad*, 68–122.

74 On Las Casas, see Pagden, *European Encounters*, 51–87.

75 Odell points out the distinction between Dutch and Jesuit accounts in this regard, noting that, even when Dutch-made books relied heavily on Jesuit manuscripts (and published materials), they still carried far more by way of pictures: Odell, "Clothing, Customs, and Mercantilism."

76 Hazart, *Kerckelycke historie*, for which see the full, descriptive, assertive title cited above (chapter 1, note 107).

77 Montanus, *Gedenkwaerdige gesantschappen*, for which see *Atlas Japannensis*, 262–269 (and 268 for a roster of international victims). Montanus's description also includes a history of crucifixions, which, if a typical digression for this author, has the effect of widening the scope of his history to make it a generic Christian rather than expressly Catholic narrative.

78 Montanus, *Atlas Japannensis*, 265, and see 262 for another fairly grisly set of tortures (done to "Christians" and "martyrs" who happen to be Japanese).

79 Montanus, *Atlas Japannensis*, 266. "Singok," which is almost universally referenced in the secondary literature as "the mysterious 'boiling waters of Singok,'" may denote a set of boiling hot springs near Mt. Unzen (not far from Nagasaki) referred to by locals as "the valley of hell": *onsengoku* in Japanese, which would have been pronounced by Europeans in a form close to "Sengok" or "Singok." The word may also be a generic form of "Jigoku" (which would have been pronounced by Europeans as "Shijok" or "Shigok"), a Japanese term for hell (with thanks to David Spafford for helping to work out this puzzle).

80 Montanus, *Atlas Japannensis*, 268.

81 The engraving of "'t Ziedende Water van Singock" (inserted between pages 240 and 241 in the original Dutch edition and 266 and 267 in the English edition) offers a pastiche of pain, as it were. It is mostly unclear whether the victims are Japanese or European (Jesuits, e.g.), yet the methodical persecutors are plainly Japanese. The plate is unsigned, yet might be attributed to van Meurs himself, who makes a point of listing himself on the title page as "Plaatsnyder en Boekverkoper [Engraver and Bookseller]." Montanus, it should be noted, also recounts explicit violence and bodily pain in Formosa, where the indigenes lop off and parade their enemies' heads as "trophies of victory" (*Atlas Japannensis*, 48), and otherwise grants much attention to the gory practices of *seppuku* (112–114) and abortion (51, 70).

82 Between Nicolas Trigault's account of Matteo Ricci's expedition, printed in 1615 as *De Christiana expeditione apud Sinas*, and Jean-Baptiste Du Halde's grand geography of 1735 (*Description geographique*), comparatively few expressly Jesuit volumes appeared. The not insignificant exceptions were the publications of Martino Martini (*Novus atlas Sinensis*, 1655) and Athanasius Kircher (*China monumentis*, 1667), and both of these works debuted in Amsterdam-designed editions. On the Jesuits in China, their evangelical mission, and their reports to Europe, see Brockey, *Journey to the East*; Mungello, *Curious Land*; and Spence, *Chan's Great Continent*.

83 Ogilby [Dapper], *Atlas Chinensis*, 435 (and see 436 on "torture").

84 Wolfthal, *Images of Rape*.

85 Herodotus, *Persian Wars*, 6 (1.4).

86 On rape in the context of the Dutch Revolt, see Pipkin, "Every Woman's Fear," and "'They Were Not Humans.'" On violence in the earlier years of the Revolt, see Nierop, *Treason*, which offers a local history of "terror" (as van Nierop terms it) and its de-

scription, from both Catholic and Protestant perspectives. On the later period, see Schama, *Embarrassment of Riches*, 270–282; and, for de Hooghe's etchings, Nierop, *Romeyn de Hooghe*, 87-90.

87 John Dryden, *Amboyna, or the Cruelties of the Dutch to the English Merchants* (London, 1673); reprinted in *Works*, 12:1–77. On the play's significance in the context of Anglo-Dutch politics, see Markley, "Violence and Profits"; on its dramatic topoi of violence, see Schmidt, *Innocence Abroad*, 296–297.

88 Niekerk, "Man and Orangutan." The trope has been mostly associated with Africa and blackness: see Morgan, "'Some Could Suckle,'" and Nederveen Pieterse, *White on Black*, 30–51 ("Savages, Animals, Heathens, Races"). On European debates over apes and their association with human (specifically female) sexuality, see Schiebinger, *Nature's Body*, 75–114.

89 Nieuhof, *Voyages and travels*, 2:269.

90 Ogilby [Dapper], *Atlas Chinensis*, 696.

91 Montanus, *Atlas Japannensis*, 160, where the author attributes his report to an eyewitness account, albeit one obtained third-hand (from the reputable physician and Amsterdam regent Nicolaes Tulp, via the veteran merchant and WIC director Samuel Blommaert, who claims to have learned of the courting apes from "the King of Sambaces").

92 Struys, *Perillous*, 16; and cf. Struys, *Drie aanmerkelijke en seer rampspoedige reysen*, 17.

93 It was a narrative that became quickly codified in numerous volumes of "enlightened" travel literature and endured in the racialist "theoretical" literature of the nineteenth and even twentieth centuries. Several examples could be cited, yet see, among the earliest and most commonly quoted, Atkins, *Voyage to Guinea* (1735): "At some places the *Negroes* have been suspected of Bestiality with them [i.e., "prodigious" apes and monkeys]," Atkins writes. "And by the Boldness and Affection they are known under some Circumstances to express to our Females; the Ignorance and Stupidity on the other side [of African women], to guide or controul Lust; but more from the near resemblances are sometimes met to the Human Species, would tempt one to suspect the Fact" (108). Modern variants of the motif also reached the fine arts: the Post-Impressionist, Naïve artist Henri Rousseau pursued the theme, for example, in a painting of an Amerindian figure fighting off a gorilla, a canvas based apparently on a late nineteenth-century statue of an ape ravishing a woman. See Morris and Green, *Henri Rousseau*, 29–47 (and cf. fig. 26, Emmanuel Frémiet's disturbing *Gorilla* of 1887, and fig. 35, Rousseau's painting of a human-ape encounter).

94 Bernier, "Nouvelle division de la terre" (a slightly later version of the essay carries a mildly different title). Bernier's writings have been much studied of late. On his 1684 article, see Stuurman, "François Bernier"; and Boulle, "François Bernier." On early modern debates on race, more generally, see Livingstone, *Adam's Ancestor*; and Bernasconi and Lott, *Idea of Race*.

95 Bernier, "Nouvelle division de la terre," cited in Bernasconi and Lott, *Idea of Race*, 1–2; and see Stuurman, "François Bernier," 4.

96 Stuurman, "François Bernier," 2 (emphasis in the original); see also Hock and Mackenthun, *Entangled Knowledge* (Bernier cited on 119).

97 Greenblatt, *Renaissance Self-fashioning*. See also Lestringant, *Mapping the Renaissance World*; and Mullaney, "Strange Things."

98 Kaempfer, *History of Japan*, 19. Nieuhof's comments come in a discussion of Brahmin women, who are described as light skinned, "not inferior in complexion to [*niet zoo wit als*] the *Portuguese* or the brown *Dutch* Women." He thus conflates exotic, creole, and southern European bodies (the latter increasingly marginalized from a northwest European perspective). Nieuhof, *Voyages and travels*, 2:271; and cf. *Gedenkwaerdige zee en lantreize*, 2:144.

99 "Translator to the Reader," in Bernard, *Ceremonies and religious customs*, n.p. (note that this preface appears in the beginning of "Part II" of the third volume, which, confusingly, comes in the fourth bound volume of the six). The admiring remarks on the enlightened quality of Bernard's ensemble derive from Israel, *Radical Enlightenment*, 135. They are echoed (to support, paradoxically, a contrasting narrative of the Enlightenment) in Hunt, Jacob, and Mijnhardt, *Book That Changed Europe*; see also Hunt, Jacob, and Mijnhardt, *Bernard Picart*.

100 Behn, *Oroonoko* (quotation on 13, spelling modernized).

101 See the "Nieuwe Pascaert van Oost Indien" and "Paskaerte vande archipel en de eylanden daer omtrent gelegen," in Keulen, *Groote nieuwe vermeerde zee-atlas* (the maps are not paginated and vary in placement with different volumes). Note that violence seeps into such decorative cartography in more ways than one. In the foreground of the "Oost Indien" cartouche, a snake and mongoose snarl at one another, suggesting the correlative natural violence—human and animal alike—of the exotic world. This sense of natural violence in exotic settings was common in other media, as well. Scenes of

antagonistic (and sometimes bloody) wildlife inhabit the foreground of numerous Brazilian landscapes by the painter Frans Post, and there are also cases of exotic animal violence in illustrated volumes of natural history (for example, in Seba's "Thesaurus," as discussed in chapter 2). Even non-European *naturalia*, these images suggest, offer narratives of exotic violence.

102 These "decorative" distinctions can be observed in many of the Dutch-designed atlases of this period; see, for example, the maps of Pieter van der Aa's *Nouvel atlas*. In general, cartouches dedicated to European lands present Europe as a place of history (royal figures), military feats (arms), mythological events (allegorical figures), and technological advance (depictions of mapmakers, navigators, and their instruments); while the exotic world is depicted as a place of natural wonder (flora and fauna), ethnographic curiosa (global peoples and "customs," including images of violence), and, not least, commercial exchange (exotic products). For a contrast with this "exotic" mode of cartographic design, see the cartouches in Covens and Mortier, *Atlas nouveau*, which, even while produced in Holland, derive from French-designed maps, bearing distinctly sober—that is, not the least bit exotic—cartouches.

103 This argument adopts some of the insights of Lisa Silverman's analysis of the "epistemology of pain" in *Tortured Subjects*. Silverman explores the history and meaning of torture in the early modern French legal system and describes a similar "desacralization" of pain and torture. She observes a shift whereby suffering could be seen as less and less "Christian." "The early modern period was . . . a moment during which both the body and pain were self-consciously reconceptualized," she notes, adding that this French transformation took place "no later than the 1680s"—concomitant, thus, with the shift in sources of geography (quotations on 9–10).

104 Early modern Europe's rhetorical delineation of body types—exotic and not—may have a precedent in the ancient world, where distinctions were drawn between the bodies of Greek citizens and their slaves. As Page DuBois has argued, torture was "fundamental to classical society in that it helped to delineate not merely a social but also epistemological boundary between slaves and citizens: slaves were assumed to speak truth only under torture because, lacking the ability to reason, they lacked the ability to dissemble as their citizen-masters might." See Du-

Bois, *Torture and Truth*, 19; and also DuBois, *Slaves and Other Objects*.

105 Cf. Silverman, *Tortured Subjects*, 5; and also Myers, *Death and a Maiden*, which speaks of a "decline" of torture in the Holy Roman Empire from the mid-seventeenth century, even while arguing for the shift in its purpose and meaning (5).

106 Brancaforte describes the older tradition of invoking Christian motifs in European travel literature, which then takes on the qualities of pilgrimage: *Visions of Persia*. Merback analyzes the shift in Christian depictions of bodily pain, from a more visceral and vivid form of representation (pre-Reformation) to a more allegorical rendering of (for example) the tortured figures who join Christ in crucifixion scenes: *Thief, the Cross, and the Wheel*.

107 Asad, "On Torture."

108 See Brook, Bourgon, and Blue, *Death by a Thousand Cuts*, especially chapters 1 (quotation on 22) and 6. Brook et al. argue (without invoking specifically the sources of early modern geography discussed here): "As the sight of judicial torment was withdrawn from the public realm in Europe, an ongoing visual appetite for the sight of mutilated bodies migrated to other sources, and did so at the same time as images of the world beyond Europe began to circulate within Europe" (24). See also Bourgon, "Chinese Executions," which traces these themes into the twentieth century.

109 As Brook et al. point out, the relative dearth of available images in the West of Chinese "cruel punishments" had the effect of limiting the iconographic pool. This meant that those few images in circulation were endlessly reproduced and had a disproportionate impact—thus (as they phrase it), a "fictive déjà vu." Brook, Bourgon, and Blue, *Death by a Thousand Cuts*, 23 and 30.

110 Brook, Bourgon, and Blue, *Death by a Thousand Cuts*, 164, where the authors quote Montesquieu's contemptuous commentary on the "tyrannie" of the Qing, which is further generalized to encompass the despotism of Chinese (and Tartar) rule: "what the peoples of Asia have called punishments those of Europe have deemed the most outrageous abuse."

111 [Mason], *Punishments of China*. With text in both English and French, and twenty-two full-page engravings, the volume targeted a broadly European audience and marked the distillation in this literature of the conceit of an expressly "Chinese" culture of torture.

Epigraphs: Du Halde, *Description geographique*. The quotation comes from the "Translator's Preface" to the English edition (thus ca. 1738): *Description of the Empire*, 1:iv. While this preface is unsigned, bibliographers typically ascribe it to Emanuel Bowen, who signed the volume's maps (over which much fuss is made, otherwise, in the preface).

Ladies amusement, 4. A first edition came out just prior to February 1760, when an advertisement for the book appeared in *Gentleman's Magazine*.

1 See the citations gathered in the Oxford English Dictionary (*OED*: online edition accessed 23 April 2013, q.v. "china"), which show instances of *china ware* from the 1630s and of *china* from the mid- to late seventeenth century. Cf. also Yang, *Performing China*, 3–6.

2 Gordon-Smith, "Influence of Jean Pillement."

3 See the *OED* online edition (accessed 23 April 2013), q.v. "ottoman," "Java," and "mocha"; for "India," see the *OED* hard-copy edition (1933; reprint ed. Oxford: Oxford University Press, 1970), vol. 5, 204. Note that *ottomane* was first deployed in French as such in 1729, after which this usage quickly spread to other European languages. India, as a geographic term, was famously affixed to America in 1493, yet it still retained a sense related to South and Southeast Asia, and this gained traction over the seventeenth century—after which the term *India* came into greater use as a type of fabric. *Java* was used allusively from the late eighteenth century, yet regularly thereafter; while *mocha* was used as a term for coffee already from 1762.

4 On the burgeoning interest in luxury goods at this time, see Berg and Eger, *Luxury*; Berg, "Pursuit of Luxury"; McCants, "Exotic Goods"; and Vries, "Luxury in the Dutch Golden Age," which points out the breadth of such consumption beyond the so-called elites of Europe.

5 This is not to suggest that such place-name usages were entirely new: compare *damask* for a fabric affiliated with Damascus, used already in the fourteenth century. Yet the breadth and frequency of the early modern phenomenon suggest a whole new order of usages. To the instances already cited might be added *Muslin* for fabrics from Mosul, from the early to mid-seventeenth century; *Persian* for woolen rugs but also (and more frequently) for silk liners, in both cases from ca. 1700; *Morocco* for leather binding, from the early to mid-eighteenth century; *Trinidado* for tobacco, from the turn of the seventeenth century;

and *Coromandel* for a kind of lacquered furniture, which comes into use in the nineteenth century. Perhaps the most direct and immediate instance of this geo-linguistic transformation is *Siamoise*, a term used in the late seventeenth century for "a new cloth . . . produced in imitation of the ambassadors robes" following a visit to the French court by Siamese envoys in 1684: see Jacobson, *Chinoiserie*, 38.

6 Cf. Brown, "Thing Theory."

7 "Translator's Preface," in Du Halde, *Description of the Empire*, 1:iv; *Ladies amusement*, 4. Note that the modern term *decorative* as applied to material arts occurs only from the nineteenth century—the *OED* cites an 1855 usage from Alexander Bain's *Senses and the Intellect*: "In the fancies of decorative art, nature has very little place" (ii.iv.607)—which underscores the difficulties and inaccuracies of applying the term to the range of arts that flourished in pre-Enlightenment Europe. On the "Age of Classification," see Farr, *Sex, Botany and Empire*, 20.

8 "Du Halde's Preface," in *Description of the Empire*, n.p.; "Translator's Preface," in *Description of the Empire*, 1:iv; *Ladies amusement*, 4 and passim. On the "feminine" qualities of the decorative arts, see Sloboda, "Porcelain Bodies," and Kowaleski-Wallace, "Women."

9 Smith, *Imagining the Pacific*, 1–39 (quotation on 22).

10 See Harley et al., *History of Cartography*, especially vol. 1 (*Cartography in Prehistoric, Ancient, and Medieval Europe and the Mediterranean*). On the rise of Dutch mapmakers, especially in the field of extra-European cartography, see Zandvliet, *Mapping for Money*.

11 Some of these varieties are discussed in Zandvliet, *Mapping for Money*, where he notes that maps were often inventoried with paintings and material arts (210–212 and passim). See also Barber and Harper, *Magnificent Maps*; and Kagan and Schmidt, "Maps and the Early Modern State," which discusses the civic, national, and royal contexts of map display.

12 Heijbroek and Schapelhouman, *Kunst in kaart*.

13 Baldaeus, *Naauwkeurige beschryvinge*, and Hendrick Doncker, *Peninsula Indiæ citra Gangem* (ca. 1680). The South Asia map was regularly reprinted in the atlases of R. and J. Ottens (e.g., *Atlas maior*, ca. 1730) and by the leading German mapmaker of the day, Johann Baptist Homann, whose firm kept the map in circulation well into the eighteenth century under the name of "Homann Erban [Heirs]" (e.g., in 1733 and ca. 1745 editions).

14 Which is not to suggest that other frontispieces to works of geography did not also advertise the riches of the exotic world. But the contrast between Dutch-produced and other contemporary works could be striking: cf. Du Halde, *Description geographique*, which lacks a proper frontispiece and whose title page itself provides a relatively drab textual announcement of the book's title, with a small, unremarkable, chinoiserie vignette.

15 Nicolaes Visscher's *Novissima et Accuratissima Totius Americae Descriptio* appeared in the mid-seventeenth century (the first edition is dated ca. 1658) and in all subsequent atlases of the Visscher firm. The map then appeared—to cite just a few well-known examples—in a version engraved by Gerrit Lacasz. van Schagen, printed in the exceedingly popular (and widely translated) history of America by Montanus, *Nieuwe en onbekende weereld* (Amsterdam, 1671); in another 1671 edition, this time produced in London by John Ogilby, who scratched out and revised the dedication (see figure 109); and in a popular variant printed in Amsterdam (1680) by Justus Danckerts, which reverses the lower cartouche and scotches the upper cartouche to fit a reproportioned page. The map is discussed in greater detail in Schmidt, "Impulse of Mapping."

16 Honour, *European Vision*, 157–158.

17 Francis Lamb [after N. Visscher], *Novissima et Accuratissima Totius Americae Descriptio per Johanem Ogiluium Cosmographum Regium* (London, [1671]). Ogilby mildly modifies some of the cartography—the Great Lakes are adjusted slightly—but most of the changes relate to nomenclature (Anglicized) and to the dedicatory cartouche (to Anthony Ashley, Baron of Wimburne).

18 The map appeared originally in a Paris edition of 1683 as the "Carte de la Nouvelle France et de la Louisiane Nouvellement decouverte" (engraved by Nicholas Guerard), then in a second, revised edition of 1697, "Carte d'un Nouveau Monde entre le Nouveau Mexique et la Mer Glaciallein," in this case printed in Utrecht and engraved by Gaspar Bouttats. Berchem's upper cartouche is discussed below.

19 "Ameriki opisanie" (Description of America), in Hübner, *Zemnovodnago kruga kratkoe opisanie*.

20 "America," in Blaeu, *Atlas major*, where the placement of the American volume and its frontispiece varies by the language of the edition; and cf. Nicolaes Berchem, "Allegory of America" (black and brown ink with brown and gray wash over black chalk; incised for transfer), Metropolitan Museum of

Art (accession no. 59.208.90). Note that Berchem's drawing and Blaeu's print clarify the gender of the allegory: she is unambiguously female, which is less obvious on the Visscher map, where the figure is oddly androgynous.

21 Hendrick Doncker, *Pas-caert van Guinea, vertoonende de Tand-kust, Qua Qua-Kust en de Goudkust van C. das Palmas tot R. da Volta* (Amsterdam, ca. 1665), with several later editions.

22 Montanus, *Nieuwe en onbekende weereld*, 144; Montanus, *Gedenkwaerdige gesantschappen*, 296; Dapper, *Gedenkwaerdig bedryf*, 405, 463; Dapper, *Asia*, facing 202.

23 John Smith after William Vincent, *The Indian Queen* [Anne Bracegirdle as Semernia] (London, ca. 1690).

24 Behn, *Widdow ranter*, which was written ca. 1688–1689, first performed (posthumously) in 1689, and published in 1690. Cf. John Dryden and Sir Robert Howard, *The Indian Queen* (1664).

25 The original print was published ca. 1689 with the caption. The National Portrait Gallery has another version, printed without the caption, that it dates "early eighteenth century" (NPG D788), and another variant published by Edward Cooper dated ca. 1700–1725 (NPG D19499).

26 The Silesian glass cup and van Schoor tapestry are discussed in Honour, *European Vision*, 148–149. Note that the headdress of the cut-glass figure resembles another variant of the Indian Queen–Bracegirdle print published ca. 1700 (a copy of which is in the National Portrait Gallery: see NPG D790). The tapestry was designed ca. 1700 by Lodewijck van Schoor after a cartoon by van Schoor (figures) and Pieter Spierincx (background), and it was woven in Brussels "in an undetermined workshop," according to the captioning of the National Gallery of Art, Washington, D.C. (inv. no. 1950.6.1).

27 See *John Cotterell China-Man & Glass-seller. At the Indian Queen & Canister against the Mansion House* (ca. 1750). There was also an Indian King, which likewise sold "all sorts of fine China ware" alongside sundry exotica: *Charles Vere At the Indian King* (ca. 1772); and see the discussion in Eaton, "Nostalgia for the Exotic."

28 See—one of several examples—"King Ashurnasirpal II, King of Assyria (883–859 B.C.), Review of Prisoners," a set of carved reliefs from the North-West Palace at Nimrud, ca. 865–860 B.C.E. (British Museum, object nos. WA 124537, 124549, and 124552). Parasols also appear on Greek vases and in Roman lit-

erature—for example, Ovid's *Ars Amatoria*, where it is meant to embody the quality of gallantry: "Be sure and hold her parasol over her; and clear a way for her if she's hemmed in by the crowd; fetch a stool to help her on to the couch; and unlace or lace up the sandals on her dainty feet" (*Ars Amatoria*, II, 209–212).

29 Doncker, *Pas-caert van Guinea, vertoonende de Tand-kust, Qua Qua-Kust en de Goud-kust van C. das Palmas tot R. da Volta*. "Qua Qua" refers to the region in between the Ivory and Gold Coasts.

30 Cf. Eco, "Innovation and Repetition."

31 Johannes van Keulen, *Pas-kaart vande zee kusten inde boght van Niew* [sic] *Engeland tusschen de Staaten Hoek en C. de Sable* [i.e., from Cape Cod through Canada]. The map appeared on its own and in van Keulen's *Groote nieuwe vermeerde zee-atlas* (1688), a maritime atlas published in French, English, Italian, Spanish, and Dutch editions, thus granting the map (and the New England palm trees) extensive circulation. It was also picked up in other atlases—for example, in Gerard van Keulen's *De groote nieuwe vermeerde zee-atlas* (Amsterdam: Van Keulen, 1709).

32 Bartholomew Gosnold, *'t Noorder Gedeelte van Virginie* (n.d.); also printed in Aa, *Naaukeurige versameling*. Van der Aa was the likely printer of the original map (and perhaps its designer). The vignette presumably depicts an encounter between Gosnold and the Penobscot in the region of Cape Elizabeth, Maine. See also Egmond and Mason, " 'People Who Eat Raw Fish,' " which offers an illustration, from this same geographic moment, of *arctic* palms (as background landscape for Inuit).

33 See the manuscript illustrations in Blussé and Falkenburg, *Nieuhofs beelden*, where the case is made (in Falkenburg's contribution) that palms in the van Meurs prints were inspired by, and may have derived from, Ming porcelain. They thus demonstrate how a proto-chinoiserie style—exotic motifs—moved dizzyingly from Chinese sources to European ones to ersatz Chinese ones (from Ming porcelain to van Meurs's engravings to the later seventeenth-century delftware that replicated van Meurs's Chinese scenes).

34 Cf. Cañizares-Esguerra, *Puritan Conquistadors*, where the traditional argument—that the map offers an anti-Catholic polemic—is summarized and endorsed.

35 Maarten de Vos, *America (Vier Werelddelen)* (ca. 1595): "Europa machte mich der Welt, Godt mir bekandt / Gold, das sonst Heeren macht, liess mich zur Sclavin werden / Ich ben bey Reichtum arm in meinem eigen Land / Weil meine Eide wird geführt

auf andre Erden." The poem and the allegorical print are discussed in Schmidt, *Innocence Abroad*, 135–136; see also Vandenbroeck, *Beeld van de andere*, which reproduces the German version of the print and discusses others that appeared in the late sixteenth century. Honour, *European Vision*, 117, discusses an Italian variant of this allegorical theme as sketched and painted by the Verona artist Paolo Farinati.

36 Udemans, *Geestelyck roer*, 96–97, 122–123, and see also 101–105.

37 Jacob Cats, "Op den handel die met Indiaen of ander vergelegen volck gedreven wert," in *Invallende gedachten*, 79.

38 Pietz, "Problem of the Fetish [I–III]."

39 Pietz, "Problem of the Fetish, II," especially 40–41.

40 Pietz, "Problem of the Fetish, II," 24.

41 Pietz discusses, for example, the writings of Willem Bosman, a Dutch merchant active on the Gold Coast: Bosman, *Nauwkeurige beschryving*.

42 There is one further irony, which points in the other direction: that the material objects obtained by Europeans from Africa and America—where these objects, abundantly present, may indeed have been treated as mere trifles—functioned as fetishes for their new European owners, who housed them in costly cabinets of curiosity and otherwise accorded them the status of elite, exotic specimens. Cf. Freedberg's discussion of "the turning of exotic and imported objects into fetishes or into things bound to be fetishized" in "Science, Commerce, and Art" (quotation on 415).

43 Jan van Kessel, *Europe*, *Asie* [Asia], *Africque* [Africa], and *Americque* [America], oil on copper, Bayerische Staatsgemäldesammlungen. The four central panels measure ca. 48.5 × 67.5 cm, while the sixteen smaller panels of each composition (thus 64 total) measure ca. 14.5 × 21 cm. The paintings are collectively dated 1664–1666, although two of the central panels are signed and more concretely dated— *Europe* is dated 1664, and *America* is dated 1666— and these years are taken to demarcate the ensemble's manufacture. On the paintings and their production, see Krempel, *Jan van Kessel*; Schneider, *Still Life Painting*, 156–169; Teixeira, *Allegory of the Continents*; and Baadj, "World of Materials." On the concept of continents as they developed over these years, see Lewis and Wigen, *Myth of Continents*.

44 The painting of America is a mild exception to the series' overall design insofar as the allegorical figure is not completely obvious—it could conceivably

be the third principal figure, the woman dancing through the rear with a boy. Furthermore, the "live" figures are less distinctively and less fully costumed, although the latter condition—seminudity—may be part of the logic of the composition. The seated woman on the left, who wears only a scanty skirt, would seem to fill the main allegorical role: she and Europe both sit stage left, while Africa and Asia occupy positions stage right. Van Kessel may have placed her a bit more discreetly in the composition owing to her immodest cover-up. He may also have wished, more basically, to vary the compositions among the panels. America, in all cases, might be singled out for her lack of religious accoutrements. Once again, however, this may be part of the logic of the composition, a way to indicate the New World's unique lack of religious understanding (or so it was proposed).

45 The literature on van Kessel is meager. Along with the materials cited above, see Baadj, "Monstrous Creatures," which pays special attention to the artist's working methods. Van Kessel not only drew inspiration from other visual artists but also collaborated with several of them throughout his career. Among this group was Erasmus Quellinus, who is sometimes listed as co-painter for the Munich series. This is based on a 1681 inventory for Jan Gillis, an Antwerp silversmith in possession of a set of *Continents* allegedly by van Kessel and Quellinus. As van Kessel was known both to replicate his paintings and to allow others to do the same—we know of at least one variation of the *Continents*, and it would not be too surprising to find more—this archival notation cannot be definitively attached to the Munich paintings (which have been in German collections from at least the early eighteenth century). In all events, Quellinus certainly worked with van Kessel on other projects and may well have contributed to the Munich panels by painting the human figures.

46 The Blaeu maps are catalogued and a version of them reproduced in Schilder, *Monumenta Cartographica Neerlandica*, vol. 5. The maps appeared in several states and editions—1608, 1612, 1624—and the plates ultimately landed in the hands of Nicolaes Visscher, who used them for his mid-century products. Typical for Dutch geography in their broad reach, the maps were further printed, in slightly modified form, in Venice. Note that Blaeu also published a monumental world map with the same form.

47 There are also correlations with the decorative arts, where one material or form comments, as it were, on another: see Hellman, "Nature of Artifice."

48 Nieuhof, *Gezantschap*. Insofar as this volume appeared in 1665, it is safe to say that the central panel of *Asia*, generally dated 1664–1666, was painted in 1665 or 1666.

49 The statue of the Buddha on a pedestal is modeled after an engraving of "Ninifo" in Nieuhof, *Gezantschap* (2:86), while the standing figure in the center-right niche is a variation of the Great Khan from the Nieuhof–van Meurs frontispiece (cf. figure 5).

50 Many of these borrowings are summarized in Teixeira, *Allegory of the Continents*; see 101 and 126 for the examples cited. On the decorative arts, see, for example, Grigsby, "Nieuhoff's *Embassy*," and Odell, "Porcelain."

51 Which is to say: van Kessel may have been a "great" natural history painter, yet this requires a reconceptualization of how we understand and judge the seventeenth-century art of natural history, which was more of a process of pillaging, evidently, than an ad vivum "art of describing." Cf. Alpers, *Art of Describing*, for the traditional view.

52 Jan Brueghel the Elder, *The Temptation in the Garden of Eden* (ca. 1600, oil on panel, 53 × 84 cm, Victoria and Albert Museum). There are several versions of this painting, most nearly identical, some with subtle changes, and some that reverse the composition. The "London" horse is identical (although not the gallinule and the penguin) to the left-side horse in a variant of the painting now in the Carmen Thyssen-Bornemisza Collection: Jan Brueghel the Elder, *The Garden of Eden* (ca. 1610–1612, oil on panel, 59.4 × 95.6 cm, on deposit at Museo Thyssen-Bornemisza).

53 Teixeira, *Allegory of the Continents*, 107–108 and 115–116 (yet note Teixeira's mistaken attribution of the armadillo, which is borrowed from Clusius [*Exoticorum*, 109] rather than Gesner). Perhaps the most "cited" text in the composition was Piso et al., *Historia naturalis Brasiliae*, which supplied van Kessel with scores of models—American fauna are distributed throughout the globe's continents—and van Kessel also mined the recently published natural history of Francisco Hernández de Toledo, *Nova plantarum, animalium et mineralium Mexicanorum historia* (Rome, 1651). The very range of these materials attests to the breadth of van Kessel's borrowings—from sources of the North and South Netherlands, from Spanish and Italian naturalists, and so on—and this offers yet another instructive comparison with the production techniques of exotic geography.

54 Several of the material objects also derive, just as do the *naturalia*, from secondary visual sources.

The elaborate sculpture in *Africa* of a female figure on a deer comes from a Pieter Boel *vanitas* painting of 1663, where it is meant to stand for the riches of the world—and certainly bears no connection to things "African." On that continent, in particular, and the decorative jumble that surrounds her, see Massing, *Image of the Black*, 349–352 (which also discusses *America*).

55 Barthes, "Monde-objet."

56 Schama, *Embarrassment of Riches* (quotation on 160); Schama, "Perishable Commodities."

57 Hochstrasser, *Still Life and Trade*.

58 This, of course, is an oversimplification of Dutch still-life painting, which could also combine forms, textures, media, and the like. The point, all the same, is to highlight the self-conscious mixtures of provenance in van Kessel's *Continents*, which is among the chief messages of the ensemble and of the mode of exotic geography that it exemplifies.

59 The Buddha—extracted from a van Meurs print, "Ninifo afgod der wellust" (Nieuhof, *Gezantschap*, 2:86)—may be a combination of Mi-lo-fo and the god of good fortune (the so-called laughing Buddha): see Lach and Van Kley, *Asia*, vol. 3, book 4, figure 335 (with annotation). The pagoda, which would become a fixture in the design of eighteenth-century decorative arts, also derives from a van Meurs–Nieuhof engraving, "Porcellyne Tooren" (Nieuhof, *Gezantschap*, 1:108–109).

60 Visual references to cannibalism are both subtle and not: the Eckhout-derived figure of a Tapuya (Tarairiú) woman, replicated in the form of a statue (in the center-right rear niche), carries a human limb in her hand and straw backpack. Meanwhile, a grisly feast of human flesh is depicted in a painting within the painting, "hanging" allusively above the scene of sati.

61 The Bible is the Antwerp edition of the so-called Louvain Bible, printed originally in 1547 and later by Plantin: see Teixeira, *Allegory of the Continents*, 15.

62 Schneider, *Still Life Painting*, 159–162.

63 Vries and Woude, *First Modern Economy*, 309–311.

64 The dancer, like the Brahmin, derives from a print in van Linschoten: see Teixeira, *Allegory of the Continents*, 100.

65 These "American" mixtures are discussed more fully in Schmidt, "Mapping an Exotic World."

66 For the engraved and carved shell (*turbo marmoratus*), see Bergvelt, *Wereld binnen handbereik*, 47

(cat. 64); for the porcelain teapot, see Honour, *European Vision*, 165 (cat. 140).

67 Behn, *Oroonoko*, 40; and cf. Thomas Harriot, *A briefe and true report of the new found land of Virginia* (1588), republished in 1590 (Frankfurt am Main) with engravings by the de Bry atelier after John White. On Behn's geographic sensibilities (she invokes the "seraglio," thus Asia, in her description of the African princess Imoinda: *Oroonoko*, 18), see Yang, "Asia Out of Place." On the Harriot images and their production, see Gaudio, *Engraving the Savage*, which underscores the materiality of these engravings, a reading that adds yet another tactile quality to Behn's description. And for a comparable example of a lacquered exotic body, in this case nonfictional, see the description of Mai, the Ra'iatean who was shipped to London by James Cook, introduced to British society by Joseph Banks, and described by a contemporary English observer—in terms remarkably reminiscent of Behn's image of Oroonoko—as "a specimen of pale, moving mahogany, highly varnish'd; not only varnish'd, indeed, but curiously veneer'd" (cited in Fara, *Sex, Botany and Empire*, 122–123).

68 Rumphius, *Herbarium Amboinense*, Preface (n.p. [sig. ***r]).

69 Temple, "Upon the Gardens of Epicurus," in *Miscellanea. The Second Part* (London, 1690), 57–58; for which see Temple, *Gardens of Epicurus*, 53–54 (emphasis added).

70 Temple, *Miscellanea*, 58–59 (*Gardens of Epicurus*, 54–55). On the Cape Colony garden, cultivated under the auspices of the Dutch East India Company and known as "the Company's garden," see Fleischer, "Company's Garden."

71 The term *sharawadgi* (or *sharawaggi*) persists in early modern print, popularized by several eighteenth-century writers—the *OED* lists usages by Alexander Pope and Horace Walpole—and is revived in the twentieth century, when it appears in scholarly literature on architecture and garden history. As for its origins, while the term does not match up to any bona fide Chinese word, it may relate to a Japanese word cited by Kaempfer: "When Dutchmen, accompanied by the German Engelbert Kaempfer (1651–1716), visited the gardens at Kyoto in the late seventeenth century they noted the 'irregular but agreeable' features 'artfully made in imitation of nature,' and the Japanese words sorowaji or shorowaji suggesting asymmetry. It would appear that sharawadji is a corruption of the Japanese, filtered through Dutch, probably misheard by the seventeenth-century visitors to the Japanese

gardens at Kyoto. Temple probably picked the word up from Dutchmen who had visited Japanese gardens." See Curl, "Sharawadgi" (with similar definitions in other reference works).

72 Smith, *Imagining the Pacific*, 22.

73 Smith, *Imagining the Pacific*, 23, citing (with full approval) Joppien, "Dutch Vision of Brazil," where Joppien discusses the *Anciennes Indes* tapestries along with other components of the Mauritian oeuvre.

74 Smith, *Imagining the Pacific*, 1–39 and passim. Smith's arguments reverberate in a wide-ranging essay by Martin Kemp, who proposes that exotic artifacts, by their inherently hybrid nature, do not evince "historical meta-realities"—historical narrative—a theory that suggests to Kemp an absence of colonial and imperial ideology (or at least the sort of ideologies ascribed to such objects by postcolonial critics): Kemp, " 'Wrought by No Artist's Hand.' "

75 Hooghe, *Indes Orientales*, Introduction (n.p.). For lacquered furniture and its potential for narrative, see Lasser, "Reading Japanned Furniture."

76 Findlen, *Possessing Nature*, where the discussion pertains primarily to Baroque Italy (and thus overlooks developments in and sources from the Netherlands).

77 The technology of stereotype developed, in fact, in the later eighteenth century and initially for print. Yet the uses, motives, and concepts behind it expanded on earlier atelier practices: to find the most cost-effective way to extract profit from the least amount of labor and material, and thus to replicate and duplicate whenever circumstances allowed. Printing exotic images, which pertained to things and spaces Europeans often knew little about, made this a viable strategy more often than not. On the practices and effects of such replications, see Eco, "Innovation and Repetition."

78 See Piso et al., *Historia naturalis Brasiliae*, 270 and 280, which depict per engraving images of Tupinambá and Tapuya (Tarairiú) couples, respectively. These illustrations closely resemble the paintings by Eckhout and presumably follow original sketches done in preparation for the paintings. These now lost sketches are likely the basis of similar (to the engravings) sketches done by Zacharias Wagenaer. See the reproductions in Whitehead and Boeseman, *Portrait of Dutch Seventeenth Century Brazil*, 235 (Piso and Marcgraf engravings), 269–272 (Eckhout paintings), and 257–258 (Wagenaer watercolors). The van Meurs materials are in Montanus, *Nieuwe en onbekende*

weereld (1671), 359 (engraved illustration based on the African woman or "Molher Negra" [see fig. 87] and the Tapuya man [Wagenaer's "Omem Tapuya"]) and 363 (engraved illustration based on the Tapuya woman or "Molher Tapuya" [see fig. 169] and, very loosely, the Tapuya man); and in Nieuhof, *Gedenkwaerdige zee en lantreize* (1682), 218 (engraved illustration based on the Tupinambá couple [Wagenaer's "Molher Brasilianae" and "Omem Brasiliano"]) and 224 (engraved illustration based on the Tapuya couple). Note that, in the case of the van Meurs illustrations, the images in some cases more closely resemble drawings from the journal of Caspar Schmalkalden—another presumed set of copies from lost originals—for which see Whitehead and Boeseman, *Portrait of Dutch Seventeenth Century Brazil*, 267–268. In all events, van Meurs made the engravings his own by revising and modifying them, and by combining various elements in the original drawings. Post's illustrations—which served as a source for hundreds of paintings done from the 1650s through 1670s—were used for the prints in Barlaeus, *Rerum per octennium in Brasilia*.

79 Baldaeus, *Naauwkeurige beschryvinge*; Dapper, *Asia*. On Angel's role as conduit for the original drawings, see Stolte, *Angel's Deex-Autaers*, especially 68–101; and Bergvelt, *Wereld binnen handbereik*, 186–187 (cat. 413). The Baldaeus prints are attributed to Coenraet Decker, while the Dapper engravings would have been the work of the van Meurs atelier.

80 *Athanasii Kircheri e Soc. Jesu China monumentis* (Amsterdam: Johannes Janssonius van Waesberge and Elizer Weyerstraten, 1667); and *Athanasii Kircheri e Soc. Jesu China monumentis* (Amsterdam: Jacob van Meurs, 1667), the latter a pirated edition.

81 Bernard, *Ceremonies et coutumes* (the Asia volume was printed ca. 1729); Aa, *Galerie agreable*. The printing history of these images—far more convoluted than this brief summary can possibly convey—are partially worked out in Veldman, "Familiar Customs," and Wyss-Giacosa, *Religionsbilder*, 228–252.

82 Kusukawa, "Uses of Pictures." See also Kusukawa, "Leonhart Fuchs"; and Kusukawa, *Picturing the Book of Nature*.

83 Cf. Baldaeus, *Naauwkeurige beschryvinge* (1672), frontispiece, and Hendrick Doncker, *Peninsula Indiæ citra Gangem hoc est Orae celeberrimae Malabar & Coromandel cum adjacente insula non minus celebratissima Ceylon* (ca. 1680). The original version of this map is exceedingly rare, yet the design was replicated by later printers and atlas makers, including, for ex-

ample, Johann Baptist Homann and his heirs (there is a 1733 version attributed to the French cartographer Guillaume de L'Isle) and Reinier and Josua Ottens in their *Atlas maior* (ca. 1740).

84 The Kändler design, executed by his assistants Johann Friedrich Eberlein and Peter Reinke, proved immensely popular and was produced in a larger and smaller format. It also inspired several variations by other *modelleurs* working for other porcelain factories (and in Meissen): see Honour, *European Vision*, 169 (cat. 142). Note that allegorical figures made from porcelain were designed particularly for the dessert course of a grand dinner, replacing less durable pieces made of sugar paste or wax. While the latter forms might have been more flexible in their design and fabrication, the porcelain pieces were plainly more enduring, and they thus fixed, by the mid-eighteenth century, specific exotic images and messages into the scheme of elite dinners.

85 Vries, *Curieuse aenmerckingen*; on which see Roeper and Wildeman, *Reizen op papier*, 48, which describes the massive and "exotic" output of this author.

86 Veldman, "Familiar Customs," 104.

87 Hooghe, *Indes Orientales*; Aa, *Galerie agreable*.

88 On the cabinet (which sold at auction on 24 June 2008: Christie's sale 2811, lot 273), see Bergvelt, *Wereld binnen handbereik* (essays), 86 and cat. 83. Note that, while the right front panel bears de Hooghe's image of the manufacture of lacquer ("Lakwerken"), the left shows his depiction of sugar production ("Sucreries du Bresil / Brasilise Suykerwerken"), which is itself a replication based on Frans Post's Brazilian illustrations. In both cases, the cabinet panels would have afforded the artist a perfect, print-like rectangle to work with: hardly the unwieldy space of "decorative" arts imagined by Smith.

89 Stalker and Parker, *Treatise of japaning*, title page (emphasis added); *Ladies amusement*. Note that both Weigel and Schenk had close connections with cartographers and geographers—for example, with Johann Baptist Homann and Gerard Valck, respectively—and produced several variations of their books, also printed by members of their extended families.

90 See the samples reproduced in Rudi, *Exotische Welten*.

91 Hoftijzer, *Van der Aa*, which notes that the printer's widow "was one of the richest women of Leiden" and that his daughter and heir was worth over 100,000 guilders (87).

92 Aa, *Nouvel atlas*. As the title page announces: "Suivant les nouvelles observations de Mrs. de l'Academie Royale des Sciences, & rectifié sur les relations les plus recentes des plus fidéles voyageurs."

93 Aa, *Naaukeurige versameling*, title page (italics added). This old-wine-in-a-new-bottle strategy had a prior and rich history in Dutch publishing: compare the precedent of Cornelis Claesz. and Barent Langenes as described in Roeper and Wildeman, *Reizen op papier*, 138.

94 Aa, *Galerie agreable*, where the printer offers his product as "un Ouvrage de plaisir & d'utilité" (Preface, n.p.).

95 For a comprehensive, page-by-page description of the atlas, including photographs of every sheet (also reproduced digitally), see Krogt, *Koeman's Atlantes Neerlandici*, vol. 4A: 1.

96 Clunas, *Pictures and Visuality*, 46; and cf. Ginzburg's discussion of erotic imagery, where he makes a distinction among sets of images that circulate in distinct spheres, for example private and public ("two iconic circuits [let us call them that]"): Ginzburg, "Titian" (quotation on 79).

97 Nieuhof, *Gezantschap*. The unsigned frontispiece, an identical version of which was printed for the French edition published that year, and which was used and adopted for the German, Latin, and English editions, is generally attributed to Jacob van Meurs.

98 See Blussé and Falkenburg, *Nieuhofs beelden*, fol. 23 (following p. 32), and cf. the manuscript frontispiece, with an altogether different design, following p. 30. Note the not inconsequential fact that Nieuhof, naturally, never met the emperor.

99 Editions of Nieuhof's book are detailed in Landwehr, *VOC*, 539–544. See also Sun, *Wandlungen*, 316 (ill. 268), 336 (ill. 300), 394 (ill. 400, depicting the "viceroy"), and 422 (ill. 433), all of which appeared before the close of the seventeenth century.

100 Du Halde, *Ausführliche Beschreibung*, frontispiece; for which see Sun, *Wandlungen*, 482 (ill. 520), and cf. ills. 416 and 468.

101 Pelka, *Ostasiatische Reisebilder*, plates 77–86, reproduces images of the cabinet before it suffered damage in World War II (the lower part, lost in the war, was not likely part of the original design). A similarly designed *Aufsatzschreibtisch*, also attributed to the van Soest atelier (ca. 1705) and now in the Bayerisches Nationalmuseum, Munich, likewise adopts the van Meurs–Nieuhof frontispiece for its central panel: see Eikelmann, *Wittelsbacher*, 259–263.

102 Bremer-David, "Six Tapestries."

103 *The Emperor on a Journey*, Beauvais, ca. 1690–1705. Different versions of the tapestry have varying measurements—the Getty Museum's tapestry (see plate 20), for example, has different dimensions than one sold recently by Christie's: see Bremer-David, "Six Tapestries," and cf. Christie's London, Sale 8033, lot 13, 7 July 2011; http://www.christies.com/LotFinder/LotDetailsPrintable.aspx?intObjectID=5461626 (accessed 7 May 2013).

104 Which can also be said for the inlaid cabinet in the Grassi Museum and the *Aufsatzschreibtisch* in the Bayerisches Nationalmuseum, both of which count likewise as luxury objects.

105 It is hardly coincidental that this motif gained traction in this period also across other media and genres. It was precisely in these years that Montesquieu began to posit that the king of France favored a form of government akin to that of the Persian and Turkish sultan—Oriental despotism, in other words: see, for example, Letter 37 of the *Lettres persanes*, first published in Amsterdam in 1721 (Montesquieu, *Persian Letters*, 91).

106 Nieuhof, *Gezantschap*, and Aa, *Galerie agreable*; and cf. the variations in Thévenot, *Relations* (for which see Sun, *Wandlungen*, 401 [ills. 407]), and—as late as 1810!—Eberhard August Wilhelm von Zimmermann, *Taschenbuch der Reisen*, 12 Jahrgänge (Leipzig: G. Fleischer, 1802–1813), Jahrg. 9 (1810) (for which see Sun, *Wandlungen*, 596 [ill. 685]).

107 For Nieuhof's manuscript description of the boulder-banging beggar, see Blussé and Falkenburg, *Nieuhofs beelden*, 44, where the author notes the religious context of the scene. None of the other figures on the plaque—a strikingly large, blue and white glazed faience tableau—come from the manuscript drawing, yet they do relate to other prints designed by van Meurs's atelier (discussed below). The tin-glazed earthenware punch bowl (Fitzwilliam Museum accession no. C.2415-1928) bears the monogram SVE: Samuel van Eenhoorn, who was active at the Grieksche A Factory from 1678 to 1686.

108 The cylindrical bottle is dated by the British Museum (accession no. AN358086001) ca. 1710–1720, although the latter year makes more sense based on the publication date of Weigel's pattern book (ca. 1720). Helen Espir ascribes the vase's painting to Preissler, who worked at that time in Breslau, while the British Museum also lists Ignatius Bottengruber (who worked in Breslau, as well) as a possible painter: Espir, *European Decoration*, 136–137. For Nieuhof's descrip-

tion of the prostrate figure, see Blussé and Falkenburg, *Nieuhofs beelden*, 44; for the Qalandar, see Dapper, *Syrie*, 260.

109 Kiby, *Exotismen*, 79–80 and 274–275 (plates 64–66); see also Eikelmann, *Wittelsbacher*, 298–301. The mendicant is painted into the décor of the lodge's kitchen, which also contains ceramic tiles, a fairly common kitchen feature. Along with other exotic motifs, the tiles depict solemn biblical and religious scenes (Stations of the Cross, e.g.), which should caution us not to take such domestic décor too lightly.

110 Whitehead and Boeseman, *Portrait of Dutch Seventeenth Century Brazil*; and see Freedberg, "Science, Commerce, and Art," where Freedberg contrasts these Dutch-derived exotic materials from their Lincean counterparts—works from the Accademia dei Lincei in Rome—characterizing the former as entrepreneurial, commercial, and colonial, and the latter as aristocratic, "sometimes libertine" (394).

111 Whitehead and Boeseman, *Portrait of Dutch Seventeenth Century Brazil*, 107–140, where the authors also describe a Dutch tapestry series (of which there are no known samples); Buvelot, *Eckhout*, 35–36 and 146 (n. 140).

112 Two examples, both with hunting scenes, are reproduced in Bergvelt, *Wereld binnen handbereik*, 158 (cats. 328–329). The Gemeentemuseum shell (cat. 329), mounted by Elias van de Velde in 1660, makes clear the convergence of global hunting by including an "Indian" figure with bow and arrow along with two other non-Indian hunters. Some shells also had Post-derived scenes: see Corrêa do Lago, *Frans Post* (2003), 86–87.

113 The cup, presently in the Historisk Museum at the University of Bergen, bears the date 1653 inscribed into the coconut; the mounting, however, is likely from the early nineteenth century (as per registration text, object no. BY 00513). The female figure combines three separate Eckhout portraits, which occupy three separate, majestic canvases: the so-called *Tapuya Woman*, who carries a tumplined *straw* backpack (as opposed to a cloth satchel, as on the coconut) laden with human limbs; the *Tupinambá Woman*, who bears a child in her right arm, likewise close to her breast; and the *African Woman*, who handles a young child with her left hand. All three paintings were executed in Brazil in 1641, yet the coconut carver would have likely worked from a sketched copy or printed variation of these portraits done sometime after 1647.

114 On the relative value of coconut cups in this period, see the curatorial description of a similar co-

conut cup, dated ca. 1630, in the collection of the Victoria and Albert Museum (object no. M.39-1970): "By the mid-16th century [coconut shells] had declined in popularity, as more unusual materials became available in Western Europe. The mounts on coconut cups of this date are usually much plainer than earlier ones.... From the 13th century coconuts and other organic materials such as shells and ostrich eggs were highly valued in Western Europe for their rarity and exoticism.... Coconut cups continued to be produced in the 17th century, but they were no longer considered as 'curiosities' unless they were intricately carved": http://collections.vam.ac.uk/item/O78573/cup/ (accessed 1 July 2011). See also Spiess, "Asian Objects."

115 Van der Aa's print appears in the second of three China tomes (tome 57), bearing the title "Les mendians Chinois se font des blessures pour avoir l'aumone." See also the van Meurs–Dapper volumes on Africa (with a manacled figure on the frontispiece) and on Persia and the Mogul empire (a bound figure roped around the neck): Dapper, *Naukeurige beschrijvinge* and *Asia*. Note that the cangue image also made its way into Bernard's *Ceremonies et coutumes*, where it regained its earlier religious reading.

116 See Dapper, *Gedenckwaerdig bedryf*, 477; and cf. Cortes, *Voyage en Chine*, 443 and 456 (fol. 166r and 169v). De la Cortes seems to have made use of a Chinese encyclopedia, which would have placed the origin of the image at one more (at least) remove.

117 The drug pot is catalogued as late seventeenth-century blank (white) Japanese porcelain, overdecorated in Delft (Groninger Museum, inv. NAP 96). The reverse side features a Chinese official on horseback with attendants and comes from an altogether separate engraving in Petrus II Schenk, *Nieuwe geinventeerde Sineesen* (Amsterdam, ca. 1700-1725). See Jörg, "Some Items."

118 A repurposed drug pot did not have a handle, however, so the form relates also to an ale or beer mug, perhaps a stout goblet or even a roemer. For its use as a drinking vessel, specifically for alcohol, see Jörg, "Some Items." For a similar-sized tankard—in this case, purpose designed—also with a Nieuhof-derived scene (a "mendicant"), see Eikelmann, *Wittelsbacher*, 399.

119 The Dapper cangue scene also appeared on a set of embroidered silk wall coverings, now in Munich; these are discussed below.

120 See Jörg, "Some Items," which lists the drug pot as blank (white) Japanese porcelain of the late seventeenth century, overdecorated in Delft (Groninger Museum, inv. NAP 97).

121 Johannes van Keulen, *Nieuwe Pascaert van Oost Indien* (ca. 1680–1689); and cf. van Keulen, *Paskaerte van de archipel en de eylanden daer omtrent gelegen* (ca. 1680), which shows a bound prisoner who appears to confront his executioner, begging for mercy (although this time in the Levant: see fig. 105).

122 In fact, the motif may have been veritably common, and it makes a serendipitous appearance in David Mitchell's imaginative reconstruction of the exotic world of Dutch commerce: "From a carpet bag at his feet, Vorstenbosch produces two porcelain figurines in the Oriental mode. One is an executioner, axe poised to behead the second, a kneeling prisoner, hands bound and eyes on the next world" (Mitchell, *Thousand Autumns*, 11).

123 The tea-bowl and saucer (16.9 cm diameter) are made of hard-paste porcelain and, although manufactured in Meissen, were painted outside of the workshop by the little-known artist Lauche (signed on the reverse: "Lauche fecit"). The museum file for the set in the British Museum (inventory no. AN 237672001) lists a version with the same motif sold at auction (Christie's, 2 July 1984, lot 215).

124 Cortes, *Voyage en Chine*, 455 (fol. 169r) and cf. 456 (fol. 169v). This theme and motif, and the frank admiration it expresses for imperial China's "graded system of punishment," is echoed a century after de las Cortes in the account of his fellow Jesuit Du Halde. Montesquieu, by contrast, condemned the Qing regime for its harsh treatment of "aristocrats": see Brook, Bourgon, and Blue, *Death by a Thousand Cuts*, 162–166.

125 Aa, *Galerie agreable*, where the prints appear in the third of the three China tomes (tome 58). The image of the tickled-tormented woman also appears in the Dapper–van Meurs China volume, but it does not appear to have made it into the material arts (unlike the caning scenes, as discussed below). This image may have been simply too risqué.

126 Stalker and Parker, *Treatise of japaning*, plate 18. The volume includes several other designs based on print geography, particularly the books of Jacob van Meurs. A version of the Nieuhof–van Meurs cangued figure, who appears on the frontispiece of the *Gezantschap* and in one of the mendicant prints, features as part of a design "For a Standish Pon Inke & Paper w[hi]ch allso [sic] sarve [serve] for a Comb Box" (plate 7). And images taken from scattered van Meurs engravings of Chinese religious practices are

used in "A Pagod Worshipp in the Indies" (plate 17)—a caption that describes exotic religion per se rather than the design's possible use (e.g., for a cabinet). In general, the Stalker and Parker volume exhibits numerous such descriptive vignettes—plates that depict exotic social customs, religious practices, and the like—alongside the mere "decorative" designs that feature the sort of flowers, birds, insects, and other fare taken as typical chinoiserie.

127 Stalker and Parker, *Treatise of japaning,* title page. Despite titular calls for "japanning"—cf. *Ladies amusement; or, Whole art of japanning made easy*—volumes such as Stalker and Parker's aimed to address a range of fields; they were more properly manuals for material arts.

128 Both figures may also seem less obviously "Chinese" in appearance, yet the Stalker and Parker engravings were relatively crude, such that other, clearly and intentionally "Oriental" figures—standing before pagodas, wearing mandarin costumes, sporting Qing-style mustaches, and the like—nonetheless lack the more careful detailing and refined shaping of van Meurs's prints.

129 See Eikelmann, *Wittelsbacher,* 264–269; and Pelka, *Ostasiatische Reisebilder,* 52–23 and plates 71–76. The wall panels suffered damage in World War II and were subsequently removed from earlier settings, yet archival material confirms their prior use in more domestic (as opposed to stately) contexts. The intensively dark ground of the textiles suggests a design meant to imitate lacquer: deep black with reds, greens, and gold. The panel that bears the two caning motifs also includes one of the cangue vignettes, confirming that the designer, by intent, presented scenes of exotic violence.

130 Bedroom design and alcoholic paraphernalia had vastly different contexts and meanings, needless to say, in premodern Europe. The room in the Residenz that housed the wall coverings had a more public role than a modern bedroom, retaining some manner of political function. That said, it was among the smaller rooms of the Residenz and designed to offer some degree of refuge from affairs of state. Drinking paraphernalia had long been associated with a rich history of rituals, some of which may have related to violence (e.g., hunting). It seems important, all the same, to note the form of these particular scenes of violence: distinctly *exotic* motifs.

131 On early modern "mass" consumption, particularly as it pertains to global objects, see Bermingham, "Consumption of Culture"; Vries, "Luxury";

Vries, *Industrious Revolution*; and McCants, "Exotic Goods."

132 Kaempfer, *Amoenitatum exoticarum*; van der Aa, *Galerie agreable.*

EPILOGUE

Epigraphs: *Catalogue of the Portland Museum,* iv. Note that those persons who may prefer "order and method" also fall under the rubric of "true Lover[s] of Science": the distinction is thus between a majority that loves exotic variety and a minority of *cognoscenti*—namely, enlightened men of "science."

Translator's preface, in Bernard, *Ceremonies and religious customs,* 4:ii (emphasis added). The anonymous translator identifies himself merely as "A Gentleman some time since of St. John's College in Oxford"—someone who allies himself with the ranks of the learned, in other words, or what the author of the Portland Museum catalogue might call a *cognoscente.*

1 Kaempfer, *Amoenitatum exoticarum politico-physico-medicarum fasciculi V* [Five fascicles of exotic pleasures regarding politics, physics, and medicine]; and Johnson, *Prefaces,* 4:4 ("Preface" for John Hughes). See also Knellwolf, "Exotic Frontier," which notes how "the exotic became associated with the sensual appeal of faroff, mainly tropical, climes only during the eighteenth century" (10).

2 The full title of the Latin compendium published by Charles de l'Écluse (better known by his Latin name Clusius) indicates its thoroughly natural-historical interests: *Exoticorum libri decem, quibus animalium, plantarum, aromatum, aliorumque peregrinorum fructuum historiae describuntur* [Ten books of exotica: the history and uses of animals, plants, aromatics and other natural products from distant lands]. The book was printed in Leiden in 1605 by the atelier of Raphelengius (heirs of Frans van Ravelingen). See further Egmond, *World of Carolus Clusius*; and Ommen, *Exotic World of Carolus Clusius.*

3 *Ladies amusement,* 3–4 and passim. Note that variants of the word *chinoiserie* were also entering the contemporary vocabulary of design: an inventory of 1715 speaks of a "bureau de marquetterie les figures ala [*sic*] chinoisses." See Eikelmann, *Wittelsbacher,* 259.

4 *Catalogue of the Portland Museum,* iii–iv, which speaks both to the exotic objects and to their display; and see also the comments of Mary Delany ("agreeable confusion"), who visited the Portland collection, in Delany, *Autobiography and Correspondence,* 4:238 (also cited in Sloboda, "Displaying Materials").

Note that the objects collected by the Duchess of Portland were predominantly material arts of exotic disposition and *naturalia* extracted from the exotic world.

5 Montagu (still known as Elizabeth Robinson, yet months from her marriage to Edward Montagu) cited in Sloboda, "Displaying Materials," 463; Montesquieu, *Persian Letters*, 20; and William Temple, "Upon the Gardens of Epicurus," in *Miscellanea. The Second Part* (London, 1690), 58. See also the comments of the French Jesuit priest and painter Father Attiret, who described the great gardens he had seen in China (in 1743) as "a beautiful disorder": Baltrušaitis, *Jardins en France*, 23. And compare, only slightly later in the century, the observation by Louis-Antoine, Comte de Bougainville of the "beautiful disorder" he witnessed in the tropical islands of the Pacific (in the 1760s): Bougainville, *Voyage*, 244–245.

6 *Catalogue of the Portland Museum*, iv. Note that "Methodist" had at least two meanings that pertain to its usage in the Portland catalogue. On the one hand, the term was used in natural history for those who (as the word implies) favored the organization of species according to a particular schema or method; on the other hand, it implied a methodical or even precisionist approach, more broadly, to matters of organization and design.

7 Du Halde, *Description geographique*, "Preface" (n.p.); and see also "Translator's Preface," in Du Halde, *Description of the Empire*.

8 Johann Gaspar Scheuchzer, "Introduction by the Translator," in Kaempfer, *History of Japan*, (n.p.); and see also the "Author's Preface" (n.p.), which conveys a similar sentiment. On Scheuchzer—of an illustriously learned Zurich family—see Beer, "Johann Gaspar Scheuchzer."

9 *Ceremonies and religious customs*, ii.

10 Heller, "Linnaeus on Sumptuous Books."

11 Mandeville, *Travels*, 14 and passim.

12 "To the Reader," in Olearius, *Voyages & travels*, where Olearius notes, as well, how geography "instructs . . . efficaciously." Compare the perfect distillation of geography's dual agenda in a comment by John Locke, who observed—in the context of reading Holland-made sources—that the genre comprised "a very good mixture of delight and usefulness": Locke, *Thoughts Concerning Education*, Appendix, 324 (cited in Carey, "Travel").

13 Rochefort, *History of the Caribby-Islands*, 50; see also Sloboda, "Displaying Materials," 463 ("cunning confusion").

14 *Catalogue of the Portland Museum*, iv.

15 Rumphius, *Herbarium Amboinense*, Preface (n.p.). The Dutch version speaks of "onvolmaakte Chaos"—namely, incomplete or imperfect chaos. Note that, although their publication dates lie deep in the eighteenth century, Rumphius's comments were penned no later than the 1690s. See Rumphius, *Ambonese Curiosity Cabinet*, lxxx–lxxxi, which details the volumes' preparation and also discusses, inter alia, the "digestion" by Rumphius of exotica. See also Scheuchzer, "Introduction by the Translator," ("digressions") in Kaempfer, *History of Japan* (n.p.); and Bernard, *Ceremonies and religious customs*, 4:ii, which clarifies the proper—"methodical"—digestion of textual exotica.

16 Kaempfer, "Author's Preface," in *History of Japan*, ii.

17 "Translator's Preface," in *Description of the Empire*, 1:ii.

18 This moment, of course, is the Saidian moment described in *Orientalism* and discussed in this book's Introduction. His many critics notwithstanding, Said is surely correct to speak of the development of ideological "Orientalism," particularly in English and French texts, from the middle of the eighteenth century. He misses, however, the prehistory of this moment, as established in sources of exotic geography from ca. 1670–1730. Studies that focus on the ample production of imperial exoticism, particularly in this post-1750 moment, include (along with Said, *Orientalism*) Ogborn, *Indian Ink* (on England and print); Grigsby, *Extremities* (on France and painting); and Brückner, *Geographic Revolution* (on the United States and maps).

19 *Ladies amusement*, 4.

20 *Charles Vere At the Indian King, The Corner of Salisbury Court, Fleetstreet No. 81, London* (1772); on which see Eaton, "Nostalgia for the Exotic."

21 McClellan, "Watteau's Dealer"; and Glorieux, *À l'Enseigne de Gersaint*, which points out just how much of Gersaint stock comprised objects of "exotic" flavor (in terms of both materials and motifs).

22 An aesthetic of exoticism and an aesthetic of pleasure could also blend with an aesthetic of enlightenment, of course: see Kavanagh, *Enlightened Pleasures*.

[BIBLIOGRAPHY]

Aa, Pieter van der. *Atlas nouveau et curieux des plus celebres itineraires.* 2 vols. Leiden: Pieter van der Aa, ca. 1714.

———. *L'atlas soulagé de son gros & pesant fardeau.* Leiden: Pieter van der Aa, ca. 1700.

———. *La galerie agreable du monde.* 66 parts. Leiden: Pieter van der Aa, ca. 1729.

———. *De gedenkwaardige West-Indise voyagien, gedaan door Christoffel Columbus, Americus Vesputius, en Lodewijck Hennepin.* Leiden: Pieter van der Aa, 1704.

———. *Grand theatre historique, ou Nouvelle histoire universelle tant sacrée que profane.* 5 vols. Leiden: Pieter van der Aa, ca. 1703.

———. *Naaukeurige versameling der gedenk-waardigste zee en land reysen na Oost en West-Indien.* 28 vols. Leiden: Pieter van der Aa, 1707–1708.

———. *Nouveau petit atlas, ou Nouvelles cartes géographiques.* 3 parts Leiden: Pieter van der Aa, ca. 1710.

———. *Le nouveau theatre du monde, ou La geographie royale.* Leiden: Pieter van der Aa, 1713.

———. *Nouvel atlas, très-exact et fort commode pour toutes sortes de personnes, contenant les principales cartes geographiques.* Leiden: Pieter van der Aa, 1714.

Ackerman, James S. "Early Renaissance 'Naturalism' and Scientific Illustration." In *The Natural Sciences and the Arts: Aspects of Interaction from the Renaissance to the Twentieth Century*, ed. Allan Ellenius. Stockholm: Almqvist and Wiksell International, 1985.

Aken-Fehmers, Marion S. van, et al. *Delfts aardewerk: Geschiedenis van een nationaal product.* 4 vols. Zwolle: Waanders; The Hague: Gemeentemuseum Den Haag, 1999–2007.

Alden, John, and Dennis Landis, eds. *European Americana: A Chronological Guide to Works Printed in Europe Relating to the Americas, 1493–1776.* 6 vols. Providence: John Carter Brown Library; New York: Readex Books, 1980–1997.

Allard, Carel. *Orbis habitabilis oppida et vestitus, centenario numero complexa* [...] *Des bewoonden waerelds steden en dragten, in een honderd-getal begreepen.* Amsterdam: Carel Allard, ca. 1685.

Alpers, Svetlana. *The Art of Describing: Dutch Art in the Seventeenth Century.* Chicago: University of Chicago Press, 1983.

———. "The Mapping Impulse in Dutch Art." In *Art and Cartography: Six Historical Essays*, ed. David Woodward, 51–96. Chicago: University of Chicago Press, 1987.

Anderson, Benedict. *Imagined Communities: Reflections on the Origin and Spread of Nationalism.* Rev. ed. London: Verso, 2006.

Apianus, Petrus. *Cosmographicus liber* (1524). Rev. ed. Antwerp: Arnold Birckman, 1533.

Asad, Talal. "Muslims and European Identity: Can Europe Represent Islam?" In *The Idea of Europe: From Antiquity to the European Union*, ed. Anthony Pagden, 209–227. Cambridge: Cambridge University Press, 2002.

———. "On Torture, or Cruel, Inhuman, and Degrading Treatment." *Social Research* 63, no. 4 (1996): 1081–1109.

Atkins, John. *A Voyage to Guinea, Brazil, and the West-Indies.* London: Caesar Ward and Richard Chandler, 1735.

Baadj, Nadia Sera. "'Monstrous Creatures and Diverse Strange Things': The Curious Art of Jan van Kessel the Elder (1626–1679)." Ph.D. dissertation, University of Michigan, 2012.

———. "A World of Materials in a Cabinet Without Drawers: Re-framing Jan van Kessel's *The Four Parts of the World.*" In *Meaning in Materials: Netherlandish Art, 1400–1800,* ed. H. Perry Chapman, Ann-Sophie Lehmann, and Frits Scholten, 202-237. Nederlands Kunsthistorisch Jaarboek, 62. Leiden: Brill, 2013.

Baggerman, Arianne. *Een drukkend gewicht: Leven en werk van de zeventiende-eeuwse veelschrijver Simon de Vries.* Amsterdam: Rodopi, 1993.

Bailey, Gauvin Alexander. "'Le style jésuite n'existe pas': Jesuit Corporate Culture and the Visual Arts." In *The Jesuits: Cultures, Sciences, and the Arts, 1540–1773,* ed. John O'Malley et al., 38–89. Toronto: University of Toronto Press, 1999.

Baldaeus, Philip. *Naauwkeurige beschryvinge van Malabar en Choromandel, der zelver aangrenzende ryken, en het machtige eyland Ceylon: nevens een omstandige en grondigh doorzochte ontdekking en wederlegginge van de afgoderye der Oost-Indische heydenen.* Amsterdam: Johannes van Someren and Johannes Janssonius van Waesberge, 1672.

———. *A true and exact description of the most celebrated East-India coasts of Malabar and Coromandel; as also of the Isle of Ceylon.* In Churchill, *Collection of voyages,* 3:563–901.

Baltrušaitis, Jurgis. *Jardins en France, 1760–1820.* Paris: Caisse National des Monuments Historiques et des Sites, 1978.

Barber, Peter, and Tom Harper. *Magnificent Maps: Power, Propaganda and Art.* London: British Library Publishing, 2010.

Barkey, Karen. *Empire of Difference: The Ottomans in Comparative Perspective.* Cambridge: Cambridge University Press, 2008.

Barlaeus, Caspar. *Rerum per octennium in Brasilia et alibi nuper gestarum, sub praefectura illustrissimi Comitis I. Mauritii, Nassoviae, &c.* Amsterdam: Ioannis Blaeu, 1647.

Barthes, Roland. "Le monde-objet." In *Essais critiques,* 19–28. Paris: Seuil, 1964.

Beekman, E. M., ed. and trans. *Fugitive Dreams: An Anthology of Dutch Colonial Literature.* Amherst: University of Massachusetts Press, 1988.

Beer, G. R. de. "Johann Gaspar Scheuchzer, F.R.S., 1702–1729." *Notes and Records of the Royal Society of London* 6 (Dec. 1948): 56–66.

Behn, Aphra. *Oroonoko* (1688). Ed. Joanna Lipking. New York: W. W. Norton, 1997.

———. *The Widdow Ranter or, The history of Bacon in Virginia.* London: James Knapton, 1690.

Bekker, Balthasar. *De betoverde weereld.* 4 vols. Amsterdam: Daniel van den Dalen, 1691–1693.

Benjamin, Walter. "The Work of Art in the Age of Mechanical Reproduction." In *Illuminations: Essays and Reflections,* ed. Hannah Arendt, trans. Harry Zohn. New York: Schocken, 1968.

Benton, Lauren. *A Search for Sovereignty: Law and Geography in European Empires, 1400–1900.* New York: Cambridge University Press, 2010.

Berg, Maxine. "In Pursuit of Luxury: Global History and British Consumer Goods in the Eighteenth Century." *Past and Present* 182 (Feb. 2004): 85–142.

Berg, Maxine, and Elizabeth Eger, eds. *Luxury in the Eighteenth Century: Debates, Desires and Delectable Goods.* Basingstoke: Palgrave Macmillan, 2002.

Berger, Shlomo. "An Invitation to Buy and Read: Paratexts of Yiddish Books in Amsterdam, 1650–1800." *Book History* 7 (2004): 31–61.

Bergvelt, Ellinoor, and Renée Kistemaker, eds. *De wereld binnen handbereik: Nederlandse kunst- en rariteitenverzamelingen, 1585–1735.* 2 vols. Zwolle: Waanders, 1992.

Berkvens-Stevelinck, C. M. G., et al. *Le Magasin de l'Univers: The Dutch Republic as the Centre of the European Book Trade.* Leiden: E. J. Brill, 1992.

Bermingham, Anne. "The Consumption of Culture: Image, Object, Text." In *The Consumption of Culture, 1600–1800: Image, Object, Text,* ed. Anne Bermingham and John Brewer, 1–20. London: Routledge, 1995.

Bernand, Carmen, and Serge Gruzinski. "La redécouverte de l'Amérique." *L'homme* 32, nos. 122–124 (April–Dec. 1992): 7–35.

Bernard, Jean-Frédéric, and Bernard Picart. *The ceremonies and religious customs of the various nations of the known world.* 6 vols. London: William Jackson and Claude Dubosc, 1733–1737.

———. *Ceremonies et coutumes religieuses des tous les peuples du monde.* 8 vols. Amsterdam: J. F. Bernard, 1723–1743.

Bernasconi, Robert, and Tommy Lee Lott, eds. *The Idea of Race*. Indianapolis, IN: Hackett, 2000.

Bernier, François. "Nouvelle division de la terre, par les différentes espèces ou races d'hommes qu habitent, envoyée par un fameux voyageur à M. l'Abbé de la ***** à peu prés en ces termes." *Journal des Sçavans* 12 (24 April 1684): 133–140.

Betteridge, Tom. *Sodomy in Early Modern Europe*. Manchester: Manchester University Press, 2002.

Beverley, Robert. *The history and present state of Virginia, in four parts* (1705). 2nd ed., rev. and enl. London: B. and S. Tooke, 1722.

Bindman, David, and Henry Louis Gates, Jr., eds. *The Image of the Black in Western Art: From the "Age of Discovery" to the Age of Abolition*. Part 1: Artists of the Renaissance and Baroque. Cambridge, MA: Harvard University Press, 2010.

Bisaha, Nancy. *Creating East and West: Renaissance Humanists and the Ottoman Turks*. Philadelphia: University of Pennsylvania Press, 2004.

Blackburn, Robin. *The Making of New World Slavery: From the Baroque to the Modern, 1492–1800*. London: Verso, 1997.

Blaeu, Joan. *Atlas major*. Amsterdam: Joan Blaeu, 1662–1672.

Bleys, Rudi. *The Geography of Perversion: Male-to-Male Sexual Behavior Outside the West and the Ethnographic Imagination, 1750–1918*. New York: New York University Press, 1995.

Blom, Frans. "Picturing New Netherland and New York: Dutch-Anglo Transfer of New World Information." In *The Dutch Trading Companies as Knowledge Networks*, ed. Siegfried Huigen, Jan L. de Jong, and Elmer Kolfin, 103–126. Leiden: Brill, 2010.

Blussé, Leonard, and R. Falkenburg, eds. *Johan Nieuhofs beelden van een Chinareis, 1655–1657*. Middelburg: Stichting VOC, 1987.

Bodart-Bailey, Beatrice M., ed. and trans. *Kaempfer's Japan: Tokugawa Culture Observed*. Honolulu: University of Hawaii Press, 1999.

Bogaert, Abraham. *Historische reizen door d'oostersche deelen van Asia*. Amsterdam: Nicolaas ten Hoorn, 1711.

Bok, Marten Jan. "European Artists in the Service of the Dutch East India Company." In *Mediating Netherlandish Art and Material Culture in Asia*, ed. Thomas DaCosta Kaufmann and Michael North. Amsterdam: Amsterdam University Press, 2014.

Boogaart, Ernst van den. "Books on Black Africa: The Dutch Publications and Their Owners in the Sev-enteenth and Eighteenth Centuries." *Paideuma: Mitteilungen zur Kulturkunde* 33 (1987): 115–126.

———. *Het verheven en verdorven Azië: Woord en beeld in het* Itinerario *en de* Icones *van Jan Huygen van Linschoten*. Amsterdam: Het Spinhuis, 2000.

Boogaart, Ernst van den, Hendrik Richard Hoetink, and Peter James Palmer Whitehead. *Johan Maurits van Nassau-Siegen, 1604–1679: A Humanist Prince in Europe and Brazil*. The Hague: Johan Maurits van Nassau Stichting, 1979.

Borris, Kenneth, and G. S. Rousseau, eds. *The Sciences of Homosexuality in Early Modern Europe*. New York: Routledge, 2007.

Bosman, Willem. *Nauwkeurige beschryving van de Guinese Goud- Tand- en Slave-Kust: nevens alle desselfs landen, koningryken, en gemenebesten, van de zeeden der inwoonders, hun godsdienst, regeering, regtspleeging, oorlogen, trouwen, begraven, enz.* Utrecht: Anthony Schouten, 1704.

———. *A new and accurate description of the coast of Guinea, divided into the Gold, the Slave, and the Ivory Coasts*. London: James Knapton et alia, 1705.

Boswell, James. *The Life of Samuel Johnson* (1768). 2 vols. New York: George Dearborn, 1837.

Boterbloem, Kees. *The Fiction and Reality of Jan Struys: A Seventeenth-Century Dutch Globetrotter*. Basingstoke: Palgrave Macmillan, 2008.

———. " 'Met een beschaafder Penne . . . ': The Making of *Drie aanmerkelijke en seer rampspoedige reysen*: A Case of Early-Modern Ghostwriting." *Jaarboek voor Nederlandse Boekgeschiedenis* 15 (2008): 34–50.

Bougainville, Louis-Antoine, Comte de. *A voyage round the world*. Trans. John Reinhold Forster. London: J. Nourse, 1772.

Boulle, Pierre H. "François Bernier and the Origins of the Modern Concept of Race." In *The Color of Liberty: Histories of Race in France*, ed. Sue Peabody and Tyler Stovall, 11–27. Durham, NC: Duke University Press, 2003.

Bourgon, Jérôme. "Chinese Executions: Visualising Their Differences with European Supplices." *European Journal of East Asian Studies* 2, no. 1 (2003): 153–184.

Bourguet, Marie-Noëlle, Christian Licoppe, and Heinz Otto Sibum, eds. *Instruments, Travel and Science: Itineraries of Precision from the Seventeenth to the Twentieth Century*. London: Routledge, 2002.

Bowers, J. Z., and R. W. Carrubba. "Drug Abuse and Sexual Binding Spells in Seventeenth-Century Asia: Essays from the *Amoenitatum Exoticarum* of

Engelbert Kaempfer." *Journal of the History of Medicine and Allied Sciences* 33 (July 1978): 318–343.

Boym, Michael. *Flora Sinensis*. Vienna: M. Rictius, 1656.

Brancaforte, Elio Christoph. *Visions of Persia: Mapping the Travels of Adam Olearius*. Cambridge, MA: Harvard University Press, 2003.

Braun, Georg, and Frans Hogenberg. *Civitates orbis terrarum*. 6 vols. Cologne: Apud P. Gallaeum, 1572–1617.

Bremer-David, Charissa. "Six Tapestries from *L'histoire de l'empereur de la Chine*." In *French Tapestries and Textiles in the J. Paul Getty Museum*, 80–97. Los Angeles: J. Paul Getty Museum, 1997.

Brienen, Rebecca Parker. *Visions of Savage Paradise: Albert Eckhout, Court Painter in Colonial Dutch Brazil*. Amsterdam: Amsterdam University Press, 2006.

Brockey, Liam Matthew. *Journey to the East: The Jesuit Mission to China, 1579–1724*. Cambridge, MA: Harvard University Press, 2007.

Brook, Timothy, Jérôme Bourgon, and Gregory Blue. *Death by a Thousand Cuts*. Cambridge, MA: Harvard University Press, 2008.

Brown, Bill. "Thing Theory." *Critical Inquiry* 28 (2001): 1–22.

Brückner, Martin. *The Geographic Revolution in Early America: Maps, Literacy, and National Identity*. Chapel Hill: University of North Carolina Press, 2006.

Bruijn, Cornelis de. *Aanmerkingen over de printverbeeldingen van de overblyfzelen van het oude Persepolis, onlangs uitgegeven door de Heeren Chardin en Kempfer, waer in derzelver mistekeningen en gebreken klaer worden aengewezen*. Amsterdam: R. and G. Wetstein, J. Oosterwyk, and H. van de Gaate, 1714.

———. *Cornelis de Bruins Reizen over Moskovie, door Persie en Indie: verrykt met driehondert konstplaten, vertoonende de beroemste lanttschappen en steden, ook de byzondere dragten, beesten, gewassen en planten, die daer gevonden worden: voor al derzelver oudheden, en wel voornamentlyk heel vitvoerig die van het heerlyke en van oudts geheele werrelt door befaemde Hof van Persepolis, by de Persianen Tilulminar genaemt*. Amsterdam: Willem and David Goeree, 1711.

———. *Reizen van Cornelis de Bruyn, door de vermaardste deelen van Klein Asia, de eylanden Scio, Rhodus, Cyprus, Metelino, Stanchio, &tc mitsgaders de voornaamste steden van Egypten, Syrien en Palestina, verrijkt met meer als 200. kopere konstplaaten, vertoonende de beroemdste landschappen, steden, &tc*. Delft: H. van Krooneveld, 1698.

———. *Travels into Muscovy, Persia, and part of the East-Indies*. 2 vols. London: A. Bettesworth et al., 1737.

———. *Voyage au Levant, c'est à dire dans les principaux endroits de l'Asie Mineure, dans les isles de Chio, de Rhodes, de Chypre &c. De même que dans les plus considerables villes d'Egypte, de Syrie, et de la Terre Sainte; enrichi de plus de deux cens taillesdouces*. Delft: Henri de Kroonevelt, 1700.

———. *A Voyage to the Levant: or, Travels in the principal parts of Asia Minor, the islands of Scio, Rhodes, Cyprus, &tc*. London: Jacob Tonson and Thomas Bennet, 1702.

Bruijn, Jaap R., and Femme S. Gaastra. "The Dutch East India Company's Shipping, 1602–1795, in a Comparative Perspective." In *Ships, Sailors and Spices: East India Companies and their Shipping in the 16th, 17th and 18th Century*, ed. Jaap R. Bruijn and Femme S. Gaastra, 177–208. NEHA-Series III, no. 20. Amsterdam: NEHA, 1993.

Brummett, Palmira, ed. *The "Book" of Travels: Genre, Ethnology, and Pilgrimage, 1250–1700*. Leiden: Brill, 2009.

Bry, Theodor de. *Collectiones peregrinationum in Indiam Occidentalem et Indiam Orientalem, XXV partibus comprehensæ*. Frankfurt am Main: De Bry, 1590–1629.

Buvelot, Quentin, ed. *Albert Eckhout: A Dutch Artist in Brazil*. The Hague: Royal Cabinet of Paintings Mauritshuis, 2004.

Cañizares-Esguerra, Jorge. *Puritan Conquistadors: Iberianizing the Atlantic, 1550–1700*. Stanford, CA: Stanford University Press, 2006.

Carey, Daniel. "Travel, Geography, and the Problem of Belief: Locke as a Reader of Travel Literature." In *History and Nation*, ed. Julia Rudolph, 97–136. Lewisburg, PA: Bucknell University Press, 2006.

Caron, François. *Rechte beschryvinge van het machtigh Koninghrijck van Iappan, bestaende in verscheyde vragen, betreffende des selfs regiering, coophandel, maniere van leven, strenge justitie &c*. The Hague: Johannes Tongerloo, 1661.

Caron, François, and Joost Schouten. *A True Description of the Mighty Kingdoms of Japan and Siam* (1663). Ed. C. R. Boxer. London: Argonaut Press, 1935.

Carrillo Castillo, Jesús. "'The World Is Only One and Not Many': Representations of the Natural World in Imperial Spain." In *Spain in the Age of Exploration, 1492–1819*, ed. Chiyo Ishikawa, 139–157. Seattle: Seattle Art Museum, 2004.

A catalogue of the Portland Museum, lately the property of the Duchess Dowager of Portland, deceased: Which will be sold by auction, by Mr. Skinner and Co. on Monday the 24th of April, 1786 . . . [London, 1786].

Catesby, Mark. *The natural history of Carolina, Florida, and the Bahama Islands. Containing the figures of birds, beasts, fishes serpents, insects, and plants.* 2 vols. London: M. Catesby, 1731–1743.

Cats, Jacob. *Invallende gedachten op voorvallenden gelegentheden.* Amsterdam: J. J. Schipper, 1655.

Cavanaugh, Alden, and Michael Yonan, eds. *The Cultural Aesthetics of Eighteenth-Century Porcelain.* Farnham, Surrey: Ashgate, 2010.

Chardin, John [Jean]. *Voyages de Monsieur le Chevalier Chardin, en Perse, et autres lieux de l'Orient.* 3 vols. Amsterdam: Jean Louis de Lorme, 1711.

Chartier, Roger. "Crossing Borders in Early Modern Europe: Sociology of Texts and Literature." *Book History* 8 (2005): 37–50.

———. *Forms and Meanings: Texts, Performances, and Audiences from the Codex to the Computer.* Philadelphia: University of Pennsylvania Press, 1995.

———. "Genre Between Literature and History." *Modern Language Quarterly* 67 (March 2006): 129–139.

———. *The Order of Books: Readers, Authors, and Libraries in Europe Between the Fourteenth and Eighteenth Centuries.* Trans. Lydia G. Cochrane. Stanford, CA: Stanford University Press, 1994.

Chen, Bianca. "Digging for Antiquities with Diplomats: Gisbert Cuper (1644–1716) and his Social Capital." *Republics of Letters: A Journal for the Study of Knowledge, Politics, and the Arts* 1, no. 1 (1 May 2009). Available at http://rofl.stanford.edu/node/36.

Churchill, Awnsham, and John Churchill, eds. *A collection of voyages and travels.* 6 vols. London: Awnsham and John Churchill, 1704 [vols. 1–4] and 1732 [vols. 5–6].

Chytraeus, David. *De ratione discendi, et ordine studiorum in singulis artibus recte instituendo.* Wittenberg [s.n.], 1564.

Clark, Stuart. *Vanities of the Eye: Vision in Early Modern European Culture.* Oxford: Oxford University Press, 2007.

Clarke, T. H. *The Rhinoceros from Dürer to Stubbs, 1515–1799.* London: Sotheby's Publications, 1986.

Clunas, Craig. *Pictures and Visuality in Early Modern China.* London: Reaktion, 1997.

Clusius, Carolus. *Exoticorum libri decem, quibus animalium, plantarum, aromatum, aliorumque peregrinorum fructuum historiae describuntur.* [Leiden]: Raphelengius, 1605.

Cohen, Jeffrey Jerome. "Pilgrimages, Travel Writing, and the Medieval Exotic." In *The Oxford Handbook of Medieval Literature in English*, ed. Elaine Treharne and Greg Walker, 611–628. Oxford: Oxford University Press, 2010.

Columbus, Christopher. *The Diario of Christopher Columbus's First Voyage to America, 1492–1493.* Trans. and ed. Oliver Dunn and James E. Kelley, Jr. Norman: University of Oklahoma Press, 1989.

———. *The Four Voyages: Being His Own Log-Book, Letters and Dispatches with Connecting Narratives.* Ed. J. M. Cohen. Harmondsworth: Penguin, 1969; reprint ed., 1992.

———. *Select Documents Illustrating the Four Voyages of Columbus.* Trans. and ed. Cecil Jane, Works issued by the Hakluyt Society, 2nd ser., no. 65 and 70. London: Hakluyt Society, 1930–1933.

Comenius, Johann Amos. *Orbis sensualium pictus, hoc est Omnium fundamentalium in mundo rerum, et in vita actionum, pictura et nomenclatura.* Nuremberg: Michael Endter, 1658.

Cook, Harold J. *Matters of Exchange: Commerce, Medicine, and Science in the Dutch Golden Age.* New Haven, CT: Yale University Press, 2007.

Cooper, Alix. *Inventing the Indigenous: Local Knowledge and Natural History in Early Modern Europe.* New York: Cambridge University Press, 2007.

Cooper, Frederick, and Ann Laura Stoler, eds. *Tensions of Empire: Colonial Cultures in a Bourgeois World.* Berkeley: University of California Press, 1997.

Corrêa do Lago, Bia. *Frans Post e o Brasil Holandês na coleção do Instituto Ricardo Brennand = Frans Post and Dutch Brazil in the collection of Instituto Ricardo Brennand.* Recife: Instituto Ricardo Brennand, 2003.

Corrêa do Lago, Pedro, and Bia Corrêa do Lago. *Frans Post, 1612–1680: Catalogue Raisonné.* Milan: 5 Continents, 2007.

Cortes, Adriano de las. *Le voyage en Chine d'Adriano de las Cortes s.j. (1625).* Ed. Pascale Girard, trans. Pascale Girard and Juliette Monbeig. Paris: Chandeigne, 2001.

Cortés, Hernán. *Letters from Mexico.* Trans. and ed. Anthony Pagden. New Haven, CT: Yale University Press, 2001.

Cosgrove, Denis. *Apollo's Eye: A Cartographic Genealogy of the Earth in the Western Imagination.* Baltimore: John Hopkins University Press, 2001.

Court, Pieter de la. *Interest van Holland, ofte Gronden van Hollands-welvaren.* Amsterdam: Joan. Cyprianus vander Gracht, 1662. Rev. ed. [*Aanwysing der heilsame politike gronden en maximen van de republike van Holland*]. Leiden: Hakkens, 1669.

Covens, Johannes, and Cornelis Mortier. *Atlas nouveau, contenants toutes les parties du monde.* Amsterdam: Covens and Mortier, 1730.

Cox, Edward Godfrey. *A Reference Guide to the Literature of Travel: Including Voyages, Geographical Descriptions, Adventures, Shipwrecks and Expeditions.* 4 vols. Seattle: University of Washington Press, 1935.

Curl, James Stevens. "Sharawadgi." In *A Dictionary of Architecture and Landscape Architecture.* 2000 (accessed online at Encyclopedia.com, 11 January 2011).

Curtis, Neal. "'As If': Situating the Pictorial Turn." *Culture, Theory and Critique* 50 (2009): 95–101.

———, ed. *The Pictorial Turn.* New York: Routledge, 2010.

Dackerman, Susan. "Dürer's Indexical Fantasy: The Rhinoceros and Printmaking." In *Prints and the Pursuit of Knowledge in Early Modern Europe*, ed. Susan Dackerman, 164–171. Cambridge, MA: Harvard Art Museums; New Haven, CT: Yale University Press, 2011.

Dam, Jan Daniël van. *Delffse porceleyne: Dutch delftware, 1620–1850.* Trans. Lynne Richards. Zwolle: Waanders; Amsterdam: Rijksmuseum, 2004.

Dantzig, Albert van. "Willem Bosman's 'New and Accurate Description of the Coast of Guinea': How Accurate Is It?" *History in Africa* 1 (1974): 101–108.

Dapper, Olfert. *Asia: of Naukeurige beschryving van het rijk des Grooten Mogols, en een groote gedeelte van Indiën [. . .] beneffens een volkome beschryving van geheel Persie, Georgie, Mengrelie en andere gebuur-gewesten.* Amsterdam: Jacob van Meurs, 1672.

———. *Gedenkwaerdig bedryf der Nederlandsche Oost-Indische Maetschappye, op de kuste en in het keizerrijk van Taising of Sina.* Amsterdam: Jacob van Meurs, 1670.

———. *Naukeurige beschrijvinge der Afrikaensche gewesten, van Egypten, Barbaryen, Libyen, Biledulgerid, Negroslant, Guinea, Ethiopien, Abyssinie getrokken uit verscheyde hedendaegse lantbeschryvers en geschriften van bereidse onderzoekers dier landen.* Amsterdam: Jacob van Meurs, 1668.

———. *Naukeurige beschryving der eilanden, in de Archipel der Middelantsche Zee.* Amsterdam: Wolfgang, Waesberge, Boom, Someren and Goethals, 1688.

———. *Naukeurige beschryving van gantsch Syrie, en Palestyn of Heilige Lant.* Amsterdam: Jacob van Meurs, 1677.

Darnton, Robert. *The Business of Enlightenment: A Publishing History of the Encyclopédie, 1775–1800.* Cambridge, MA: Harvard University Press, 1979.

Daston, Lorraine, and Katharine Park. *Wonders and the Order of Nature, 1150–1750.* New York: Zone Books, 1998.

Davids, Karel. "Amsterdam as a Center of Learning in the Dutch Golden Age, c. 1580–1700." In O'Brien et al., *Urban Achievement*, 305–323.

Defoe, Daniel. *A plan of the English commerce: Being a compleat prospect of the trade of this nation, as well the home trade as the foreign.* London: Charles Rivington, 1728.

Delany, Mary Granville Pendarves. *The Autobiography and Correspondence of Mary Granville, Mrs. Delany.* Ed. Augusta Waddington Hall, Lady Llanover, 6 vols. (1861–1862). Repr., New York: AMS Press, 1974.

Dew, Nicholas. "Reading Travels in the Culture of Curiosity: Thévenot's Collection of Voyages." *Journal of Early Modern History* 10 (2006): 39–59.

Dickenson, Victoria. *Drawn from Life: Science and Art in the Portrayal of the New World.* Toronto: University of Toronto Press, 1998.

Donaldson, Ian. "Samuel Johnson and the Art of Observation." *ELH [English Literary History]* 53 (1986): 779–799.

Drijvers, Jan Willem. "Cornelis de Bruijn and Gijsbert Cuper: A Skilled Artist and a Learned Discussion." In Sancisi-Weerdenburg and Drijvers, *Through Travellers' Eyes*, 89–107.

Drijvers, Jan Willem, Jan de Hond, and Heleen Sancisi-Weerdenburg, eds. *"Ik hadde de nieusgierigheid": De reizen door het Nabije Oosten van Cornelis de Bruijn (ca. 1652–1727).* Mededelingen en Verhandelingen Ex Oriente Lux, vol. 31. Leuven: Peeters, 1997.

Dryden, John. *The Works of John Dryden.* Vol. 12, ed. Vinton A. Dearing. Berkeley: University of California Press, 1994.

Du Halde, Jean-Baptiste. *Ausführliche Beschreibung des Chinesischen Reiches und der großen Tartarey.*

4 vols. Rostock: Johann Christian Koppe, 1747–1756.

———. *Description geographique, historique, chronologique, politique, et physique de l'empire de la Chine et de la Tartarie Chinoise.* 4 vols. Paris: P. G. Le Mercier, 1735.

———. *A description of the Empire of China and Chinese-Tartary, together with the Kingdoms of Korea and Tibet: Containing the geography and history (natural as well as civil) of those countries.* 2 vols. London: T. Gardner for Edward Cave, 1738–1741.

DuBois, Page. *Slaves and Other Objects.* Chicago: University of Chicago Press, 2003.

———. *Torture and Truth.* New York: Routledge, 1991.

Duran, Shimon ben Tsemach. *Sefer ha-Tashbets* [The Book of Tashbets]. Ed. Rabbi Meir Crescas. 3 parts. Amsterdam: Jochanan Levi Rofe, 1738–1741.

Earle, T. F., and K. J. P. Lowe, eds. *Black Africans in Renaissance Europe.* Cambridge: Cambridge University Press, 2005.

Eaton, Natasha. "Nostalgia for the Exotic: Creating an Imperial Art in London, 1750–1793." *Eighteenth-Century Studies* 39 (2006): 227–250.

Eco, Umberto. "Innovation and Repetition: Between Modern and Post-Modern Aesthetics." Special issue: The Moving Image, *Daedalus* 114 (Fall 1985): 161–184.

Eeghen, Isabella H. van. *De Amsterdamse boekhandel, 1680–1725.* 5 vols. Amsterdam: Scheltema & Holkema, 1960–1978.

———. "Arnoldus Montanus's Book on Japan." *Quaerendo* 2 (1972): 250–272.

Egmond, Florike. *The World of Carolus Clusius: Natural History in the Making, 1550–1610.* Perspectives in Economic and Social History, vol. 6. London: Pickering and Chatto, 2010.

Egmond, Florike, and Peter Mason. " 'These are People Who Eat Raw Fish': Contours of the Ethnographic Imagination in the Sixteenth Century." *Viator: Medieval and Renaissance Studies* 31 (2000): 311–360.

Eikelmann, Renate. *Die Wittelsbacher und das Reich der Mitte: 400 Jahre China und Bayern.* Munich: Hirmer, 2009.

Emerson, John. "Sir John Chardin." In *Encyclopaedia Iranica*, vol. 5 (1991–1992), 369–377.

Emmer, Pieter. *The Dutch Slave Trade, 1500–1850.* New York: Berghahn, 2006.

Emmer, Pieter, and Wim Klooster. "The Dutch Atlantic, 1600–1800: Expansion Without Empire." *Itinerario* 23, no. 2 (1999): 48–69.

Espir, Helen. *European Decoration on Oriental Porcelain, 1700–1830.* London: Jorge Welsh Books, 2005.

Evans, R. J. W., and Alexander Marr, eds. *Curiosity and Wonder from the Renaissance to the Enlightenment.* Aldershot: Ashgate, 2006.

Evelyn, John. *Sculptura: or, The history and art of chalcography, and engraving in copper* (1662). 2nd and rev. ed. London: J. Murray, 1769.

Exquemelin, Alexander. *De Americaensche zee-roovers.* Amsterdam: Jan ten Hoorn, 1678.

Fabian, Johannes. *Time and the Other: How Anthropology Makes Its Object.* New York: Columbia University Press, 1983.

Fanon, Frantz. *The Wretched of the Earth.* Trans. Richard Philcox. New York: Grove Press, 2004.

Farr, Patricia. *Sex, Botany and Empire: The Story of Carl Linnaeus and Joseph Banks.* New York: Columbia University Press, 2003.

Fernández-Armesto, Felipe. *Amerigo: The Man Who Gave His Name to America.* New York: Random House, 2007.

Ferrier, Ronald W., ed. *A Journey to Persia: Jean Chardin's Portrait of a Seventeenth-Century Empire.* London: I. B. Tauris, 1996.

Findlen, Paula. *Possessing Nature: Museums, Collecting, and Scientific Culture in Early Modern Italy.* Berkeley: University of California Press, 1994.

Fleischer, Alette. "The Company's Garden and the (Ex)change of Nature and Knowledge at Cape of Good Hope (1652–1700)." In Roberts, *Centres and Cycles*, 101–128.

Forrer, Kuniko. *François Halma (1653–1722): Een bio-bibliografisch onderzoek naar een boekverkoper tijdens de overgang van de zeventiende naar de achttiende eeuw.* Doctoraalscriptie [M.A. thesis], University of Amsterdam, 2005.

Foucault, Michel. *Discipline and Punish: The Birth of the Prison.* Trans. Alan Sheridan. New York: Pantheon, 1977.

———. "What Is an Author?" In Foucault, *Language, Counter-Memory, Practice: Selected Essays and Interviews*, ed. Donald F. Bouchard, 113–138. Ithaca, NY: Cornell University Press, 1977.

Franits, Wayne E. *Dutch Seventeenth-Century Genre Painting: Its Stylistic and Thematic Evolution.* New Haven, CT: Yale University Press, 2008.

———. *Paragons of Virtue: Women and Domesticity in Seventeenth-Century Dutch Art.* Cambridge: Cambridge University Press, 1995.

Freedberg, David. "Science, Commerce, and Art: Neglected Topics at the Junction of History and Art

History." In *Art in History/History in Art: Studies in Seventeenth-Century Dutch Culture*, ed. David Freedberg and Jan de Vries, 376–428. Santa Monica, CA: Getty Publications, 1991.

Frijhoff, Willem, and Marijke Spies. *Dutch Culture in a European Perspective*, vol. 1: *1650: Hard-Won Unity*. New York: Palgrave Macmillan, 2004.

Froude, James Anthony. "England's Forgotten Worthies." In *Short Studies on Great Subjects*, rev. ed., 4 vols. London: Longmans, Green, 1886–1888.

Fuller, Mary C. *Remembering the Early Modern Voyage: English Narratives in the Age of European Expansion*. New York: Palgrave Macmillan, 2008.

———. *Voyages in Print: English Travel to America, 1576–1624*. Cambridge: Cambridge University Press, 1995.

Gaskell, Ivan. "Tobacco, Social Deviance, and Dutch Art in the Seventeenth Century." In *Looking at Seventeenth-Century Dutch Art: Realism Reconsidered*, ed. Wayne Franits, 68–77. Cambridge: Cambridge University Press, 1997.

Gaudio, Michael. *Engraving the Savage: The New World and Techniques of Civilization*. Minneapolis: University of Minnesota Press, 2008.

———. "The Space of Idolatry: Reformation, Incarnation, and the Ethnographic Image." *Res* 41 (Spring 2002): 72–91.

Geerts, A. J. C. *Catalogue des livres japonais de feu M. le docteur A. J. C. Geerts*. Leiden: Brill, 1887.

Genette, Gérard. *Paratexts: Thresholds of Interpretation*. Trans. Jane E. Lewin. Cambridge: Cambridge University Press, 1997.

Gibbon, Edward. *The History of the Decline and Fall of the Roman Empire*. 6 vols. London: Strahan and Cadell, 1776–1789.

Ginzburg, Carlo. "Titian, Ovid, and Sixteenth-Century Codes for Erotic Illustration." In *Clues, Myths, and the Historical Method*, trans. John and Anne Tedeschi, 77–95. Baltimore: Johns Hopkins University Press, 1989.

Glorieux, Guillaume. *À l'Enseigne de Gersaint: Edme-François Gersaint, marchand d'art sur le Pont Notre-Dame (1694–1750)*. Paris: Editions Champ Vallon, 2002.

Gnirrep, Kees. "De intekenaren op de *Reizen door Klein Asia* 'van Cornelis de Bruijn (1698)." *Jaarboek voor Nederlandse Boekgeschiedenis* 8 (2001): 59–72.

———. *De Levant in kleur: Cornelis de Bruijn, Voyage au Levant (1700), een experimentele kleurendruk*. Amsterdam: Universiteitsbibliotheek, 1997.

Goedings, Truusje. "Kaartkleurders en de technische aspecten van het kleuren in de zestiende en zeventiende eeuw." In Heijbroek, *Kunst in kaart*, 95–129.

———. "Kunst- en kaartafzetters: Gekleurde prenten en kaarten." In Nierop, *Romeyn de Hooghe*, 204–221.

Goinga, Hannie van. "Schaduwbeelden: Vrouwen in het boekenvak in de vroegmoderne tijd: een nieuw terrein van onderzoek." *Jaarboek voor Nederlandse Boekgeschiedenis* 12 (2005): 13–28.

Good, Anne. "The Construction of an Authoritative Text: Peter Kolb's Description of the Khoikhoi at the Cape of Good Hope in the Eighteenth Century." *Journal of Early Modern History* 10 (2006): 61–94.

Gordon-Smith, Maria. "The Influence of Jean Pillement on French and English Decorative Arts Part Two: Representative Fields of Influence." *Artibus et Historiae* 21, no. 42 (2000): 119–163.

Greenblatt, Stephen J. *Marvelous Possessions: The Wonder of the New World*. Chicago: University of Chicago Press, 1991.

———. *Renaissance Self-Fashioning: From More to Shakespeare*. Chicago: University of Chicago Press, 1980.

Grigsby, Darcy Grimaldo. *Extremities: Painting Empire in Post-Revolutionary France*. New Haven, CT: Yale University Press, 2002.

Grigsby, Leslie. "Johan Nieuhoff's *Embassy*: An Inspiration for Relief Decoration on English Stoneware and Earthenware." *The Magazine Antiques* 143 (1993): 172–183.

Groesen, Michiel van. *The Representations of the Overseas World in the De Bry Collection of Voyages (1590–1634)*. Library of the Written Word, vol. 2. Leiden: Brill, 2008.

Groot, Erlend de. *The World of a Seventeenth-Century Collector: The Atlas Blaeu-Van der Hem*. 't Goy-Houten: HES & De Graaf, 2006.

Guy, Basil. " 'Ad Majorem Societatis Gloriam': Jesuit Perspectives on Chinese Mores in the Seventeenth and Eighteenth Centuries." In Porter and Rousseau, *Exoticism in the Enlightenment*, 66–85.

Hakluyt, Richard. *The principal navigations, voiages, traffiques and discoueries of the English nation, made by sea or overland . . . at any time within the compasse of these 1500 yeeres*. 3 vols. London: G. Bishop, R. Newberie and R. Barker, 1598–1600.

Hall, Catherine, ed. *Cultures of Empire: Colonizers in Britain and the Empire in the Nineteenth and*

Twentieth Centuries. Manchester: Manchester University Press, 2000.

Hall, Edith. *Inventing the Barbarian: Greek Self-Definition Through Tragedy*. Oxford: Clarendon Press, 1989.

[Hamel, Hendrik]. *'t Oprechte journael, van de ongeluckige reyse van 't jacht de Sperwer: Varende van Batavia na Tyowan en Fermosa, in 't jaer 1653[,] en van daer na Japan, daer schipper op was Reynier Egbertsz. van Amsterdam*. Amsterdam: Gillis Joosten Saagman, ca. 1670.

Hannema, Kiki. "'Groot gelt gespilt': De boekuitgaven van de Bruijn." In Drijvers, Hond, and Sancisi-Weerdenburg, *"Ik hadde de nieusgierigheid,"* 21–42.

Harley, J. B. *The New Nature of Maps: Essays in the History of Cartography*. Ed. Paul Laxton. Baltimore: Johns Hopkins University Press, 2001.

Harley, J. B., et al., eds. *The History of Cartography*. 6 vols. Chicago: University of Chicago Press, 1987–.

Hartog, François. *The Mirror of Herodotus: The Representation of the Other in the Writing of History*. Trans. Janet Lloyd. Berkeley: University of California Press, 1988.

Hay, Denys. *Europe: The Emergence of an Idea*. Edinburgh University Publications: History, Philosophy and Economics, vol. 7. Edinburgh: Edinburgh University Press, 1957.

Hazart, Cornelius. *Kerckelycke historie van de gheheele wereldt*. Antwerp: Michiel Cnobbaert, 1667–1671.

———. *Sots-caproen met verscheyden bellen behanghen ende gheschoncken voor een nievw iaer aen Arent Montanvs ghevschen woorden-dienaer tot Schoonhoven*. Antwerp: Michiel Cnobbaert, 1669.

Heiden, Frans Jansz. van der. *Vervarelijke schip-breuk van't Oost-Indisch jacht Ter Schelling, onder het landt van Bengale*. Amsterdam: Johannes van Someren, 1675.

———. *Vervarelyke schip-breuk van't Oost-Indisch jacht Ter Schelling, onder het landt van Bengale*. Amsterdam: Jacob van Meurs and Johannes van Someren, 1675.

Heijbroek, J. F., and M. Schapelhouman, eds. *Kunst in kaart: Decoratieve aspecten van de cartografie*. Utrecht: HES, 1989.

Helgerson, Richard. *Forms of Nationhood: The Elizabethan Writing of England*. Chicago: University of Chicago Press, 1992.

Heller, John L. "Linnaeus on Sumptuous Books." *Taxon* 25 (1976): 33–52.

Hellman, Mimi. "The Nature of Artifice: French Porcelain Flowers and the Rhetoric of the Garnish."

In Cavanaugh and Yonan, *Cultural Aesthetics*, 39–64.

Heniger, J. *Hendrik Adriaan van Reede tot Drakenstein (1636–1691) and Hortus Malabaricus: A Contribution to the History of Dutch Colonial Botany*. Rotterdam: A. A. Balkema, 1986.

Hennepin, Louis. *Beschryving van Louisiana, nieuwelijks ontdekt ten zuid-westen van Nieuw-Vrankryk*. Amsterdam: Jan ten Hoorn, 1688.

———. *Description de la Louisiane*. Paris: Sebastien Hure, 1683.

———. *A new discovery of a vast country in America*. London: M. Bentley et al., 1698.

———. *Nouveau voyage d'un pais plus grand que l'Europe avec les reflections des enterprises du Sieur de la Salle, sur les mines de St. Barbe, &c*. Utrecht: Antoine Schouten, 1698.

———. *Nouvelle decouverte d'un tres grand pays situé dans l'Amerique*. Utrecht: Guillaume Broedelet, 1697.

———. *Nouvelle decouverte d'un tres grand pays situé dans l'Amerique*. Leiden: Pieter van der Aa, 1704.

Herodotus. *The Persian Wars*. Vol. 1: Books 1–2, trans. A. D. Godley. Cambridge, MA: Harvard University Press [Loeb Classical Library], 1920.

Herrera, Antonio de. *Historia general de los hechos de los Castellanos en las islas y tierra firme del Mar Oceano*. 4 vols. Madrid: Emplenta Real [Juan Flamenco and Juan de la Cuesta], 1601–1615.

Hesselink, Reinier H. "Memorable Embassies: The Secret History of Arnoldus Montanus' *Gedenkwaerdige Gesantschappen*." *Quaerendo* 32, nos. 1–2 (2002): 99–123.

Heylyn, Peter. *Cosmographie in four bookes. Containing the chorographie and historie of the whole world, and the principall kingdomes, provinces, seas, and isles thereof*. 4 vols. London: W. W. for Henry Seile, 1652.

Hochstrasser, Julie. *Still Life and Trade in the Dutch Golden Age*. New Haven, CT: Yale University Press, 2007.

Hock, Klaus, and Gesa Mackenthun. *Entangled Knowledge: Scientific Discourses and Cultural Difference*. Münster: Waxmann, 2012.

Hodgen, Margaret T. *Early Anthropology in the Sixteenth and Seventeenth Centuries*. Philadelphia: University of Pennsylvania Press, 1964.

Hoetink, B., ed. *Verhaal van het vergaan van het jacht de Sperwer en van het wedervaren der schipbreukelingen op het eiland Quelpaert en het vasteland van Korea (1653–1666) met eene beschrijving van dat rijk door Hendrik Hamel uitgegeven.* Werken Uit-gegeven door de Linschoten-Vereeniging, vol. 18. The Hague: Martinus Nijhoff, 1920.

Hoftijzer, Paul. "Dutch Printing and Bookselling in the Golden Age." In *Two Faces of the Early Modern World: The Netherlands and Japan in the 17th and 18th Centuries,* ed. W. J. Boot and Yozaburo Shirahata, 59–67. Kyoto: International Research Center for Japanese Studies, 2001.

———. "Metropolis of Print: The Amsterdam Book Trade in the Seventeenth Century." In O'Brien et al., *Urban Achievement,* 249–363.

———. *Pieter van der Aa (1659–1733): Leids drukker en boekverkoper.* Hilversum: Verloren, 1999.

Hond, Jan de. "Cornelis de Bruijn (1652–1726/7): A Dutch Painter in the East." In *Eastward Bound: Dutch Ventures and Adventures in the Middle East,* ed. Geert Jan van Gelder and Ed de Moor, 51–80. Amsterdam: Rodopi, 1994.

———. " 'Den Vermaarden Cornelis de Bruyn': Een Korte Biografie." In Drijvers, Hond, and Sancisi-Weerdenburg, *"Ik hadde de nieusgierigheid,"* 9–20.

Honour, Hugh. *The European Vision of America.* Cleveland: Cleveland Museum of Art, 1975.

Hooghe, Romeyn de. *Les Indes Orientales et Occidentales et autres lieux.* Leiden: Pieter van der Aa, ca. 1700 (facsimile ed., Amsterdam: Van Hoeve, 1979).

———. *Schouburgh der Nederlandse veranderingen, geopent in ses tooneelen, waer op de wisselbeurten des Vereenigde Staets door den Fransen oorlog gebrouwen, in historiele sinnebeelden, vertoont en beschreven zijn.* Amsterdam: Romeyn de Hooghe, 1674.

Hornius, Georgius. *Georgi Horni orbis politicus, imperiorum, regnorum, principatuum, rerum publicarum.* Leiden: Cornelius Driehuysen, 1668.

Hostetler, Laura. *Qing Colonial Enterprise: Ethnography and Cartography in Early Modern China.* Chicago: University of Chicago Press, 2001.

Hübner, Johann. *Zemnovodnago kruga kratkoe opisanie. Iz staryia i novyia gegrafii po voprosam i otvietam chrez Iagana Gibnera sobranoe* [A brief description of the terraqueous globe. Collected by Johann Hübner from ancient and modern geography by way of questions and answers]. Moscow [s.n.], 1719.

Hulme, Peter. *Colonial Encounters: Europe and the Native Caribbean, 1492–1797.* London: Routledge Kegan & Paul, 1987.

———. "Tales of Distinction: European Ethnography and the Caribbean." In *Implicit Understandings: Observing, Reporting, and Reflecting on the Encounters Between Europeans and Other Peoples in the Early Modern Era,* ed. Stuart B. Schwartz, 157–197. Cambridge: Cambridge University Press, 1994.

Hung, Wu. *The Double Screen: Medium and Representation in Chinese Painting.* London: Reaktion, 1996.

Hunt, Lynn, Margaret Jacob, and Wijnand Mijnhardt, eds. *Bernard Picart and the First Global Vision of Religion.* Los Angeles: Getty Research Institute, 2009.

———. *The Book That Changed Europe: Picart and Bernard's Religious Ceremonies of the World.* Cambridge, MA: Harvard University Press, 2010.

Israel, Jonathan I. *Radical Enlightenment: Philosophy and the Making of Modernity, 1650–1750.* Oxford: Oxford University Press, 2001.

Jackson, Anna M. F., and Amin Jaffer, ed. *Encounters: The Meeting of Asia and Europe, 1500–1800.* London: Victoria and Albert Museum, 2004.

Jacobson, Dawn. *Chinoiserie.* London: Phaidon, 1993.

Jay, Martin. *Downcast Eyes: The Denigration of Vision in Twentieth-Century French Thought.* Berkeley: University of California Press, 1993.

Johns, Adrian. *The Nature of the Book: Print and Knowledge in the Making.* Chicago: University of Chicago Press, 1998.

———. *Piracy: The Intellectual Property Wars from Gutenberg to Gates.* Chicago: University of Chicago Press, 2009.

Johnson, Samuel. *Prefaces, biographical and critical, to the works of the English poets.* 10 vols. London: J. Nichols et al., 1779–1781.

———. *The vanity of human wishes: The tenth satire of Juvenal imitated.* London: R. Dodsley, 1749.

Jones, Adam. "Decompiling Dapper: A Preliminary Search for Evidence." *History in Africa* 17 (1990), 171–209.

Jong, Jan de, et al., eds. *Het exotische verbeeld, 1550–1950: Boeren en verre volken in de Nederlandse kunst.* Nederlands Kunsthistorisch Jaarboek, 53. Zwolle: Waanders, 2003.

Joppien, Rüdiger. "The Dutch Vision of Brazil: Johan Maurits and His Artists." In Boogaart et al., *Johan Maurits van Nassau Siegen,* 296–376.

Jörg, Christiaan. "Some Items of Dutch-Decorated Oriental Porcelain." *Transactions of the Oriental Ceramics Society* 65 (2000–2001): 143–148.

Jorink, Eric. *Reading the Book of Nature in the Dutch Golden Age, 1575–1715*. Trans. Peter Mason. Brill Studies in Intellectual History 191. Leiden: Brill, 2010.

Kaempfer, Engelbert. *Amoenitatum exoticarum politico-physico-medicarum fasciculi V, quibus continentur variae relationes, observationes & descriptiones rerum Persicarum & Ulterioris Asiae.* Lemgo: Henrici Wilhelmi Meyeri, 1712.

———. *De beschryving van Japan, behelsende een verhaal van den ouden en tegenwoordigen staat en regeering van dat ryk.* The Hague: P. Gosse and J. Neaulme, and Amsterdam: Balthasar Lakeman, 1729.

———. *Exotic Pleasures: Fascicle III, Curious Scientific and Medical Observations.* Trans. Robert W. Carrubba, Library of Renaissance Humanism. Carbondale, IL: Southern Illinois University Press, 1996.

———. *The history of Japan.* Trans. J[ohann] G[aspar] Scheuchzer. London: J. G. Scheuchzer, 1727.

Kagan, Richard. *Clio and the Crown: The Politics of History in Medieval and Early Modern Spain.* Baltimore: Johns Hopkins University Press, 2009.

Kagan, Richard, and Benjamin Schmidt. "Maps and the Early Modern State: Official Cartography." In *History of Cartography*, vol. 3: *Cartography in the European Renaissance*, ed. David Woodward, 661–680. Chicago: University of Chicago Press, 2007.

Kaufmann, Thomas DaCosta. "An Independent Dutch Art? A View from Central Europe." *De zeventiende eeuw* 13 (1997): 359–369.

———. *Toward a Geography of Art.* Chicago: University of Chicago Press, 2004.

Kavanagh, Thomas M. *Enlightened Pleasures: Eighteenth-Century France and the New Epicureanism.* New Haven, CT: Yale University Press, 2010.

Kemp, Martin. "'Wrought by No Artist's Hand': The Natural, the Artificial, the Exotic, and the Scientific in Some Artifacts from the Renaissance." In *Reframing the Renaissance: Visual Culture in Europe and Latin America, 1450–1650*, ed. Claire Farago, 177–196. New Haven, CT: Yale University Press, 1995.

Keulen, Johannes van. *De groote nieuwe vermeerde zee-atlas ofte water werelt.* 2 vols. Amsterdam: Van Keulen, 1688.

Kiby, Ulrika. *Die Exotismen des Kurfürsten Max Emanuel in Nymphenburg: Eine kunst- und kulturhistorische Studie zum Phänomen von Chinoiserie und Orientalismus im Bayern und Europa des 16. bis 18. Jahrhunderts; seine politische Relevanz.* Studien zur Kunstgeschichte, vol. 53. Hildesheim: Georg Olms, 1990.

Kircher, Athanasius. *China monumentis, qua sacris quà profanis, nec non variis naturae & artis spectaculis, aliarumque rerum memorabilium argumentis illustrata.* Amsterdam: Johannes Janssonius van Waesberge and Elizer Weyerstraten, 1667.

———. *La Chine d'Athanase Kirchere de la Compagnie de Jesus, illustrée de plusieurs monuments tant sacrés que profanes, et de quantité de recherchés de la nature & de l'art.* Amsterdam: Johannes Janssonius van Waesberge and Elizer Weyerstraten, 1670.

Knellwolf, Christa. "The Exotic Frontier of the Imperial Imagination." *Eighteenth-Century Life* 26 (2002): 10–30.

Knellwolf, Christa, and Robert P. Maccubin, eds. *Exoticism and the Culture of Exploration*, Special Issue of *Eighteenth-Century Life*. Durham, NC: Duke University Press, 2002.

Koeman, Cornelis. *Atlantes Neerlandici: Bibliography of Terrestrial, Maritime and Celestial Atlases and Pilot Books, Published in the Netherlands Up to 1880.* 6 vols. Amsterdam: Theatrum Orbis Terrarum, 1967–1985.

Kolb, Peter. *Caput Bonae Spei hodiernum, das ist: Vollständige Beschreibung des Africanischen Vorgebürges der Guten Hofnung.* Nürnberg: Peter Conrad Monath, 1719.

———. *Naaukeurige en uitvoerige beschryving van de Kaap de Goede Hoop . . . na waarheit beschreven.* Amsterdam: Balthazar Lakeman, 1727.

Kolfin, Elmer, and Esther Schreuder, eds. *Black Is Beautiful: Rubens to Dumas.* Zwolle: Waanders, 2008.

Kolfin, Elmer, and Jaap van Veen, eds. *Gedrukt tot Amsterdam: Amsterdamse prentmakers en -uitgevers in de Gouden Eeuw.* Zwolle: Waanders, 2011.

Kowaleski-Wallace, Elizabeth. "Women, China, and Consumer Culture in Eighteenth-Century England." *Eighteenth-Century Studies* 29 (1995–1996): 153–167.

Krempel, Ulla. *Jan van Kessel d. Ä., 1626–1679: die vier Erdteile.* Munich: Alte Pinakothek, 1973.

Krogt, Peter van der. *Koeman's Atlantes Neerlandici.* Vol. 4A: 1, "The *Galérie agréable du monde* by Pieter van der Aa." Houten: HES & De Graaf, 2012.

Kusukawa, Sachiko. "The 'Historia Piscium' (1686)." *Notes and Records of the Royal Society of London* 54 (May 2000): 179–197.

———. "Leonhart Fuchs on the Importance of Pictures." *Journal of the History of Ideas* 58 (1997): 403–427.

———. *Picturing the Book of Nature: Image, Text, and Argument in Sixteenth-Century Human Anatomy and Medical Botany*. Chicago: University of Chicago Press, 2012.

———. "The Uses of Pictures in the Formation of Learned Knowledge: The Cases of Leonhard Fuchs and Andreas Vesalius." In Kusukawa and Maclean, *Transmitting Knowledge*, 73–96.

Kusukawa, Sachiko, and Ian Maclean, eds. *Transmitting Knowledge: Words, Images, and Instruments in Early Modern Europe*. Oxford: Oxford University Press, 2006.

Lach, Donald, and Edwin J. Van Kley. *Asia in the Making of Europe*. 3 vols. Chicago: University of Chicago Press, 1965–1993.

The ladies amusement; or, Whole art of japanning made easy (ca. 1760). 2nd ed. London: Robert Sayer, ca. 1762.

Landwehr, John. *Studies in Dutch Books with Coloured Plates Published 1662–1875: Natural History, Topography and Travel Costumes and Uniforms*. The Hague: Junk, 1976.

———. *VOC: A Bibliography of Publications Relating to the Dutch East India Company, 1602–1800*. Ed. Peter van der Krogt. Utrecht: HES Publishers, 1991.

Lange, Petrus de. *Wonderen des werelds*. Amsterdam: M. W. Doornick, 1671.

Lasser, Ethan. "Reading Japanned Furniture." In *American Furniture*, ed. Luke Beckerdite, 169–190. Milwaukee: Chipstone Foundation, 2007.

Latour, Bruno. *Science in Action: How to Follow Scientists and Engineers Through Society*. Cambridge, MA: Harvard University Press, 1987.

Law, John. "On the Methods of Long Distance Control: Vessels, Navigation and the Portuguese Route to India." In *Power, Action and Belief: A New Sociology of Knowledge?* ed. John Law, Sociological Review Monograph 32, 231–260. London: Routledge and Kegan Paul, 1986.

———. "On the Social Explanation of Technical Change: The Case of the Portuguese Maritime Expansion." *Technology and Culture* 28 (1987): 227–252.

Lestringant, Frank. *André Thevet: Cosmographe des derniers Valois*. Geneva: Librairie Droz, 1991.

———. *Mapping the Renaissance World: The Geographical Imagination in the Age of Discovery*. Trans. D. Fausset, intro. Stephen Greenblatt. Cambridge, MA: Polity, 1994.

Lewis, Martin W., and Kären Wigen. *The Myth of Continents: A Critique of Metageography*. Berkeley: University of California Press, 1997.

Linschoten, Jan Huygen van. *Itinerario: Voyage ofte schipvaert, van Ian Huygen van Linschoten naer Oost ofte Portugaels Indien*. Amsterdam: Cornelis Claesz, 1596.

Livingstone, David N. *Adam's Ancestor: Race, Religion, and the Politics of Human Origins*. Baltimore: Johns Hopkins University Press, 2008.

Locke, John. *Some Thoughts Concerning Education*. Ed. John W. and Jean S. Yolton. Oxford: Clarendon Press, 1989.

Loomba, Ania. "Periodization, Race, and Global Contact." *Journal of Medieval and Early Modern Studies* 37 (Fall 2007): 595–620.

Mancall, Peter. *Envisioning America: English Plans for the Colonization of North America, 1580–1640*. Boston: Bedford/St. Martin's, 1995.

———. *Hakluyt's Promise: An Elizabethan's Obsession for an English America*. New Haven, CT: Yale University Press, 2007.

Mandeville, John. *The Travels of Sir John Mandeville*. Trans. and ed. C. W. R. D. Moseley. London: Penguin, 1983.

[Männling, Johann Christoph, ed.]. *Dapperi exotici curiosi continuatio*. Frankfurt and Leipzig: Michael Rohrlach, 1718.

———. *Dapperus exoticus curiosus: Das ist des vielbelesenen Hn. Odoardi Dapperi Africa- America- und Asiatische Curiositäten*. Frankfurt: Michael Rohrlach, 1717.

Margócsy, Dániel. *Commercial Visions: Science, Trade, and Visual Culture in the Dutch Golden Age*. Chicago: University of Chicago Press, 2014.

———. "A Museum of Wonders or a Cemetery of Corpses? The Commercial Exchange of Anatomical Collections in Early Modern Netherlands." In *Silent Messengers: The Circulation of Material Objects of Knowledge in the Early Modern Low Countries*, ed. Sven Dupré and Christoph Lüthy, 185–215. Berlin: LIT Verlag, 2011.

———. "'Refer to Folio and Number': Encyclopedias, the Exchange of Curiosities, and Practices of

Identification Before Linnaeus." *Journal of the History of Ideas* 71 (2010): 63–89.

Markley, Robert. *The Far East and the English Imagination, 1600–1730.* Cambridge: Cambridge University Press, 2006.

——. "Violence and Profits on the Restoration Stage: Trade, Nationalism, and Insecurity in Dryden's *Amboyna.*" *Eighteenth-Century Life* 22 (1998): 2–17.

[Mason, George Henry]. *The Punishments of China.* London: William Miller, 1801.

Mason, Peter. "Ethnographic Portraiture in the Eighteenth Century: George Psalmanaazaar's Drawings of Formosans." *Eighteenth-Century Life* 23, no. 3 (1999): 58–76.

——. *The Lives of Images.* London: Reaktion, 2001.

Mason, Peter, and Florike Egmond. "Albert E(e)ckhout, Court Painter." In Buvelot, *Albert Eckhout,* 109–127.

Massing, Jean Michel. *The Image of the Black in Western Art.* Vol. 3, part 2: "From the Age of Discovery to the Age of Abolition: Europe and the World Beyond." Ed. David Bindman and Henry Louis Gates, Jr. Cambridge, MA: Harvard University Press, 2011.

McCants, Anne E. C. "Exotic Goods, Popular Consumption, and the Standard of Living: Thinking About Globalization in the Early Modern World." *Journal of World History* 18 (2007): 433–462.

McClellan, Andrew. "Watteau's Dealer: Gersaint and the Marketing of Art in Eighteenth-Century Paris." *Art Bulletin* 78 (1996): 439–453.

McKenzie, D. F. *Bibliography and the Sociology of Texts.* Cambridge: Cambridge University Press, 1999.

McLuhan, Marshall. *Understanding Media: The Extensions of Man.* New York: McGraw-Hill, 1964.

Meersbergen, Guido van. "De uitgeversstrategie van Jacob van Meurs belicht: De Amsterdamse en 'Antwerpse' edities van Johan Nieuhofs *Gezantschap* (1665–1666)." *De zeventiende eeuw* 26 (2010): 73–90.

Merback, Mitchell B. *The Thief, the Cross, and the Wheel: Pain and the Spectacle of Punishment in Medieval and Renaissance Europe.* Chicago: University of Chicago Press, 1999.

Merian, Maria Sibylla. *Metamorphosis insectorum Surinamensium, ofte Verandering der Surinaamsche insecten.* Amsterdam: For the Author and Gerard Valck, [1705].

Meserve, Margaret. *Empires of Islam in Renaissance Historical Thought.* Harvard Historical Studies 158. Cambridge, MA: Harvard University Press, 2008.

Mignolo, Walter D. *The Darker Side of the Renaissance: Literacy, Territoriality, and Colonization.* 2nd ed. Ann Arbor: University of Michigan Press, 2003.

Miller, David Philip, and Peter Hanns Reill, eds. *Visions of Empire: Voyages, Botany, and Representations of Nature.* New York: Cambridge University Press, 1996.

Mitchell, David. *The Thousand Autumns of Jacob de Zoet.* New York: Random House, 2011.

Mitchell, W. J. T. *Picture Theory: Essays on Verbal and Visual Representation.* Chicago: University of Chicago Press, 1994.

Montanus, Arnoldus. *Atlas Japannensis: being remarkable addresses by way of embassy from the East India Company of the United Provinces to the Emperor of Japan.* London: John Ogilby, 1670.

——. *Gedenkwaerdige gesantschappen der Oost-Indische Maetschappy in 't Vereenigde Nederland, aen de Kaisaren van Japan.* Amsterdam: Jacob van Meurs, 1669.

——. *De nieuwe en onbekende weereld, of, Beschryving van America en 't Zuid-land.* Amsterdam: Jacob Meurs, 1671.

Montesquieu, Charles-Louis de Secondat, Baron de. *Lettres persanes.* Cologne [Amsterdam]: Pierre Marteau [Jacques Desbordes], 1721.

——. *Persian Letters.* Trans. and ed. C. J. Betts. Rev. ed. Harmondsworth: Penguin, 2004.

Morgan, Jennifer L. "'Some Could Suckle over Their Shoulder': Male Travelers, Female Bodies, and the Gendering of Racial Ideology, 1500–1770." *William and Mary Quarterly,* 3rd series, 54 (1997): 167–192.

Morris, Frances, and Christopher Green, eds. *Henri Rousseau: Jungles in Paris.* London: Tate Publishing, 2005.

Mullaney, Steven. "Strange Things, Gross Terms, Curious Customs: The Rehearsal of Cultures in the Late Renaissance." *Representations* 3 (1983): 40–67.

Mungello, David E. *Curious Land: Jesuit Accommodation and the Origins of Sinology.* Honolulu: University of Hawaii Press, 1989.

Munting, Abraham. *Naauwkeurige beschryving der aardgewassen.* Utrecht: François Halma and Leiden: Pieter van der Aa, 1696.

Müsch, Irmgard. "Albertus Seba's Collection of Natural Specimens and its Pictorial Inventory." In Albertus Seba, *Cabinet of Natural Curiosities*, 7–12. Cologne: Taschen, 2005.

Myers, William David. *Death and a Maiden: Infanticide and the Tragical History of Grethe Schmidt.* DeKalb: Northern Illinois University Press, 2011.

Nederveen Pieterse, Jan. *White on Black: Images of Africa and Blacks in Western Popular Culture.* New Haven, CT: Yale University Press, 1992.

Niekerk, Carl. "Man and Orangutan in Eighteenth-Century Thinking: Retracing the Early History of Dutch and German Anthropology." *Monatshefte* 96 (2004): 477–502.

Nierop, Henk van. *Treason in the Northern Quarter: War, Terror, and the Rule of Law in the Dutch Revolt.* Trans. J. C. Grayson. Princeton, NJ: Princeton University Press, 2009.

Nierop, Henk van, et al., eds. *Romeyn de Hooghe: De verbeelding van de late Gouden Eeuw.* Zwolle: Waanders, 2008.

Nieuhof, Johan. *L'Ambassade de la Compagnie Orientale des Provinces Unies vers L'Emperour de la Chine, ou Grand Cam de Tartarie.* Leiden: Jacob van Meurs, 1665.

———. *An embassy from the East-India Company of the United Provinces, to the Grand Tartar Cham Emperour of China.* London: John Macock, 1669.

———. *Gedenkwaerdige zee en lantreize door de voornaemste landschappen van West en Oostindien.* Amsterdam: Widow of Jacob van Meurs, 1682.

———. *Het gezantschap der Neêrlandtsche Oost-Indische Compagnie, aan den grooten Tartarischen Cham, den tegenwoordigen keizer van China.* Amsterdam: Jacob van Meurs, 1665.

———. *Voyages and travels into Brasil and the East-Indies: Containing an exact description of the Dutch Brasil, and divers parts of the East-Indies.* In Churchill, *Collection of Voyages*, 2:1–369.

Noordegraaf, Leo, and Thera Wijsenbeek-Olthuis. "De wereld ontsloten: Aanvoer van rariteiten naar Nederland." In Bergvelt and Kistemaker, *Wereld binnen handbereik*, 39–50 [essays].

O'Brien, Patrick, et al., eds. *Urban Achievement in Early Modern Europe: Golden Ages in Antwerp, Amsterdam and London.* Cambridge: Cambridge University Press, 2001.

Odell, Dawn. "Clothing, Customs, and Mercantilism: Dutch and Chinese Ethnographies in the Seventeenth Century." In Jong et al., *Exotische verbeeld*, 139–159.

———. "Porcelain, Print Culture and Mercantile Aesthetics." In Cavanaugh and Yonan, *Cultural Aesthetics*, 141–158.

Ogborn, Miles. *Indian Ink: Script and Print in the Making of the English East India Company.* Chicago: University of Chicago Press, 2007.

Ogilby, John [Olfert Dapper]. *Asia, the first part. Being an accurate description of Persia, and the several provinces thereof, the vast empire of the Great Mogol, and other parts of India, and their several kingdoms and regions.* London: John Ogilby, 1673.

———. *Atlas Chinensis: Being a second part of a relation of remarkable passages in two embassies from the East-India Company of the United Provinces, to the vice-roy Singlamong and general Taising Lipovi, and to Konchi, emperor of China and East Tartary.* London: Thomas Johnson, 1671.

Ogilvie, Brian W. *The Science of Describing: Natural History in Renaissance Europe.* Chicago: University of Chicago Press, 2006.

Olearius, Adam. *The voyages & travels of the ambassadors sent by Frederick Duke of Holstein, to the Great Duke of Muscovy, and the King of Persia* (1647). Trans. John Davies. London: Thomas Dring and John Starkey, 1662.

Ommen, K. van, ed. *The Exotic World of Carolus Clusius, 1526–1609.* Leiden: Leiden University Library, 2009.

Ortelius, Abraham. *Parergon, sive Veteris geographiae aliquot tabulae* (1579). Rev. ed. Antwerp: Officina Plantiniana, 1592.

———. *Theatrum orbis terrarum.* Antwerp: Gilles Coppens de Diest, 1570.

Pagden, Anthony. *European Encounters with the New World: From Renaissance to Romanticism.* New Haven, CT: Yale University Press, 1993.

Pelka, Otto. *Ostasiatische Reisebilder im Kunstgewerbe des 18. Jahrhunderts.* Leipzig: Hiersemann, 1924.

Pepys, Samuel. "My Collection of Frontispieces." In *Catalogue of the Pepys Library at Magdalene College, Cambridge*, ed. Robert Latham, vol. 3: *Prints and Drawings*, part 1: General, 87–175. Cambridge: Boydell and Brewer, 1980.

Persepolis illustrata, or, The ancient and royal palace of Persepolis in Persia. London: S. Harding, on the Pavement in St. Martin's Lane, 1739.

Peter the Great: An Inspired Tsar. Amsterdam: Hermitage, 2013.

Peters, Marion. "Nepotisme, patronage en boekopdrachten bij Nicolaes Witsen (1641–1717), burgemeester van Amsterdam." *Lias: Sources and Documents Relating to the Early History of Ideas* 25 (1998): 83–134.

———. "Nicolaes Witsen and Gijsbert Cuper: Two Seventeenth-Century Dutch Burgomasters and Their Gordian Knot." *Lias: Sources and Documents Relating to the Early History of Ideas* 16 (1989): 111–151.

———. *De wijze koopman: Het wereldwijde onderzoek van Nicolaes Witsen (1641–1717), burgemeester en VOC-bewindhebber van Amsterdam*. Amsterdam: Bert Bakker, 2010.

Pfaff, Sybille. *Zacharias Wagener, 1614–1668*. Hassfurt [s.n.], 2001.

Pietsch, Theodore W. "Louis Renard's Fanciful Fishes." *Natural History* 98 (1984): 58–67.

———. "Samuel Fallours and His 'Sirenne' from the Province of Ambon." *Archives of Natural History* 18 (1991): 1–25.

Pietz, William. "The Problem of the Fetish, I." *Res* 9 (Spring 1985): 5–17.

———. "The Problem of the Fetish, II." *Res* 13 (Spring 1987): 23–45.

———. "The Problem of the Fetish, III." *Res* 16 (Autumn 1988): 105–123.

Pipkin, Amanda. "Every Woman's Fear: Stories of Rape and Dutch Identity in the Golden Age." *Tijdschrijft voor Geschiedenis* 122, no. 3 (2009), 290–305.

———. "'They Were Not Humans, but Devils in Human Bodies': Depictions of Sexual Violence and Spanish Tyranny as a Means of Fostering Identity in the Dutch Republic." *Journal of Early Modern History* 13 (2009): 229–264.

Piso, Willem, et al. *Historia naturalis Brasiliae*. Leiden: F. Hackius and Amsterdam: Lodewijk Elzevier, 1648.

———. *De Indiae utriusque re naturali et medica libri quatuordecim*. Amsterdam: Lodewijk and Daniel Elzevier, 1658.

Porter, Roy, and G. S. Rousseau, eds. *Exoticism in the Enlightenment*. Manchester: Manchester University Press, 1989.

Postma, Johannes. *The Dutch in the Atlantic Slave Trade, 1600–1815*. Cambridge: Cambridge University Press, 1990.

Pratt, Mary Louise. *Imperial Eyes: Travel Writing and Transculturation*. London: Routledge, 1992.

Purchas, Samuel. *Hakluytus posthumus, or Purchas his pilgrimes*. 4 vols. London: William Stansby, 1624–1625.

Quinn, David B., ed. *The Hakluyt Handbook*. 2 vols. Works issued by the Hakluyt Society, 2nd ser., no. 144–145. London: Hakluyt Society, 1974.

Raven, Charles E. *John Ray: Naturalist*. 2nd ed. Cambridge: Cambridge University Press, 1950; reissued 1986.

Ray, John. *Further Correspondence of John Ray*, ed. Robert W. T. Gunther. London: Ray Society, 1928.

Reed, Marcia, and Paola Demattè. *China on Paper: European and Chinese Works from the Late Sixteenth to Early Nineteenth Century*. Los Angeles, CA: Getty Publications, 2011.

Reede tot Drakenstein, Hendrik Adriaan van. *Hortus Indicus Malabaricus*. 12 vols. Amsterdam: Joannis van Someren and Joannis van Dyck [final vols. Widow of Johannes van Someren, Heirs of Jan van Dyck, Hendrik Boom, and Widow of Dirk Boom], 1678–1693.

Reitsma, Ella. *Maria Sibylla Merian and Daughters: Women of Art and Science*. Amsterdam: Rembrandt House Museum; Los Angeles: J. Paul Getty Museum; Zwolle: Waanders, 2008.

Remmert, Volker R. "'Docet parva pictura, quod multae scripturae non dicunt': Frontispieces, Their Functions, and Their Audiences in Seventeenth-Century Mathematical Sciences." In Kusukawa and Maclean, *Transmitting Knowledge*, 239–270.

———. *Picturing the Scientific Revolution: Title Engravings in Early Modern Scientific Publications*. Early Modern Catholicism and the Visual Arts Series, vol. 4. Philadelphia: Saint Joseph's University Press, 2011.

Renard, Louis. *Fishes, Crayfishes and Crabs: Louis Renard's Natural History of the Rarest Curiosities of the Seas of the Indies*. Ed. Theodore W. Pietsch, 2 vols. Baltimore: Johns Hopkins University Press.

———. *Poissons, ecrevisses et crabes de diverses couleurs et figures extraordinaires, que l'on trouve autour des Isles Moluques, et sur les cotes des Terres Australes*. 2 vols. Amsterdam: Louis Renard, 1718.

Rennie, Neil. *Far-Fetched Facts: The Literature of Travel and the Idea of the South Seas*. Oxford: Oxford University Press, 1995.

Ridley, Glynis. *Clara's Grand Tour: Travels with a Rhinoceros in Eighteenth-Century Europe*. London: Atlantic, 2004.

Rietbergen, P. J. A. N. "Zover de aarde reikt: De werken van Johan Nieuhof (1618–1672) als illustratie van het probleem der cultuur- en mentaliteitsgeschiedenis tussen specialisatie en integratie." *De zeventiende eeuw* 17 (1986): 17–40.

Roa-de-la-Carrera, Cristián A. *Histories of Infamy: Francisco López de Gómara and the Ethics of Spanish Imperialism.* Trans. Scott Sessions, foreword by David Carrasco. Boulder: University Press of Colorado, 2005.

Roberts, Lissa. *Centres and Cycles of Accumulation in and Around the Netherlands During the Early Modern Period.* Berlin: LIT, 2011.

Rochefort, Charles de. *Histoire naturelle et morale des iles Antilles de l'Amerique.* Rotterdam: Arnout Leers, 1658.

———. *The history of the Caribby-Islands, viz. Barbados, St. Christophers, St. Vincents, Martinico, Dominico, Barbouthos, Monserrat, Mevis, Antego, &c. in all XXVIII.* Trans. John Davies. London: Thomas Dring and John Starkey, 1666.

Roeper, V. D., Boudewijn Walraven, and Jean-Paul Buys, eds. *Hamel's World: A Dutch-Korean Encounter in the Seventeenth Century.* Amsterdam: SUN, 2003.

Roeper, V. D., and G. J. D. Wildeman. *Reizen op papier: Journalen en reisverslagen van Nederlandse ontdekkingsreizigers, kooplieden en avonturiers.* Jaarboek van het Nederlands Scheepvaart Museum Amsterdam. Zutphen: Walburg, 1996.

Rubiés, Joan-Pau. "Instructions for Travellers: Teaching the Eye to See." *History and Anthropology* 9 (1996): 139–190.

———. *Travel and Ethnology in the Renaissance: South India Through European Eyes, 1250–1625.* Cambridge: Cambridge University Press, 2000.

———. "Travel Writing as a Genre: Facts, Fictions and the Invention of a Scientific Discourse in Early Modern Europe." *International Journal of Travel and Travel Writing* 5 (2000): 5–33.

Rudi, Thomas. *Exotische Welten: Der Schulz-Codex und das frühe Meissener Porzellan.* Munich: Hirmer, 2010.

Rumphius, Georgius Everhardus. *D'Amboinsche rariteitkamer.* Amsterdam: François Halma, 1705.

———. *The Ambonese Curiosity Cabinet.* Trans. and ed. E. M. Beekman. New Haven, CT: Yale University Press, 1999.

———. *Herbarium Amboinense / Het Amboinsche kruid-boek.* Ed. Joannes Burmannus. 6 vols. Amsterdam: François Changuin, Jan Catuffe, Hermanus Uytwerf; The Hague: Pieter Gosse, Jan Neaulme, Adriaan Moetjens, Antony van Dole; Utrecht: Steven Neaulme, 1741–1750.

———. *Thesaurus imaginum piscium testaceorum.* Leiden: Pieter van der Aa, 1711.

Sacks, David Harris. "Richard Hakluyt's Navigations in Time: History, Epic, and Empire." *Modern Language Quarterly* 67 (March 2006): 31–62.

Said, Edward W. *Culture and Imperialism.* New York: Knopf, 1993.

———. *Orientalism.* New York: Random House, 1978.

Salmon, Thomas. *Hedendaegsche historie, of tegenwoordige staet van alle volkeren.* Trans. M. van Goch, 3 vols. Amsterdam: Isaak Tirion, 1729–1731.

Sancisi-Weerdenburg, Heleen. "Through Travellers' Eyes: The Persian Monuments as Seen by European Travellers." In Sancisi-Weerdenburg and Drijvers, *Through Travellers' Eyes,* 1–35.

———. "'Yver, aendacht en naerstigheit': Verblijf in Persepolis." In Drijvers, Hond, and Sancisi-Weerdenburg, *"Ik hadde de nieusgierigheid."* 129–142.

Sancisi-Weerdenburg, Heleen, and Jan Willem Drijvers, eds. *Through Travellers' Eyes: European Travellers on the Iranian Monuments.* Achaemenid History, vol. 7. Leiden: Nederlands Instituut voor het Nabije Oosten, 1991.

Schama, Simon. *The Embarrassment of Riches: An Interpretation of Dutch Culture in the Golden Age.* New York: Knopf, 1987.

———. "Perishable Commodities: Dutch Still-Life Painting and the 'Empire of Things.'" In *Consumption and the World of Goods,* ed. John Brewer and Roy Porter, 478–488. London: Routledge, 1993.

Schiebinger, Londa. *Nature's Body: Gender in the Making of Modern Science.* Boston: Beacon, 1993.

———. *Plants and Empire: Colonial Bioprospecting in the Atlantic World.* Cambridge, MA: Harvard University Press, 2004.

Schiebinger, Londa, and Claudia Swan, eds. *Colonial Botany: Science, Commerce, and Politics.* Philadelphia: University of Pennsylvania Press, 2004.

Schilder, Günter. *Monumenta Cartographica Neerlandica,* vol. 5: *Tien wandkaarten van Blaeu en Visscher = Ten Wall Maps by Blaeu and Visscher.* Alphen aan den Rijn: Canaletto, 1996.

Schmidt, Benjamin. "Accumulating the World: Collecting and Commodifying 'Globalism' in Early Modern Europe." In Roberts, *Centres and Cycles,* 128–154.

———. "The Atlas Van der Hem and the Culture of Print Geography." In *The Atlas Blaeu–Van der Hem,* ed. Günter Schilder et al., vol. 8: *History of* the Atlas and the Making of the Facsimile, 190–202. Houten: HES & De Graaf, 2011.

———. "The Dutch Atlantic: From Provincialism to Globalism." In *Atlantic History: A Critical Appraisal*, ed. Jack P. Greene and Philip D. Morgan, 163–187. Oxford: Oxford University Press, 2009.

———. *Innocence Abroad: The Dutch Imagination and the New World, 1570–1670*. Cambridge: Cambridge University Press, 2001.

———. "Mapping an Exotic World: The Global Project of Dutch Geography Circa 1700." In *The Global Eighteenth Century*, ed. Felicity Nussbaum, 19–37. Baltimore: Johns Hopkins University Press, 2003.

———. "On the Impulse of Mapping, or How a Flat Earth Theory of Dutch Maps Distorts the Thickness and Pictorial Proclivities of Early Modern Cartography (and Misses Its Picturing Impulse)." *Art History* 35 (2012): 1036–1050.

Schneider, Norbert. *Still Life Painting in the Early Modern Period*. Trans. Hugh Beyer. Cologne: Benedikt Taschen, 1990.

Schouten, Joost. *Notitie van de situatie, regeeringe, macht, religie, costuymen, traffijcquen, ende andere remercquable saecken, des Coninghrijcks Siam*. The Hague: Aert Meuris, 1638.

Schouten, Wouter. *Oost-Indische voyagie, vervattende veel voorname voorvallen en ongemeene vreemde geschiedenissen, bloedige zee- en landt-gevechten tegen de Portugeesen en Makassaren; belegering, en verovering van veel voorname steden en kasteelen*. Amsterdam: Jacob van Meurs and Johannes van Someren, 1676.

Schwartz, Gary. "The International Identity of the Netherlands." *Schwartzlist*, no. 212 (also published in *Het Financieele Dagblad*, 19 June 2004, p. 25).

Schwartz, Vanessa. *Spectacular Realities: Early Mass Culture in Fin-de-siècle Paris*. Berkeley: University of California Press, 1998.

Seba, Albertus. *Locupletissimi rerum naturalium thesauri accurata descriptio, et iconibus artificiosissimis expressio, per universam physices historiam*. 4 vols. Amsterdam: J. Wetstein, W. Smith, and J. Janssonius van Waesberge, 1734–1735 and 1758–1765.

Segalen, Victor. *Essay on Exoticism: An Aesthetics of Diversity*. Trans. and ed. Yaël Rachel Schlick. Durham, NC: Duke University Press, 2002.

Senebier, Jean. *Essai sur l'art d'observer et de faire des experiences*. 3 vols. Geneva: J. J. Paschoud, 1802.

Shapin, Steven. "The Invisible Technician." *American Scientist* 77 (1989): 554–563.

———. "Pump and Circumstance: Robert Boyle's Literary Technology." *Social Studies of Science* 14, no. 4 (1984): 481–520.

———. *The Scientific Revolution*. Chicago: University of Chicago Press, 1996.

———. *A Social History of Truth: Civility and Science in Seventeenth-Century England*. Chicago: University of Chicago Press, 1994.

Shapin, Steven, and Simon Schaffer. *Leviathan and the Air-Pump: Hobbes, Boyle, and the Experimental Life*. Princeton, NJ: Princeton University Press, 1985.

Shapiro, Barbara J. *A Culture of Fact: England, 1550–1720*. Ithaca, NY: Cornell University Press, 2003.

Silverman, Lisa. *Tortured Subjects: Pain, Truth, and the Body in Early Modern France*. Chicago: University of Chicago Press, 2001.

Singy, Patrick. "Huber's Eyes: The Art of Scientific Observation Before the Emergence of Positivism." *Representations* 95 (2006): 54–75.

Sloboda, Stacey. "Displaying Materials: Porcelain and Natural History in the Duchess of Portland's Museum." *Eighteenth-Century Studies* 43 (2010): 455–472.

———. "Porcelain Bodies: Gender, Acquisitiveness, and Taste in Eighteenth-Century England." In *Material Cultures, 1740–1920: The Meanings and Pleasures of Collecting*, ed. Alla Myzelev and John Potvin, 19–36. Burlington, VT: Ashgate, 2009.

Smith, Bernard. *Imagining the Pacific: In the Wake of the Cook Voyages*. New Haven, CT: Yale University Press, 1992.

Smith, Pamela H. "Science in Motion: Recent Trends in the History of Early Modern Science." *Renaissance Quarterly* 62 (2009): 345–375.

Spary, Emma C. "Scientific Symmetries." *History of Science* 43 (2004): 1–46.

Spence, Jonathan. *The Chan's Great Continent: China in Western Minds*. New York: W. W. Norton, 1998.

Spiegel, Gabrielle. "The Task of the Historian." *American Historical Review* 114 (2009): 1–14.

Spiess, Karl-Heinz. "Asian Objects and Western European Court Culture in the Middle Ages." In *Artistic and Cultural Exchanges Between Europe and Asia, 1400–1900: Rethinking Markets, Workshops and Collections*, ed. Michael North, 9–28. Farnham, Surrey: Ashgate, 2010.

Spon, Jacob, and George Wheler. *Voyage d'Italie, de Dalmatie, de Grece, et du Levant, fait aux années 1675 & 1676*. 2 vols. Amsterdam: Henry and Theodore Boom, 1679.

Stagl, Justin, and Christopher Pinney. "From Travel Writing to Ethnography." *History and Anthropology* 9 (1996): 121–124.

Stalker, John, and George Parker. *A treatise of japaning and varnishing, being a compleat discovery of those arts.* Oxford: John Stalker and George Parker, 1688.

Standaert, Nicolas. "Seventeenth-Century European Images of China." *China Review International* 12 (Spring 2005): 254–259.

Stavorinus, J. S. *Reize van Zeeland over de Kaap de Goede Hoop, naar Batavia, Bantam, Bengalen, enz.* 2 vols. Leiden: A. and J. Honkoop, 1793.

Stolte, Carolien. *Philip Angel's Deex-Autaers: Vaisnava Mythology from Manuscript to Book Market in the Context of the Dutch East India Company, c. 1600–1672.* New Delhi: Manohar, 2012.

Struys, Jan Jansz. *Drie aanmerkelijke en seer rampspoedige reysen, door Italien, Griekenlandt, Lijflandt, Moscovien, Tartarijen, Meden, Persien, Oost-Indien, Japan, en verscheyden andere gewesten.* Amsterdam: Jacob van Meurs and Johannes van Someren, 1676.

——. *The perillous and most unhappy voyages of John Struys, through Italy Greece, Lifeland, Moscovia, Tartary, Media, Persia, East India, Japan, and other places in Europe, Africa, and Asia.* Trans. John Morrison. London: Samuel Smith, 1683.

Stuurman, Siep. "François Bernier and the Invention of Racial Classification." *History Workshop Journal* 50 (Autumn 2000): 1–21.

Sun, Ying. *Wandlungen des europäischen Chinabildes in illustrierten Reiseberichten des 17. und 18. Jahrhunderts.* Frankfurt am Main: Peter Lang, 1996.

Swan, Claudia. "The Uses of Realism in Early Modern Illustrated Botany." In *Visualizing Medieval Medicine and Natural History, 1200–1550,* ed. Jean A. Givens, Karen M. Reeds, and Alain Touwaide, 239–249. Aldershot: Ashgate, 2006.

Sweet, James H. "Mutual Misunderstandings: Gesture, Gender and Healing in the African Portuguese World." *Past and Present* 203 (2009, Supplement 4): 128–143.

Teixeira, Dante Martins. *The "Allegory of the Continents" by Jan van Kessel "The Elder" (1626–1679): A Seventeenth-Century View of the Fauna in the Four Corners of the Earth.* [Petrópolis]: Index, [2002].

Temple, William. *Upon the Gardens of Epicurus, with other Seventeenth-Century Garden Essays,* ed. Albert Forbes Sieveking. London: Chatto and Windus, 1908.

Terwen-De Loos, J. *Nederlandse schilders en tekenaars in de Oost: 17de-20ste eeuw.* Amsterdam: Rijksmuseum, 1972.

Thévenot, Jean de. *Gedenkwaardige en zeer naauwkeurige reizen van den Heere de Thevenot.* Trans. G. v. Broekhuizen. 3 vols. Amsterdam: Jan Bouman, 1681–1682.

——. *The Travels of Monsieur de Thevenot into the Levant.* Trans. Archibald Lovell. London: Henry Clark, 1687.

Thévenot, Melchisédech. *Relations de divers voyages curieux qui n'ont point esté publiées et qu'on a traduit ou tiré des originaux des voyageurs françois, espagnols, allemands, portugais, anglois, hollandois, persans, arabes & autres orientaux.* 4 vols. Paris, 1663–1696.

Tobin, Beth Fowkes. *Picturing Imperial Power: Colonial Subjects in Eighteenth-Century British Painting.* Durham, NC: Duke University Press, 1999.

Toussaint, Jacques, and Anne Verbrugge. *Un cabinet, un roi, une ville / Een kunstkast voor Willem III.* Namur: Société Archéologique de Namur, 2004.

Trexler, Richard C. "Making the American Berdache: Choice or Constraint?" *Journal of Social History* 35 (2002): 613–636.

——. *Sex and Conquest: Gendered Violence, Political Order, and the European Conquest of the Americas.* Ithaca, NY: Cornell University Press, 1995.

Turnovsky, Geoffrey. *The Literary Market: Authorship and Modernity in the Old Regime.* Philadelphia: University of Pennsylvania Press, 2010.

Udemans, Godefridus. *'t Geestelyck roer van 't coopmans schip, dat is: Trouw bericht, hoe dat een coopman, en coopvaerder, hem selven dragen moet in syne handelinge, in pays ende in oorloge, voor Godt, ende de menschen, te water ende te lande, insonderheyt onder de heydenen in Oost- ende West-Indien.* Dordrecht: Fransoys Boels, 1638.

Uffenbach, Zacharias Conrad von. *Merkwürdige Reisen durch Niedersachsen Holland und Engelland.* 3 vols. Ulm: Johann Friedrich Gaum, 1753–1754.

Ulrichs, Friederike. *Johan Nieuhofs Blick auf China (1655–1657): Die Kupferstiche in seinem Chinabuch und ihre Wirkung auf den Verleger Jacob van Meurs,* Sinologica Coloniensia, vol. 21. Wiesbaden: Harrassowitz, 2003.

Valentyn, François. *Oud en Nieuw Oost-Indiën.* 5 vols. Amsterdam: Gerard Onder de Linden and Dordrecht: Joannes van Braam, 1724–1726.

Vandenbroeck, Paul. *Beeld van de andere, vertoog over het zelf: Over wilden en narren, boeren en bedelaars*. Antwerp: Koninklijk Museum voor Schone Kunsten, 1987.

Van Eerde, Katherine S. *John Ogilby and the Taste of His Times*. Folkestone: Dawson and Sons, 1976.

Veen, Jaap van der. "Met grote moeite en kosten: De totstandkoming van zeventiende-eeuwse verzamelingen." In Bergvelt and Kistemaker, *Wereld binnen handbereik*, 51–69 [essays].

Veldman, Ilja M. "Familiar Customs and Exotic Rituals: Picart's Illustrations for *Cérémonies et coutumes religieuses de tous les peuples*." *Simiolus: Netherlands Quarterly for the History of Art* 33 (2007/2008): 94–111.

Venbrux, Eric. "'Wild and Barbaric Manners': The Exotic Encountered in a Dutch Account of Australian Aborigines in 1705." In Jong et al., *Exotische verbeeld*, 160–181.

Verhoeven, Garrelt, and Piet Verkruijsse, eds. *Iovrnael ofte gedenkwaerdige beschryvinghe vande Oost-Indishe reyse van Willem Ysbrantsz. Bontekoe van Hoorn: Descriptieve bibliographie, 1646–1996*. Zutphen: Walburg, 1996.

Verhoeven, Gerrit. "'Brought Together at Great Effort': The Place of Author, Publisher, and Reader in the Genesis of the Early Modern Travel Guide." *Quaerendo* 34 (2004): 240–253.

Verkruijsse, Piet, and Chunglin Kwa, eds. *Aap, vis, boek: Linnaeus in Amsterdam*. Zwolle: Waanders, 2007.

Verstegen, Richard. *Theatrum crudelitatum haereticorum nostri temporis*. Antwerp: Adrien Hubert, 1587.

Vesalius, Andreas. *De humani corporis fabrica*. Basel: Ex officina Joannis Oporini, 1543.

Vespucci, Amerigo. *Letters from a New World: Amerigo Vespucci's Discovery of America*. Ed. Luciano Formisano, trans. David Jacobson, foreword by Garry Wills. New York: Marsilio, 1992.

Vickers, Michael. "The Views of Persepolis by William Marshall and Wenceslaus Hollar in Sir Thomas Herbert's *Travels*." In Sancisi-Weerdenburg and Drijvers, *Through Travellers' Eyes*, 59–69.

Vries, Boudien de. "Vrouw en boek: Een speurtoch naar de 'onzichtbare' vrouw in de boekenwereld." *Jaarboek voor Nederlandse boekgeschiedenis* 12 (2005): 7–12.

Vries, Jan de. "The Dutch Atlantic Economies." In *The Atlantic Economy During the Seventeenth and Eighteenth Centuries: Organization, Operation, Practice,* and Personnel, ed. Peter Coclanis, 1–29. Columbia: University of South Carolina Press, 2005.

———. *The Industrious Revolution: Consumer Behavior and the Household Economy, 1650 to the Present*. New York: Cambridge University Press, 2008.

———. "Luxury in the Dutch Golden Age in Theory and Practice." In Berg and Eger, *Luxury in the Eighteenth Century*, 41–56.

Vries, Jan de, and Ad van der Woude. *The First Modern Economy: Success, Failure, and Perseverance of the Dutch Economy, 1500–1815*. Cambridge: Cambridge University Press, 1997.

Vries, Marleen de. "Published . . . and Exploited: On Eighteenth-Century Best-Seller Authors, Lying Publishers, Sneaky Privileges and Shared Authorship." *De achttiende eeuw* 37 (2005): 36–52.

Vries, Simon de. *Curieuse aenmerckingen der bysonderste Oost en West-Indische verwonderens-waerdige dingen*. 4 vols. Utrecht: Johannes Ribbius, 1682.

———. *Groot historisch magazijn*. Amsterdam: Aert Dircksz. Ooszaen, 1688.

———. *Groot historisch schouwtooneel*. 3 vols. Amsterdam: Jan Bouman, 1680–1682.

———. *Groote historische rariteit-kamer*. 3 vols. Amsterdam: Jan Bouman, 1682–1684.

Waals, Jan van der. "Exotische rariteiten: Afbeeldingen en voorwerpen van vreemde volkeren." In Bergvelt and Kistemaker, *Wereld binnen handbereik*, 153–168 [essays].

Wagenaer, Zacharias. *The "Thierbuch" and "Autobiography" of Zacharias Wagener*. Ed. Christina Ferrão and José Paulo Monteiro Soares, trans. David H. Treece and Richard Trewinnard. Dutch Brazil, vol. 2. Rio de Janeiro: Editura Index, 1997.

Welie, Rik van. "Patterns of Slave Trading and Slavery in the Dutch Colonial World, 1596–1863." In *Dutch Colonialism, Migration and Cultural Heritage*, ed. Gert Oostindie. Leiden: KITLV Press, 2008.

Westermann, Mariët. *A Worldly Art: The Dutch Republic, 1585–1718*. 2nd ed. New Haven, CT: Yale University Press, 2005.

Wey Gómez, Nicolás. *The Tropics of Empire: Why Columbus Sailed South to the Indies*. Cambridge, MA: MIT Press, 2008.

White, John. *The true pictures and fashions of the people in that parte of America now called Virginia, discowred by Englishmen*. In Thomas Harriot, *A briefe and true report of the new found land of Virginia*, plates 1–23. Frankfurt am Main: Theodor de Bry, 1590.

Whitehead, Peter, and Marinus Boeseman. *A Portrait of Dutch Seventeenth-Century Brazil: Animals, Plants and People by the Artists of Johan Maurits of Nassau*. Amsterdam: North-Holland, 1989.

Wilkie, Everett C., Jr. "The Authorship and Purpose of the *Histoire naturelle et morale des iles Antilles*, an Early Huguenot Emigration Guide." *Harvard Library Bulletin*, 2nd ser., 2, no. 3 (1991): 26–84.

Wills, John E., Jr. "Author, Publisher, Patron, World: A Case Study of Old Books and Global Consciousness." *Journal of Early Modern History* 13 (2009): 375–433.

——. *Embassies and Illusions: Dutch and Portuguese Envoys to K'ang-hsi, 1666–1687*. Cambridge, MA: Harvard University Press, 1984.

——. *Pepper, Guns, and Parleys: The Dutch East India Company and China, 1662–1681*. Cambridge, MA: Harvard University Press, 1974.

Willughby, Francis, and John Ray. *De historia piscium libri quatuor*. Oxford: [University Press at the] Sheldonian Theatre for the Royal Society, 1686.

——. *Ornithologia libri tres*. London: John Martyn, 1676.

Winichakul, Thongchai. *Siam Mapped: A History of the Geo-body of a Nation*. Honolulu: University of Hawaii Press, 1994.

Wintle, Michael. *The Image of Europe: Visualizing Europe in Cartography and Iconography throughout the Ages*. Cambridge: Cambridge University Press, 2009.

Witsen, Nicolaes. *Noord en Oost Tartarye, ofte bondig ontwerp van eenige dier landen en volken, welke voormaels bekent zijn geweest* (1692). 2nd ed. 2 vols. Amsterdam: François Halma, 1705.

Wittfogel, Karl August. *Oriental Despotism: A Comparative Study of Total Power*. New Haven, CT: Yale University Press, 1957.

Wolff, Larry. *Inventing Eastern Europe: The Map of Civilization on the Mind of the Englightenment*. Stanford, CA: Stanford University Press, 1994.

Wolfthal, Diane. *Images of Rape: The "Heroic" Tradition and its Alternatives*. Cambridge: Cambridge University Press, 1999.

Wyss-Giacosa, Paola von. *Religionsbilder der frühen Aufklärung. Bernard Picarts Tafeln für die "Cérémonies et Coutumes religieuses de tous les Peuples du Monde."* Wabern bei Bern: Benteli, 2006.

Yang, Chi-ming. "Asia Out of Place: The Aesthetics of Incorruptibility in Behn's *Oroonoko*." *Eighteenth-Century Studies* 42 (2008): 235–253.

——. *Performing China: Virtue, Commerce, and Orientalism in Eighteenth-Century England, 1660–1760*. Baltimore: Johns Hopkins University Press, 2011.

Zandvliet, Kees. *De groote waereld in't kleen geschildert: Nederlandse kartografie tussen de middeleeuwen en de industriële revolutie*. Alphen aan den Rijn: Canaletto, 1985.

——. *Mapping for Money: Maps, Plans, and Topographic Paintings and Their Role in Dutch Overseas Expansion During the Sixteenth and Seventeenth Centuries*. Amsterdam: Batavian Lion International, 1998.

Zech, Marieke. " 'Inde Werelt vol Drucks': Vrouwen in de boekhandel." *Historica* 23, no. 1 (2000): 22–24.

[ACKNOWLEDGMENTS]

Exotic journeys are almost invariably exuberant rides, and this one was no exception. It has led me to all sorts of rare-book libraries, into museum galleries and storage depots, to showrooms and backrooms of map and print collections, and to many memorable workshops and symposia. All of this travel entailed countless kindnesses, and I am grateful for the literary-scholarly protocol that allows me to thank all of those who made this project such a wonderful experience, intellectually and otherwise.

The arc of the project included three incredibly productive points of research and writing, which conveniently fell at the beginning, middle, and end of the process. The major themes and outlines of the book were conceptualized over the course of a near-perfect year at the Institute for Advanced Study in Princeton, which afforded an ideal environment to think, along with fantastic colleagues to think with. I am grateful for the intellectual camaraderie of and cogent feedback from the terrific group of scholars who spent that year with me (and the faculty who hosted us), including Peter Arnade, Herman Bennett, Mario Biagioli, Jonathan Israel, Richard Kagan, Michael Lackner, Martha Newman, and Heinrich von Staden. I am equally grateful to the American Council of Learned Societies for their support that year in the form of a Frederick Burkhardt Fellowship. This early work on texts, maps, and images—two-dimensional sources, as I came to think of them—made me understand that I needed to consider more carefully three-dimensional objects, media, and material culture; and I had the stupendous good fortune to be able to do this at the Victoria and Albert Museum in London. The V&A, with its incomparable collection of objects and curators, provided the best possible submersion in the decorative arts I could have hoped for. I am grateful for the patience and generosity of my colleagues that year, who fielded endless questions and permitted innumerable curatorial indulgences as I tried to learn how to think through objects: Glenn Adamson, Marta Ajmar, Chris Breward, Richard Checketts, Christine Guth, Anna Jackson, Kirstin Kennedy, Ethan Lasser, Reino Leifkes, Alex Marr, Leslie Miller, Liz Miller, and Linda Sandino. Once again, too, I am correspondingly indebted to the support of a granting organization, in this case the amazingly creative (and admirably generous) Mellon Foundation, whose New Directions Fellowship launched my work in truly new directions. Finally, I finished the book in the delightful confines of the Netherlands Institute for Advanced Study in Wassenaar, where I received support from the Royal Netherlands Academy of Arts and Sciences. NIAS proved a superb place to complete the manuscript, and I was able to benefit, once again, from a warmly supportive group of scholars, including Gert Oostindie, Aviva Ben-Ur, Karel Davids, Alison Games, Henk den Heijer, Jim Jasper, Tod Jones, Wim Klooster, and Kati Röttger.

I am fortunate to have had backing, along the way, from several granting agencies. I am grateful to the British Academy, Getty Research Institute, Huntington Library, and Fulbright Program for their support. I am also indebted to the stimulating workshops at the various institutions where I was invited to present material from this project: at Yale (and the Beinecke Rare Book and Manuscript Library), Harvard (and the Fogg Art Museum), Columbia (and its Queen Wilhelmina workshops), Brown (and the John Carter Brown Library), USC (and its Early Modern Studies Institute), and UCLA (and the Clark Library). And I am pleased to thank, as well, the many audiences of talks presented at various venues: in Ann Arbor, Austin, Baltimore, Boston, Buffalo, Claremont, Columbus, Denver, Durham, Hartford, Iowa City, Irvine, Los Angeles, Miami, Milwaukee, Pasadena, Pittsburgh, Princeton, Riverside, Santa Barbara, Stanford, and, closer to home, Seattle, where a fabulous conference on "Space and Place in the Early Modern World" brought wonderful speakers to share their work, as well (with a special call out to Ricardo Padrón, Larry Silver, and my co-organizer of that conference, Louisa Mackenzie). A bit further afield, I received great feedback from seminars in Amsterdam, Antwerp, Basel, Cambridge, Copenhagen, Duisburg, Erlangen, Galway, Ghent, Glasgow, Istanbul, Leiden, London, Montreal, Munich, Paris, Turku, Vancouver, Venice, and Wassenaar.

And to the people along the way, who shared their own work, offered thoughtful feedback on mine, nurtured early versions of the project, answered ongoing queries, took me into their archives and storage rooms, hosted me at their institutions and homes, with far more than collegial kindness, I am immensely grateful. Many thanks (with apologies for the roster-like accounting) to Victoria Avery, Daniela Bleichmar, Leonard Blussé, Wietse de Boer, Charissa Bremer-David, Arndt Brendecke, Susanna Burghartz, Jorge Cañizares-Esguerra, Brian Considine, Hal Cook, Lúcia

Costigan, Rudolf Dekker, Sven Dupré, Julie Emerson, Felipe Fernández-Armesto, Paula Findlen, James La Fleur, Dagmar Freist, Susanne Friedrich, Mary Fuller, William Goetzmann, Jos Gommans, Michiel van Groesen, Evan Haefeli, Randy Head, Paul Hoftijzer, Lynn Hunt, Margaret Jacob, Adam Jones, Christiaan Jörg, Benjamin Kaplan, Thomas DaCosta Kaufmann, Valerie Kivelson, Catherine Labio, Inger Leemans, Susan Legêne, Peter Mancall, Dániel Margócsy, Peter Mason, Wijnand Mijnhardt, Joe Miller, Felicity Nussbaum, William O'Reilly, Anthony Pagden, Mark Peterson, Ted Pietsch, Amanda Pipkin, Judith Pollmann, Sumathi Ramaswamy, Marica Reed, Peter Reill, Lissa Roberts, Jessica Roitman, Neil Safier, Ariadne Schmidt, Stephanie Schrader, Jonathan Sheehan, Pamela Smith, Nico Stehr, Philip Stern, Carolien Stolte, Sanjay Subrahmanyam, Taina Syrjämaa, Jan De Vries, Mariët Westermann, Bronwen Wilson, Anne Woollett, and Kees Zandvliet.

Archives and libraries and museums took me away from my home institution, the University of Washington, yet this project would never have been possible without the support of colleagues and friends in Seattle. Many thanks to members of the Early Modern Research Group, including Marshall Brown, Selim Kuru, Estelle Lingo, Stuart Lingo, and Geoff Turnovsky. I am grateful to my chair over the years of this book's composition, R. Kent Guy, who provided support not only in mundane ways—leave and teaching release—but scholarly, as well; and to members of my home department (some, alas, gone), who offered everything from rich feedback for long chapters, to precise citations for arcane footnotes, to warm friendship and convivial hospitality. Thanks especially to Susan Glenn, Jim Gregory, Richard Johnson, David Spafford, Lynn Thomas, Simon Werrett, and to the late, dear Stephanie Camp. And to my graduate students along the way, from whom I have learned so much: Brad Bouley, Genevieve Landis Carlton, Sean Cocco, Dominic Hall, Steve Schillinger, and Emma Hinchliffe, research assistant par excellence, who contributed heroic labors, late in the day, in the service of pictures. I also received timely funding from the University of Washington, and I would like to acknowledge the support of the Hanauer Faculty Fellowship and Hanauer Discretionary Fund, the Simpson Center for the Humanities, the Center for Western European Studies, the Royalty Research Fund Fellowship, and the Keller and Gellert Faculty Fellowships.

My editor at Penn, Jerry Singerman, supported this project from the start, and he has been remarkably helpful throughout the process. I am grateful to him for his smart and incisive feedback, and for his efficient and expert conversion of the manuscript into this final book. I would also like to thank Joyce Ippolito, whose sharp eye improved the manuscript considerably, and Noreen O'Connor-Abel.

Finally, there are the "families" that nurtured this book in ways that go well beyond footnotes and archives, fellowships and conferences. I began this project in Princeton, where I had the unstinting support of my in-laws, Charles and Janet

Townsend. They made that year-long stay—and the numerous others that followed—an unalloyed success, and for their many layers of hospitality and generosity over the years I am sincerely indebted to them. I also worked on this book for great stretches in the Netherlands, where I lucked into a second adopted family, who have offered me over the years far more warmth, friendship, and kindnesses than I could ever have imagined possible. I am deeply grateful to Henk and Tine van Nierop for countless glasses of wine, lovely Ottolenghi dinners, and engaging late-night conversations covering all manner of topics, including (even) the invention of exoticism. They somehow made each stay in Amsterdam more *gezellig* than the last, which is quite a feat of friendship. Finally, to those who put up with this project over the years, both at home and abroad, enduring innumerable working trips and marathon museum sessions, pressing deadlines and chapter revisions, I owe more than measly thanks. I am profoundly grateful to my daughter, Isabel, who not only made those trips and sessions such incredible fun; she also taught me how to look at and think about visual sources and material objects—what lovely lessons!—and her remarkably precocious critical skills, even as they made me feel inept at times, contributed enormously to my own efforts to see these materials with fresh eyes. And to my constant editor-cum-companion in life, Louise Townsend—an old pro in more ways then she realizes—I am also profoundly indebted and hugely appreciative for everything. Her intelligent criticisms, sympathetic readings, and patient explications, time and again, have made this book much better than it otherwise would have been, and I am way in hock to her. This time—I promise!—you get that exotic trip to . . . .

ACKNOWLEDGMENTS

[INDEX]

Page references in bold refer to illustrations.

animal motifs. *See* exotic fauna

Art d'observer (Senebier), 139

Asad, Talal, 11, 223, 339n27

Asia (Dapper): images, **29, 243**; India, 175; *naturalia,* 114; Ogilby and, 56; parasol motif, 242; sexual violence, 216; source material, 368n79; torture descriptions, 199, 359n61, 371n115

Asia Minor (de Bruijn). *See Levant* (de Bruijn)

Asie (van Kessel), **259, 268**; central panel, 269, 271, 272; source material, 264, 366n48

Atkins, John, 361n93

Atlas Chinensis (Ogilby/Dapper), 56, **57,** 345n67. *See also Gedenkwaerdig bedryf* (Dapper)

Atlas Japannensis (Montanus), 56, **58,** 328–29, 340n45, 345n67. *See also Japan* (Montanus)

Atlas major (Blaeu), 39, 238, **240,** 284, 349n6, 364n20

Atlas nouveau (Covens and Mortier), 362n102

atlas production, 35, 39, 56, 345n74, 362n102

Atlas soulagé (van der Aa), 33

Attiret, Father, 373n5

Augsburg Confession (1530), 206

Ausführliche Beschreibung des Chinesischen Reichs und der grossen Tartarey (Du Halde), **298.** *See also Description geographique, historique, chronologique, politique, et physique de l'empire de la Chine* (Du Halde)

author-illustrator disconnect. *See* illustrations, acquisition and production of

authorship, 20; acquisition of original journals, 49–51; author-figure conceit, 103–5, 139–40, 347n92, 354n108, 354n118; bookmaker role, 27–28, 48–54, 70–74, 93, 106–7, 264, 344n47, 344n56; de Bruijn and, 98, 119, 147, 153; changes in approaches to, from Renaissance to early modern period, 69–74; conflation of Montanus and Dapper and, 42–43, 70, 343n30; decentering effect of pictures, 124, 347n91; of images, 53–54, 97–101, 103–5, 158, 159; parochialism and, 78. *See also* illustrations, acquisition and production of; impersonal, disordered style

autopsia, 347n102, 352nn88–89; authorial assumptions and, 103–5, 139–40, 354n108, 354n118, 354n122; de Bruijn and, 86, 119, 127, 145, 153–54, 158, 161; early modern faith in, 86, 119, 127–28; Jesuit geography as, 78; limited value of, 72–73, 76–77, 97; natural history and, 130–35; Persepolis images and, 155–59; as selling point, 59, 119, 139, 163, 195; vs. semblance of sight, 20, 136–39, 159, 161; sight metaphor and, 339n36, 348 (epigraphs), 349n6; truth claims and, 72–73, 129, 154–55, 158, 159. *See also* spectacle and spectatorship; travel literature; visuality of Dutch exotic geography

backlash against/criticism of exotic geography, 22–23, 355n125; Du Halde's criticism, 106–7, 226, 230, 289, 299, 328; Montanus *Japan,* criticism of, 77–78, 140–44, 173, 328–29, 355n124; scholarly criticism, 156–59, 161, 286. *See also* order and method

Bacon, Francis, 128

Bain, Alexander, 363n7

Baldaeus, Philip. *See Malabar*

Banks, Joseph, 343n35, 367n67

Barlaeus, Caspar, 346n85, 358n46, 368n78

Barthes, Roland, 270, 271

Baumgartner, Johann Wolfgang, 245, **248**

Bayeren, Abraham van, 270

Beekman, E. M., 338n18, 347n92

Behn, Aphra, 244, 364n24. *See also Oroonoko* (Behn)

Bekker, Balthasar, 342n19

Bell, Johann Adam Schall von, 213

Bennet, Thomas, 342n29

Bentinck, Margaret Cavendish, Duchess of Portland. *See* Portland Museum

Benton, Lauren, 339n25

Bentvueghels (society of Dutch and Flemish artists), 145

Berchem, Nicolaes (America cartouches), 235–50; lower cartouche, 235, **236,** 253–55, **254,** 364n20; meanings of, 252–57, 272; parasol motif, 236, 241–50, 253, 257; replication and imitation of, 237–49, 281–82, 284; as standard iconic depiction of America, 235–38, 284; upper cartouche, 235, **252,** 252–53

Bernard, Jean-Frédéric, 43, 124. *See also Ceremonies et coutumes religieuses*

Bernier, François, 218–21

Bernigeroth, J. M., **298**

Beverley, Robert, 124–25

Blaeu, Joan (mapmaking firm): *Atlas major,* 39, 238, **240,** 284, 349n6, 364n20; Martini's map of China, 65; Post and Eckhout illustrations, 279, 308

Blaeu, Willem (mapmaking firm), 35; continents maps, **263,** 366n46; reputation, 53; Wagenaer and, 189

Bleiswyk, François van, **34**

Bleys, Rudi, 181, 357n30, 357n35

blindness and geographic description, 136–37, 139, 161, 354n113

Bloemaert, Cornelis, **88**

Blommaert, Samuel, 361n91

Blue, Gregory, 362n108, 362n109, 362n110

Boel, Pieter, 367n54

Bogaert, Abraham, 155–56, 355n138

Bontekoe, Willem, 51, 164, 342n26, 343n31

bookmaking and bookmakers. *See* authorship; branding of Dutch exotic geography; Dutch print ateliers as standard-setters; illustrations, acquisition and production of; publishing process; *specific bookmakers*

Bort, Balthasar, 350n29

Bosman, Willem, 143, 365n41

Boswell, James, 24, 81

Boterbloem, Kees, 350n36, 358n44

Boucher, François, 333, **334**

Bourgon, Jérôme, 362n108, 362n109, 362n110

Bowen, Emanuel, 363 (epigraph)

Boym, Michael, 135, 351n54

Bracegirdle, Anne, 244–45

Brancaforte, Elio Christoph, 362n106

branding of Dutch exotic geography: van der Aa and, 7, 49, 53, 64, 71, 118, 290–91, 293–94, 369nn92–93; con-

289, 328, 330, 333; America motifs, 245–49, **246**, **247**; cartouches, importance as motif sources, 233; decontextualization of exotic motifs, 246–47, 274, **275**, 277–78, 322–23; decorative arts term and, 363n7; Dürer's rhinoceros image, 345n61; Eckhout images, 308–12, **310**, **311**, 356n14, 358n46, 370n113; exotic place names and, 227–28; Kessel panels and, 261–62, 269–70; maps as, 232; van Meurs-Dapper images, 55, 314–22; van Meurs-Nieuhof Great Khan image, **299**, 299–302, **300**, **301**, 312, 369n101; van Meurs-Nieuhof mendicants images, 302–8, **304**, **305**, 312–13, 370n107, 371–72n126; palm tree motif, 251, 305; pattern books and, 287–89, 319–20, 326–28, 372n128; replication habit, 279; torture motifs, **299–300**, **300–301**, **304–6**, 308, 312–22, **316**, 321, 371n122, 372n129, 372n130. *See also* curiosity cabinets (collector's cabinets); glass, examples of; iconic circuits; lacquering; porcelain; Portland Museum; tapestries; transmediation

McKenzie, Donald, 48

Merback, Mitchell B., 362n106

merchants of exotic goods, 245–46, **248**, **332**, 333, 364n27

Merian, Maria Sibylla: drawing from life, 91, 134–35, 353n106; images, 40, **134**; publication process, 124, 352n68

Metamorphosis insectorum Surinamensium (Merian), 40, **134**

metapictures, 108, 351n49. *See also* framing device

Meurs, Jacob van (atelier), 27–28; Aa's republication of, **293**, 319, 320, 326, 371n125; authorship and, 27–28, 51–55, 70, 78, 264, 344n56; branding, 25, 27, 28, 42, 56, 62, 70, 74, 110–11; career details, 49, 92–93; collaborations, 35, 99, 100, 104, 164, 216, 345n64, 359n56; competition with, 56, 62, 100; control over publication, 42–43, 349–50n21; criticism of, 106; as engraver, 39, 49, 54, 92–93, 295, 360n81; impersonal, digressive style, 70, 73–75, 78, 274, 329, 354n122; Nieuhof's journals and (*See* "Iournaal" [Nieuhof]); Ogilby collaboration, 42, 53, 65, 216, 236, 345n66, 349–50n21; output, 33, 41; pirating by, 68, 346n86; pricing, 126; success, 80–81; torture as spectacle, 224, 318–19; translation publication, 92, 216, 342n29; visual-pictorial emphasis, 28, 85, 86, 92–99, 302, 344n58. *See also* *Africa* (Dapper); *America* (Montanus); *Asia* (Dapper); *Gedenkwaerdig bedryf* (Dapper); *Gedenkwaerdig bedryf* (Dapper), Cortes source images; *Gedenkwaerdige zee en lantreize* (Nieuhof); *Gezantschap der Neêrlandtsche Oost-Indische Compagnie* (Nieuhof); *Gezantschap der Neêrlandtsche Oost-Indische Compagnie* (Nieuhof), frontispiece of; *Japan* (Montanus); Meurs images/frontispieces; *Naukeurige beschryving van gantsch Syrie* (Dapper); *Oost-Indische voyagie* (Schouten); *Reysen* (Struys)

Meurs, Jacob van, images/frontispieces from: van der Aa *Galerie,* **293**, 320; borrowing from material arts, 350n27, 365n33; Dapper *Africa,* 60; Dapper *Asia,* **29**, **243**; Dapper *Gedenkwaerdig bedryf,* **57**, **98**, **99**, **192**, **293**, **314**, **317**, **318**; Dapper *Syrie,* **185**; Montanus *Amer-*

ica, **32**, **242**; Montanus *Japan,* **58**, 104, 143, 212, 218; Nieuhof *Gedenkwaerdige zee en lantreize,* **93**, **115**, **184**, **281**; Nieuhof *Gezantschap,* 26, 61, **95**, **96**, **114**, **136**, 295–96, **297**, 303; replication in exotic geography, 264, 280–81, 294, 296–99, 313, 345n63, 359n63, 366n49, 371n125; replication in material arts, 288, 299–309, 316–22, 367n59, 369n101, 370n107, 371–72n126, 372n128; Schouten *Oost-Indische voyagie,* 141, **194**; sources, 54–55, 94–97, 106, 279–81, 295–96, 308, 350n27, 351n54, 354n108, 365n33, 368n78; Struys *Reysen,* 165, **177**; style, 94, 97, 110, 115, 118, 150, 213–14, 224, 241–42, 250, 251, 262, 264, 270. *See also Gezantschap der Neêrlandtsche Oost-Indische Compagnie* (Nieuhof), frontispiece of

Mitchell, David, 371n122

Mitchell, W. J. T., 108, 351n49

mocha (term), 228, 363n3

Monstrorum historia (Aldrovandi), 266

Montagu, Elizabeth, 328

Montanus, Arnoldus, 9; biographical information, 71; conflation with Dapper, 42–43, 70, 343n30; output, 42–43; as stay-at-home writer, 73–74, 76, 213, 354n122, 361n91. *See also America* (Montanus); *Japan* (Montanus)

Montesquieu, Charles-Louis de Secondat, Baron de: Oriental despotism, 224, 362n110, 370n105, 371n124; *Persian Letters,* 17, 328, 370n105

Mortier, Cornelis, 362n102

Mostaert, Jan, 187

motifs and iconographies, 271–72, 337n4, 340–41n51. *See also* aesthetic of exoticism; Berchem, Nicolaes (America cartouches); cartouches; chinoiserie; decontextualization of exotic world; Eckhout, Albert; Eckhout, Albert, replication of his images; exotic fauna; feathers, as exotic motif; flowers and exotic plants; iconic circuits; material arts; pagoda motif; palm tree motif; parasol motif; replication of images; snakes/serpents, as exotic motif

Mulder, J., 90

Munnicks, Johannes, 131

Muscovy (de Bruijn): criticism of, 155–59; images, **44**, **121**, **146**, **149**, **150**, **151**, **152**, **155**; Persepolis images, **151**, **152**, **153**, 156–60, 353n95, 355n138, 356n147; pricing, 43, 126, 343n34; replication of images from, 159–60; sight metaphor, 82, 86, 158, 348 (epigraph); torture descriptions, 198; visual-pictorial emphasis, 43, 123, 147, 153–61, 351n60, 353n95, 355n134

Naaukeurige versameling (van der Aa), 71, 291, 365n32

Naauwkeurige beschryvinge (Baldaeus). *See Malabar*

Nantes, Edict of (1598), 47

narrative: aesthetic of exoticism and, 289; blending of texts and, 27–28, 51, 53, 76, 106, 347n92; illustrations and, 100–101, 104–7, 159, 253; material arts and, 231, 278, 301–2, 307. *See also* Jesuit geography; travel literature

Nassau-Siegen, Johan Maurits van. *See* Johan Maurits, prince of Nassau-Siegen

parasol motif: as all-purpose marker of exoticism, 140, 241–45, 247–50, 322, 357; Berchem's "America" cartouche, 236, 241–50, 253, 257; material arts, 300, 313, 315, 322; meanings, 247, 249–50, 253, 364–65n28; van Meurs engravings, 94, 241–42, 250, 295

paratexts: appeal of exotic geography and, 56–59; as characteristic of Dutch geography, 18, 39, 48, 55, 81, 101; van Meurs and, 25, 28, 42, 73

Parergon (Ortelius), 84, 339n36

Park, Katharine, 125, 356n149

Parker, Robert, 228, 288, 319–21, 326

parochialism, 74; Du Halde and, 80–81; in earlier geographic publishing, 8–10, 15, 64–65, 75–76, 346n85, 347n101; lack of commercial success and, 78; order and method and, 331, 332–33

Pas-caert van Guinea (Doncker), **241**, 245, 249, 256, 257, 282

Pas-kaart vande zee kusten inde boght van Niew [*sic*] *Engeland tusschen de Staaten Hoek* (van Keulen), **250**, 323, 365n31

Paskaerte vande archipel en de eylanden daer omtrent gelegen (van Keulen), **221**, **222**, 371n121

patronage, 68, 159. *See also* Johan Maurits, prince of Nassau-Siegen; Witsen, Nicolaes

Peace of Westphalia (1648), 5, 166, 209

Peninsula Indiæ (Erben), **235**, 270, 284, 368–69n83

Pepys, Samuel, 122, 345n72, 351n65

Persepolis illustrata (Harding), 160

Persepolis images: de Bruijn's images, **151**, **152**, **153**, 156–60, 353n95, 355n138, 356n147; Chardin's images, **156**, 157–59; Kaempfer's images, **157**, **158**, 356n148

Persian Letters (*Lettres persanes,* Montesquieu), 17, 328, 370n105

Peter the Great, 147, 148, 237, 351n55

Picart, Bernard, 35, 43, 55, 342n19. *See also Ceremonies et coutumes religieuses*

Pietz, William, 255–57, 270, 365n41

Pillement, Jean-Baptiste, 228, 288–89. *See also Ladies amusement* (Pillement)

Pinney, Christopher, 74–75

Piso, Willem. *See Historia naturalis Brasiliae* (Piso)

plants. *See* exotic flora

Poissons, ecrevisses et crabes (Renard), 41, 124, 126, 130, 131

political structure, Dutch, 46, 47

Poliziano (Angelo Ambrogini), 214

porcelain, 371n122; china term and, 228; drug pots, 315–16, 371n117, 371n118; examples, **275**, 284, 305, **306**; as motif source, 350n27, 365n33; pattern books for, 289; uses, 369n84. *See also* delftware

Portland Museum, **327**; exotic pleasure and, 330; as "promiscuous assemblage," 324–26, 328, 333, 372–73n4

Portugal, 346n77, 347n101

Post, Frans: exotic landscape and, 7; exotic natural violence theme, 362n101; Johan Maurits patronage, 91, 308; replication of his images, 279–80, 308, **310**, 340n51, 368n78, 369n88

postcolonial studies, 15, 21, 23, 339n27

Poussin, Nicolas, 214

Praetorius, Herr, 159, 353n95, 355n138

prefaces, function of, 56–59

Preissler, Ignaz, 305–6

pricing of books, 36–39, 43, 126, 343n34

Principal navigations, voiages, traffiques and discoueries (Hakluyt), 8, 64, 86, 338n18

print runs, 41, 119, 342n21, 342n22

privileges, state, 41–42, 50–51, 100, 103, 343n40, 348n108

pronk still life painting, 7, 270–71

Psalmanazar, George, 347n89

publishing process: color printing, 44–45; high costs, 62; improvements in quantity and quality, 31; print run quantities, 41, 119, 342n21, 342n22; technological production advantages, 42, 119–20. *See also* authorship; illustrations, acquisition and production of

Punishments of China (Mason), 224–25, 362n111

Purchas, Samuel, 9

quarto format, 39

Quellinus, Erasmus, 366n45

race, 21, 167, 218–21, 223, 361n98

Ramusio, Giovanni Battista, 86, 346n85

rape. *See* sexual violence

Ray, John, 119–24, 129, 351n63

realism, 278. *See also* autopsia; Eckhout, Albert; Merian, Maria Sibylla; natural history; Persepolis images; Rumphius, Georg; still life painting; truth claims

Reede tot Drakenstein, Hendrik Adriaan van. *See Hortus Indicus Malabaricus* (Reede tot Drakenstein)

Reinke, Peter, 369n84

Reizen over Moskovie, door Persie en Indie (de Bruijn). *See Muscovy* (de Bruijn)

Reizen van Cornelis de Bruyn, door de vermaardste deelen van Klein Asia (de Bruijn). *See Levant* (de Bruijn)

Relación del viaje (Cortes). *See Gedenkwaerdig bedryf* (Dapper), Cortes source images

Relations de divers voyages curieux (M. Thévenot), **63**

religion: confessional boundaries, 11–12, 77, 78, 80, 360n77; desacralization of violence, 21, 211–14, 222–23, 362n103; fetish concept and, 256; iconography of, 3–4, 252–53, 257, 271–72; images' instructive value, 124–25, 129; limited interference in Dutch printing, 46; New World's perceived lack of, 271–72, 366n44; persecution of Christians outside Europe, 8, 142, 173, 210–12, 223, 339n29, 360n77, 360n78, 360n79; violence, intra-European, and, 205–9, 215, 223. *See also* Jesuit geography; parochialism

Rembrandt van Rijn, 187, 214, 352n89

Remmert, Volker R., 349n13

Renard, Louis, 41, 124, 126, 130, 131

replication of images: van der Aa and, 54, 92, 289–94, 314–15, 319, 337n1, 359n63, 359n67; Baldaeus *Malabar,* 54, 233, 281, 284; Berchem's *America* cartouches, 237–49, 281–82, 284; de Bruijn's images, 159–60, 351n62, 356n147; as common practice, 54, 92, 279–81,